Making the
Big Red Machine

Making the Big Red Machine

*Bob Howsam and the
Cincinnati Reds of the 1970s*

Daryl Smith

Foreword by Lee May

McFarland & Company, Inc., Publishers
Jefferson, North Carolina, and London

LIBRARY OF CONGRESS CATALOGUING-IN-PUBLICATION DATA

Smith, Daryl Raymond.
  Making the Big Red Machine : Bob Howsam and the Cincinnati
Reds of the 1970s / Daryl Smith ; foreword by Lee May.
    p.   cm.
  Includes bibliographical references and index.

  ISBN 978-0-7864-3980-5
  softcover : 50# alkaline paper ∞

  1. Cincinnati Reds (Baseeball team)   2. Howsam, Robert L.
3. Anderson, Sparky, 1934–   4. Baseball — Ohio — Cincinnati —
History — 20th century.   5. Baseball managers — Ohio —
Cincinnati — Biography.   I. Title.
GV875.C65.S65   2009
796.357′640977178 — dc22   2008051012

British Library cataloguing data are available

On the cover: Players on the 1976 Reds team left to right — Bench
(C), Rose (3B), Concepcion (SS), Morgan (2B), Perez (1B), Foster
(LF), Geronimo (CF), Griffey (RF); (inset) Bob Howsam (courtesy
Cincinnati Reds)

Manufactured in the United States of America

*McFarland & Company, Inc., Publishers
  Box 611, Jefferson, North Carolina 28640
  www.mcfarlandpub.com*

It is vital to give credit where credit is due. The people of Cincinnati are indebted to Bob Howsam for the way he ran their ball club for thirteen seasons. I am indebted to him for sharing his insights with me in a series of interviews from May 2005 to December 2007. He shared his philosophies and principles for running an organization. Most of the philosophies that were behind the Big Red Machine came directly from Bob Howsam. A few of the principles I discovered on my own as I studied Mr. Howsam and the Big Red Machine.

Mr. Howsam deeply admired the knowledge of Branch Rickey, general manager of the Brooklyn Dodgers from 1943 to 1950, and Rickey's willingness to share that knowledge with others. Mr. Howsam, too, was gracious enough to do that with many general managers during and since his tenure in the major leagues. He was also kind enough to share them with you and me. For that we should all be thankful.

ACKNOWLEDGMENTS

As always, a successful project has many hands and minds. Let me thank John Sloan and Vicki Caruana, fellow authors and believers from Fellowship Bible Church, who helped me begin to chart this voyage. Thanks for my good friends Andy Katayama, Bob Berger, Jeff Nelson, and Jeff Wesley who provided healthy feedback during the writing. Thanks to Midge Smith, Mary Shouse, Rachel Reynolds, and Erin Reder for editing help. I appreciate the staff at the Public Library of Cincinnati and Hamilton County and the Kenton County Library for their research assistance. Gratitude is also extended to the Carrizosa family for their hospitality and support in Arizona.

Thanks to many of the staff of the Big Red Machine for sharing their insights with me and for those great years with the Big Red Machine: Sparky Anderson, Alex Grammas, George Scherger, Chief Bender, Dick Wagner, and Bob Howsam. Thanks to Greg Rhodes, Jarrod Rollins, Chris Eckes, Rob Butcher, and other staff of the Reds and Reds Hall of Fame for assistance and encouragement. Greg Rhodes has done yeoman's work in preserving the rich history of the Reds for the people of Cincinnati. Thanks to Scott Belmer and Rich Ritchie of Robin Imaging who did the photo work. Thanks also to Chris Boland and John Griffith at the College of Mount St. Joseph for their excellent work in photo advising.

Finally, thanks to my wife Laura for her understanding and support throughout this project and for the sacrifices that she and all four of my children — Ryan, Stephanie, Andrew and Brent — made. Finally, thanks to the Lord Jesus Christ for the ability to see, think, and write.

TABLE OF CONTENTS

FOREWORD BY LEE MAY

They called me the "Big Bopper." That was fine with me. I always wanted to be a home run hitter when I was growing up. My favorite player was Harmon Killebrew, who played for the Washington Senators and then the Minnesota Twins when they moved north. I wanted to be just like Killebrew and hit a lot of homers. I did: I hit 354 of them.

I loved playing baseball, and some of my best days were playing for Cincinnati. I was there when we became the Big Red Machine and we sure could hit the ball. Between me, Johnny Bench, and Tony Perez, there were a lot of long balls hit. We powered the team right into the World Series with Baltimore when we met up with Brooks Robinson.

I know a lot of folks around Cincinnati were upset when I was traded to Houston. But if you think they were upset, that was nothing compared to me. I can't repeat what I said when I heard the news. Joe Morgan was the lucky one in that trade, he got to come to Cincinnati.

I went on to play ball for eleven more seasons with the Astros, Orioles, and Royals, but I'll never forget those great days with Cincinnati. If you are like me and like to look back at the good old days, this book is for you. You'll read about the trade that made me so mad and other memorable things that happened during the Big Red Machine days. Enjoy!

Lee May, Cincinnati, Ohio

PREFACE

Complete and total domination. The 1976 Cincinnati Reds had just swept the entire baseball postseason. Neither the New York Yankees nor the Philadelphia Phillies had so much as slowed the Big Red Machine as it rolled to its second consecutive world championship. Never had a team been so dominant in postseason play.[1] It is doubtful that a team ever will be again. The Reds maintained a ten-year run in which they were a force of nature in the National League and, for the most part, baseball as a whole.

The team lives on in American sporting lore. Travel around this country and tell a man in his late thirties or forties that you are from Cincinnati. Almost without fail, he will immediately connect the city to its greatest team. This happens in Texas, California, Washington — everywhere. I know because I have done it. To explain this phenomenon, you must understand how the Reds were built and run. Sustained greatness never happens by accident. Others have written about what the team did and how they did it, but this is the story of *why* that greatness occurred.

This book follows Cincinnati's Reds from 1967 to 1979, focusing on the years 1970 to 1976 when they dominated baseball. I began by asking the question, "Why was the Big Red Machine so great"? Everyone knows those teams were great, but what made them great? Was it talent? There are a lot of talented teams that do not become great. This book is an exploration of why the Reds achieved greatness. The book begins with the circumstances that led to the introduction of a new leadership team, plays out the team's greatness on the field and tells how it all unraveled.

Essentially my answer to the greatness question is leadership. In particular — through a series of interviews, personal reflections, and research — the answer to my question came down to one man, Bob Howsam, the general manager and chief architect of the Big Red Machine. I have had extensive interviews with Mr. Howsam as well as his top two assistants in the organization. Mr. Howsam was of great assistance and this book in part is a look at the team through his eyes. I also interviewed Sparky Anderson, the manager, and several of his coaching staff. Further information was gathered from newspaper articles written at the time as well as players' autobiographies.

This book is first and foremost intended to be a baseball story. It is also full of leadership principles. If the reader isn't interested in the principles, it is still a great story. For the careful reader, there is more.

There have been a number of books written on the Big Red machine. Most have been stories about what they did. Most contain anecdotes from the players. One such title is *Men of the Reds Machine*, written in 1977 by Ritter Collett. *Cincinnati and the Big Red Machine*, by Robert Walker, examines how the city of Cincinnati tied its identity to the Reds. The great Cincinnati sports writer Bob Hertzel published a very popular book, *The Big Red Machine*, in 1976. An interesting read, it chronicles the team from 1970 to 1975, with the primary focus on the 1975 team. There are no recent books on the club.

This book takes a different view. It is a view from the top — and behind the scenes — the backdrop to the greatness we saw on the field. The only book that comes close in flavor is entitled *Big Red Dynasty*, by John Erardi and Greg Rhodes, published in 1997. Their fine book examines the team using a headlines or blog approach, with interesting facts, figures, and charts. Additionally they assembled the finest collection of photos available from that era. Erardi and Rhodes both encouraged me to write this book, which relies heavily on interviews with firsthand sources.

I leave you with this challenge. Ask a middle-aged man from any part of the country who his favorite baseball team was when he was a kid. Eight times out of ten he will say the Big Red Machine. He will name five or six starters off that team, even if he can't name four or five starters from any team in the 1980s, a decade later. I hope that this book brings back great memories for baseball fans from that era that will be shared with their children as they attempt to pass along the specialness of the Big Red Machine.

INTRODUCTION

The story of the Big Red Machine actually begins in St. Louis. Or perhaps it begins in southern Colorado. Then again, it probably begins back in Cincinnati, after all.

Cincinnati was founded by a group of settlers in 1788. It is nestled along the banks of the Ohio River directly across from a smaller tributary squirting out of Kentucky, the Licking River. Its location helps to explain its identity. Most Americans, who are notoriously bad at all geography outside of their local towns, think of Ohio as "way up North" and Kentucky as "way down South." The fact that these two share a 664-mile border catches most by surprise.

Geography aside, Cincinnati's location makes it a unique blend of two cultures, southern and midwestern. Conservative southern values, along with the vibrant factory life of the burgeoning industrial revolution of the early twentieth century, melded into one. Many boys of the early twentieth century grew up on farms in Kentucky and left for jobs in "the big city" when they finished high school. Some would commute back home on weekends, glutting U.S. Routes 25 and 42 before President Dwight Eisenhower initiated the building of the interstate system. Cincinnati is regarded as being a conservative town and proud of it. Civic pride runs high, normalcy and steady progress is cherished. Many Cincinnatians regard the city as the finest in the nation, a well-kept secret. They would just as soon keep it that way; they don't want it to grow too big.

Originally known as Losantiville, it was renamed Cincinnati in 1790 by the governor of the Northwest Territory, Gen. Arthur St. Clair, who was a member of an organization of Revolutionary War soldiers called the Society of the Cincinnati. The society took its name from Quinctius Cincinnatus, an ancient Roman military leader.[1] The Cincinnati area is commonly referred to as "the Tri-State" by locals, because it is located in southwest Ohio and includes parts of Kentucky across the river and Indiana just to the west. Hills surround the downtown area — some call it "the City of Seven Hills." The famed American poet, Henry Wadsworth Longfellow, paid a visit to the city and fell in love with its beauty. He referred to it as the "Queen City of the West." The moniker has stuck to this day. After the turn of the twentieth century, the city was heavily settled by people of German descent. As a result Catholic and Lutheran churches are scattered across the city.

A mere four years after the end of the Civil War, a man who was very fond of the relatively new game of baseball arrived at a controversial, if not revolutionary, idea. He would pay an entire team to play the game. Until this point in American history few had been paid to play games. Baseball was considered a leisure activity, a recreation, a hobby. Aaron Champion viewed it as a game as well, but a game that was beginning to have bragging rights, as towns and cities fielded amateur teams to compete against one another. The rivalry between cities was becoming intense. Champion, an attorney, wanted his city and team to be the best. He hired Harry Wright, a former cricket player, who was considered the best baseball player in America, as player-manager. Cincinnati fielded the first all-professional team of nine players in 1869. Nowadays the average American cannot fathom life without professional sports, but at one time it was professional sports that were unfathomable.

That first professional team was also a machine of sorts. They traveled from town to town playing local organizations and they won every time. In those days baseball games were strictly the domain of adults and older teenagers. Children played the game, but only on sandlots and never in an organized manner. The team's record that first year was 57–0. They sported mustaches, wore knee britches with long red socks, and adopted the moniker "Cincinnati Red Stockings."

The win streak continued into the next year, 1870, with the team notching 130 consecutive victories before eventually losing their first game, 8–7 in extra innings.[2] They were among the charter members of the newly formed professional league, the National League (NL), in 1876. Other members included Chicago, Boston, St. Louis, New York, and Philadelphia. They were kicked out of the league in 1880 for renting out their ballpark on Sundays and selling beer at games, but they still traveled and played in what was known as the American Association. They reentered the National League in 1889, and shortly thereafter, in 1901, the rival American League (AL) sprang up.

In 1903, Pittsburg (they would not add the "h" until 1911) owner Barney Dreyfuss and Boston Americans owner Henry Killilea — whose teams had won their respective leagues — decided to pit the champions of the two leagues against each other in a nine-game tournament; they called it the World Series. Boston, which later became the Red Sox, won the very first series 5–3 with the help of a pitcher named Cy Young.[3]

The Reds would not become familiar with the Series until the year 1919 when, as NL pennant winners, they played the Chicago White Sox. This Series is well known but not for the baseball that was played. A group of unscrupulous gamblers influenced a number of White Sox players, a wonderful player was perhaps unjustifiably implicated, and the Chicago "Black Sox" and Shoeless Joe Jackson became infamous across America. By the way, the Reds did win the Series 5–3.

The Reds watched from afar as the New York Yankees of George "Babe"

Ruth and Lou Gehrig dominated the 1920s and 1930s. They would finally reach the Series again in 1939 when they lost to those Yankees 4–0. They returned one year later and this time were victorious 4–3 over the Detroit Tigers. The rest of the 1940s were barren of postseason action.

The 1950s produced many wonderful baseball memories during the post–World War II boom, but no trips to the World Series for the Reds. The era boasted Gus Bell (father of Buddy), Wally Post, Ted Kluszewski, and the Reds' first African-American player of note, Frank Robinson.

The Reds surprised the NL in 1961, winning the league title by four games over the Dodgers. In the Series, they met the M&M boys, the Yankees of Mickey Mantle and Roger Maris who sort of broke Babe Ruth's record of sixty homers in one season. The season had been expanded from 154 to 162 games in 1961 with the addition of the Los Angeles Angels and the Washington Senators expansion teams to the American League. Maris had fifty-nine home runs in 154 games, and hit his sixty-first on the last day of the regular season. Mantle sat on the bench during the Series, with a painful and bloody abscess on his hip,[4] but the Reds were still no match for the Yankees and were defeated 4–1.

Another significant event in the life of the Reds occurred in 1961 when long-time owner Powel Crosley died. Crosley was perhaps one of the most brilliant business leaders in American history and yet would be one of the least-known among the greats. He certainly does not have the name recognition of a Carnegie, Rockefeller, or Wrigley. His business ventures were as varied as they were brilliant.

Crosley's first business was selling mail-order automobile parts for Ford's Model T, among other vehicles. One day shortly after this period he went out to buy a radio for his son. When he discovered how expensive radios were, he bought the parts separately and built the radio himself, saving quite a bit of money. Hence, he invented an affordable radio for the American consumer and went into production. By 1922 Crosley was the leading radio manufacturer on the planet. He migrated into radio broadcasting and later entered television. Along the way he invented and produced several different types of antennas, phonographs, a small airplane (called the Moonbeam), and cameras.

Crosley had a flair for manufacturing. His self-named company produced household appliances like stoves, refrigerators, and ovens by the thousands from its Cincinnati plant. His refrigerator was the first to boast shelves in the door. He invented a refrigerator that worked off of a kerosene stove, called the Crosley Icyball, that could be used in tropical climates and rural areas without electricity. He even introduced a small and affordable automobile, produced from the 1930s to the 1950s.[5]

But he is best remembered in Cincinnati for the team he owned and for the field they played on. The Reds' home since 1912 had been Redland Field. It was a quaint ballpark not unlike those later emulated at the beginning of the twenty-first century. It lay on the west side of town at the intersection of Findlay and Western Avenues, about four miles from the center of Cincinnati. When Crosley purchased the team in 1934, the field was renamed by the board of directors in honor of the new owner and for the enterprises he ran. It was the second to be named for an owner and his empire (following by eight years Chicago's Wrigley Field). In modern times it is routine to name a stadium after an organization but not the owner. Such practices bring huge revenues to the home team in naming rights. In those days it was done to simply honor influential people.

Crosley purchased the financially troubled club in the midst of the Great Depression to ensure that it stayed in Cincinnati. It was a theme that would be repeated in the city. His great entrepreneurial mind immediately affected the running of the Reds. They were the first team to travel by air to a ballgame — to Chicago to play the Cubs in 1934.[6] In 1935 lights were installed at Crosley Field facilitating the first night game in baseball history. Attendance jumped by 400 percent, injecting new revenue into the financially strapped club. The Reds enjoyed two pennants under Crosley's reign. After his death in 1961, his heirs sold the team to the general manager that had been hired the previous year, Bill DeWitt.

Shortly after Crosley's passing, the Reds were one of the first to face a crisis that other teams would face throughout the end of the twentieth century —

Owner Bill DeWitt purchased the team from Powel Crosley's heirs. He stands inside Crosley Field circa 1963. His desire to move the team to the suburbs triggered a chain of events that would lead to the Big Red Machine (photograph courtesy Roadwest Publishing [Jack Klumpe Collection]).

December 5, 1966, press conference: a watershed event in the history of Cincinnati. Francis Dale (center), publisher of the *Cincinnati Enquirer* and head of the new eleven-man ownership group, announcing that the group is buying the team from Bill DeWitt (right), as Cincinnati mayor Gene Ruehlman looks on. The change in ownership precipitated the need for a new general manager (photograph courtesy Roadwest Publishing [Jack Klumpe Collection]).

the need for a new stadium and the fight over where it would be built and who would pay for it. It was a fight with an unintended byproduct that changed the course of the Reds.

DeWitt was wealthy, but not filthy rich. He guided the Reds in the early 1960s with a firm and frugal hand. He was both owner and general manger. He realized that he needed a new stadium to compete with bigger-city ball clubs. On an early wave of a developing trend, he wanted to build a new ballpark away from the downtown area, in the suburbs. He targeted a developing area known as Blue Ash, roughly twelve miles northeast of downtown, near one of the three newly built interstate highways running through Cincinnati, I-71. The city fathers were mortified. Yes, they wanted a new stadium but they wanted it downtown, not uptown.

At about that time discussions were to get underway with Paul Brown, a legendary football coach who had been dislodged from his job with the team that bore his name. The idea was hatched to build a stadium downtown that would house the Reds and a new football team. New York had recently done the same thing with the Mets and Jets; they played in multipurpose Shea Stadium. DeWitt wanted no part of this idea. He threatened to sell — and to sell to outside interests. Fearful that the city would lose the Reds ball club altogether, a group of eleven concerned businessmen bought DeWitt out. The new owners, very civic minded but unfamiliar with running a sports team, wisely realized that they lacked the baseball knowledge necessary to run the club. They needed a new general manager, someone good.

1

A New Beginning

January 22, 1967, was an unseasonably warm and windy day, perhaps foreshadowing better times blowing into Cincinnati. Inside the packed *Cincinnati Enquirer* conference room bursting with notepads, microphones, and TV cameras, the atmosphere was like a bellowing furnace. The new Reds ownership group had finished their two-week hunt and were about to introduce the man who would lead the Reds. All the local media plus the wire services were there. This was in the days before ESPN so there were not a lot of national media, but with the Cincinnati Reds local coverage was enough.

Frank Dale, the head of the ownership group, introduced the new general manager. Before the press sat a bespectacled, respectable-looking man. His hair neatly trimmed, his frame large, his voice sure. He was the quintessential American businessman of the postwar era. His name was Robert L. Howsam.

It was a new era for Cincinnati baseball. Owners and college administrators often refer to "a new era" when they introduce a new leader or coach. It is a truthful statement but with misleading connotations. Whenever a new leader or coach comes into an organization, it is always a new era. By definition, it has to be a new era but it does not have to be a good one.

The words "new era" have such a positive sound. However sometimes change is bad. Sometimes the new era is worse than the old one. Ask many a college athletic director after they hire a new football or basketball coach. For example, years after the Reds press conference, Army would hire a new football coach, Todd Berry, and proudly announce it was a new era. It certainly was: Army went on to notch its longest losing streak in history, nineteen games.

This however would be a good era, an era unknown until this time in Cincinnati and outside of New York, relatively unknown in baseball as a whole. The Reds had been to the postseason roughly every twenty years—1919, 1939, 1940, and 1961. But things were about to change.

To understand the Big Red Machine without understanding Bob Howsam is like trying to understand the fledgling thirteen states without understanding George Washington. Born on February 28, 1918, Howsam was part of what Tom Brokaw has dubbed "the greatest generation." That generation was raised in the Depression, fought World War II, pulled the plow of the postwar boom, and sent the first man to the moon. Though that description fits many of

Howsam's contemporaries, his individual life deserves more attention. Insight into Bob Howsam's life gives insight into the Big Red Machine.

Howsam was born in the mile-high city of Denver, Colorado, to Lee and Mary Howsam. Lee Howsam, of British ancestry, emigrated from Canada as a boy. Mary was a Colorado native. Bob was the younger of two boys, Earl being the older. When Bob was eight the family moved to the fertile San Luis Valley, 250 miles by road south by southwest of Denver. It is a place that takes your breath away with both its beauty and its altitude. The valley, bordered by the Sangre de Cristo Mountains on the east and the San Juan Range to the west, is home to one of the earth's wonders: the Great Sand Dunes National Monument. The largest sand dunes in North America rise over 750 feet into the air. Medano Creek runs nearby in spring and early summer and literally disappears into the Colorado sand. It remains a favorite Colorado tourist attraction to this day.

Lee Howsam had gone into partnership with the son of a Russian immigrant who came from a family of expert beekeepers. They decided to open a beekeeping business in La Jara, a small, dusty town at the southern edge of the valley, about twenty miles north of the New Mexico border. There was lots of pollen from the nearby flowers, natural vegetation, and vegetables raised by local farmers in the fertile valley. In this era, before widespread refrigeration and freezing, the San Luis Valley provided the only supply of vegetables for Los Angeles and the southern California basin. Vegetables from the East were shipped in part of the year. Later in the year local California produce was used.

Bob Howsam: the quintessential businessman of the post–World War II era. His arrival would usher in an era of success unknown before or since in Cincinnati (photograph courtesy the Cincinnati Reds).

But for about a two-month period the only produce available was from the high fertile valleys of Colorado near the Howsam beekeeping operation.

Unhappy with the local education their children were receiving, Lee and Mary sent their children to the Los Angeles area, 900 miles to the west, to attend school. They stayed with Mary's brother who lived near a side entrance to the MGM Studios. Bob received a good education for the year, but the real excitement was that several movie stars from *Our Gang* attended his school. The next year Bob lived with family friends in Redland, California.

In the summer of 1933, the local Colorado school administrators were replaced. Assured that education would improve, Lee and Mary brought Bob back for the remainder of his school years, where he could also help with the family business. To earn extra cash, Bob helped load California-bound produce on railroad cars for twenty-five cents an hour. The cash was helpful and the extra muscle paid dividends for Bob who was by now six foot two and a star on the local high school basketball team. The team did well and reached the state semi-finals where they were defeated by Denver West. They might have beaten the big Denver school but their center was out with the mumps.[1]

Bob Howsam liked baseball and girls. Baseball in those days was a game played mostly by older teenagers and adults—Carl Stotz was still a few years away from developing Little League baseball for boys, in Williamsport, Pennsylvania. With no organized games for youngsters, Bob was relegated to sandlot pick-up games. However American Legion ball was available for high-school-aged boys. Due to his large frame, Bob played first base. Most small towns had teams of young men that played in a state league and La Jara was no exception. Bob was their batboy; occasionally they would let him play. Barnstorming teams were popular in that day and some "big names" came through on such clubs. Babe Didrikson, probably the greatest female athlete in American history, came through with the bearded House of David team. Even more thrilling for Howsam was the game against the Kansas City Monarchs with Satchel Paige on the mound. Howsam was fortunate enough to get into that game and face the man who said, "Don't look back, something might be gaining on you." Paige didn't look back against Howsam—he struck him out swinging. If you're going to strike out against a barnstormer, Satchel Paige would be your first choice.[2]

Girls were another matter. Deane Christianson, his high school sweetheart, lived in nearby Sanford. One day she asked a favor of her beau. Could he arrange a date for her friend who was coming in from Denver for a few days? Bob got his friend Johnny Platt to accompany Deane's friend, Janet, and they all enjoyed the local dance that evening.

As high school ended Bob set his sights on the big state school in Boulder, the University of Colorado. Enrolling there, he joined Alpha Sigma Phi fraternity and began studying, planning on becoming a high school coach. A few months after arriving, during a pick-up football game, the ball was thrown out of bounds and rolled down a hill. It fell near the feet of a beautiful girl. Bob looked up and smiled. It was Janet. Carpe diem, Bob thought, seize the day. He asked her to go "coking" on the spot.

"Coking" dredges up thoughts of a secluded city alley, littered with trash and reeking of a foul stench—pale bodies, silhouetted behind a dumpster, with arms moving around their faces. In those days "coking" was more benign—it was inviting a girl out to get a Coca-Cola. "The Sink" was the place, and five cents was the price. The Sink was the local soda fountain where couples often went to converse on dates.

Soon, though, Howsam was intent on returning to the San Luis Valley to help his dad run the family business. Exhibiting the foresight and practicality that would mark his life, Howsam switched to the Barnes Business School in Denver for the remainder of his studies. As these drew to a close, war loomed on the horizon. Hitler was moving across eastern and western Europe.

Again showing foresight, Howsam began to prepare for the inevitable for men born in the late 1910s and early 1920s—war. He enrolled in flying training at Adams State Teachers College (now Adams State College) in Alamosa, Colorado, a mere fifteen miles from where he had grown up. The training was excellent, as the San Luis Valley provided tricky winds where a pilot could hone his skills much like a sailor in rough seas. After finishing at Alamosa, he transferred to Parkersburg, West Virginia, where he completed training and then, in turn, instructed for a while.

In 1943 he entered the Navy Air Corps as an ensign and was assigned to Corpus Christi, Texas; Dallas, Texas; Hutchinson, Kansas; and finally Floyd Bennett Field in New York. It may not seem as glamorous as flying fighters over Europe or the Pacific but it was reserved for a select few. The men assigned to Floyd Bennett were required to take up newly arrived planes and put them through tests. If they checked out, the pilots would then deliver them to a naval air station somewhere in the United States where they would pick another plane and deliver it to another naval air station. The process would be repeated until they arrived back at Floyd Bennett. Howsam was not flying just one model of airplane. Unlike cars, which are fairly interchangeable, airplanes differ greatly. They differ in procedures, take-off speeds, and—most importantly—landing and approach speeds, configurations, and handling in the wind. Doing this job required both intelligence and versatility. Howsam's wind training in Alamosa and his intelligence from birth and schooling paid high dividends.

Like most veterans of that era, Bob Howsam rarely talks about those days. Almost all of the men of his generation served; to them it was nothing special. After the war he returned to his hometown, La Jara, where he helped get the family business back up and running again. His father Lee had taken ill during the war and the business had been greatly scaled back. With Bob's help, the business was back on its feet and booming. They signed honey contracts with Burleson's in Texas, and Sue Bee in Sioux City, Iowa, and delivered locally to grocery stores like Safeway. Bob Howsam figured he had found his life calling and purpose—beekeeping in La Jara, Colorado.[3] That all changed with a visitor from Washington, D.C.

Bob Howsam married well in every sense of the word. Concerning his trip to the soda fountain to go "coking": "It was the best 5 cents I ever spent," he says. Janet only wanted to know one thing then. Was Bob still seeing Deane? If so, Janet Johnson was not about to take a friend's boyfriend.

Janet Johnson was a beautiful woman, resembling Donna Reed in *It's a Wonderful Life*. She is as beautiful on the inside as she is on the outside — a loving, kind, and compassionate person. She takes a quiet but genuine interest in others, all of this and she came from a good family. Good in every sense of the word.

Bob and Janet dated steadily from that day in 1936 through 1938. Bob decided he had found the woman he wanted to spend the rest of his life with but he needed the blessing of her parents. Some would find this an outdated way of pursuing a woman but it was the custom of the time and still serves smart men well in the twenty-first century.

He was more nervous than usual about meeting "her dad." Not uncommon for most men, it was a big step. Janet was her father's only natural child (he also had an adopted daughter) and Bob could only imagine that Daddy wouldn't let his girl go easily. There was another thing standing in the way. Not only was her dad large in stature and of high reputation, he was a U.S. senator from Colorado, Edwin "Big Ed" Johnson.

Ed Johnson was born to a Swedish father and English mother in 1884. Raised on a cattle ranch in Nebraska, he homesteaded after marriage in Colorado and managed a mill and elevator cooperative. He rose through local politics, losing his first bid for school superintendent in 1914. He kept trying and eventually was elected to the Colorado General Assembly, lieutenant governor, and governor, and finally the U.S. Senate in 1936.[4] He was serving the first of three Senate terms by the time Bob Howsam met him. He was a "Jeffersonian Democrat" serving from a highly Republican state. His secret was that he worked on behalf of the people and they loved him for it. A great recipe for any politician but one rarely followed.

Good fortune was with Howsam on the day he first met Janet's father. Howsam was to rendezvous with Senator Johnson in a conference room of a Denver hotel where the senator was having conferences. When Howsam knocked on the door, Jim McKelvey, a big rancher and family friend of the Howsams, opened it. "Jim, what are you doing here?" asked young Bob. "Let me introduce you to a friend of mine, this is Senator Johnson," said Jim McKelvey, who later disappeared. An intermediary made that first meeting a lot easier for the nervous Howsam. Bob later realized that Senator Johnson, who knew so many people in Colorado, had looked for the connection and arranged for McKelvey to be there to help Bob. The elder Johnson took an immediate liking to young Howsam. Dad and Mom's blessing quickly followed, and Robert Howsam and Janet Johnson were married on September 15, 1939, almost three years to the day since the Coca-Cola at The Sink.

Janet, or "Janny," as Howsam affectionately calls her, supported him through flight training and lived with his parents in La Jara while Bob was serving during the war. His parents helped care for Bob and Janet's first son, Robert Jr., born in 1942, and later Edwin, born in 1944.

Late in 1946 "Big Ed" approached Howsam. He wanted Bob to go to Washington to be his administrative assistant. After discussions with his parents and Janet, Bob agreed. He spent six months in 1947 helping run Senator Johnson's Washington office. While there, he was the office manager, making sure that the senator saw to the important stuff. As Bob would later report, "I got a lot of office procedures crammed into my head in those six months."[5]

Another unexpected offer came in the middle of 1947. The old Western League had been a vibrant baseball factory in the early part of the twentieth century but during the war it was considered expendable and left to wither on the vine. Several businessmen wanted to resurrect the league to provide entertainment to the postwar American public in the West, where there was no TV and no major-league baseball. St. Louis was then the most western major league outpost.

Ed Johnson had been asked to be the unpaid president of the Western League. Denver was to be part of the league that would also consist of Omaha, Pueblo, Des Moines, Sioux City, and Johnson's old hometown, Lincoln, Nebraska. He asked Howsam to go out and become the executive secretary of the league until a permanent man could be found. Essentially, Howsam, age twenty-nine, was asked to get the league up and running.

Professionally Howsam knew flying, beekeeping, office procedures and little else. When you have no clue what you are doing, it is best to find someone who does. A mentor is invaluable. Howsam sought one immediately; his name was George Trautman. He was a willing savior to the young businessman.

Trautman was the president of the National Association of Professional Baseball Leagues, essentially the minor leagues. Through his tutelage, Howsam drafted a league constitution, schedule, and policies, plus hired the umpires. The league was up and running by the summer of 1947. He spent hours on the road before interstate highways were built, visiting parks and overseeing operations.

Shortly after the first season, the Denver owners had news for him. They wanted out, completely out. The team was for sale. Howsam saw a window of opportunity. He again set out to seize the moment.

Bob called his dad and his brother. They used money from the family honey business they had sold when Howsam went to Washington, plus all of Bob's savings, and scraped together the $75,000 necessary to buy the Denver Bears. He was thirty years old and now owned his own ball club.

Everyone chipped in. Dad was interim president, Mom and Janet counted tickets, Dad and Janet delivered season tickets personally to fans, sons Robert and Edwin worked as unpaid grounds crew. Howsam himself did a little bit of everything. As he likes to say, they were mom and pop, but they weren't bush league.[6] Everyone had to pitch in, especially at first. Bob was still committed to be the league's executive secretary through 1948. He divided his attention between executive secretary duties and helping to run the Bears, where he did everything that was left over, including helping the kids with the grounds crew duty. It was a trial by fire and it was invaluable in molding his young mind to handle the two sides of baseball, the business side and the athletic side. It would serve him well years later when he understood the entire gamut of baseball operations inside and out. Before he was entirely ripped in two, a replacement arrived as executive secretary. He could now devote himself to the Bears.

Even before he purchased the club, Howsam saw its most pressing need. It was a big one. The ballpark, Merchant's Park, was like many at the time. It was not a place you would really want to take your family: a wooden fire trap and termite heaven.[7]

Howsam contacted the mayor of Denver, Ben Stapleton. A popular man, he had been mayor for twelve years. Stapleton told Howsam that there was a city dump ready to close on the west side of town; they could have the dump site for a ballpark. Not the most attractive piece of real estate in town, but the price was right: $1. The deal was to be closed after the November election. Two unfortunate events then occurred, one for the mayor and one for Howsam. The mayor lost his job and Howsam lost his land deal. The new mayor had a new asking price, $32,000.[8]

Not ideal, but it was the best option he had. Howsam bought the dump. Many Bronco fans of the sixties through the nineties had no idea that they were walking on the site of an old dump when they entered Mile High Stadium. The Howsam family spent many Sundays walking the outfield of Mile High, picking up bottles and other debris that had worked its way to the surface. It was a family tradition. The new ballpark was christened Bears Stadium when it opened in August 1948.

Soon thereafter Howsam was faced with one of the first real tests of his resolve. There comes a moment like this in every leader's life. In fact there are many such moments, if your tenure is long. However the first one is often the most fearful, especially for a young adult. If a young person doesn't handle the first one right, the others can become more daunting or they may not come at all. Churchill put it best: "There comes a time in every man's life when he is called upon to do something very special; something for which he and only he has the capabilities, has the skills, and has the necessary training. What a pity if the moment finds the man unprepared."

Howsam's moment came during the 1949 season. He was sitting with Mike Gazella, the extremely popular manager of the Bears. The team had nearly won the pennant the previous season. The discussion was centered on changes that needed to be made in how the ball club was being run. Bob Howsam saw things one way, Mike Gazella the other. The changes were not all that major but Gazella's neck stiffened. He didn't want to change. Howsam pressed. Finally Gazella put his cards on the table. I am not going to change and I won't have to go because I have so much fan support that you can't fire me — I am too popular. That's the gist of what Gazella said and it was a moment of truth. Howsam paused, then pulled the trigger. He didn't want to fire Gazella, but Gazella's words had forced him to do it.[9]

The press went nuts. How could a young general manager like Howsam fire a successful manager and former Yankee player like Gazella. Shouldn't Gazella know best? How Howsam could do it was simple: he not only was the general manager, he was the owner, a luxury most GMs do not have. Unlike owners who sometimes hire and fire willy-nilly, out of arrogance (the young George Steinbrenner of the Yankees comes to mind), Howsam had thought out these types of scenarios in advance. He had anticipated the possibility in advance and knew what he had to do. He was able to do this because he had a good handle, even early in his career, on the principles important to running a ball club. He was willing to stick to those principles, popular or not. At this point they were not popular.

Howsam quickly put it behind him. If you are going to be the leader you have to learn to take the heat and move on.[10] He was confident that he had made the correct decision — and it turned out he was right.

Earl Browne finished out the year and managed the 1950 season. Browne was replaced by Andy Cohen, the former New York Giant, and the Bears won their first title in 1952. Crowds were coming through the turnstiles in record numbers. The Bears drew nearly a half a million people to their games in 1949, more than two major-league teams that season and an all-time minor-league record. Howsam was named *Sporting News* Minor League Executive of the Year in 1951 and again in 1956.

Attendance began to slip in the mid–1950s as Denverites were getting increasing options for their entertainment dollars. Howsam sensed that Denver was hungry for a higher level of baseball. There are essentially four levels of baseball at the minor-league level (Rookie, A, AA, AAA) — the more A's, the higher the level of baseball. Howsam wanted a AAA club, but there weren't any available. Each major league team had an arrangement with one city for one AAA club.

Howsam got his opportunity, though, in 1955. The Athletics were moving from Philadelphia to Kansas City, pushing the baseball frontier westward. The Yankees had a AAA club in Kansas City — the Blues — and they were now for sale. Howsam bought them and moved them. Denver was now AAA.

"Fan conscious" would be a descriptor for Bob Howsam throughout his baseball life. Howsam's sense for what the fan wanted was at times uncanny. It was a trait that would persist his entire career. Simply put, he believed that fans wanted a good team, a clean ballpark, and friendly service at a fair price. That isn't rocket science but it was rare in baseball in those days and sometimes in these. As he likes to say about fans, you can't just open the gates and expect them to come; you have to give them a reason to come. Success shortly followed the step up to AAA and the Bears won the league title and the Junior World Series in 1957. Attendance was again on the rise.

Howsam was in his mid thirties and didn't enter the game as an adult until the age of twenty-nine. Some wondered, how could a young GM be so baseball savvy having never played the game professionally? The simple answer for Bob Howsam's early success was his willingness to seek mentors and to learn from them. He had several but only one was famous.

After George Trautman, who taught Howsam how to set up a minor league, there was Jack Zeller who lived in Ft. Worth, Texas. He and Howsam drove all over the dusty plains of Texas from hamlet to hamlet, visiting ballparks in the late 1940s and early 1950s. They kept the radio off as Howsam picked Zeller's mind for every nugget of baseball wisdom. Zeller had been the general manager of the Detroit Tigers. Under his watch the Tigers had won a World Series and another American League pennant in the 1940s. When Howsam ran the Bears, the bald-headed Zeller was the chief scout for the Boston Braves with whom the Bears had a working agreement.[11] Howsam sensed Zeller's knowledge of the game and his knowledge of how to find talent, and he thirsted to drink heavily from that fountain of knowledge.

Later the Bears began a working relationship with the Pittsburgh Pirates in the early 1950s. It was there that Howsam met Billy Myers who had played professionally as a shortstop for seven years, mostly for Cincinnati. He knew baseball and had great stories and a great eye for talent. He taught Howsam what to look for in players.[12] He was invaluable to Howsam's education. Howsam had played the game but never thought about what he was doing when he was playing, just like many ballplayers. The game takes on a new perspective when you are in charge of running a team.

The great advantage in running a high-level minor-league club is the exposure you get to the major league operations of your parent club. When the Denver club jumped from A to AAA, the Yankees became their parent club. It was through this opportunity that Howsam met his second most valuable baseball mentor.

The Yankees were and had been at the pinnacle of baseball for more than thirty years. Their general manager was George Weiss. What Howsam saw in Weiss amazed him. He was an organizational wonder. He believed in surrounding himself with good people. He gave them clear guidelines and policies to follow and then let them do their jobs. What he could do above all was read people. He hand picked them and knew their nuances and how to communicate with them. For example, to one scout "fair" might mean a player is okay. To another, "fair" might mean "sign him right away." Weiss never watched the players, he trusted that to the scouts, but knew how to read what the scouts were really saying. Weiss was in charge of the organizational levers and he had great people at work when he pulled them. Under his watch as the Yankees farm director, scouting director, general manager, and then president, New York won nineteen World Series titles.[13]

How does one find a mentor? In Howsam's experience, it is something that occurs naturally. Howsam believes the process begins when you run into a person that you automatically feel comfortable with. Howsam looked for two qualities in a mentor, saying, "you can tell that he is a learned person in what he is talking about and ... he has ... integrity — the ability that makes you feel that what he is saying is factual and the truth." A person's ability to know what he was doing and to communicate honestly was highly esteemed by Bob Howsam.

Others among Howsam's circle of mentors were Senator Johnson and his own father, Lee Howsam. But without a doubt the most important baseball person in Bob Howsam's life was Branch Rickey of the Brooklyn Dodgers who integrated baseball with Jackie Robinson in 1947.

To look at Branch Rickey only through the lens of his most famous contribution to baseball is to appreciate only one detail of a grand portrait. Rickey actually spent only a fraction of his long baseball career with the Dodgers. The majority of his professional life was spent with the St. Louis Cardinals. St. Louis shared a common heritage with other baseball Meccas, it had two baseball teams: the Cardinals and the Browns. Chicago had the Cubs and White Sox. The City of Brotherly Love had the Phillies and the Athletics. No city was bigger on baseball than New York, who had the Yankees, the Giants, and Rickey's future employer, the Dodgers. Rickey felt that to compete with a huge city like New York, which had a bigger fan base and bigger wallet, he would have to scrap. And scrap he did. He invented the farm system, a novel idea in 1917.

If Rickey found a boy who knew how to pick up a baseball, he signed him. Off he went to the minors to be developed, and there was plenty of room in the minors. The Cardinals eventually had over thirty minor-league teams. To put that in perspective, the St. Louis club now has six. Sometimes there would be half a dozen teams in a league and they were all Rickey's players. Good coaching, which is so key to player development, was rare in those days outside of the minor leagues.[14]

America was not as consumed with sports in the first part of the twentieth century as it is today. More important, with hard work on the farm or factory there was less discretionary time for men to coach young boys. Lighted ballparks were not known in major-league parks until the late 1930s; on amateur fields they were unheard of. Most ball playing was done during the day for boys, or during the evenings in the longer summer days. The average player in Little League today receives better coaching than most eighteen-year-olds did in the 1940s. So when a young man got to the minor leagues there was a lot to do. Rickey would have upwards of six hundred players in the minors in a given year. Most never saw the major leagues, but a few did. Through Rickey, the Cardinals became a baseball power — he was the architect of the famed Gashouse Gang.

Bob Howsam first met Branch Rickey when his Bears were playing against Pueblo, a Brooklyn Dodgers minor league club. Later Howsam heard Rickey speak at a minor-league convention. He was mesmerized, recalling Rickey as one of the greatest speakers he had ever heard. Rickey had earned his law degree from the University of Michigan and Howsam is convinced that Rickey could have been successful in any field that he chose to enter. Howsam had the utmost respect for Ricky—for his baseball intellect, his drive, his passion, and most of all for his character.

Howsam actually got to know Rickey after Branch joined Pittsburgh in 1950. The Denver Bears became an affiliate of the Pittsburgh Pirates. Howsam traveled down to Huntsville, Texas, where Pittsburgh had a camp. Howsam asked Rickey if he could follow him as he directed the pitcher's workouts. There were about six mounds lined up, and Rickey would walk down the row with his secretary, Ken Blackburn, in tow. As he walked he inspected the pitchers, making comments that Blackburn recorded on his notepad. Blackburn would type up the notes and have them on Rickey's desk by the next morning.

At the next day's meeting with Rickey, the coaches and scouts would go over the notes. Branch would say things like "this pitcher will advance rapidly" or "this one won't make it." It was by watching and listening to Rickey that Howsam really honed his eye for talent. He calls Rickey the greatest judge of talent he ever saw.

Eventually Rickey took Howsam under his wing. He brought him to his major league camp in Fort Pierce, Florida, where Rickey would put on demonstrations and drills personally. One of his favorites was to teach players to run faster. Rickey loved speed. He believed speed could help on offense and defense. There is an old adage: "there are two things you can't coach, height and speed." Rickey believed the former but not the latter. He felt you could teach a youngster to get faster. The key was the stride — the longer the stride, the faster the player. Rickey would mark off chalk lines in the grass. The first distance he would chalk off was six feet. He would have the players run, touching the chalk marks with their foot on each stride. Then he would gradually lengthen the chalk marks, to six and a half feet and then farther from there. Again, he would have the players run across the field on the markers, lengthening their stride; the longer the stride, the faster the player. The average stride was seven and a half feet. The ideal stride, according to Rickey, was nine feet.

While at his camps, Howsam further scrutinized how Rickey evaluated talent. Like a trainer of thoroughbred horses who was able to identify that rare horse that has a chance at the Kentucky Derby, Rickey could quickly identify which players had a chance at the majors.

It is called "tacit knowledge" in the business world, knowledge that is hard to put into words. It is like trying to describe to someone how you remain balanced on a bicycle. You can explain that you must sit on the seat and push the pedals, but that doesn't get to the heart of the matter of riding a bike. It is something that you must learn through observation and more so through trial and error, with a few skinned knees along the way. So it is with talent evaluation. Slowly, through his own travels with other mentors and interaction with Rickey, Howsam picked up the tacit knowledge of player evaluation. It was a skill that would serve him well.

Howsam and Rickey spoke frequently on the phone and would often share information about players. One day Howsam spotted a young player for the Kansas City Monarchs of the Negro Leagues. He called Rickey and said, "Mr. Rickey, you have got to see this guy." It just so happened that the Monarchs were due to play a game at Forbes Field in Pittsburgh the next week. Rickey said he would go over and check him out. Howsam didn't hear anything for a week, so he called Rickey. Had Rickey seen this special ball player? Rickey was indignant, "Who wants to sign a thirty-six-year-old second baseman?" Amazingly the Monarchs had two men named Banks on the team. The thirty-six-year-old played that day and Ernie Banks did not. Before Rickey could get a look at the latter, he had been signed by the Cubs.[15] Chicago fans have no idea how close Ernie Banks came to being "Mr. Pirate." Bob Howsam was developing an eye for talent on par with his mentors.

From Jack Zeller and Billy Myers, Howsam learned how to scout for talent. Rickey honed those skills and taught him how to run a farm system and develop players. From George Weiss he learned the importance of organization and surrounding himself with good people. Bob Howsam now had the two jobs of the general manager well under control, the business side and the baseball side. However this young general manager's attention was about to turn elsewhere.

2

ENTERING THE BIG TIME

"Where to go from here?" That was Bob Howsam's question for Big Ed Johnson. He was sitting in his car, in front of his father-in-law's apartment one spring evening in 1959. They felt they had attained all they could with the Denver Bears. The Bears had begun as a new Class A franchise in 1947 in an old, dilapidated park. Howsam and crew had built a new stadium and won three pennants and one Junior World Series title in their first eleven seasons as owners. Attendance was climbing ever higher in the late 1950s.

Howsam knew that it wouldn't last forever—the novelty wears off and competition for entertainment dollars continues to come—thus the conversation with Big Ed Johnson in the car in 1959. Somehow—the idea seemed to bubble up and gain momentum as the conversation ensued—they realized that the next step was the big time, the major leagues.

There was only one problem. Baseball had and still has a monopoly. A man could not start his own major-league team or league. It's against the law. Maybe the law could be changed, Big Ed suggested. Howsam was excited by the idea, but the practical side of him realized that he couldn't do it on his own. So he called his mentor, Branch Rickey, who at the time was out of a job.

Rickey had had two and a half decades of success with the St. Louis Cardinals. His teams had won five pennants and four World Series titles, the best-known of which was the Gashouse Gang of 1934. After St. Louis, Rickey had turned the Brooklyn Dodgers around. Integrating baseball in 1947 with Jackie Robinson and other shrewd moves brought Brooklyn to the World Series for the fourth time in their history. His teams or the ones he left behind won seven National League pennants in ten years, and the Dodgers won the World Series title in 1955.

Unfortunately for Rickey, the majority owners of the Dodgers had decided to sell the ball club in 1950. The new majority owner was Walter O'Malley who realized that the ball club had become Rickey's. O'Malley wanted it to be his. This was not the first time this song had been sung, nor would it be the last. Paul Brown was the founding coach of the Cleveland franchise of the All-America Football Conference (AAFC). He was so important to the team that they named it after him. The Browns began play in 1946. They dominated the AAFC and then shocked the football world by continuing the domination when they joined the older and more established NFL in 1950. Like Rickey, Brown was revolutionary in his ideas and strategies, and altered how the game was played. Unfortunately for Brown, the Cleveland Browns owners wanted to sell in 1961. The new buyer was Art Modell. He soon realized that the ball club was really Brown's. Modell wanted it to be his. He fired Brown just like Walter O'Malley fired Branch Rickey. It was the "twisted golden rule" in play. He who owns the gold makes the rules. Both owners later left their faithful and fanatic followers and moved their teams to greener pastures in other cities. Walter O'Malley went on to become beloved in Los Angeles.

After Rickey left Brooklyn he was lured to the Pittsburgh Pirates organization but it was not a good fit. He lasted only five years there. By that time he was seventy-three years old. His family begged him to retire, slow down, and enjoy his remaining years. That is when he got the call from Bob Howsam.

In 1959 the baseball landscape was tilted heavily to the eastern United States. The Dodgers and Giants had just left their long-time homes in New York for the West Coast. Aside from these two franchises, the farthest west that major-league baseball ventured was Kansas City, smack dab in the middle of the continental United States.

There were many large cities that were hungry for a baseball team, many of them in the center of the country. Minneapolis, Dallas, Houston, and Denver all wanted a big-league ball club. But those who ran professional baseball were not interested. Things seemed pretty good from their perspective. There was more demand than supply of teams, and that was a good situation for ownership. That situation is in stark contrast to the early twenty-first century when it took the Montreal Expos more than a year to find a new home.

Rickey latched onto the idea of forming a new league with Howsam. They had a great working relationship, ideas, and mutual respect. They quickly compiled a list of cities: Denver, Houston, Dallas/Ft. Worth, Minneapolis/St. Paul, Buffalo. Interested owners included actress Susan Hayward's husband in Atlanta, Jack Kent Cooke in Toronto, and M. Donald Grant who was part of a New York City group. The New York delegation was led by Bill Shea and he quickly joined Rickey and Howsam as the principal movers and shakers behind the proposed league. How the name for the proposed league was coined is not clear, but it was apropos, the Continental League.[1]

The would-be founders would be disappointed. They got a bill proposed in the Senate to put baseball under antitrust legislation and limit the number of players a major-league club could protect. These measures would in essence open the way for a third major league. They lobbied Congress hard, but in the end they were turned down by a vote of 73–12.

To help quell the storm after the vote, the baseball powers promised franchises to Houston and New York right away. Additionally, they promised that all the cities would eventually get franchises. Minneapolis got the Twins in 1961 when they moved from Washington, where they were known as the Senators.

The next year Bill Shea was able to secure the expansion Metropolitans (the Mets) for New York, where their ballpark long bore his name in recognition of his passion for New York baseball. Meanwhile Houston got the expansion Colt .45s that same season. Atlanta got the Milwaukee Braves four years later.

The rest were left out in the cold for years. Dallas got the Rangers in 1972 after the second Washington Senators franchise moved there. Toronto got the Blue Jays in 1977. Denver finally got the Rockies in 1993. And Buffalo never got a franchise at all; they bid unsuccessfully against Denver and Miami for expansion teams in the early 1990s. Indianapolis and Oklahoma City also desired major league clubs in the 1960s and were left hungry.

Howsam did not have time or energy to put into grieving the loss of the Continental League, however. He had other business at hand.

Phone calls were an important part of Bob Howsam's life. Before the advent of e-mail and faxes, the options for doing business were straightforward—in person, by snail mail, or by phone. Face to face is always preferable in order to read nonverbal cues but it requires travel. In the 1940s and 1950s commercial air travel had not become viable yet. Rail took time, as did bus and car, especially across the expansive western United States. For a man like Howsam who wanted to get business done, the phone was crucial.

One day Howsam got a call from Lamar Hunt in Dallas. Hunt was the son of H. L. Hunt, the Texas oil magnate. He was interested in owning a professional football franchise. Like Howsam, Rickey, and Shea in baseball, Hunt had been unable to secure a football franchise for Dallas. So he wanted to do what any sensible young millionaire would do—start his own football league.

Unlike baseball, football was not protected from competition by upstart leagues. Hunt was proposing a rival to the NFL, which would be called the AFL. He knew Howsam and his reputation and wanted him to start a franchise in Denver. To Howsam and the family-owned business, Rocky Mountain Empire Sports, it was an attractive offer. Bear's Stadium sat mostly empty from September to April each year. A professional football franchise would provide entertainment and generate income in those down months. So while he had been lobbying for the Continental League, Howsam had also been getting a new football team going in Denver. When the AFL got underway, Howsam wanted to get the fans involved with the club, so he sponsored a team-naming contest for local residents. A western theme won—the Broncos.

Opening Night in September 1960 was a harbinger. Less than twenty thousand people came to the first game, leaving over fifteen thousand seats empty. The Broncos were also received in a lukewarm manner by the Denver press. The football landscape in the late 1950s and early 1960s was much different than what it is today. College football was king, and the University of Colorado Buffaloes were just a few miles up the road in Boulder.

Professional football was considered by many to be a sort of bush league, the kind of thing respectable people didn't associate with. Several college stars of the 1930s, 1940s, and 1950s never played professionally. It is not that they weren't drafted or that the professional teams had no interest in them. Rather, the players had no interest in professional football. For example, Jay Berwanger, the first winner of the Heisman Trophy, was picked first in the first NFL draft, but decided not to play pro ball. The second Heisman winner, Clinton Frank, passed up pro football to go into the advertising business. The third, Larry Kelley, didn't want to be known as a professional football player and went into teaching. Davey O'Brien, the fourth Heisman winner, almost passed up pro football for geology; he ended up playing for two years but then left the NFL to join the FBI. Nile Kinnick, the fifth Heisman winner, passed up football for law school. Les Horvath, the 1944 Heisman winner, initially turned down the NFL for dental school.[2]

Perceptions began to change in 1958 when a young Johnny Unitas led the upstart Baltimore Colts to an exciting overtime win against the mighty New York Giants in the NFL Championship game, later known as "the Greatest Game Ever Played." It was one of the first professional championship games ever broadcast on television.

A mere two years later, the Broncos and the rest of the AFL were struggling to get off the ground just as the NFL was coming of age. On the field, the Broncos were not very strong. Frank Tripucka, Gene Mingo, and Lionel Taylor were the headline players. A couple of early-season snows were welcomed by the local ski resorts but proved disastrous to the young club. Less than six thousand people showed up to see the Broncos play the New York Titans.[3] The Broncos completed the season with four wins, nine losses and one tie on the field — and they were broke at the box office. Howsam's family and the Broncos lost $270,000 in one year.[4] They were not alone. Teams in Oakland, Buffalo, and New York City were all losing money. Some could afford it more than others. Hunt's Dallas Texans[5] were reported to have lost a million dollars — a princely sum at the time. Lamar Hunt's father, H. L. Hunt, is reported to have said, "At this rate my son will be out of money in fifty years." Howsam was out of money right then.

The Howsam family and Rocky Mountain Empire Sports were faced with a dilemma. Should they risk their entire financial future and try again the next season, crossing their fingers for better weather and press or cut their losses and maintain financial viability? Howsam chose the latter, wisely. It was not just the Broncos who went on the market. The Broncos, Denver Bears, and Bears Stadium would all have to be sold.

Howsam's chief concern was that the Broncos and especially the Bears remain in town. He had an attractive out-of-town offer, but he feared that bidder John Monfrey would take the teams to San Antonio. So instead he sold the team to a group of Denver buyers, for less money. The Bears would stay in Denver as would the Broncos.

Howsam and Janny took one last Sunday walk around Bears Stadium, a place where their boys Robert and Edwin had grown up, helping their dad pick up trash. They shed some tears and said good-bye to the family business that had become so much a part of their lives during the previous fourteen years. The family honey business was gone and now the family sports business was gone, too.

What was next? Clearly not the major leagues in Denver and clearly not the professional football big time with the Broncos. Howsam and a friend purchased some office space in the Cherry Creek Shopping Center. At age forty-three, he settled down there and began to sell a fairly new product known as mutual funds. He figured he had found his calling for the rest of his professional days as an investment representative.

Three years later the phone rang again. Howsam's mentor, Branch Rickey, was on the line and wanted Howsam's help. Rickey was in a predicament in St. Louis. August Busch Jr. of the Budweiser beer empire[6] had purchased the Cardinals in 1953. "Gussie," as he was known, expected to win World Series titles in the same manner that he was intent on winning the beer wars. The Cardinals had come close just once, in 1957, when they finished second to the Milwaukee Braves for the National League title.

The Pirates had let Rickey go at the end of the 1954 season. He had been in retirement since that time but not happily. Busch figured that Rickey could help him. Busch had great respect for Rickey and brought him to St. Louis in 1962 as a "senior consultant." His duties were to help scout, develop players, and provide expertise to the front office.

There were problems, though. When Busch purchased the club, he'd asked his inner circle who knew the most about baseball. When Dick Meyer mentioned that he had been a catcher in seminary, Busch handed him the reins of the ball club as executive vice president. Under Meyer there was actually a good baseball man, Bing Devine, who had been the general manager since 1958. A St. Louis native, Devine had been around baseball and the Cardinals for most of his life. He knew the game, as Meyer knew beer. Enter Branch Rickey. He was not welcomed by Meyer and Devine, but Busch wanted him there. They were forced to work as a trio—a classic case of too many cooks in the kitchen.

By August 1964 Busch's patience and trust in Devine had run out after more than ten years and not one trip to the World Series, even though for most of those years they had one of the all-time greatest and most-respected players, Stan "the Man" Musial. Busch fired Devine. He now had Meyer at the helm of the club and Rickey as special assistant. Meyer wasn't qualified to be general manager and Rickey wasn't interested. St. Louis needed a general manager. That's why Howsam's phone was ringing.

Howsam had been giving financial advice and selling mutual funds fairly successfully for more than two years. Unlike Rickey, he was content. He and Janet were Coloradans through and through. They loved Denver. Howsam agreed to visit St. Louis and then came back to Denver to talk it over with Janet. He asked her what she wanted to do. She was fully supportive of whatever Bob wanted to do. This was likely his only shot at the big leagues, a shot he figured would never come from his financial advising office. It was too good an opportunity to pass up. He told Busch and Rickey that he would come.

What he found in the front office upon his arrival surprised him. Many of Cardinals' franchise procedures were not up to par with those of the AAA Bears. For example, there were no season ticket sales. All ticket purchases were of the walk-up, day-of-the-game variety. There were other procedures he wanted straightened out immediately. Now it was time for Howsam to make a phone call.

Howsam had met Dick Wagner during Howsam's days with the Bears while Wagner was running the Lincoln Chiefs. Wagner was now running a radio station in Salina, Kansas. A keen businessman with an eye for detail, Wagner was just the one to tighten the hatches of the Cardinals' business ship. Howsam also knew that the Cardinals would be leaving their long-time home, Sportsman's Park, for a new, downtown, multipurpose stadium the next year. Howsam had experience in this area through his Bears Stadium days. Wagner had also been through the drill twice during his career. Howsam wanted Wagner to oversee that project as well.

On the field, the Cardinals were solid. Howsam had entered a pretty good baseball situation. The Cards had a tremendous pitcher in Bob Gibson. They had a future two-time All-Star, Tim McCarver, behind the plate. Bill White and Ken Boyer were strong at first and third. And Devine had secured a fine young outfielder in a mid-year acquisition from the Cubs, Lou Brock.

When Howsam arrived in late August 1964, the Cardinals were in fourth place, nine games behind the Phillies. Howsam began to survey the situation and plan for next year. Then the Phillies began to collapse. The Phillies were led by a crafty manager, Gene Mauch, All-Star Jim Bunning on the mound, and a rookie named Richie Allen,[7] but none of them could halt the Phillies' slide. Leading by six and a half games with twelve games remaining, the Phillies fell apart. Going into the last weekend of the season, the Reds had overtaken the Phillies and led the Cards by ½ game. With the Reds hosting the Phillies on Friday and Sunday of the last weekend of the season, the Phillies won both games. Meanwhile the Cardinals needed to beat the lowly Mets just once in a three-game series to win the pennant. They lost games one and two before winning the last game of the season to leapfrog the Reds and win the National League crown by one game. From fourth place in August, the Cardinals had made it into the World Series.

In the Fall Classic the Cardinals faced the Yankees in Mickey Mantle's last great season. Mantle hit three home runs and had eight RBIs, but the Yankees still lost. Bob Gibson won Games Five and Seven. A workhorse on the mound, he was voted the Series MVP. The Cardinals were World Champions.

Gussie Busch was elated, as was Bob Howsam but Howsam knew this wasn't his team. It was Bing Devine's club. Devine deserved the credit. He had built the club, while Howsam had just happened to enter in time for the party. But after the celebrations, Howsam turned his attention to building the ball club in his own image.

There were problems in St. Louis. The press—and therefore the fans—were not enamored with Bob Howsam. He replaced a well-liked and respected man in Bing Devine. Howsam couldn't fault the fans. He liked Devine, too. It wasn't his idea to fire him. He simply took the opening that was available. Around St. Louis a few viewed Howsam as Branch Rickey's pet.

Rickey wasn't well-liked in St. Louis either. Never one to mince words, he had suggested that Stan Musial retire after the 1962 season. Musial had a good year hitting, but Rickey thought his star had faded in the field. Musial returned for 1963 and hit only .255 before ending his career.

Things didn't get any better for Rickey when Busch fired Devine. The press and the fans figured that Rickey was behind it. He wasn't, but that didn't matter. The front-office personnel also suspected that Rickey was to blame for losing the popular Devine. Politics took over and some people loyal to Devine decided that Rickey would pay.

Rickey was a man full of energy, always on the go. He would walk and dictate notes to his secretary, usually a man, who followed him around. Rickey didn't want to take the time to write things down. At the end of the day, he would bring the notes to one of the other secretaries who would then transcribe the notes. That is where they found their opportunity.

Rickey asked the secretaries to type up the memo to himself and to send it to Dick Meyer. Rickey had said in the notes that "if and when" the Cardinals were out of the pennant race in 1964, the Cardinals should bring up certain players from the minors, that others should be sent down, and still others replaced. The secretaries typed it up. They also typed up a separate memo and sent it over to the *St. Louis Post-Dispatch*. It was in the paper the next day. Somewhere in the process the key phrase "if and when" was left out.[8] So it was printed that Rickey wanted to rid the team of certain players. It wasn't true but that didn't seem to matter. That's the way it often is with the press. The truth may not sell newspapers but shades of the truth do.

The uproar was predictable. Gussie Busch and Meyer were in a predicament. How could they settle the fans and the press and yet do the best thing for the ball club? Sometimes it takes a lot of courage to do the right thing. It may be unpopular and it might not be understood in the short term. The path of least resistance, of pandering, is often the easier path. The best thing in this case would have been to investigate what had really occurred. To clarify it and explain it to all. But that would have taken time, energy, and courage. When the heat was on Busch and Meyer chose the path of least resistance. They fired Branch Rickey.

Most fans, dependent on the local newspaper for their information in the days before the Internet and talk radio, felt it was the right thing to do. "Rickey should never have said those things," they thought — of things he had never said to begin with. Those who leaked the false story kept working in the organization. That is often how it works with politics. Those with a grudge to hold, rational or not, choose a target for their fury, take aim, and fire. The irony is that often the target is not really responsible for the initial offense after all. Branch Rickey didn't cause Devine to be fired, it was Mr. Busch's decision, but loyalists didn't see that or didn't want to see it. You are not going to aim at the owner, especially when he writes your paycheck and owns the beer company.

Howsam in turn, was in a quandary. His mentor, his friend, and the one who had brought him to St. Louis had been fired and unjustly fired at that. What was he to do? He could stay on and continue the work or he could resign in protest. He mulled the decision over. He was not one to make a hasty decision. He liked to think things over, weigh all his options, look at the pros and cons, make as rational and right a decision as possible. After much thought he made up his mind — he would resign in protest.

He called Rickey and told him what he had decided. Rickey turned on him in an instant. "No you will not, you must not," Rickey said. "This is your chance. You need to stay and run the ball club." Resigning on his behalf, he said, would do no one any good and certainly would not change Gussie Busch's mind. He told Howsam to stay — and so he did.

Front-office upheaval aside, Howsam turned his attention to the club, the 1964 World Series Champions. He realized that he deserved no credit for the club's success. He simply was the caretaker for what Devine had left him. It was time to move into the future.

Howsam's most pressing decision was who to hire as the new manager. His World Series manager, Johnny Keane, had resigned the day after the Series and bolted for the Yankees. Rumors were floating around in August that when Busch axed Devine he planned to fire Keane as well but wanted to wait until the end of the season. Furthermore, Busch was rumored to be interested in Willie Mays's old manager from the Giants, Leo Durocher, as Keane's replacement. All that changed after the unexpected pennant and Busch decided to offer Keane a lucrative contract. Keane said no and handed in a resignation letter instead. Interestingly, his letter was dated September 28, a week before the season ended.

Busch indeed was interested in pursuing Durocher and wanted to sign him once Keane left. Busch told Howsam about it. Howsam did some checking; the word around the league was that Durocher was great in the dugout but that you had to keep an eye on him on the road because he could be a bit wild. He liked more than his fair share of liquor and was a regular at the card table and race track.[9] The last thing Howsam wanted was a manager who needed a babysitter on the road. He nixed the Durocher idea. They finally settled on young Red Schoendienst, a Cardinal player through 1963 and a coach for Keane in 1964.

The 1965 season was a disappointment. The Cardinals had their nucleus back from the 1964 World Champions. Gibson was still on the mound, and White, Boyer, McCarver, and Brock were in the field. But they just didn't click, as White, Boyer, and shortstop Dick Groat tailed off offensively. The Cards finished seventh, well back of the first-place Dodgers who had two primary weapons, Sandy Koufax and Don Drysdale. Their offensive weapons were few, if steady, but with a couple of nuclear missile launchers on the mound, you don't need much offense.

Howsam looked at the Cardinals' farm system and was not impressed with what was coming up. He decided that the only way to improve the talent on the club was to trade for it. He had learned from Rickey that it was better to trade a player one year too early than one year too late. He felt that Boyer and popular shortstop Dick Groat might be nearing the end of their careers, so he dealt them at the end of the 1965 season while he could still get something for them. Howsam's eye for talent was going to be tested at the major-league level.

The problems in the front office continued. Not ugly, not loud, not obnoxious, not unworkable, but problems nonetheless. Howsam grew increasingly frustrated in having his decisions approved by Dick Meyer. Meyer was a good businessman but he didn't have the baseball knowledge and experience that Howsam had. Furthermore Howsam was used to having a free hand. In Denver he was the majority owner, president, and general manager. St. Louis was a new situation for him. He felt that sometimes a decision needed to be made right away and that the GM needed the freedom to pull the trigger. Sometimes opportunity is fleeting. A trade may be on the table one minute, a good trade, a trade you want to make. But half a day later it is off the table. That half a day to get approval from your boss could be costly.

Once he did get the trades approved by Meyer they were not popular in St. Louis, with the fans or the press. Groat and Boyer had been extremely popular players and Boyer was the NL MVP in 1964. But Howsam had learned with his firing of Gazella years earlier that decisions might stir negative press and fan reaction, and that he had to ignore the flak and move on.

The authority irritants aside, Howsam continued to deal in 1966. Howsam felt he had some good young arms coming up, among them Steve Carlton, though he still didn't see much offensively in the farm system. So he dealt pitcher Ray Sadecki for Orlando Cepeda in mid-season. In 1965 Howsam had traded experience for youth. This time he was searching for proven bats. After the season Howsam dealt for Roger Maris. The moves were good ones but not enough to overcome Los Angeles. The Dodgers finished in first again, this time twelve games ahead of the Cardinals.

Though they had come up short, the Cards were well positioned for the upcoming 1967 season. At the end of the year, Gussie Busch threw his annual large party for his whole business empire. It was mostly for his brewing business but Bob and Janet Howsam and a few others were also invited from the Cardinals organization. It was a gala event at a nice hotel in Los Angeles. Frank Sinatra and other high rollers were in attendance. As the party went on into the evening, the Howsams had one of those moments. "How in the world did we get here, rubbing elbows with these people?" they wondered. "We are just a couple of kids from Colorado." "I am the son of a beekeeper," Howsam thought. Mentally stepping outside of the party, they became observers and couldn't believe what they were seeing. They were blown away. Bob and Janet began to giggle like a couple of schoolkids.

The laughter was interrupted by a butler. "Excuse me, Mr. Howsam, Mr. Busch would like to see you in another room."

It was odd to get pulled into a side room to see Mr. Busch during a party. Normally one doesn't get pulled aside at a party unless it is urgent — the kids are sick with the babysitter, someone has died, something like that. But the Howsam's two boys were grown and out of the house, though Edwin was in the Marines and on his way to Vietnam. And no one they knew was on their deathbed.

It was due to a phone call that Mr. Busch wanted to see Howsam, but it wasn't the U.S. Marine Corps on the phone, it was the Cincinnati Reds. Francis Dale, president of the new Reds ownership group that had bought the club from DeWitt, had called Gussie asking permission to speak with Bob Howsam about coming to Cincinnati. Busch had given them permission.

Busch asked Howsam what he thought. Howsam responded that to be courteous he ought to at least check out the situation. Busch told Howsam that the Reds would be calling and that he would hate to lose him, but that Howsam would have to make up his own mind about the situation.

Here was Howsam at a cocktail party rubbing elbows with Frank Sinatra, happy that things had gone so well in his major-league debut, realizing that he was very fortunate, and now, out of the blue, someone wanted him to walk away from all of that and come to a new, unknown place.

Howsam was stunned. He returned to the party and told Janet what had happened. His mind went into a very familiar place, analysis mode. He began to examine all the pros and cons, all the angles.

In order to weigh all the information, you have to *get* all the information. Howsam decided that the only way to get all the information was to visit with the Cincinnati people. When the Reds called, he agreed to come have a look and an interview. It was to be a two-way inspection, one for Howsam and one for the ownership group.

St. Louis's central location made it an ideal airline hub and it was home to one of the largest airlines in the world, TWA. Therefore it offered a neutral site for a meeting — the St. Louis Hilton Hotel. Three members of the five-man search committee flew into St. Louis in mid–January 1967 and were met by

Howsam. The committee was chaired by Bill Williams. The other two committee members making the trip were Raymond (Barry) Busse and Bill DeWitt, Jr. DeWitt had remained with the club after his father had sold it.[10]

The group exchanged pleasantries and sat down for a powwow. The committee told Howsam what they were looking for. They wanted a proven baseball man with major league general manager experience and a man who was familiar with building and moving into a new stadium. Howsam was both. His record with the Bears and Cardinals was solid, and he had moved clubs into both Bears and Busch Stadiums.

The committee also wanted a man who was conscientious of the fan and dedicated to making baseball an exciting, interesting, family event. Finally, they wanted a general manager who was dedicated to building an extensive farm system. Again, with Howsam's experience in promotions, both with the Bears and Cardinals, as well as his minor-league experience, he fit the bill perfectly.

Then came the kicker. Whoever got the job would have total authority to run the baseball operation. The general manager would consult with the ownership group on fiscal matters, but all baseball calls would be his alone. Howsam's heart jumped and his mind reflected on his number one frustration in St. Louis, the chain of command and having to get final approval from Dick Meyer. The song Cincinnati was singing had a nice melody. Howsam told them that before he could accept an offer, if one should come, he would need to talk it over with Mr. Busch and Janet.

As they gathered around the large table at the St. Louis Hilton, Bill Williams was seated next to Howsam. A piece of paper with notes caught Bob Howsam's eye. He couldn't miss it as it was in plain sight. On the paper was written "60,000 TOP." When the compensation question issue came up, as it inevitably would, Howsam knew what their top offer would be.[11]

Howsam (making $35,000 with St. Louis) didn't want to appear greedy and he knew that if the Reds won, then the money would come, so he told them that he wouldn't come for less than $45,000. The Reds could obviously live with that.

The Reds' offer contained much more than a $10,000 pay increase from what Howsam was making in St. Louis; it included the free-reign clause. He would run the club without interference, unlike in St. Louis. The fact that a non-baseball man had had the final say there had been frustrating to a baseball man who had known the luxury of calling the shots in Denver for fourteen years and calling them very successfully. It was not that Howsam was an egomaniac. On the contrary, he was widely considered to be a gentleman and duly humble. But Howsam believed strongly in a number of things, one of which was that if he was going to be successful, he wanted the free reign to be successful. If he was going to fail, and he certainly didn't expect to, he didn't want it because he'd been reigned in. He wasn't power hungry, he was freedom hungry.

It is still an issue for general managers today. Theo Epstein, "Boston's Boy Wonder," resigned from his post for two months in the fall of 2005 over a similar issue. He protested his lack of freedom to call the shots under team President Larry Lucchino and disagreed over the direction of the club. When that was rectified, he returned to the Red Sox front office.

Control is also an issue for coaches in other sports. Seattle Seahawks head coach Mike Holmgren was on the verge of resignation at the end of the 2004 season. One major issue was a front office that was not reading the same sheet of music. When that was rectified by team owner Paul Allen, the Seahawks took off and went to the Super Bowl the next season. If the top leadership is not in harmony, it is very difficult for an organization to enjoy success, especially long-term success.

Bob Howsam was in a quandary. He was happy in St. Louis and he was making a comfortable salary for the time.[12] Janet was happy in St. Louis, but Bob asked her what she wanted. "I want whatever you want," replied his biggest supporter. The Cardinals were poised, cocked, and loaded for a championship run in 1967, and Howsam had worked hard to bring them to that point. Yet there was potentially a very attractive offer in another city, for a ball club that probably was not going to contend for the league title in 1967. He decided that, in a way, he would let August Busch make the decision for him.

What would Busch say? In his heart, Howsam knew what he wanted Busch to say, "please stay." There was a very clear way that Busch could get that message across in Howsam's mind. Offer him more control and offer him a multi-year deal. It was Busch's policy that all front-office people, including the GM, worked on one-year contracts. It was a good policy for ownership because it made things a lot easier and a lot less expensive if they needed to let someone go (such as Devine and Rickey), but it provided little security and peace of mind to the front-office personnel. Beside the salary increase and control of the club, Cincinnati was offering a three-year deal.

The day came to approach Busch. Howsam laid out all that Cincinnati was offering him. He also made it very clear that he was happy in St. Louis and happy to be working for Busch. Busch's response made the decision very easy. "Well, you know, Bob, we only offer one-year deals here, maybe you ought to look into that Cincinnati offer."[13]

Whether Busch had Howsam's best interest in mind or was having second thoughts about having him at the helm, no one will ever know. But it certainly did not come across as "please stay." Howsam had his answer ready when the Reds called.

3

THE NEW ERA BEGINS
January–April 1967

January 22, 1967, bore the first faint hints of the dawn of the Big Red Machine. The conference room of the *Cincinnati Enquirer* was jammed with reporters. The local press, television stations, and the Reds' longtime flagship radio station WLW were on hand.

Bob Howsam leaned into the microphone and made a few introductory comments. He told them how delighted he was to be with the Reds and how he saw it as a great opportunity to be in a good baseball town. He thanked the ownership group for bringing him in. He made it clear that he wasn't all that familiar with the organization, so he asked that they not ask about specifics because he just couldn't answer those. Press conference over; it was time to figure out some of those specifics. His first mission was to figure out what ammunition was already in the Reds' arsenal.

Cincinnati in the 1940s and '50s had a blue-collar feel: meatpacking, machinery, tool-and-dye operations. It was the heart of the Midwest, as Pat Summerall said. Many of the men who worked in these trades played semi-professional sports on the weekend. One of those men was from Anderson Ferry, a suburb of Cincinnati. It was seven miles downstream from the center of the city and named for the ferry that transported cars and other machinery back and forth across the Ohio River. The man liked to take his son along to the weekly football contests, played without facemasks, but otherwise with uniforms, pads and helmets. Pete Rose liked watching his dad play football and himself played in local Pop Warner leagues and in high school as a halfback. But Rose's real love was baseball and he played it with blue-collar grit. His dad taught him to switch-hit and insisted from his first days of baseball playing that he do it, even if it meant that he got fewer hits at the beginning.

Rose and his friends made it a contest trying to sneak into Reds games after school. It wasn't hard to sneak into Crosley Field but Rose excelled at it, even at a young age. By the time he reached Western Hills High School, the athletic director of the Mustangs, Arch McCartney, knew that here was a gritty young ballplayer. McCartney wasn't the last to see the grit—and the talent. Unfortunately McCartney only got to see that talent in action for two years.

Before Pete Rose could enjoy the fruits of the field, he needed to learn the labor of the books.

Disappointed that he was not offered a spot on the football team his sophomore year, due to his small size, Rose copped an attitude. He began to run with the wrong crowd and skipped class often. When he was in class he wasn't paying attention and he found trouble in the hallways between classes; fists flew often. His dad laid down the law on several occasions and Pete promised to reform but didn't. His report card at the end of the year served as his wake-up call. He had passed phys ed and nothing else. He had failed the tenth grade. That snapped him out of the attitude, and he hit the books hard the next year and thus was able to play both football and baseball. Yet when he reached his senior year he was unable to play high school sports, because it was his fifth year of school.

So instead he signed up to play ball for an amateur team based in Lebanon, Ohio, a team that played in a Dayton, Ohio, league, three nights a week. Pete had been a catcher growing up but played second base for Lebanon. He was tearing up the league while his uncle Buddy was a local scout for the hometown Reds. Uncle Buddy began to watch Rose and got Phil Seghi of the Reds to sign him in 1960 for $7,000.

There was no amateur draft in those days, a club could sign whomever, wherever, for whatever if they had interest and the prospect would sign. Pete had just graduated from high school when he signed. As a result, Seghi told Pete that he could wait until the next spring and report to the Reds or be sent midseason to Geneva, New York, though he cautioned Rose against the latter. Pete thought for half a second and opted for Geneva. He was ecstatic. College baseball was not then very popular or widespread. The road to the big leagues went through the minors and Rose wanted to make it to the big leagues.

At first it didn't look like that would happen. When Rose arrived in upstate New York the players were set, battle-hardened and in shape. Rose, having played only three days a week, wasn't ready. Plus there was a young Cuban already stationed at second base. Pete struggled mightily, so much so that he was on the verge of giving up. The reports from Geneva back to the Reds were not glowing concerning the youngster. Uncle Buddy wrote a letter to Pete's dad encouraging him to speak with Pete about his prospects. His dad traveled to Geneva to help convince Pete to stay. The visits helped — Rose did stay. He was often the last person off of the practice field. He had some skills that needed honing. He rarely left when practice officially ended, something that continued throughout the minor leagues.

Rose finished the season and, with a fresh start in the spring, he was assigned to Tampa in the Florida State League. There he tore up the league with a .350 average and thirty triples and was named player of the year. The next year he was in Macon, Georgia, where he continued to pound out triples and doubles and hit .330.

One thing Rose never struggled with was his moxie and risk taking. In those days players would pile into station wagons and other such vehicles to travel from town to town for games. They would often leave right after an away game and drive back to Macon through the night. It could get monotonous. On one such trip Rose was sitting in the back of the station wagon on top of the equipment. It was stuffy and he was bored. He eased the back window down without anyone noticing, then deftly crawled out of the window and up to the top of the car while they were rolling along at 65 mph. The breeze and air felt good as he lay on top of the station wagon. Reinvigorated, he decided to make sure the driver was awake. Crawling across the top of the speeding car, he dropped his face down onto the windshield. The driver almost had a heart attack.[1]

Spring training in 1963 was a turning point for the young second baseman. He had played two and one-half years of minor-league ball. He was fast but did not possess blazing speed — and was definitely not big in stature or muscle. He resembled a plumber more than a professional athlete. But in the minors he had earned a reputation as a hard-nosed, gritty player, with a solid glove and consistent bat. More than anything he was known for his hustle. Whitey Ford, the great New York Yankee pitcher saw him in action that spring and said, "there goes Charlie Hustle." The moniker stuck for his entire career.

The Reds' manager then was Fred Hutchinson. "Hutch," a uniquely talented and insightful man, was like a father to many of the players. He had everyone's respect and admiration, without pandering to players, a rare feat then and even more so now. Rose caught Hutchinson's eye. Hutch wanted to bring Rose north to start the season with the club, but he was practically alone in his opinion.

Not many of the established veterans wanted Rose on the club. They found him brash and cocky. The prevailing thought was that Rose needed to learn his place and wasn't ready. The minorities thought differently. Frankie Robinson, as Frank Robinson was known then, was the leader of the group and also happened to be the best player on the team. He, along with Vada Pinson and Leo Cardenas, took a liking to the youngster from the west side. Robinson would later say that they saw Rose as an outsider, someone who had to overcome the odds, just like them.[2] They sided with Hutch in thinking that Rose should be on the team.

Opening Day in Cincinnati is a really big deal. It is the unofficial start to spring and to new life in Cincinnati. As the oldest professional team, Cincinnati has the honor each year of hosting baseball's Opening Day against another National League team on an early Monday in April. In the American League two clubs share the honors on a rotating, biannual basis. In the National League it is always Cincinnati against someone, and the game is played in Cincinnati. On Tuesday the rest of the league begins play as the Reds are idle, and then everyone plays on Wednesday and the season is underway. It is the same thing every year, a tradition.[3]

Given the hoopla in Cincinnati, the Opening Day starting pitcher is a topic of much conversation and anticipation, an honor bestowed upon the finest starting pitcher on the team. But the other talk of the day is about the newcomers, the rookies who have earned a starting position, a rare feat at the major league level.

When the 1963 team began their season in Cincinnati on April 8, they had a rookie leadoff hitter, Peter Edward Rose, penciled in to play second base. His first at-bat spoke volumes. The umpire shouted "Play ball!" and Pete Rose walked to the left side of the plate for the first time at Crosley Field as a big league player. On the mound stood Pittsburgh Pirate pitcher Earl Francis, a six foot two, 215-pound right-hander. Rose settled into his now familiar crouched batting stance. Francis went into his wind-up and pitched; Rose saw the ball

Frank Robinson (left) — known then as "Frankie" — and Willie Mays pose with lumber in hand. Robinson was one of the leaders of the Reds and one of the few who wanted the cocky second baseman Pete Rose to join the team in 1963 (photograph courtesy Roadwest Publishing [Jack Klumpe Collection]).

leave his hand and tracked it as it sailed toward him. He watched it go by and into the catcher's mitt, just as he had been trained. "Ball one!" called home plate umpire Jocko Conlan. Conlan with great irritation then looked directly at Rose who was looking back wide-eyed toward the catcher. "Listen, rookie, don't look back here at me. I don't need no help with my calls."

Rose, scared to death, never said a thing and turned around to face Francis again. The next pitch the process was repeated. Rose watched the ball go into the catcher's mitt for ball two. The third pitch had the same result. By this time Conlan figured out that the rookie wasn't questioning his ability, it was how he batted, strange as it seemed. Francis's next pitch also was a ball and Rose took off for first, flying.[4] The Crosley Field crowd erupted with its approval, embracing the rookie from that moment. Rose seemed to be an odd duck but a good one.

At the end of the year Rose had good stats, a .263 batting average with 170 hits, and an impressive validation — he was voted NL Rookie of the Year. He was almost everything Hutch wanted in a leadoff hitter. A smart player, patient, with a good eye that could differentiate between balls and strikes with laser accuracy. This gave teammates a feel for the opposing pitcher's stuff, the type of pitches in his arsenal, and his command of those pitches on a given day.

Rose could also jump-start the team, getting on base regularly, giving the Reds a good chance of scoring early. Whether it was through hits or walks, his good on-base percentage (OBP), as it is known today, was key. As a bonus it is good for the leadoff man to be a fast runner so that he is a threat to steal, putting additional pressure on the pitcher. Though he was patient and possessed a good eye, Rose was not especially fast. Stolen bases would not be a large part of his repertoire. Now his big league career was off and running — with a walk.

Another good-looking rookie arrived on the scene two years later, in 1965, a youngster from Cuba named Tony Perez. Baseball had a long history in Cuba. Sailors coming to port to load sugar shortly after the U.S. Civil War introduced Cubans to the game. They caught on quickly, forming their own leagues less than twenty years later. Nonblack players from Cuba began arriving in the National League early in the twentieth century. The Reds had a deep relationship with Cuban baseball, as the Havana Sugar Kings had served as the Reds' Class-AAA affiliate in the 1950s.

Tony Perez was born in Ciego de Avila, Cuba, in 1942. As he finished high school, he began working in a Havana sugarcane factory. Tony Pacheco, a scout for the Reds, signed him to a minor-league contract in 1960. Perez said a tearful good-bye to his family. He feared he would not see them for a long time.[5] Relations between the United States and Castro's recently announced communist government were strained. Indeed, Perez would be one of the last players to legally leave Cuba to pursue baseball in the United States.

Like Rose, Perez was sent to Geneva, New York. Perez was skinny and played second base. When Rose arrived, they moved Perez to third. Rose had received a nice bonus to sign with the Reds. Perez was not a "bonus baby" and therefore was the one who was moved. Perez spent two seasons at Geneva, where he clubbed twenty-seven home runs his sophomore season. The Reds didn't get too excited. Geneva was a Class D league club, the lowest wrung on the ladder at the time. Perez was promoted to Class B at Rocky Mount, South Carolina, in 1962, then to Class A in Macon, Georgia, a year after Rose left there. He made a splash at AAA San Diego in 1964 with thirty-four home runs. The Reds then thought he might be ready to play first base in the major leagues.

Perez was twenty-three years old when he broke into the Reds' lineup, platooning at first base. He hit a respectable .260 in 1965, with twelve home runs and forty-seven RBIs in his part-time role. His first blast was perhaps his most memorable of the season. The bases were full when Perez hit a home run off Atlanta Braves pitcher Denny LeMaster on April 13, 1965.

Perez burst onto the national sports scene in the 1967 All-Star Game at "the Big A" in Anaheim, a game that went into extra innings. A similar event with a much different outcome took place thirty-five years later at the 2002 All-Star Game in Milwaukee. That 2002 game speaks volumes about the state of baseball in the twenty-first century. AL Manager Joe Torre and his NL counterpart, Bob Brenly, fearing not to play every single player, inserted everyone into the lineup during the nine innings, while nervously joking that they hoped the game wouldn't go into extra innings, though it was a close contest. As fate would have it, the game reached the end of the ninth inning deadlocked and the managers were out of players, or so they said. Both managers had starters on the mound that had only pitched two innings each, but the managers felt they shouldn't "over pitch" them in an All-Star Game, that it wouldn't be fair. (Contrast that with the 1967 classic when several pitchers went three innings and one went four.)

In 2002, Baseball Commissioner Bud Selig called the two managers over after ten innings. They pleaded their case and after the eleventh inning, with the game still tied, the commissioner called the game finished on the spot. Instead of rectifying the problem by telling the managers to manage properly, baseball invented a gimmick to solve the manager's lack of courage. They dictated that the All-Star Game winning league would host the Opening Game of the World Series (and thus four of the seven games if necessary). It was a good way to add importance to the All-Star Game, but unnecessary to solve the problem of managers not having the courage to manage.

It hadn't been like that in 1967. The game was in the fifteenth inning and was going to go all night until the winner was determined on the field. Jim "Catfish" Hunter had been on the mound for four innings when Tony Perez decided the game with a deep ball over the left-field fence that ended the game and gave the victory to the National League, 2–1. By the way, four pitchers remained in the bullpen unused by the 15th inning and Tom Seaver was in his

Tony Perez was awarded the All-Star MVP trophy for his fifteenth-inning home run in the 1967 classic at the "Big A" in Anaheim. Here NL President Warren Giles presents Perez the trophy in Crosley Field a few days later. Crosley's Longines clock can be seen in the background. Perez, a member of the Big Four, was the first try at the third-base puzzle (photograph courtesy Roadwest Publishing [Jack Klumpe Collection]).

first inning of work. Back then managers knew how to manage; they didn't live in fear of the players they coached.

Howsam had a rule of thumb: you need to know your personnel. When it came to players, he felt that if you watched a player every day for thirty days, you would have a true gauge of what kind of ballplayer he was. If you see a player in just one series, or when a visiting team comes in for a few games, you can't get an accurate assessment of the player, but after thirty days you refine your estimate and it becomes precise, if you know what you are looking for. After seeing Rose and Perez for thirty days, he knew he had some talent. So Howsam had a gritty blue-collar kid from the West Side at second base and a young Cuban at third. It was a start. But he also needed to build his team in the front office. It was there that he next turned his attention.

There are essentially four parts of a major-league front office. There is scouting, which is the beginning of the pipeline. Scouting identifies the young players that teams want to draft and sign. Next is player development, which is responsible for bringing the drafted players along through the minor-league system. There is the business side of the front office, handling hiring, firing, ticket sales, marketing, TV contracts, travel reservations, etc. Finally, there is baseball operations, which oversees the manager and the team's players.

To handle the business side, Howsam turned again to an old friend, Dick Wagner. Wagner had left the St. Louis Cardinals after he helped Howsam and the Cards move into Busch Stadium in 1965. From there he'd moved to Los Angeles where a brash, confident entrepreneur from the television and communication world, Jack Kent Cooke, had purchased the Lakers basketball team in 1965. His Lakers then played in the Los Angeles Sports Arena in the shadow of the Coliseum. Tired of the management of the dimly lit and drabby Arena, Cooke wanted an upscale venue, befitting his Lakers. He located a spot in Inglewood, a suburb of Los Angeles, and there he would build his monument, Jack Kent Cooke's Great Western Forum, but he needed someone to oversee the project. He had heard of Dick Wagner's good work on Busch Stadium and lured Wagner out to Los Angeles. About five months into the project, though, Dick Wagner's phone rang. It was Bob Howsam. Could Wagner meet him over a meal?

Bob and Janet Howsam flew to California and met Dick and Gloria Wagner for lunch at the space-age dining room at the Los Angeles International Airport. Howsam asked Dick to come and run the business side of the Reds. He needed someone with ability to run the business side without oversight and someone he could trust. Howsam would run the baseball talent side. He told Wagner that he was his first choice. Eager to rejoin baseball and Howsam, Wagner said yes in a heartbeat. Howsam was delighted.

There is an old saying that behind every good man is a better woman. The statement is often true, though no longer politically correct. It can also be said that behind any great CEO or general manager is a very competent secretary. Once a CEO finds such a person, he or she doesn't want to let them go. This person shields the boss, acts as a gatekeeper, keeps him or her organized, and covers his or her backside. In reality the person has very little official power or authority, but unofficially they have a ton. Nixon found Rose Mary Woods while he was a young representative in Congress and took her through the ranks all the way to the White House. Howsam had such a person in St. Louis and he didn't want to lose her. He'd persuaded Lorraine Holzborn to come to Cincinnati.

Howsam also wanted to bring some other front-office talent with him from St. Louis. Every good CEO tries to bring good people with him or her when they leave one organization for another. Lee Iacocca was famous for it. When he was fired from Ford Motor Company by Henry Ford after turning over a one-billion-dollar profit, Iacocca asked Bill Ford if he could bring a little book along with him. In the book Iacocca had the names of rising stars within Ford Motor, with A, B, and C ratings. Bill Ford agreed. Iacocca made good use of the book. He pursued a number of the rising stars and persuaded them to join his new team at Chrysler, often in positions of increased responsibility from those they had held at Ford.[6]

"It's not what you know, it's who you know." In America that is a disparaging remark, but it isn't necessarily a bad thing. Hiring good people is hard to do. There are more vacancies than there are good people to fill them. Good people are rarely floating around available and organizations try desperately to hold onto the good ones they have. So it helps to know people who know good people.

Iacocca knew that you don't take employees from an organization simply because they are your buddies (though some of that does go on). You take them because they are proven performers who you can trust to get the job done. Bob Howsam knew the same thing. When going into uncharted territory, tested, reliable help is invaluable. Perhaps the old adage should be changed to "it is not who you know, but who you know who knows you can get the job done." Leaders rely heavily on networks because they want to acquire proven talent.

Howsam's loyal and capable assistant Dick Wagner was Howsam's first hire for his front office Big Four. Wagner's behind the scenes work would affect the Reds for sixteen years and baseball for four decades (photograph courtesy Roadwest Publishing [Jack Klumpe Collection]).

Howsam now had the proven Wagner but there was another guy he wanted, Chief Bender. Not Charles Albert "Chief" Bender, whose mother was Ojibwe and father a German immigrant,[7] and who was a tremendous pitcher for the Philadelphia Athletics, with a career record of 210–127, landing him in the Hall of Fame. Although he was as solid as it gets on the mound, he is not the Bender Howsam wanted. He wanted "the other Chief Bender."

Sheldon "Chief" Bender is another member of Brokaw's Greatest Generation. Born in St. Louis, he grew up a Cardinals and Browns fan.[8] Some of Sheldon's early baseball was played against the boys one neighborhood over, Joe Garagiola and Yogi Berra. Bender was drafted by the Browns but didn't make the team. He went through chiropractic school before World War II called. He signed up for the navy and went to the marines. He was assigned to the Pacific Fleet and was shipped to the Solomon Islands.[9] It was there that he received his toughest mission. He was to accompany the fourth Marine Raider Battalion in a raid on one of the Solomon Islands, New Georgia. The mission for Bender and his mates was to go ashore and attack the heavily fortified Japanese from behind.

It was on this mission that Bender earned a souvenir from the Japanese that he carries to this day — a bullet about an inch from his left hip. The young Bender had never been on a plane but his first flight would be a memorable one. He was put on an aircraft to be evacuated for treatment of the bullet wound. The flight did not last long. The plane was shot down on takeoff by a Japanese Zero and crash-landed in the harbor. He and the crew hid in the water until they could be rescued and evacuated, this time by ship. After mending, Bender returned to tough fighting in Guam, where many were killed.

When the war ended Bender was shipped to California where he debated between chiropractics and baseball. He felt the urge to go home and he joined the Cards as a player in 1948. A year later a Winston-Salem writer named Spencer asked if it was okay to call him "Chief." Sheldon Bender was a little embarrassed about the nickname, but agreed. After a while Bender began to resist; he was "Shel," after all. Walt Shannon, the Cardinals farm director, sat him down and taught him a valuable lesson. "Shel, nobody will remember 'Sheldon Bender,' but everybody will remember 'Chief Bender.'" Bender stopped resisting and it almost came back to haunt him.

One day the other Chief Bender visited an Athletics minor-league game in Moultrie, Georgia. When his wife heard people calling Sheldon "Chief," she was furious. How could some little white guy from St. Louis shoplift her husband's moniker? But the storm ended as quickly as it erupted. While his wife was irate, the first Chief Bender didn't seem to care in the least. There were now two Chief Benders in the world.

Soon thereafter Sheldon "Chief" Bender migrated to coaching and managing in the minors. He spent most of his minor-league time in various Georgia towns, primarily Albany. Bing Devine eventually brought him to the

Cardinals front office in 1958 to help in player development. When Howsam replaced Devine, he asked Bender, whom he had known from Denver Bears days, to help familiarize him with the Cardinals organization.

Howsam planned on handling the baseball operations in Cincinnati, Wagner the business side, and they hoped that Bender would handle player development. Bender was very happy in his hometown of St. Louis. He had spent twenty enjoyable years in the Cardinals' organization. Howsam was asking him to make a lateral move to a new town. It was a hard decision but in the end his love and respect for Bob Howsam got him to pack his bags and move 350 miles east to the Queen City.

Howsam had his eye on another St. Louis talent, too—George Kissell. Kissell was the Cardinals' bench coach, and in Howsam and Bender's view, one of the best men in baseball in instructing young players. The Cardinals were furious. They called the Reds ownership group with a message: "Tell Howsam to quit taking our people." The ownership group came to him. "Bob, you just can't take anybody else from St. Louis."

Howsam blushed. "Well, you can't blame me." There were others he wanted but he stopped. He didn't take any Cardinal talent again, at least for a while.

Taking stock as he entered his first season with the Reds, Howsam had three-quarters of his front office's "Big Four." He had two future stars on the field, Rose and Perez. It was not a bad start.

4

MORE TALENT, LITTLE IMPROVEMENT
1967–1969

Oklahoma's favorite son is Mickey Mantle, at least when it comes to the national pastime. He is the most famous and beloved baseball player of all time in the Sooner State. Born and raised in Commerce, Oklahoma, the switch-hitting, homer-hitting prodigy with blue eyes and blonde hair caught the imagination of baseball fans across the country in the 1950s. In many ways he and Willie Mays, with the cross-town New York Giants, were the symbols of the game in a kind of golden age of baseball.

Little boys across the dusty plains of Oklahoma idolized Mantle. In a small schoolroom in Binger, 250 miles southwest of Mantle's hometown, a teacher asked each student, "What do you want to be when you grow up?" A pudgy little brown-haired boy in the back raised his hand. "I want to be a baseball player." His classmates giggled. Another year and the class was asked the same thing, "What do you want to be when you grow up?" The same little boy shot up his hand. "I want to be a baseball player." Everyone giggled again. The next year the same scenario unfolded, "What do you want to be when you grow up?" "I want to be a baseball player." No one laughed at John Bench this time.

Bench was growing up and filling out. He starred for Binger High, not as a catcher but on the mound where he primarily played. He was a young Babe Ruth in that he was an excellent pitcher but he also hit very well.

Tony Robello, a Reds scout for the area, came to see Bench one day. There were scouts from several teams in attendance. Most left midway through the game, which turned out to be their loss. Bench pitched early in the game and in the late innings moved behind the plate. Robello was still there watching and was impressed. He had found a player, not a pitcher but a catcher.

Scouts live busy lives. They often shuffle between small towns, commuting late at night after the conclusion of ball games in order to be in the next town to run a baseball camp the next morning and then see the next prospect play. Perhaps that's why so many scouts left the game early that day, they had a deadline to meet or a place to be. They had seen enough of Bench on the mound and at bat to get an idea of the type of player he was; it was time to move on. Or perhaps they wanted to get to the local diner for supper at a decent time that night or get back and go for a quick swim in the hotel pool before dark. Who knows the reasons they left but at least one stayed and that made all the difference in the baseball world. It pays to stay until the job is done.

The Reds signed Bench upon his high school graduation, with their second-round pick of the amateur draft in June 1965. They had chosen a third baseman in the first round. When Howsam arrived in Cincinnati, Bench was scheduled to be the starting catcher at Buffalo, their AAA club, after tearing up the AA Carolina League in his second minor-league season.

The Reds were mediocre in 1967, Howsam's first at the helm as GM. They finished 87–75, fourteen games back of the Cardinals. The St. Louis Cardinals Howsam had built were terrific that year. The Cards were led by Lou Brock, Bob Gibson, Curt Flood, and Orlando Cepeda, whom Howsam had traded for in 1966. They easily overcame the Los Angeles Dodgers who had won the NL in 1965 and '66. One reason they did so was that the Dodgers' Sandy Koufax, with a choice between his career and having a left arm, wisely chose the arm and retired after the 1966 season at the age of thirty-one. The Dodgers were never the same.

The Reds had a couple of finds of their own in 1967. After primarily playing Tony Perez at first base for his first two years, the Reds made a series of changes. They moved Perez from first to third, and he responded brilliantly at the plate, hitting .290, with twenty-six home runs and 102 RBIs, earning the MVP award in his first All-Star Game, the fifteen-inning affair in Anaheim. His play at third base was another story; he seemed to be a clubber at the plate and a bit of a clunker at third.

The move of Perez from first allowed the Reds to work another promising youngster into the lineup — Lee May, or, as he became known in Cincinnati, "Big Lee May." To this day, fans in Cincinnati hear the name Lee, and immediately Big Lee May's face comes to mind.

In the pre-steroid era, Lee May was a big man in baseball. As such he was also labeled "the Big Bopper." Six foot three and well above 200 pounds, he never wore slim pants. In 1967, young and full of promise, May split time at first with a power hitter who struck out too much, Deron Johnson. Even while splitting time with Johnson, May hit twelve home runs, with fifty-seven RBIs, batting .265. He played so well that the Reds traded Johnson to the Atlanta Braves at the end of the season. Big Lee May then hit .290, with twenty-two homers and eighty RBIs in his first full season as a regular in 1968.

The Perez move to third was not the only change of the year. Another involved a not-so-big man who'd arrived with promise one year before Howsam, in 1966. Pete Rose had anchored the Reds at second base since his 1963 Rookie of the Year season. However, there was a young infielder coming up through the organization whose play was stirring strong sentiment that he deserved to be on the field. His name was Tommy Helms. Helms made the club in 1966 as a third baseman and promptly followed Rose's lead, earning Rookie

Lee May, a.k.a. "The Big Bopper," receives his Reds Rookie of the Year Award from longtime sports writer Earl Lawson. Lee May was part of the original Big Four, a big man in baseball's pre-steroid era (photograph courtesy Roadwest Publishing [Jack Klumpe Collection]).

of the Year. When the Reds wanted to make room for May at first and moved Perez to third, that left the Rookie of the Year with no position. The Reds had a hole in the outfield (vacated by Deron Johnson) and the versatile Rose was sent to right, not the young Helms. Helms got Rose's spot at second. The Reds now had three of their "Big Four" on the field, as Howsam's first season rolled along.

During his first year on the job, Howsam had time to look around the organization to see what was needed. He had no intention of changing much until he had a better handle on the operation. This also gave him time to evaluate his front-office personnel in order to assess their strengths and weaknesses. He kept many of the personnel he inherited. Some left for other opportunities and unfortunately a few had to be dismissed because they did not want to go in the direction Howsam was moving the organization — or because they were disloyal. Those were but a handful.

Great leaders know that you have to get the right people into the organization to go in the right direction. In baseball this applies to both the front office and on the field. Jim Collins calls this getting the right people on the bus.[1] If you get the right people on the bus, you will get to where you want to go. If you don't get the right people on the bus, it doesn't matter where you want to go, you won't get there. You have to get the right people on the bus and the wrong people off of the bus.

In the major leagues, the people who first invite people to get on the bus are the scouts. They are the ones out there beating the bushes, finding the talent. It is often a thankless job, with lots of miles down two-lane roads in the middle of the night, stopping at small inns in tiny towns. In those days a major-league club generally had a half dozen scouts at a time, each responsible for a territory.

Scouting has been essential to baseball almost from its professional origins. The rules for acquiring that talent were fundamentally changed in 1965. Up until that point, teams would find a young man they wanted and offer him a contract. If multiple teams were interested in a player, a bidding war could break out, which was good for the player's financial fortunes. If he was a really good player, the teams would offer him a bonus to sign the contract — hence the term "bonus baby," used when a lot of money was paid to a teenager to sign.

Historically the New York Yankees had the best team and hailed from the largest city, with the most press, and thus they had the most fame and the largest network of contacts. Therefore they had a huge advantage in finding and signing the best players. This in turn allowed them to *stay* the best team, which helped them find and sign the best players, a never-ending cycle. This was probably the primary reason for the advent of the amateur baseball draft in 1965. Each team still scouted but a draft was held the first week of June (to coincide with high school graduation). Each team took turns in selecting a player. The team with the worst record got to draft first and the best team drafted last.

Originally there were no set number of rounds to the draft. Teams would drop out when they had taken all the players they desired. The Reds went thirty-two rounds in the inaugural 1965 draft. Contrast that with Bob Howsam's first draft with the Reds in 1967 when they tapped seventy-two players, illustrating Howsam's desire to grab many players to develop a few good ones. Once a player was selected, he could only sign with the drafting club. This helped to keep costs down because there was no competition in the bidding. The only time a team would offer a bonus was to entice the youngster to skip college, leave college early, or come play their sport. For example, a talented youngster might be offered a football scholarship to college while the baseball club tried to entice him toward a baseball career.

After the end of that first year, one thing Howsam realized was that he needed to expand the scouting operation. The Reds had seven full-time scouts at the time. Howsam needed someone to expand and lead this band of men to make sure they had direction and coordination. His answer was found in two siblings.

The Bowen brothers were both baseball insiders. Bob Howsam met Rex Bowen when Rex was running the Pittsburgh Pirates baseball camp for Branch Rickey in Fort Pierce, Florida. Howsam was impressed with Bowen's eye for talent and his ability to develop it. His most famous finds for the Pirates were

Rex Bowen (standing here with his scouts circa 1968) was brought over from Pittsburgh to run the scouting program. He was forceful, opinionated, and had a great eye for talent. His brother Joe is in the back row with glasses (photograph courtesy Roadwest Publishing [Jack Klumpe Collection]).

Bill Mazeroski and Maury Wills. Rex eventually moved up in the Pirates organization. Howsam called him late in 1967 and asked him to come over to run the Reds scouting department. It promised increased responsibilities over what he had in Pittsburgh. Rex said yes and brought along his younger brother Joe.

Rex Bowen was very detailed when it came to player evaluation. He had lots of major-league experience and was very knowledgeable about the game. As a result he was ardent in his opinions and feelings, and he was outspoken with his views. Rex felt strongly that he knew what he was doing and that what he said should be given weight, often the most weight. His forcefulness could be offensive to some and he wasn't afraid to ruffle feathers.

Joe Bowen was several years younger than Rex. He was quieter than his brother, with better people skills, but also a good baseball man. He was bent toward being very orderly in how he carried out his business. Joe was tasked to look at every top prospect in America once they were identified. In that way, at least one person had seen them all in order to help develop the preferred draft sequence.

Initially Rex was kept in the office, taking care of the administration. Soon Howsam and the Bowens realized that administrative work was better suited for Joe, who was well organized. This freed Rex to do what he did best, look for talent. So Joe became the head of the scouting department, while Rex became the chief scout. Not only do you have to get the right people on the bus, but you have to get them in the right seat.

The Bowen brothers joined the Reds for the 1968 season. They proved to head a formidable scouting department. The Bowen brothers in scouting, Chief Bender in player development, Dick Wagner running the business end, and Bob Howsam heading the baseball side: Bob Howsam's front-office "Big Four" was in place. He had his folks on the front-office bus. They would stay together during Howsam's entire tenure and beyond.

September is a time for baseball tryouts. As of September 1, major-league teams can expand their rosters from the normal twenty-five up to forty. The minor-league seasons generally end in late August. Teams that are not in contention for a postseason birth generally use this time to bring young players up and see if they can hack it in the big leagues. There has been many a player who has shined in the minors, but quickly faded under the lens of the big leagues. September is a chance to see if they will shine or fade.

The Reds were well back in September 1967 and they had a problem behind the plate. Johnny Edwards was not spectacular but had been a steady and dependable backstop for the Reds for seven seasons. As the 1967 season wore on, something bizarre began to happen. Edwards began to have trouble getting the ball back to the pitcher. As absurd as it sounds, Edwards began to throw the ball over the pitcher's head, to his side, or bounce it to him. It was like watching a seven-year-old at a Little League game. At first it was dismissed, as people thought that it would pass. It didn't, though, and concern began to grow.

A poor defensive catcher is a huge liability in the game. Would-be base steal-ers seem to gain speed as well as confidence. Players who are not base-stealing threats begin to take chances from first to second. Pitchers, who as a breed are already prone to developing unhealthy psyches, get unnerved. "My catcher can't get the ball back to me, what's next?" Something had to be done. Edwards needed to get better or be replaced.

September was a test for the young catcher from Binger, Oklahoma. Still only nineteen, Johnny Bench was a couple of years away from the big leagues, the Reds' front-office thought. He'd played only four months at the Class-AAA level. On August 28, 1967, Bench emerged from the dugout and took his place behind the plate at Crosley Field. He went 0-for-3 in the game and was lifted in the ninth inning for pinch hitter Chico Ruiz with a runner on second. Chico Ruiz pinch-hitting for Johnny Bench would not be a common occurrence in coming years.

Bench's September numbers were not spectacular. He hit .163 with a homer in only eighty-six at-bats, but defensively he was phenomenal. Base stealers beware: Bench "had a gun." As a former pitcher, his young arm was strong and accurate. More importantly he had what was known as a "quick release." That is baseball jargon for the time between when a catcher receives the pitched ball in the mitt, emerges from the catcher's crouch to the throwing position, and lets the ball fly. Bench could also pounce on a ball like a puma on its prey. The Reds saw Bench's potential and they had their answer. Besides, he could throw the ball back to the pitcher. What was the name of the guy who Lou Gehrig replaced? That's how Edwards felt. He was traded to the Cardinals five months after the season ended.

The Cardinals won the pennant and the World Series in 1967 with the team Bob Howsam had assembled. They returned to the Series in 1968 with all eight regulars and the vast majority of pitchers from the Howsam era. The irony is that after a one-year stint by Stan Musial in 1967, Bing Devine was back in the general manager's seat. The man that Howsam had replaced in 1964 left Howsam a World Championship team. Howsam, in turn, had left Devine a team that went to two World Series in a row, winning one and coming within a missed slide by Lou Brock of winning another, a pretty fair trade between the executives.

The Reds were poised to make a similar run in 1969. The potential they saw in Bench had been quickly realized. He had hit .275, with fifteen home runs and eighty-two RBIs, on his way to winning Rookie of the Year in 1968, the Red's third award winner in seven years. The Reds now had their "Big Four" in place on the field: Rose, Perez, May, and Bench, plus another Rookie of the Year in Helms. The player's bus seemed to have the right passengers on board. Things were definitely bright for the Reds; it looked to be a promising year.

Sometimes promise is not realized, however. The National League had added two expansion franchises, the Padres in San Diego, and the first international team, the Expos in Montreal. As the league swelled to twelve teams, it was split into two divisions, the Eastern and Western. Before they would go along with the deal, the Chicago Cubs insisted on being in the Eastern Division with the New York Mets. As the second-largest city at the time, Chicago wanted to be with the Big Apple. The St. Louis Cardinals, in turn, insisted on being with the Cubs, they weren't about to be separated from their longtime bitter rival. They had enough clout to make it happen. So St. Louis and Chicago went to the East, while Cincinnati and Atlanta, hundreds of miles to the east, went to the West.

That made the Reds' prospects even brighter. Howsam's two-time National League Champion Cardinals were in the other division. The Reds were in the West where the Los Angeles Dodgers were still mourning the loss of Koufax. As an expansion franchise, the Padres were no threat. The Houston Astros didn't have much, so that left the Atlanta Braves with Hank Aaron and the San Francisco Giants with the Willies: Mays and McCovey. It came down to the Braves and the Giants. Rico Carty emerged from nowhere to bolster Aaron in Atlanta and led the Braves to the title. Meanwhile the East saw one of the greatest playoff races ever between the New York Mets, Pittsburgh Pirates and Chicago Cubs. The Cubbies' rival, the Cardinals, finished well back, while Gil Hodges' Amazin' Mets took the title.

The Reds were a disappointing third in the West—four games back of the Braves. The ingredients seemed to be there but the results were not. That is a puzzle for any general manger or any leader in general. When all the players seem to be in place but performance isn't what it should be, the question becomes what is needed to get over the hump? Howsam had a "Big Four" on the field and in the front office yet third place was all they could attain. Some suspected that the problem could be at the helm.

The press speculated that Howsam himself was not in the most secure position. The new owners had signed him to a three-year deal in 1967. That deal was about to expire and ownership was not quick about renewing it. They too had been disappointed with the finishes. Things seemed to be going in the right direction but not as quickly as they had hoped. Eventually Howsam was offered a new contract at the end of the 1969 season. Shortly after signing the new contract, Howsam restated his primary goal as general manager. "I'm trying to build the number-one organization in baseball." Notice that he did not say that his goal was to win championships. He certainly wanted to win a championship, and not just one, but his primary and overarching goal was to build an organization that would allow Cincinnati to win championships. As far as Howsam was concerned, this was putting the horse before the cart.

The other man at the helm, Manager Dave Bristol, was inherited by Bob Howsam. He seemed to be a good baseball man to Howsam and therefore he'd had no reason to remove him when he arrived, so he hadn't. Three years later

Bob Howsam (right) inherited Manager Dave Bristol when he came to the Reds. Here Bristol helps Howsam cut his fiftieth birthday cake. Twenty months later Howsam fired him (photograph courtesy Roadwest Publishing [Jack Klumpe Collection]).

he had a fourth-, fourth- and third-place finish to show for it, with better players every year. The team seemed to have gone as far as it could. It wasn't far enough. Howsam dismissed Bristol as manager on October 8, 1969. It was not a popular decision around town, in the press, or with the players. Howsam had faced that before.

As my youth pastor Carlin Dempsey and others have said, "Everything rises and falls on leadership." On the field leadership comes first and foremost from the manager. Howsam believed it and now he was about to test it.

5

A New Captain
October 1969

All Howsam's trusted advisors were gathered around him. It was how he liked to make decisions. He would gather his inner circle, the Big Four, and they would discuss the issue at hand. Howsam would ask questions and then sit back and listen — actually listen. He would ask his people to ask questions; he would probe. That is sometimes rare for a person at the top, who usually prefers speaking to listening. Dick Wagner was there and Tom Seeberg, the publicity guy. From the talent side, Chief Bender and the Bowen brothers were in attendance, as well as advance scout Ray Shore. The day's question: who should manage the Cincinnati Reds?

Often Howsam would hold a discussion while taking mental notes. He wanted his advisors to present their case as thoroughly and as well thought out as possible. He wanted the background, all the facts, the pros and cons, and the opportunity to think about them. He would then thank everyone for their input and send them away.

Afterward he would mull the decision over. With the exception of trades, he didn't like to make big decisions in a hurry. As he says, "I liked to sleep on it." He often felt that his subconscious worked on a problem overnight, for when he awoke the solution sometimes seemed obvious.

Leaders make decisions all the time, big ones and little ones. Leaders are paid to make good decisions. Not every decision they make is the right one but the majority of calls, especially the big ones, better be right or the leader won't be the leader for long. But the final decision in Cincinnati was Bob Howsam's, always his. As in St. Louis, he wanted the opportunity to succeed or fail on his own.

Howsam felt strongly that you had to think over a decision and then make it, be firm in it and move on. He would later say,

> I didn't have a problem making decisions. I figured there [were] too many
> people working in jobs and in baseball ... looking over their shoulder, looking
> back ... afraid to do what they have to do to be successful because they are
> afraid to make a decision. I wasn't going to do that. Decisions were never a
> problem with me. I guess it wasn't because I had an ego but it was because I

felt it was the only way I was going to be successful. That's why I went to Cincinnati ... because I was going to run the whole show. You just have to make a decision; there are too many people, general managers in particular, that are more interested in their jobs than in doing a good job. But if you do a good job, you don't have to worry, that's the thing.

After looking things over and checking some background information, he would then call the inner circle back to inform them of the decision he had made. There are as many decision-making styles as there are leaders; this was Howsam's style. He used it well.

Decisions actually fell into two other categories for Bob Howsam. The most important were those that needed to be thought out in advance. This pertained especially to trades. Howsam felt it was vital to think through various trade scenarios in advance, so that if a trade presented itself, he could say yes or no, with confidence, on the spot.

The final category was decisions that were easy because they were covered by detailed policies and procedures that were followed faithfully. A very simple example of this approach was that each year Howsam sent a Thanksgiving turkey to each front-office employee to show his appreciation for their efforts. He didn't need to stop just before Thanksgiving and ask himself, "What do I do this year?" The policy was well thought-out and established so he didn't need to take time to make that decision year in and year out. He could focus on other things.

There were actually several meetings on the managerial question. At their first meeting, lots of names were thrown out. Some were those of veterans with impressive experience. Dick Williams had managed the Boston Red Sox to the 1967 American League pennant. He was available but his name didn't raise much interest for Howsam. He wanted a younger, more energetic manager that could put some life in the ball club. Leo Durocher's name surfaced; he was then with the Chicago Cubs. Howsam had entertained that idea in St. Louis and he still wasn't interested. Charlie Metro had managed for Howsam in Denver. Howsam checked into his availability and also for a New York Mets coach.

Finally, Tom Seeberg, the public relations man, spoke up. What about Georgie Anderson?[1] Howsam's eyes lit up but Chief Bender's did not. His mind drifted back to another time and another place, a warm evening in Jacksonville, Florida, in 1964.

Bender had gone down to Florida to scout a minor league game. At the time George Anderson was the manager for Jack Kent Cooke's Toronto Maple Leafs minor league club. He was as fiery as they came. This particular game Toronto was playing against the Cardinals Class-AAA club, the Jacksonville Suns. The Suns were managed by Harry "The Hat" Walker. Walker violated an unwritten rule in the eighth inning and that is when the trouble started.

Several such unwritten rules exist in baseball. They are not formally codified but if you break one of these norms you might as well insult the cook at Thanksgiving dinner — wrath will follow. For example, if a pitcher throws at a batter, that pitcher can expect a "plunk" on the back the next time he comes up to bat. If the pitcher doesn't come up to bat later in the game, retribution can come at another time, sometimes years later. Roger Clemens threw at the New York Mets catcher Mike Piazza on July 8, 2000. Protected by the designated hitter rule, Clemens had nothing to fear. Three months later in the World Series, with Clemens pitching against Piazza in Yankee Stadium, he threw part of a broken bat at Piazza. Again, with the designated hitter in his home park, Clemens had nothing to fear. Then he played an interleague game against the Mets in 2002 at Shea Stadium — and had to bat. Facing Sean Estes, Estes did his duty and the ball sailed behind Clemens, one year and 327 days after Clemens hit Piazza. Baseball players don't forget.

Another unwritten rule deals with bunting, and this is the one violated by Harry Walker on that warm evening in 1964. In general, if your team is leading by five or more runs, it is considered wrong to have your batter lay down a sacrifice bunt to move a runner over to the next base late in the game. Leading the game by seven or eight runs in the eighth inning, Walker's pitcher was up to bat. He wanted to have the pitcher practice the sacrifice bunt in an actual game situation, a situation the pitcher would face in the major leagues. He signaled for the bunt. The pitcher laid one down.

When the batter bunted, Anderson went nuts. He came out of the dugout and began to yell and scream across the field at Walker. Anderson was ranting and raving like a lunatic. Bender was sitting in the stands thinking, "Boy, I'd never hire him, he can't control his temper."

In 1965 Howsam was getting ready for the season in St. Louis when he got a call from Dick Walsh, the assistant general manager of the Los Angeles Dodgers. Did Howsam need a minor league manager? He had a promising young guy he was trying to help out but the Dodgers didn't have any room. It seems that beside the incident with Walker, Anderson had committed another foible that previous season. He liked his Toronto club and announced, "If I don't win with this team, I should be fired." He didn't and therefore he was. Cooke let him go at the end of the season. Anderson had wound up back in his hometown of Thousand Oaks, California, selling used cars. He was desperate to get back into baseball. He called Walsh who didn't have room, but Walsh made a call to Howsam.

Anderson was not new to Howsam either. In fact, Walsh brought up his name by asking Howsam if he remembered the skinny second baseman in Pueblo, Colorado (a Dodgers minor-league club at the time), when Howsam was in Denver. Howsam replied, "You mean the hot-headed guy?" Howsam indeed remembered but he didn't have a need for any managers at the time.

A short time later a man named Fred Cannede called Chief Bender to tell him that his father's business needed help and that he would be unable to manage at Rock Hill, South Carolina, that year as promised. Rock Hill was a Class-

A club, near the bottom of the minors. Howsam and Bender talked it over. Could they use Anderson at Rock Hill? Bender tried to caution Howsam against it. He told Howsam about the Walker incident and Anderson's temper. Howsam listened but he also valued Dick Walsh's input; the Dodgers were a first-class organization. Howsam said, "Let's give him a chance, why don't you give him a call?"

Bender wasn't happy about it but did so. He told Anderson about the opening in Class A. "I'll take it," Anderson said before Bender could finish his sentence. "But I haven't mentioned salary," Bender said. "You give me whatever you want," was Anderson's reply. Bender agreed but decided to keep a watchful eye on the fiery skipper.[2]

George Anderson had been feisty for a long time. While playing for the Ft. Worth, Texas, Cats (a Dodgers Class-AA club) in 1955, Anderson got in a heated argument with an umpire. His manner caused Cats' radio announcer Bill Hightower to remark that Anderson reminded him of an old Cubs infielder, Sparky Adams. The name "Sparky" stuck.[3]

Bender took a couple of trips to Rock Hill in 1965 to see the thirty-one-year-old manager in action. Anderson was intense, relentless, always riding his players, on them every minute. Bender cautioned him about being so tough on the team and suggested he ease up. "You gotta get 'em to bear down," replied Anderson. "They can do better." Bender agreed but he also knew that there was a balance.

Sparky's wife, Carol, was back in Southern California until the three kids, George (Lee), Shirley, and Albert, finished school in May. When she arrived, Bender pulled her aside. You have to talk to Sparky, tell him to ease up. She sighed. She knew her husband better than anyone. "You know he's intense, that's how he's made." But she promised to talk to him.

Upon Carol Anderson's arrival, the Rock Hill team was in last place in the eight-team Western Carolinas League, seventeen games out of first. They did not have much talent. She talked with her husband. Call it a woman's touch if you will but Rock Hill had a complete turn-around in the second half of the season. They finished first, winning the race by one and one-half games. The winner of the first half of the season played the winner of the second half in a playoff to decide the league title. Anderson's team swept the best of three series; they were the champions of the Western Carolinas League. Howsam was impressed and Bender was relieved.

The next year Anderson was moved to St. Petersburg, Florida, still Class-A ball, and won the season's second half there. He did the same trick in 1967 in Modesto, California, another Class-A minor-league team. By this time Howsam was in Cincinnati and offered Anderson a promotion to manage Cincinnati's Class-AA club, Asheville, North Carolina, in the Southern League. That spring Anderson roomed with George Scherger, another minor-league manager, while helping out at the Reds spring training. While lying in his bunk one night, Sparky told Scherger, "I've got ambition. I'm going to the big leagues and when I do I'm taking you with me as a coach."[4]

After the promotion Anderson got even better results. The team was strong all year long and won the league title. Howsam knew he had something special. He didn't want to lose it. He went to Cincinnati Manager Dave Bristol, "Can you make room on your staff for Anderson? I'm afraid if we don't we are going to lose him." Bristol said he didn't have room. He was happy with his staff. It has never been Bob Howsam's policy to meddle in the manager's business. He had made his suggestion, it was rejected, that was all.

Howsam's fear was justified. When the San Diego Padres began play in 1969, Sparky's old friend Preston Gomez called. The new Padres manager wanted his friend and two-time minor-league champion manager to be his third-base coach. Anderson jumped at the chance to be in the big leagues and Howsam couldn't blame him, though he hated to see him go. Preston Gomez was a tremendous man and brought qualities that were already in Anderson to the fore.[5]

It was now a year later. Should the Reds go after Anderson to be manager? One thing attractive about Anderson to Howsam was his age. Howsam wanted an energetic young manager who could shake the ball club up. When he asked for his inner circle's view, there was one reservation — Anderson's lack of experience. Howsam knew how that could be overcome.

Anderson did have something that Howsam and all the others liked. He was a proven winner in all four years that he had managed Howsam's farm clubs. But it wasn't just the winning that Howsam liked. It was the minor-league managerial experience itself. Howsam was a great believer that major-league managers should first manage in the minors. In the minor leagues you have to ride buses, cover the field when it rains, and other humbling duties. Then when you have just about everything done for you in the majors, you appreciate it. It is the same philosophy used by some NCAA Division I basketball coaches when recruiting junior college players. A player who has to struggle at a small junior college, eating box-lunch sandwiches on the hundred-mile bus trip to the next game, appreciates things when he arrives at a big-time program.

Howsam liked the Anderson idea. Bender did too. Normally Howsam would have gone into a background check at this point. Background checks were essential to him. "You want to make sure you have the right person. If you don't go to great lengths to find out what is right and how to do it, then you are not doing your job. One reason we were successful [is that] we knew about the players we were going to trade for; we knew about them on and off the field; we knew them and their backgrounds, same way with a manager and a coach." But, a background check was not warranted for Anderson. Everyone in the room knew what Sparky stood for, the kind of man that he was. "He had a fine wife and children. He was a man of his word, willing to work hard, and not afraid to put name or neck on the line. He was very good with young players. Those are the things we had to consider," Howsam said.

Howsam decided that if he were to call it would not be to check on availability as it had been with others. It would be to offer Sparky the job. With the background check not applicable, he could offer him the job quickly and he decided to do so. There was only one problem. Anderson was on the move again. The man who had initially recommended Anderson to Howsam back in 1965, Dick Walsh, had left the Dodgers to become the California Angels general manager. He hired Lefty Phillips as his new manager. Phillips was one of Anderson's mentors and was wooing him to the Angels to be a coach. As far as connections go, Lefty Phillips had recommended Anderson to the Dodgers as a young player prospect years earlier. Baseball networks are strong and deep.

Howsam called his old friend Walsh to ask for permission to talk to Anderson. Ironically Lefty Phillips and his new coach Anderson were sitting in Walsh's office when the phone call came. Anderson had accepted the Angels third-base coaching job that very day. Walsh said he would give Howsam permission to talk to Sparky about a managerial position but not a coaching position. Howsam assured him that it was managing he wanted Anderson to do. Walsh told Howsam that he would have Anderson call him later, then hung up and gave Anderson the news and some counsel on the spot. Sparky was dumbfounded.

Anderson called Howsam later that evening from Lefty Phillips's home. They chatted about the team and about managing. Howsam asked him a number of questions. Years later Anderson would reflect back on the one that he thought that was key: "What would you do if a star pitcher walked off?"[6]

"Mr. Howsam, I could tell you a lot of things, but I don't know what I would do until I was in the situation. I can tell you one thing, I would deal with it." Anderson sensed this answer sealed the decision for him. Howsam asked Anderson if he wanted to be manager of the Reds. If so, he needed to be on a plane that night because they were planning to make an announcement the next day. Anderson packed his bags and went to the airport. The next day's announcement took everyone by surprise. Former New York Yankee pitching great and longtime Reds radio announcer Waite Hoyt asked, "Sparky who?"

George "Sparky" Anderson had several obstacles to overcome as the manager of the Reds. First and foremost was his age. Though this was an attraction to Howsam, it was a hurdle to Anderson. He was only thirty-five. To put his age in perspective, two players in the league were over forty, Willie Mays was four years his senior, and fifteen players in the National League were older. Fortunately for Anderson none of these players were on the Reds.

Anderson had an additional blessing in an odd sort of way. Anderson was blessed in that he didn't look thirty-five; he looked fifty-five. That is the lot of men who gray prematurely and Anderson was practically white. They share this fate with guys who go bald and don't buy cheap-looking toupees. When men gray early or bald early, they may look twenty years older than their actual age but they don't seem to age for the next forty years. Anderson looked prac-

Sparky Anderson was thirty-five when he was hired as the Reds manager by Bob Howsam. With his white hair he looked fifty-five. There were fifteen active players older than Anderson in the National League (photograph courtesy Roadwest Publishing [Jack Klumpe Collection]).

tically the same when he retired from baseball in 1995 at the age of sixty as the day he was hired by the Reds.

Along with his mature look, he also had a good pedigree for the job. On inspection, it is uncanny how many utility players go on to become successful managers. They seem to be rivaled only by catchers.[7] How many great baseball players can you name that went on to be successful managers? You will have to think for a while. They are a rare breed. This is something of a mystery. In today's high-salary era a great ballplayer is financially set for life. He doesn't have to manage or even coach to make a living after playing. If he has half a brain or a sound financial manager (unfortunately many don't), he can store away a few years of salary and live very comfortably for the remainder of his days. But the big money hasn't always been the case. Many generations of players had to work after baseball or even in the off-season (God forbid) to make a living. Why haven't star players more frequently gone on to become managers? The best teachers often do not make the best principals. The best engineers often don't make the best CEOs of engineering companies. The top sales people may not be the best sales supervisors. Playing and managing seem to require different stuff. It takes different skills to lead effectively than it does to play great baseball.

"Utility" is a nicer term than "sub." Utility players are like handy guys around the house. Nobody comes in and says, "My, what a nice caulking job that is around the bathtub." They may say, "Wow, what a great couch" or "I love your woodwork," but without the bathtub caulk things can get messy. A good utility player can fill in several holes, relieving tired players or filling in a few games when a star is out with a minor injury. Cesar Tovar of the Twins was probably the ultimate utility guy; he could play all nine positions and once did so all in the same game.

The other part of the equation is that utility men generally have to scrap to stay in the game. They are seemingly a bad road trip away from a ticket out of the majors. They aren't blessed with the greatest talent, so they develop versatility, grit, hustle, and a knowledge of the game. Baseball is a game of knowledge and a utility player perhaps studies harder than any other student. It helps give them that little edge to stay around another season.

It's not simply the utility role but also where they play. Utility infielders who are primarily middle infielders seem to have a better grasp on the game than do other position players. They are involved with so many plays— the routine grounder, the double play, the relay throw from the outfield, covering second on a steal, holding runners close, covering second depending on whether a batter is left- or right-handed, gathering in pop flies in shallow outfield. They are part of nearly every play. A number of current and former managers were middle infielders, including Tony LaRussa, Larry Bowa, Willie Randolph, and Ozzie Guillen. Even Leo Durocher played shortstop and second base. Casey Stengel and Jim Leyland were also utility men, but not at middle infield.

Anderson had the pedigree and, with his age in mind, he set out to select his coaching staff. As an eighteen-year-old he had reported to a team in Santa Barbara, California, where his first professional manager was George Scherger. Anderson loved him. Scherger was intense in his own right, as Bob Howsam had already found out. When Howsam arrived in Cincinnati, Ohio, Scherger was managing the Reds' minor-league affiliate in Tampa. Howsam paid a surprise visit there one evening. He came down out of the stands after a ballgame and started to enter the clubhouse but stopped when he heard a chair crash followed by Scherger yelling. Howsam smiled to himself and returned to the stands until Scherger cooled off. He then returned and greeted the surprised Scherger and they went out to dinner together. Throwing chairs in the clubhouse was fairly common in those days but by 1970 Scherger had mellowed with age. He looked like a content grandfather at age fifty. Though he only had two children at the time, Scherger would eventually have ten grandkids. He was the one guy that Anderson had to have on his staff. As promised eighteen months prior, Anderson was going to take Scherger with him to the big leagues. It was the first move he made as manager. Scherger would serve as the Reds' first-base coach. He would also be the bench coach.

"Bench coach" is an odd term for an important position. A manager can get into the game, caught up in the heat of the moment in such a way that he loses sight of the big picture. He can lose the forest for the trees. The bench coach makes sure that does not happen. A good one constantly gets the lay of the land, surveys the changing situation. Don Zimmer is the quintessential contemporary bench coach for Joe Torre. If Torre lost Zimmer it would be like losing his right arm. Who is hitting well, who should pinch hit, who isn't getting enough playing time, how can we set ourselves up for a favorable situation later in the game? In a nutshell, a bench coach reads the people and reads the situation. He is a manager's right-hand man, vice president and chief lieutenant.

Like a good vice president, the bench coach should make sure that the president doesn't get surprised or ambushed. He should funnel information that the top guy doesn't always hear. Loyalty and people skills are essential for the job. A good bench coach can make all the difference but unless you're watching them you hardly notice that they are around. They

George Scherger looked "grandfatherly" in his glasses. He was fifteen years Anderson's senior and had been Anderson's first manager in the minor leagues. Anderson promised to take Scherger to the majors with him and was good to his word (photograph courtesy Roadwest Publishing [Jack Klumpe Collection]).

don't seek the limelight; they are indispensable but almost invisible. If you have a problem or need an ear, the bench coach is your man. George Scherger was the reason Bob Howsam was not concerned about Sparky Anderson's lack of experience. Scherger was Anderson's man.

As a utility middle infielder, Anderson knew that he needed someone capable of handling his pitching staff. Dick Wagner knew a good candidate from his minor-league days. Larry Shepard had managed for Wagner's Lincoln team in 1956 and 1957. Rex Bowen seconded the nomination, knowing Shepard from the Pittsburgh Pirates. The baseball fraternity was at work again.

Slightly built with big glasses, Shepard was born in 1919 and grew up in the Dodgers' minor-league organization. He was a league leader in wins and winning percentage as the player-manager of the Billings Mustangs in both 1949 and 1950. In his managing debut in 1949, he led the club to a second-place finish. He moved on to the Hollywood Stars, where he helped pitch them to a Pacific Coast League (PCL) championship in 1952.

Shepard eventually moved on to Lincoln, Nebraska, where he was the full-time manager of the Lincoln Chiefs and led them to titles in 1956 and 1957. From Lincoln he stepped up to the Salt Lake City, Utah, Bees and managed them to the PCL title in 1959. Shepard was promoted to manage the Columbus Jets and won the International League in 1961. He developed a reputation as a fine groomer of pitchers after his 1965 Columbus team produced nine major-league pitchers. After eighteen years of minor-league managing, he finally got his first major-league position as a coach for the Philadelphia Phillies in 1967.

The Pirates tapped Shepard as their manager in 1968. His first team played about .500 ball and finished in the middle of the pack. In 1969 he had the Pirates in third place in the Eastern Division, when he was fired before the last week of the season. He was known to be a bit temperamental but he knew his stuff when it came to pitching. Dick Wagner was a big fan and Wagner was not easy to impress. Sparky knew him from his managing days in Toronto. Shepard agreed to come aboard.

For a batting coach Anderson turned to one of the most beloved Cincinnati Reds of all time. Theodore "Ted" Kluszewski was a strapping first baseman for the Reds in the 1950s. He had played football at Indiana University. His arms, particularly his biceps, were Herculean, so big that he had to cut off his uniform sleeves. He had "big guns" before the term was invented. He had three forty-homer seasons and five with over a hundred RBIs in his heyday. After a season and a half with the Pirates he was traded to the Chicago White Sox in time to play in the 1959 World Series where he hit three home runs and knocked in ten. Unlike most power hitters, "Big Klu" also could hit for average, batting more than .300 seven times.

Howsam suggested that Anderson go and talk to him. (Kluszewski owned a popular steakhouse in town.) Both Howsam and Anderson liked Ted a lot, were impressed, and thought that he would be great for the job, though he had never coached in the majors before. Kluszewski had done some roving instructing for the Reds in the minor leagues and he had wanted to coach in the majors for a long time. When Sparky offered, Big Klu relished the chance.

The missing piece was the third-base coach. Anderson wanted someone crafty and smart and got a tip about Alex Grammas from a guy in Pittsburgh. Alex Grammas grew up in Birmingham, Alabama. Of Greek descent, Grammas's family was as proud of their heritage as the characters in the film *My Big Fat Greek Wedding*. Grammas's father's story was movie material itself. He immigrated to the United States alone as a young teenager and ventured through a few cities before settling in Birmingham within a year. A few years later, after war broke out between Greece and Bulgaria, Grammas made his way back to Greece, volunteered for the army, and fought for his home country. Moving back to Birmingham when it was over, he met a "nice Greek girl," the first girl born of Greek descent in Birmingham, and they had two sons, Cameron (known as Pete) and Alex.

As a boy, Alex Grammas had the same routine for eight years. He attended his local elementary school in northern Birmingham. When school ended at 3:00 P.M., he hopped on a streetcar to the Greek Orthodox Church in southern Birmingham where he took lessons in reading, writing, and speaking Greek from 3:30 to 6:00 P.M., including Saturdays. Fortunately he found time to play some baseball and got pretty good at it. At age seventeen, he finished high school and went to Auburn University in Alabama. Once he turned eighteen, he was drafted and then spent twenty-six months in the army, including service in the mountains of Northern Luzon in the Philippines and then as part of McArthur's occupation forces in southern Japan.

When he returned from the war, Grammas joined his brother at Mississippi State, a traditional baseball power. They helped continue that rich tradition. Alex was at third and his brother at short, winning two Southeastern Conference championships in three years. He was signed by the Yankees and spent five years in the minors and then ten in the majors, with the St. Louis Cardinals, Chicago Cubs, and the Reds. His philosophy was that if you played as hard as you could, then you wouldn't have to worry about anything else. He mostly played the middle infield positions.

In 1963, a utility man for the Chicago Cubs, he sensed that his playing days were numbered. He decided to visit John Holland, the general manager of the Cubs. "Mr. Holland, I am thirty-seven years old and I would like to stay in the game. Is there a place for me?" Holland told him that a number of teams had expressed interest in him but that the Cubs also would be interested in having him manage one of their minor league clubs. "Mr. Holland, the problem is that if I go with one of those teams and get cut at the last minute in spring training, then I will be out of a job. I would just as soon go ahead and stop playing right now." Holland told Grammas that he could manage the Cubs' minor league Class-AA or Class-AAA club the next year. After meeting with Cubs' owner Phil Wrigley, it was decided that Grammas would get the Dallas–Ft. Worth Class-AA club.

After one season there, Grammas got a call from an old acquaintance, Harry Walker, who had been hired as the Pittsburgh Pirates manager. Walker had coached and managed Grammas in St. Louis and now picked Grammas to be his third-base coach. While in Pittsburgh, Grammas developed a great relationship with the General Manger Joe Brown. Joe Brown liked Alex Grammas, and Grammas liked him. When Brown fired Walker in 1967, he replaced him temporarily with Danny Murtaugh, then with Larry Shepard. Brown talked Shepard into keeping Grammas on. At the end of the 1969 season, Shepard was in turn let go as the manager. Brown told Grammas, "You will be back next year, either as the manager or as a coach."

He called Grammas a week later. "I have hired Danny Murtaugh [to return] as the manager of the Pirates." "Great," Grammas replied. "And he wants to bring in his own man." "Mr. Brown, are you trying to tell me that I am out of a job?" Grammas asked. "Well, I guess I am." "Could you at least help me out finding something else then?" Grammas requested. "I will," said Brown.

Brown was planning to attend the World Series. Bob Howsam and his manager of one week, Sparky Anderson, were going to be there too. Grammas's phone soon rang again. It was Howsam and Anderson, "Alex, would you like to come to Cincinnati as the third-base coach?" Grammas had never met Anderson.[8] It helps to have friends and networks.

Sparky Anderson had now assembled his assistants. They averaged twelve years his senior and had a combined eighty-six years of professional baseball experience, a big help to a young manager. Now, for the hardest part, he had to actually manage. Anderson told Scherger, "We're on our way." He had lots of enthusiasm. The question was whether it would translate into wins on the field.

6

THE BIG RED MACHINE
April–September 1970

Sparky Anderson met his team in late February 1970 at Al Lopez Field on the outskirts of Tampa, Florida. Like most spring training sites at the time (Dodger Town in Vero Beach aside) it was a simple ballpark. Anderson was full of enthusiasm. As he would later say, he was too naïve to even think the Reds could lose. He told Howsam and Scherger that they would win the division by ten games. His goals for the spring were to get the players in shape through a tough camp, get to know the team, and sort out the pitching. The position players were mostly settled, other than left field.

On the mound, Jim Maloney had been the stalwart and workhorse for the Reds throughout the 1960s. With a fastball timed at over ninety miles per hour, Maloney fanned many a hitter. However he had been suffering from shoulder troubles in 1969 and the Reds feared he would not recover. Maloney had been the perennial Opening Day starter. Who would lead the team on the mound now?

At the end of 1968, Howsam took a risk. He traded the longtime Reds shortstop Leo Cardenas. It was a move that was a surprise to many. Cardenas had a great reputation in the press. His range at short and his arm strength were reported to be exceptional. Howsam was not as impressed as was the press. Howsam considered Cardenas's arm and range good but not great and traded Cardenas to the Minnesota Twins for a young and promising left-handed pitcher named Jim Merritt. Lanky Merritt had gone 17–9 for the Reds in his first full season, 1969.

When the Reds opened the 1970 season at their old home park, Crosley Field, they were supposed to have been two miles to the southeast, downtown, along the banks of the Ohio River in their new ballpark by then. The ballpark, not yet named, was running late in being completed. Though the new park was not ready, the Big Four were in place on the field and the front office, and Anderson and associates were the new leaders on the field. The Reds were touted as the best team in the National League by forecasters. Everyone was cautiously optimistic after the 1969 disappointment.

Lee May was at first, Tony Perez at third, Pete Rose in right, and Johnny

Bench behind the plate. Tommy Helms was still at second, four years after chasing Rose to the outfield. Woody Woodward was at shortstop, where he split time with Darrel Chaney now that Cardenas had gone to the Twins. The Reds were waiting for a shortstop to emerge from the minors.

Left field was also a platoon situation. It didn't need to be that way. Bob Howsam had been very high on Alex Johnson. While still at St. Louis, Howsam had acquired Johnson in a multi-player deal with the Phillies. When Howsam went to Cincinnati, he acquired Johnson from the Cardinals in a trade. Now Johnson had been in left field for the Reds for two years. The man could hit. He could not get along with the press. He averaged .313 during 1968 and 1969 but he was as moody as he was talented. He carried a chip on his shoulder. The press has earned a degree of mistrust but when a player won't answer a simple question about a ballgame without getting ugly, things get tense. Howsam had

The new acquisitions for 1969 were important in the early era of the Big Red Machine. Left to right: Jim Merritt (a twenty game winner in 1970), Leon Wagner (never played a game for the Reds), Bobby Tolan (the apple of Bob Howsam's eye), and Wayne Granger (part of a formidable duo with Clay Carroll in the bullpen) (photograph courtesy Roadwest Publishing [Jack Klumpe Collection]).

tried everything to get Johnson to lighten up. He talked to him, other players talked with him, and Howsam even asked Johnson's wife to talk with him. They all tried but nothing worked. Exasperated Howsam picked up the phone, and Johnson went to the California Angels with Chico Ruiz for Jim McGlothlin, Vern Geishert and Pedro Borbon.[1]

With a hole to fill in left, the Reds turned to youth again. They had two young hitters in the organization with promise: Hal McRae, a right-hander, and Bernie Carbo, a lefty. The Reds were so high on Carbo that they had selected him with their first pick in the 1965 inaugural amateur draft, one round ahead of a young catcher named Johnny Bench. Carbo led all the minor leagues in hitting in 1969 with a .359 average.

Anderson decided that Carbo would be used against right-handers while McRae, who'd also been drafted in 1965, would get the nod against southpaws. Since most pitchers are righties, that meant Carbo would get the most starts. That was a good thing in Howsam's mind. McRae could hit but he wasn't a great defensive player, nor was he very fast. Howsam was always looking for speed.

The key figure in the speed department was in center field, Bobby Tolan. Tolan was also young and talented, one of the few bright spots in the Cardinals minor-league system when Howsam was there. Howsam had kept him in mind and watched from afar. He had been told in 1967 to stop taking Cardi-

From left to right: Tommy Helms, Johnny Bench, Pete Rose, and Alex Johnson receive awards, with Crosley's Moondeck in the background. Alex Johnson was brimming with talent — and a bad attitude that got him shipped to the California Angels (photograph courtesy Roadwest Publishing [Jack Klumpe Collection]).

nal talent, but that was only in the front office. Trading for players on the field was another matter.

Howsam was genuinely fond of Tolan. He was the type of young man you would hope your daughter married but Howsam didn't have any daughters. Thoughtful, polite, respectful, with a great smile, he was almost like a son. A son with an odd batting stance. A lefty, Tolan held the bat high over his head as if trying to knock a cobweb off of the ceiling with a broomstick. As the pitch came he would lower the bat and cock. The real excitement began once he hit the ball. To use the modern vernacular, Tolan had wheels. He was fast down the line to first and fast from first to second on the steal. He garnered twenty-six steals his first year of full-time play.

By 1968 Howsam wanted Tolan badly. Tolan had come up from the minors and was sitting on the Cardinal bench behind a well-stocked outfield. Howsam offered the Cardinals a deal: Vada Pinson for Bobby Tolan, a known quantity for an unknown. The thinking was that the team would lose a good player now for possibly a great player later.

It was a surprise and an unfair deal for the Reds in the eyes of many. Pinson had played outfield for the Reds for ten years. He had come up as a nineteen-year-old and averaged nearly .300 and twenty home runs a year. Tolan was promising but an unproven commodity, after a glowing minor league career. He had only averaged .227 in a part-time role for the Cardinals. Many great minor leaguers never pan out in the majors but this was Howsam's style. He was willing to trade a known for an unknown. Unknown to some but Howsam and his people had done their homework. The future performance was not a sure thing but there was lots of evidence that it would be good.

Bob Howsam's trading philosophy was simple, "You have to trade value to get value." Howsam loved to trade to improve a ball club. In those days, it was your only option, beside the minors, to improve your team. You couldn't go out and buy a player in the free-agent market. It didn't exist. If you didn't have what you needed in the minors, you picked up the phone and played "Let's Make a Deal."

When the famous architect Frank Lloyd Wright was asked what his best work was, Wright replied that it was his next one. Bob Howsam felt that way about his trades. They were something to be designed and planned for, just like a structure. When asked what his best trade was, his answer was always "the next one."

Howsam was interested in long-term relationships with other teams. He wanted to make a deal with a club not only now but perhaps again in the future. A good way to cut off the possibility of trades in the future was to not give any value away. In this case he had a known value in Vada Pinson and he wanted the future value of Tolan. Tolan had a great first season with the Reds in 1969 and started Opening Day in center field in 1970. To young boys in Cincinnati he was the coolest cat in town.

The Reds won on that 1970 Opening Day, beating the Montreal Expos, 5–1. Carbo started with a bang, hitting a solo home run. It was a harbinger of things to come. The Reds won often in those first three months of the 1970 season. The pitching that had been a question mark before the season began was phenomenal. The only disappointment was Maloney. Eleven days into the season he ruptured his Achilles tendon and wouldn't return until September 4. The "other Jim," Jim Merritt, drew the Opening Day start and was well on his way to twenty wins as the new leader on the mound.

Perhaps no one was as big a surprise as the man on the mound for Bat Day on June 7, 1970. Bat Day to the modern fan means that boys and girls fourteen years old and younger receive a miniature bat signed by a selected player from the home team. In 1970, it was no miniature bat, it was the real thing. Everybody fourteen and younger got one courtesy of the Reds and Hillerich & Bradsby, the company known for its "Louisville Slugger" bats. The wooden bat was twenty-nine inches long and weighed twenty-four ounces, and signed by Tony Perez. Kids would poke them in the air in unison during the cheers. I suppose that today they would be categorized as some sort of safety hazard. An

Rookie Davey Concepcion greets 1970 Rookie of the Year Bernie Carbo after his Opening Day home run. Concepcion was long a question mark, so thin early in his career that it looked as if he could barely stand (photograph courtesy Roadwest Publishing [Jack Klumpe Collection]).

usher today will take away a bat that flies into the grandstand and only return it to a spectator at the end of the game. In those days a couple thousand kids with Louisville Sluggers in their hands enjoyed a ballgame with no second thoughts about it.

On Bat Day in Cincinnati almost all the bats would have green smudge marks on them when the kids left. The old wooden seats at Crosley were painted green. When not used as a cheering instrument, the bats were tucked up between seats and arm rests where the paint would rub against them. It was a way later on to determine if the bat was an authentic "Bat Day" bat — did it have the green smudge marks on it? The green smudge marks came from fresh paint. Even though the Reds would soon vacate Crosley Field, Howsam insisted that it be kept painted and clean. He took one look at the dingy concession counters upon his arrival in 1967 and immediately ordered all of them replaced, even though they would only be used for three years. For Howsam, cleanliness was next to godliness. The ownership supported his decision despite the capital outlay required. It also exemplified a Howsam philosophy, spend money to make money but spend it wisely.

The draw on Bat Day 1970 was not only the free lumber but the starting pitcher. The guy scheduled to be on the mound was one of the most exciting in all of baseball. Wayne Simpson seemed like the second coming of Bob Gibson. When Howsam was with the Cardinals, his admiration ran deep for Cards ace Gibson. If a game had to be won, Howsam would pick Gibson to pitch it. Now with the Reds, Howsam had a young Gibson clone in rookie Wayne Simpson. In his first game of the

Wayne Simpson, the next Bob Gibson, was brilliant (13–1) for half of the 1970 season. When he and Merritt were hurt, the Machine was hampered (photograph courtesy Roadwest Publishing [Jack Klumpe Collection]).

year he had pitched a two-hit shutout against the Dodgers. In his third game he got his third win on a one-hit shutout of the Giants. Going into Bat Day, Simpson had only one loss and a low ERA. Like Gibson, Simpson was black, tall, and powerful — and had a great fastball. He beat the Mets that day for his eighth win.

A new era began three weeks later when the Reds moved from Crosley Field to Riverfront Stadium. To prepare for the move — and play on AstroTurf, the Reds worked out extensively on Houston's Astrodome outfield during a late June road trip. If Crosley was a ballpark, Riverfront was a multipurpose stadium. It was a perfectly symmetrical structure, built to house not only Howsam's Reds but Paul Brown's new team, the Bengals.

The Reds were producing high offensive numbers even with regular absences of Johnny Bench. Bench, like many others, served in the military reserves. In 1970 nearly 17 percent of major-league players were serving on reserve duty. Every team except one had a player in the reserves. Some were very notable, such as Larry Bowa and Nolan Ryan. The Reds had four: Carbo, Tolan, Chaney and Bench.[2] This meant that one weekend a month Bench would serve duty at his station in Kentucky. He was in the U.S. Army Reserve. He also was on the hook to serve two full weeks during the year. For some players that fell in the summer and their team simply had to do without their services during that time. In fact, Bench had to be excused for two days of his two-week duty so that he could play in the 1969 All-Star Game. There was some speculation that the service could affect the 1970 pennant races.

A young man in his early twenties today can barely entertain such an obligation. A professional athlete at that age cannot fathom it.[3] But for most men of Bench's generation and those prior, it was a fact of life and an accepted obligation. The draft had been instituted in 1940 as a response to the looming concern that the United States would be drawn into World War II. It had been continued essentially nonstop since that time and was unlikely to end in the near future. There was a conflict going on known as Vietnam.[4] Many who were not drafted chose to join the reserves. Some chose to join the reserves in order *not* to be drafted. Most of the games Bench missed early in his career were due to military duties. In his absence Pat Corrales donned the "tools of ignorance," catchers' gear.

The Reds' winning percentage was well above .700 through the early part of the season, reaching a crest of .737 on June 10. Winning more than seven out of every ten games was unheard of in the professional ranks. With the Reds so far in front, Howsam began to plan for the World Series. Anticipating scenarios and planning ahead were always important to him. He wanted to make a trade by the June 15 deadline to get his team a proven leader with World Series experience. He had his eye on Ron Fairly, who had been to the World Series four times with the Los Angeles Dodgers. Fairly was getting older but was still a good player and was known for his leadership. Fairly had been traded to the

Expos the previous season and they weren't interested in parting with him, so Howsam stood pat with his club.

By the All-Star Break, Sparky had his Reds at 62–26, ten games ahead of the Dodgers. At the hundred-game mark, the Reds had won seventy, a league record for one hundred games. They were on pace for 113 wins, when a hundred-win season is considered phenomenal. It was probably the finest stretch of baseball the Big Red Machine ever played. The Reds were rolling. Things were good in Cincinnati. The Reds were outdrawing the Dodgers, something that was almost unfathomable in the National League; since their move to L.A., the Dodgers had led the league in attendance eight times. As a result, the Reds were making a handsome profit. Other general managers around the league began to call Howsam for advice.

Nicknames are strange. They don't seem to be coined extemporaneously by one person, they just seem to happen. Where do they come from, who comes up with them, and are they invented or do they emerge? Some seem that they were always with us. "Murderer's Row," "the Gashouse Gang," and "the M&M boys" immediately conjure up memories of specific teams in specific eras. So it was with "the Big Red Machine."

The Reds were playing the Philadelphia Phillies in August 1969. After the Reds beat the Phillies in a 19–17 slugfest on August 3, Bob Hunter of the *Los Angeles Times* slipped a seemingly innocuous phrase into his story on the Reds, calling them a "Big Red Machine." An idea was born — or was it? Pete Rose had purchased an old, red pick-up truck during the season, at a time when pick-ups were mostly used by farmers. Rose called his truck his little red machine. Whether due to Rose or Hunter or someone else, the phrase was soon on the tongue of every Reds fan in town. Jerry Dowling, the *Cincinnati Enquirer* cartoonist, often used the theme in his sports-related cartoons. Tom Seeberg, the team's publicity director, quickly seized "the Big Red Machine" as a slogan.

It was very important to Howsam to get the Reds players noticed and covered in the press. Often the writers in New York ignore players between the Appalachian Mountains and California. That is why Howsam hired Charlie Metro, the man he had once considered to be the manager, to be his advance public relations man. Howsam would send Metro in advance of the team for interviews, armed with pictures and information on Reds players for use by local television and radio outlets. In essence Charlie Metro was to drum up interest in the Reds before they arrived in town.

Metro had a lot of help. Tom Seeberg was a top-notch publicity man from the Dodgers organization, who Howsam hired away to the Reds in the late 1960s. He was the overall publicity director. Several years earlier when both were with minor-league organizations, Sparky had recommended that Seeberg go to work for Bob Howsam if he ever had the chance. Seeberg, in turn, was the man who brought up "Georgie Anderson" in the meeting to decide on the new Reds manager. They were high school classmates. When Seeberg left for a promotion with the Dodgers, Jim Ferguson took over for Seeberg and did a great job for the rest of Howsam's tenure. The three men's publicity efforts, plus the Reds' stars' play in the All-Star Game and regular season, got the players a lot of recognition.[5] As a result, Reds players became among the most recognizable and watched athletes in all of sports. Baseball fans across the country knew of "the Big Red Machine" and how it was rolling.

Then the pistons began to ping. Wayne Simpson's shoulder began to hurt. He came out of a game against the Chicago Cubs on July 31 with an injury that initially was diagnosed as a pulled muscle. Unfortunately that diagnosis was incorrect. Upon further examination, it was determined that he had torn his rotator cuff, a group of four muscles that form a cuff at the top of the shoulder. The cuff helps to lift the shoulder up over the head and also rotate it toward and away from the body, the precise movements required for a pitcher to throw a ball. Tearing a rotator cuff actually means that a hole has developed in the rotator-cuff tendon that connects the rotator-cuff muscles to the humerus (upper-arm) bone. It can occur over time through tendonitis, the most common way, or through a sudden pop as in the case with Wayne Simpson.[6] In either case, it spells trouble for pitchers and few ever recover from it. Simpson made only two more appearances the rest of the year.

Ditto for Jim Merritt. On September 8 he was in the first inning of a game against the Giants in Candlestick Park on a cold, windy day. He uncorked a curveball and heard something pop in his elbow. He was through for the day. With a record of 20–12 at the time, he only pitched three innings the rest of the regular season.

Gary Nolan continued to be consistent, finishing 18–7. He had been another top draft choice by the Reds, taken in the first round of the 1966 amateur draft. He debuted in the majors one year later and went 14–8 as a rookie. Arm troubles plagued him in 1968 and '69 but he opened the 1970 season with a two-hit shutout of the Dodgers and never looked back.

The other starters, Jim McGlothlin and Tony Cloninger, were steady. McGlothlin looked like a grown-up Opie. He could have been mistaken for a brother of Ron Howard of *The Andy Griffith Show* and *Happy Days* fame. He had come over in the deal for Alex Johnson and went 14–10. Tony Cloninger, who had been a fifth starter, moved up to take Wayne Simpson's spot in the rotation.

Though two of the starters were ailing, the bullpen was strong. This would be the mark of every Sparky Anderson and Larry Shepard club in Cincinnati. The two stars of the bullpen were just about the most different physical specimens you could see on the mound. Wayne Granger and Clay Carroll looked a bit like Laurel and Hardy. Carroll was big and strong, built like the chicken hawk on the old Warner Brothers cartoons, with a puffed-up chest and red hair. He was a country boy from Alabama, with a southern drawl. Unlike the cartoon character Carroll didn't constantly jabber but was a great, hard thrower who could spot the ball well. He wanted the baseball; he wanted to be in the game in every tight situation.

Granger, on the other hand, was tall but slightly built, in the manner of Stan Laurel. He hailed from the North, Massachusetts. He also was a character. When teammate Tommy Helms hit the first Cincinnati home run in Riverfront Stadium, Granger decided to immortalize the shot, which had barely stayed fair, one foot above the left-field wall. Granger shimmied up the foul screen and placed an "X" with masking tape on the net. Granger had a sly sense of humor and an equally deceptive sinkerball. Granger and Carroll had fifty-one saves between them in 1970.

While the starting pitching was hurting and the bullpen was strong, Tolan was spectacular in center, hitting .316 and swiping 57 bases. Finally, the Big Four had lived up to its name. Rose hit .316 with 205 hits, May and Perez combined for seventy-four home runs and 223 RBI, and twenty-two-year-old Bench had the greatest season of them all, with a .293 batting average, forty-five home runs and 148 RBIs. In recognition of his season he was named the Most Valuable Player of the National League, the youngest ever to receive the trophy. Bench's numbers may have been even higher had it not been for his service in the Army Reserves.

While they weren't firing on all cylinders (32–30 during the last part of the season) the Reds won 102 games in 1970, the most in their history, and entered the playoffs as a formidable foe.

7

THE FIRST SERIES
October 1970

The baseball playoffs were a fairly new phenomenon, instituted the previous year. The Reds' opponent, the Pittsburgh Pirates, had survived a gritty race in the East, while they had coasted to a Western Division crown by 14½ games, exceeding Sparky's prophecy. The Pirates had beaten the Cubs and the defending World Series Champion New York Mets by five and six games respectively. Though Pittsburgh had defeated the defending World Champions, they proved to be no match for the Big Red Machine. One of the Pirates stars, Roberto Clemente, had a sub-par series, while the other standout, Willie Stargell, was tremendous. Nonetheless the Reds swept them, 3–0.

The Reds' World Series opponents were an entirely different matter. The Baltimore Orioles had won the 1966 World Series in a sweep of the Los Angeles Dodgers in Sandy Koufax's last season. Unable to repeat in 1967 or '68, the Orioles fired their manager, Hank Bauer, and replaced him with a longtime minor-league manager, the brilliant and crafty Earl Weaver. Heavily favored against the Mets in the 1969 World Series, the Mets had staged a miracle and defeated the Orioles 4–1 in one of the all-time great championship upsets. The Orioles were eager to avenge that defeat. They, like the Reds, had coasted to a division crown and swept their opponent, the Minnesota Twins, in the playoffs. It was now the clash of the titans.

The Orioles had the best defensive infield in baseball: Boog Powell at first, Davey Johnson at second, Mark Belanger at short, and Brooks Robinson at third. For a time Earl Weaver had watched, totally perplexed, as opponents came into old Memorial Stadium in Baltimore and made great diving catches and performed other spectacular infield exploits while his team seemed to make only routine plays. One day it hit him: his infielders were so good that they were making the really difficult plays seem routine. He set out to change things and ordered the grounds crew to shave the grass down, cut it really low. Additionally they watered it sparingly, so that is was hard, almost like concrete. It became, in essence, a large diamond-shaped putting green. Suddenly, it was the Orioles infielders making the great plays, while the opponents watched balls skip across the green into the outfield for base hits. The infield was like the green felt on a pool table and demanded outstanding defensive talent. The Orioles had it, most others didn't.

They were equally adept defensively in the outfield. Paul Blair could cover a position and a half in center field. Frank Robinson in right and Don Buford in left could hold their own defensively. The Orioles were good with their bats, as well. The Robinson boys, Frank and Brooks, were RBI machines, while Boog Powell was also productive at the plate. The Orioles weren't as strong as the Reds offensively but they certainly had nothing to be ashamed of.

Like the Reds, the Orioles had excellent leadership in the clubhouse. Frank Robinson would call a kangaroo court into session when needed. The court's job was to levy fines and harass those who had conducted themselves unworthily on the field. Transgressions like failing to hit the cut-off man, missing the bunt sign, and throwing errors would all be punished through pronouncements and fines of the courts, Chief Justice Robinson presiding. The informal leadership of Robinson was an immeasurable help to the formal leadership of Weaver. When a manager doesn't have to worry about keeping order, it is a weight off of his mind. It also removes the possibility of ugly confrontations between the manager and a player. In other words, when the workers take care of themselves, it is a huge benefit both to management and to the entire organization.

Earl Weaver, Baltimore's crafty manager, had baseball's best defensive infield. He had the grass shaved in Memorial Stadium to exploit the advantage (photograph courtesy Roadwest Publishing [Jack Klumpe Collection]).

The Orioles' real strength was found on the mound. They were spectacular there, with three twenty-game winners. Dave McNally was 24–9. Mike Cueller, after being a journeyman for four years, found himself in Baltimore and went 47–16 in 1969–1970. The Orioles bullpen, while not up to Cincinnati standards, was certainly reputable.

The prize egg in the Oriole pitching nest was young Jim Palmer. Flying to Cincinnati for the Series match-up, his picture adorned the front page of the *Cincinnati Enquirer* sports page. His blue eyes, fair hair and cleft chin sat atop a lean but chiseled body — he looked like a fashion model. Indeed a few years later he would be spotted in department stores across America, clad in a leading brand of underwear. Palmer's good looks were more than matched by his talent on the mound. He emerged as a twenty-year-old sensation in the 1966 World Series and he was the Orioles' third twenty-game winner in 1970.

With so much talent—only a handful of teams in baseball history could boast three twenty-game winners in a season—the question for Earl Weaver was who to start in Game One. The Game One starter has the potential to also pitch Games Four and Seven if necessary, so the decision, like so many, has ramifications down the line. Mike Cueller and Dave McNally were lefties, while Jim Palmer was a righty. Given the Reds' success against left-handers over the year (33–12 overall and 17–2 at home), Palmer got the nod. His opponent in Game One would be Gary Nolan, who shared much in common with Palmer—he was twenty-two, handsome, and much-heralded.

The temperature was fifty-seven degrees and it was a beautiful, clear, autumn day that Saturday afternoon along the banks of the Ohio River. It was the first World Series game ever played in the brand-new Riverfront Stadium. There were 51,531 in attendance to see Baseball Commissioner Bowie Kuhn throw out the first pitch. A normal-looking boy with a large afro, Michael Jackson sang the National Anthem with his four brothers.

In a playoff series, a Game One win captures the immeasurably helpful force called momentum. While the home-field advantage is less important in baseball than in most sports, momentum is coveted by all. In Game One of the

The 1970 World Series Opening Game pitchers were young, talented, and handsome. Jim Palmer (twenty-five) of the Orioles and twenty-two-year-old Gary Nolan (photograph courtesy Roadwest Publishing [Jack Klumpe Collection]).

1970 Worlds Series, the Orioles were eager to rid their mouths of the taste of the previous year's loss to the Mets. The Reds, meanwhile, were eager to show that they belonged, that "the Big Red Machine" tag was not just hype, and that the hiccups down the stretch were temporary.

The Reds got out of the gate early in the first inning with a Tolan double and Bench RBI single. They went up 3–0 on a Lee May two-run home run in the third inning, but the Orioles came back to tie it in the fifth on Boog Powell and Elrod Hendricks home runs. The real turning point of the game, and perhaps the Series, came in the bottom of the sixth with an umpire's call.

Umpires have an interesting work life. They are noticed for only one thing — when they make a mistake, which is a nice way to say "when they blow a call." They have earned the stereotype with baseball fans of being a bit overweight and not often well-liked. Rarely do you adore a worker who does his job without notice but on occasion wrecks the whole day by making one big mistake. The job can become routine. In a way, umpires have a job similar to pilots. As the old flying adage goes, "there are hours of boredom, punctuated by moments of sheer terror." For the pilot it means that normal operations are interspersed with an infrequent emergency, such as a fire. For the umpire it means that dozens of routine plays and calls are interspersed with a razor-close call with a game on the line. To make those close calls an umpire has to be in the right place. Being an umpire is first and foremost about being in the right position. They have to make the calls with their eyes, and so they have to stay in position to see the play. Calling Game One of the World Series is supposed to be an honor reserved for the best umpires.

The bottom of the sixth started with Lee May smashing a line drive down the left-field line. Brooks Robinson gloved it going toward the third-base stands, jumped, and threw from four feet into foul territory, across his body, to first. The ball bounced once on the AstroTurf and into Boog Powell's mitt to get May by a half step.

The young rookie, Bernie Carbo, then worked his way to third base on a walk and a single by Helms. Ty Cline pinch hit for Woody Woodward with one out and the game tied 3–3. Elrod Hendricks was catching with Ken Burkhart hovering behind, calling the balls and strikes. Palmer delivered the pitch and Cline smashed the ball almost straight down. The ball ricocheted high in front of home plate and Hendricks lunged forward to field the ball and fire to first to get Cline. Burkhart sprang to his left in order to call the ball fair or foul. The proper move for the umpire is to move to the left to make that call, so as not to obstruct the batter running for first base. What he didn't know and what Hendricks didn't know was that Carbo was making a mad dash from third. Palmer, who had rushed in to help field the hopper, heard Carbo's footsteps on the AstroTurf and yelled "tag him, tag him," pointing toward third.

Burkhart was straddling the third-base line when Carbo went into his slide, pushing Burkhart out of the way from underneath. Hendricks dove over

Burkhart and tagged Carbo. Meanwhile Burkhart was falling forward toward third base, trying to strain his head back over his right shoulder to see the play. Realizing that he was out of position but trying to recover, Burkhart bellowed "You're out!"

There were two problems. First, Hendricks's mitt had indeed tagged Carbo's outstretched body but the ball was not in the mitt. Second, Carbo had missed home plate while trying to slide around Burkhart. Carbo immediately leapt to his feet to argue the call with Burkhart. When he did, his foot touched the plate. Therefore he was now rightfully safe.

The stadium let out a collective groan. The fans behind home plate had a much better view of the play than Burkhart, whose back was turned. Anderson sprinted toward him. "I would like to see the picture on that one," Anderson said. "So would I," Burkhart replied.

Burkhart stood his shaky ground. After the game he admitted that he had been surprised by Carbo's dash from third. So had Alex Grammas been surprised, the third-base coach, who had not sent Carbo home. Carbo later said that he had broken for home by instinct.

In postgame interviews Burkhart said that he saw Carbo tagged "when the catcher dived at him." Asked how he could do this while falling the other way, he replied, "I don't remember how I saw it." The pictures were clear; he hadn't seen it at all.[1]

The phantom tag: Ken Burkhart's poor positioning and blown call cost the Reds Game One and changed the dynamics of the 1970 World Series. Bernie Carbo slides by as Elrod Hendricks has the ball in his right hand, not in the mitt (photograph courtesy Roadwest Publishing [Jack Klumpe Collection]).

Games can turn on a single call. If Burkhart had gotten that call right, the Reds would have led 4 to 3 with runners at first and second and one out. As it was, the very next inning Brooks Robinson gave the Orioles the lead, hitting a breaking ball over the fence, and the Reds lost the game by that one run, 4–3. One-run games seemed to be the Orioles forte. They had won forty-one of them during the season and sixteen in a row. The Reds were now down 0–1 and Baltimore had the momentum.

Game Two was played the next day, Sunday afternoon, October 11. Mike Cueller started against Jim McGlothlin. Game One home-plate umpire Ken Burkhart, as part of the standard rotation, was patrolling the right-field line and would not be a factor in further contests. He did pick up a police escort on the foul line in the second inning. A false rumor spread that a few fans were throwing things at him. Once the police arrived, they found no physical objects flying but verbal barbs, mostly good-natured, were flying and would continue for the whole game.

The Reds had hoped that Jim Merritt would be ready to go on the mound. He wasn't. Sparky left the call entirely up to Larry Shepard, who made almost all the pitching decisions. "Shep" talked with Merritt and it was clear that he wasn't able to pitch, so McGlothlin got the call. His Orioles counterpart, Mike Cueller, was an interesting character. Originally signed for the Reds by Bobby Maduro, the same man that inked Tony Perez out of Cuba, Cueller had bounced around the league for years. From the Reds, to the Cardinals, to the Astros, he arrived at Baltimore in 1969 and proceeded to win twenty-three games to share the Cy Young Award with Denny McClain. He followed that with twenty-four wins in 1970. He had a nasty screwball that broke down and away from right-handed hitters like Bench, Perez, and May.

The screwball has become a rare pitch in baseball, perhaps because it is so hard on a pitcher's forearm and elbow. The pitch is made by twisting the wrist in the opposite direction from which it normally twists. This allowed Cueller, a lefty, to have the ball break away from right-handed hitters. His curveball, of course, would break away from left-handed batters, making him a formidable opponent. The screwball was used by the great Christy Mathewson and much later by Fernando Valenzuela. But the king of the screwball was Hall of Famer Carl Hubbell who used it to strike out Babe Ruth, Lou Gehrig, Jimmy Foxx, Al Simmons, and Joe Cronin in succession —five future Hall of Famers— in the 1934 All-Star Game. Hubbell threw the pitch so often that his hand permanently turned so that the palm faced out.[2]

Cueller was as superstitious as his screwball was nasty. Among many rituals, he insisted that he and only he could pick up his glove and the ball he was using. No one could do it for him, even as a favor. He insisted that Jim Frey, a Baltimore coach, be the only one to catch his warm-up tosses before a game. Elrod Hendricks, and no one else, could stand to simulate the batter during those warm-ups. He also claimed Elrod Hendricks as his personal catcher for actual games. The Orioles normally platooned catchers; Hendricks hit left-handed and Andy Etchebarren batted right-handed; however, if Cueller was pitching, Cueller requested that only Hendricks be his battery mate, regardless of the opposing pitcher. Weaver often complied.

Neither Cueller's screwball nor superstitions spooked the Reds, as they again jumped out to the lead. The Reds had a chance to put a nail in the coffin in the third inning. They scored another run to make it 4–0, and Johnny Bench was on first base with only one out. Lee May smashed a ball into the hole between short and third, and Brooks Robinson somehow grabbed it, firing to second. Johnson fired to first to end the inning. Robinson had robbed May again.

Boog Powell made it 4–1 with a monstrous blast to dead center in the fourth inning. The pivotal inning proved to be the fifth. McGlothlin was coasting with the lead. After retiring the first batter, the Orioles followed with five singles and a fly out to tie the game. In the midst of that rally, Anderson brought into the game a twenty-year-old rookie named Milt Wilcox. Wilcox had been in the big leagues for five weeks. Standing sixty feet and six inches from Wilcox was one of the main characters in the previous day's drama, Elrod Hendricks.

The Big Bopper, Lee May, meets big Boog Powell as May is thrown out on yet another defensive gem by third baseman Brooks Robinson. May was one of only a few parts of the Big Red Machine to work properly in the Series (photograph courtesy Roadwest Publishing [Jack Klumpe Collection]).

Hendricks was a very good defensive catcher, which was fortunate for him because he was a so-so hitter, averaging .243 for the season. With the score tied, Boog Powell was at second and Brooks Robinson at first. The Reds' Ray Shore had put in his scouting report that Hendricks was a dead pull hitter, meaning that he always hit the ball to the right side of the field. In several weeks of scouting Shore had never seen Hendricks hit the ball to the left. Therefore, the infield and outfield played him to the right. Wilcox pinned the light-hitting catcher with a two-ball, two-strike count. Wilcox threw the next pitch for what he and Bench knew was strike three to end the inning. The home-plate umpire, John Flaherty, called "Ball three!"

The next pitch and following sequence was nearly as bizarre as the Carbo-Hendricks-Burkhart play the previous day. Hendricks was completely befuddled by a Wilcox fastball, expecting a change-up, and as he was swinging his spike caught in the dirt. His stride interrupted, he slapped at the ball, with his bat slicing it just inside the third-base bag for a double and two RBIs. The surprised Perez at third later said, "I played with Hendricks for five years in Puerto Rico and never saw him hit one like that." That was consistent with Hendricks, who declared that he had not hit one like that in his twelve years in the big leagues or before.[3]

Johnny Bench homered in the sixth to cut the Oriole lead to 6–5. The Orioles were threatening to score again in the top of the ninth, with their power-hitting first baseman due up next. Anderson went to the mound, skipping over the first-base foul line — it was bad luck to touch that. He wanted to discuss with his pitcher a strategy for handling Boog Powell. A new reliever who had replaced Wilcox. Teenager Don Gullett had made the Reds at the end of spring training. A southpaw from Lynn, Kentucky, a town about the size of a postage stamp, Gullett had been a three-sport star at nearby McKell High School. Notre Dame offered him a football scholarship after he scored eleven touchdowns in one game. However his baseball prowess was discovered and he was signed by a Reds scout. The Reds made it a habit to scout small towns at a time when many big-league teams wouldn't. It is a bit of a risk, as a local star may shine more due to a lack of competition than talent. The Reds were pretty sure, though, that Gullet had the talent. He spent only one year in the minors. Now he was in the World Series facing Boog Powell.

It was almost comical: a real-life David and Goliath, dapper Don Gullett, conceding four inches and sixty pounds, facing Boog Powell, six foot four and 250 pounds, with black lines under his eyes and a grimace on his face. While Gullett was scoring forty-seven points in a basketball game as a high school senior eighteen months prior, Powell had finished his eighth season in the big leagues, the reigning American League MVP. Now they met. Watching television coverage, my mother cried out, "I hope that big Boog Powell doesn't hurt that boy, it looks like he could break him in half!" It did, indeed. The bat in his hand resembled a toothpick. Gullett didn't have a sling or a stone but he had a pretty good fastball. Pitching carefully with Don Buford at first, he eventually walked Powell.

Anderson now had a new dilemma — runners on first and second with Frank Robinson due up. Conventional wisdom says to bring in the right-handed Wayne Granger to face the right-handed Robinson. Sparky figured that Gullett could handle Robinson at that stage and left him in. He was right. Robinson was called out on strikes to end the threat. But the Reds failed to score in the bottom of the ninth, the Orioles won 6–5, and the Reds went to Baltimore two games down.

The Orioles fans were smart and brutal toward opposing batters. It was unofficial policy that if you

Don Gullett was a teenager when he was asked to face former MVP Boog Powell in Game Two of the Series (photograph courtesy Roadwest Publishing [Jack Klumpe Collection]).

sat in center field in Baltimore's Memorial Stadium, you wore a white shirt to the game. In an era when some men still wore white dress shirts with skinny black ties to the ballgame, it wasn't hard to get fans to follow the unofficial center-field dress code. But teenagers helped out too. If they skipped the white dress shirt, they sported a white T-shirt. The policy was effective and the reason for it was simple. It is difficult to pick up a white ball leaving a pitcher's hand when it is coming through a background of white. It was just one more reason that the Orioles staff was the best in baseball. In an age when most ballparks have large dark walls in center field in order to give batters the benefit of an unobstructed view of pitches, Oriole fans' behavior probably seems offensive to the hitting-conscious player's union and owners. Back then it was just good baseball.

Compounding the effect of the fans' white shirts, a number of white houses were perched just above the center-field seats. Earl Weaver, the Baltimore manager, claimed that the Reds should be concerned about the white background. He asserted that this was a bigger deal than the issue of AstroTurf at Riverfront; this was the first time a World Series game had been contested on that surface.

The Reds still hoped to have Jim Merritt, their twenty-game winner, ready for Game Three in Baltimore. He was able to go five-plus innings in game two of the playoffs against Pittsburgh but again was reporting a tender elbow. It was one reason Sparky Anderson had to go with such youth on the mound. So far he had used Wilcox, twenty, and Gullett, nineteen. Between them they had eight months of big-league experience. Anderson's use of the youngsters prompted Pittsburgh Manager Danny Murtaugh to observe, "My confidence in kids goes so far but that guy Anderson is a mad man."[4]

With Merritt still unable to pitch, Sparky had Larry Shepard make the call. It would be Tony Cloninger for the Reds, who had finished the year 9–7. His opponent was Dave McNally, another of the Orioles' twenty-game winners. Sparky's mother flew in from California for the game. Mrs. Anderson wished her George good luck in the hotel lobby. It had been her first airplane flight; she was so scared that she didn't look out the window once.[5]

The game was a disaster for the Reds. The Orioles had scored four runs off Cloninger and led 4–1, with one on and one out in the bottom of the sixth when the Reds brought in their closer, Wayne Granger. A bit disgruntled because he had not been used to this point, Granger loaded the bases and then faced Orioles pitcher McNally. With two strikes on McNally Granger threw him a high fastball — just what the scouting report said *not* to throw — and McNally put it in the stands. It was the first and only grand slam hit by a pitcher in the history of the World Series. To add insult to injury, McNally finished the Reds off with a complete game, 9–3 victory. Rose declared McNally the best Baltimore had to offer.

Even more bizarre than McNally's grand slam was Larry Shepard's experience. The Reds pitching coach was in the bullpen located behind the outfield chain-link fence when the phone rang. He looked toward the dugout to see who was on the other end. He saw no one at the dugout phone. He picked up the receiver and a female voice said, "This is long distance calling for Sparky Anderson." Befuddled, Shepard answered, "I'm sorry he's not here," and hung up.[6]

The Brooks Robinson play of the day came on a Johnny Bench line drive — a diving catch to his left that he caught before Bench could drop his bat. McNally asked Robinson from the mound if he could "ride in his car this winter," referring to the automobile given to the World Series MVP. The fifth-inning gem was in addition to another Bench liner that Robinson had snared in the first.

The other Robinson also broke through in Game Three. Frank was a bit miffed at Anderson. He interpreted Anderson's Game Two remark, that he'd thought that "Gullett could handle him at this stage" to infer that he (Robinson) was over the hill and couldn't get around on a Gullett fastball. Anderson contended that he meant Gullett could handle Robinson at this stage of the year with the lighting of October, which can be tough on hitters. Robinson entered Game Three hitless for the Series, but went 3-for-4 with a home run. Cincinnati had been warned. The last line of Ray Shore's scouting report on the Orioles read, "Don't throw at Frank Robinson or do anything else to get him mad."

If Mrs. Anderson's visit didn't help the Reds, perhaps Mrs. Ruth's would. The Babe's widow was in attendance for Game Four and sent a message to the Reds clubhouse telling Sparky Anderson of her admiration for how hard he had worked to stay in the game. She requested a cap from Sparky and he gladly complied. It was a day for baseball legends. Vice President Spiro Agnew had to cancel his visit at the last minute, but the eighty-year-old former Yankee manager Casey Stengel was in attendance. They asked him to relieve for the vice president, and Stengel was glad to throw out the first pitch.

Game Four was a rematch of the Opening Game starters, Palmer and Nolan. After seven innings it looked as though a four-game sweep loomed. The Reds were down 5–3. In the top of the eighth, with Jim Palmer pitching, Tony Perez walked to start the inning and Johnny Bench singled to left. Big Lee May emerged from the dugout. Of the Big Four, only May had been hot. Weaver had seen enough and made his way to the mound to call for Eddie Watt from the bullpen. May returned to the dugout to inquire about Watt's stuff. He was told to look for a sinker and a flat slider. On the first pitch he got a sinker that didn't sink and put it 440 feet into the white shirts in the outfield stands, putting the Reds ahead. Clay Carroll pitched nearly four innings, allowing only one hit, to secure the win. Perhaps symbolically, Robinson made no great plays at third. In fact, Helms actually singled off his glove. The Reds were still alive.

A win in Game Five would return the Series to Riverfront. Though home-field advantage wasn't on the Reds minds, it sure beat batting with the white-shirt background. Plus a win would be the only way to extend the Series. Win and go home to play again, or lose and just go home.

The Orioles had Cueller scheduled to start. The Reds wanted to counter with Jim McGlothlin but like his roommate Merritt, McGlothlin developed a sore elbow after Game Two and was unable to pitch. Merritt had been hoping to come back all Series and he was pressed into duty for Game Five. The Reds scored three times in the first for a 3–0 lead. The Orioles countered with four runs in the first two innings, chasing Merritt and his sore elbow from the game. The Orioles then roughed up Wayne Granger and others that followed. Robinson robbed Bench again in the ninth with a headfirst dive into foul territory to snag a liner.

The Reds' Series was best exemplified by Big Lee May in his last at-bat in the ninth inning. As Cincinnati school children raced off their buses and into their homes on that Thursday afternoon, May was facing Cueller in the ninth. Swinging mightily to make contact, May fell to his knees in the batter's box. It wasn't a lack of trying on the Reds part. The Orioles were just too good, too experienced, and too hungry to be denied. With the game out of reach with

The Reds' fortunes rose and fell with Jim Merritt's left arm. His September sore elbow made him unfit for the Series (photograph courtesy Roadwest Publishing [Jack Klumpe Collection]).

two outs in the ninth, Sparky called Hal McRae back to the dugout and sent up little-used Pat Corrales so that he could get a bat in the World Series. He bounced out to guess who— Brooks Robinson. The Orioles took Game Five by a score of 9–3.

The Reds returned to Cincinnati beaten badly in games won and lost, but not in total scoring. Three of the five games had been settled by one run. There were probably three differences in that series: two were people-related and one a phenomenon.

Pitching had let Cincinnati down. In three of their losses they had combined leads totaling 10–0, but the pitchers could not protect those leads. A healthy Merritt and Simpson would have helped immeasurably.

In Howsam's mind, there were two things that stopped Cincinnati in the Series. One was Brooks Robinson, who was deservedly named MVP of the Series. He was unbelievable. With his signature short-billed batting helmet, he was lethal at the plate, hitting .429 with two homers and six RBIs, atoning for his miserable .053 average against the Mets the previous year. His seventeen total bases also set a record for a five-game Series. In the field he was out-of-this-world with highlight-film defensive plays in Games One, Two, Three and Five. Rarely has a man had a better Series.

The phenomenon that made a difference in the Series was experience. As Howsam said, the Reds were "slightly outclassed" overall, especially in the experience department. You either have it or you don't. Howsam had tried unsuc-

Brooks Robinson scores yet another run. Robinson destroyed the Reds at bat and in the field. It was one of the most excellent efforts in World Series history (photograph courtesy Roadwest Publishing [Jack Klumpe Collection]).

cessfully to get Ron Fairly and he would have helped. The Reds' average age of twenty-five was nearly four years junior to the Orioles. Additionally, the majority of the Orioles had played in the World Series against the New York Mets the previous year and many had been in the 1966 classic as well. The Reds had only Merritt (with the Twins in '65), Granger (Cardinals '68), and little-used Ray Washburn (Cardinals '67 and '68) with Fall Classic experience. Their youth had been a drawback, but it meant that they had many productive years to look forward to. Contrast that with the Orioles, whose star was brightly shining but would fade in a few seasons. As the Reds took stock of the Series and the season, they had high hopes for 1971. It was now their turn to think about avenging a World Series loss.

8

THE DISMAL YEAR
1971

Moms and kids in the late 1960s and early '70s had two choices for afternoon television viewing: game shows or soap operas. This was before the advent of *The Oprah Winfrey Show*. ABC's afternoon lineup was filled with three staples in the game show universe, *Let's Make a Deal*, *The Dating Game*, and *The Newlywed Game*. On the set of *The Dating Game* a young man was helping his mother, Lila, put the show together each day, but he didn't want to be doing this work for long. He was hoping to be in the radio booth at a ballpark.

Word was out that the Reds' flagship station, WLW, was searching for a new play-by-play man to replace the exiting Jim McIntyre. The new broadcaster would partner with Joe Nuxhall, the former Reds pitcher who had retired in 1966 and whom Howsam and Wagner had moved to the booth the following year.

WLW is a radio legend. Radio stations that have only three call letters, like WSM or WGN, are special. Another product of the entrepreneurial mind of Powel Crosley, WLW began broadcasting in 1922. Crosley started the radio station in his suburban College Hill home at twenty watts. Crosley was determined to make WLW the best in the nation. Constantly experimenting with new technologies, Crosley eventually boosted the station's signal to five thousand, then fifty thousand, then five hundred thousand watts. To put that in perspective, the latter is ten times the legal limit these days. My dad picked up the signal in Miami Beach on vacation but that paled in comparison with the reception that aborigines in the Australian outback sometimes got. No wonder residents of Mason, the farming community outside of Cincinnati where the WLW tower resided, sometimes reported reception in their tooth fillings.[1]

The increased power allowed Crosley to use cheaper receivers and thus build less expensive radios. The more powerful the transmitter, the less complex the radio the consumer needs. The increased power also had the benefit of beaming the station across the country.

Besides its power, WLW introduced talent that America went on to embrace. Rosemary Clooney began crooning on WLW at age thirteen, years before meeting Bing Crosby in Vermont for *White Christmas* and having a

Hollywood heartthrob for a nephew. Andy Williams and Doris Day began enter-tainment careers at WLW. Earl Hammer, better known for "John Boy" Walton, also got his start at "the Nation's Station," as it was aptly called.

The Reds' play-by-play candidate flew in from the ABC Television Cen-ter West. He had done some play-by-play for the Hawaiian Islanders of the Pacific Coast League. He thought he had his big break when he was tapped to read half-time scores and highlights for the hometown Los Angeles Lakers broadcasts. But longtime Lakers announcer Chick Hearn felt intruded upon. After a few weeks he told the Lakers radio executives "it is either the kid or me, you choose." It was an easy choice. The kid got the axe.[2]

As the business guy, it was Dick Wagner's job to hire and fire. He also presided over radio and television deals. He was impressed immediately with the youngster, no small thing when it came to Dick Wagner. The candidate had a professionalism about him that was rare for any man, but particularly for one who was only twenty-five. Wagner offered him the job on the spot, which was also rare for Wagner.[3] Al Michaels accepted.

Beginning in the 1971 season, Al Michaels called the Reds action on WLW. Dick Wagner dubbed his hiring of the twenty-five-year-old Michaels "a stroke of genius" (photograph courtesy Road-west Publishing [Jack Klumpe Collection]).

Wagner and Howsam were intent on expanding the Reds radio network. Since they drew fans from six states it only made sense to provide radio coverage in those states. By this time, the FCC had restricted WLW to fifty thousand watts, which allows decent reception within a 100-mile radius of an AM station. The Reds had a tradition called "the Reds Caravan," where Howsam, Wagner, and others from the Reds would travel to cities in the region such as Day-ton, Ohio, and meet with VIPs and others to promote the Reds. Wagner and friends also would try to enlist new stations; big ones, little ones, it didn't matter. They wanted coverage. Wag-ner's experience in the radio business helped immeasurably. He knew what it was like to sit in the radio station director's chair. He knew the things they considered. When Howsam and

Wagner arrived in 1967 Reds games were broadcast on a couple dozen stations. By the 1970s that had expanded to more than a hundred. It was one of the largest baseball networks both in number of stations and miles covered.

Wagner often would bring a broadcaster, such as Nuxhall or Michaels, along on the caravan. They would hold a luncheon and meet the local dignitaries, then jump in their car and go to the next town. It was effective. One of the Reds' biggest fans was one of the University of Nebraska assistant football coaches; he heard the games on one of Wagner's old stations out of North Platte, Nebraska, which is far closer to St. Louis than it is to Cincinnati. The Reds weren't looking to make a lot of money from radio. They wanted to cover costs and maybe make a slight profit. Their primary goal was to get their brand out. They wanted to sell the Reds, to get people attached to them instead of to another team.

This was before the advent of cable TV. Aside from NBC's Saturday *Game of the Week* there was precious little baseball on television. Radio was where it was at. Men would listen to games on their riding mowers or as they worked around the house. Boys would bring the radio down to the sandlot. When they did, Wagner wanted everyone in the Midwest and Upper South to be listening to the Reds. It was one reason that so many boys of that generation became Reds fans.

Now that the broadcasts range was extended, it was time to see if the broadcasts would be worth listening to. Michaels and others were looking forward to calling the Reds action as the team set out to make atonement for the 1970 series loss.

In the early 1970s the players were a lot closer to the public than they are today. Except for the big stars, all made about the same amount of money as a working man in Cincinnati, so they lived in modest houses in middle-class neighborhoods. Most players had off-season jobs to make ends meet. They painted houses, drove snowplows, and sold ties in department stores, among other things.

Only the biggest stars made big money. Pete Rose made headlines when he reached his goal of being the first $100,000 singles hitter in 1970. At the time the median income of a Cincinnati worker was $8,700, so Rose was making eleven times what the average person would make. He didn't have to work in the off-season.

Those who didn't need to work in the off-season found other things to do. The Reds, not unlike other clubs, formed a traveling basketball team. Fans could go to a local high school gym like Covington Catholic (in Covington, Kentucky) and see the Reds play the local firefighters and police in a charity basketball game. Young fans would go under the stands where the players stood in the tunnel waiting for introductions. You could get a Pete Rose, Johnny Bench, or Bobby Tolan autograph on your mitt in a matter of seconds, as well as a handshake and a "how ya doin,' do you play baseball?" greeting.

Unfortunately the team's medical problems continued at one such event. The Reds were playing a charity game on January 6, 1971, in Kentucky's state capitol, Frankfort. Bobby Tolan, who was pretty decent on the court, went after a loose ball. Nobody was within ten feet of him. While going for the ball, he felt a pop in his ankle. He didn't think much of it at first; it didn't really hurt. Initially he wasn't even going to go to the hospital. When he did decide to go, he found out that his Achilles tendon had snapped. The Achilles connects the lower calf muscles to the heel bone. The Reds didn't know it then but the expression "the team's Achilles heel" would have been apropos in this situation. Tolan, you see, typically had jump-started the Cincinnati Reds. Rose would lead off and often draw a walk or hit a single. A good hitter and a gifted bunter, Tolan followed and often found his way on base even if Rose had not. Stealing second was a given. He or Rose (or both) were then in scoring position. The table was then set for May, Bench, and Perez. That's how the latter trio generated 371 RBIs between them in 1970. But now Tolan was out for the entire 1971 season.

Besides the Tolan injury, the Reds had another problem. Johnny Bench wanted more money and he wasn't reporting to spring training until he got it. Bench made $40,000, good money in those days, during his 1970 MVP season. He was now asking for a three-year $500,000 deal. The two sides deadlocked. There was no free agency, so Bench's only option was to refuse to play; it was known as "holding out." In March, the two sides reached a deal. Bench reportedly had his salary doubled to $80,000 per year.

Chief Bender got a call from long time baseball scout Cliff Alexander in the spring of 1971. Alexander had a prospect he wanted Bender to see. When Alexander had a prospect he thought was worth looking at, Chief Bender listened. Alexander had recommended a young left-hander at the University of Cincinnati to the Brooklyn Dodgers years earlier. He turned out to be a pretty good one; his name was Sandy Koufax.

Alexander and Bender drove up to Ohio University. The school is sometimes confused with its better-known counterpart, the Ohio State University, the football powerhouse in the large city of Columbus. Ohio University is the other state school, located in southeastern Ohio in the sleepy town of Athens, near the West Virginia border. Alexander brought Bender to see a tall, redheaded shortstop who hailed from Dayton, Ohio. They watched the young man work out and play a game. As they drove home that evening they agreed that the player had all the tools but he wasn't a shortstop; he was a third baseman. They wanted to draft him that June but they never got the chance. The Philadelphia Phillies, with a much poorer record than the Reds, were higher in the draft order and chose Mike Schmidt of Ohio University.

It was a challenge that the Reds would face throughout the 1970s. Committed to building a winner through the draft and the farm system, they increasingly had to watch the best players get drafted before their turn came to pick.

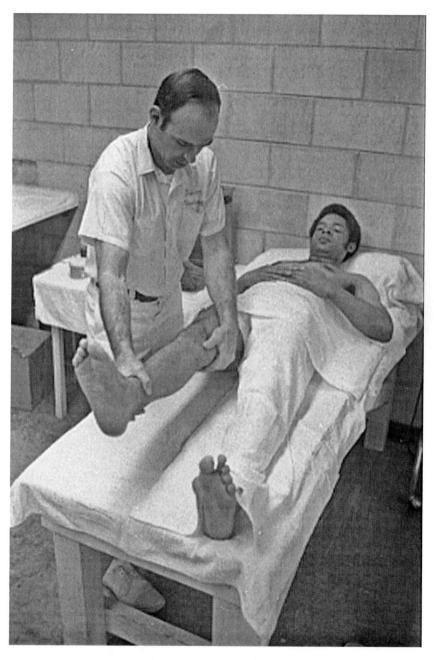

Bobby Tolan's basketball injury, a ruptured Achilles tendon, crippled him and the Reds' 1971 season (photograph courtesy Roadwest Publishing [Jack Klumpe Collection]).

In order to increase competition, teams draft in the reverse order of their finish the previous season. With the Reds consistently finishing first, they consistently drafted last. Howsam used it as an opportunity to check his scouts. If a player was drafted early in the first round, long before the Reds turn, Howsam wanted to know if he was on the Reds scouts' draft list. If he was, the conversation ended. Each scout had their territory to cover and the best players from each territory would to be identified. However, if a player was drafted who was not on a scout's list, Howsam wanted to know why. Perhaps the Reds saw a flaw that other teams didn't but Howsam wanted to make sure that it wasn't due to the fact that the Reds weren't doing their homework.

There were other visits to be made by Bender during those early years. He swung through Sioux Falls, South Dakota, to see, among others, a young outfielder named Ken Griffey. Griffey was a young left-hander who hailed from Donora, Pennsylvania, which also produced another pretty good left-handed outfielder named Stan Musial. Griffey could run, throw, and field, but he was not much of a hitter. Elmer Gray, the local scout, liked his tools and speed but his bat was such a question the Reds didn't choose him until late in the 1969 draft. After the draft Griffey verbally agreed to a contract but was called for army service at Fort Leonard Wood, Missouri. He left for the army unsigned. Afraid he would lose his prospect, Elmer Gray drove out to Missouri and inked Private Griffey right on the post. A year later, Bender was in Sioux City to check on his progress. While there he met Griffey's wife, Birdie. Bender posed for a picture alongside Birdie holding her infant son Ken Junior in her arms.

The Reds were to have had their traditional home opener in their new stadium at the beginning of the 1970 season. Project delays prevented that grand opening. Instead the move occurred two months after Opening Day. June 24, 1970, was a sad day in Cincinnati, marking the end of an era. The Reds played the San Francisco Giants in the last official game ever in Crosley Field. It had been the home of the Reds for fifty-eight years and for every World Series the Reds had ever appeared in. Many said it was time to move into a more modern stadium. It was progress. Many, the more nostalgic fans, disagreed. Crosley had a charm, an aroma, an aura about it. It was a ballpark. Grass fields, wooden structures, a moon and sun deck. Parking was arguably a problem. Built near Cincinnati's huge main post office, not far from Union Terminal rail station and among office buildings, shops and houses on the West Side before most Americans owned cars, parking was an afterthought. Seating also was limited — a capacity crowd was 29,488. Perhaps the most defining part of the park was the outfield. The grass sloped up toward the outfield walls. Beyond the right-field fence were bleachers, beyond the left-field wall was York Street and an opportunity to knock the ball right out of the park and into the street or into the parking lot across from it. However, the centerpiece of the park was just left of center field, where the old scoreboard stood high above the playing field, crowned with the famous Longines clock.

Chief Bender (left) made the rounds of the minor leagues teams on a frequent basis. At Sioux Falls, South Dakota, he poses with the regional scout Tom Goodman (right) and Ken Griffey's wife Birdie with her new baby, Ken's namesake. Junior would later autograph the photograph for Bender (photograph courtesy Sheldon Bender).

The Reds beat Juan Marichal and the Giants 5–4 that last night. Johnny Bench and Lee May hit back-to-back home runs in the eighth inning for the final runs. After Wayne Granger retired Bobby Bonds on a grounder back to the mound, there was a short ceremony. A helicopter hovered overhead and descended onto the field. Home plate was dug up and placed aboard the helicopter to be flown six miles east to the new park. The helicopter zipped right over the façade on the east side of the first-base bleachers, adorned with the Reds mustachioed mascot commemorating the centennial of professional baseball the previous season. The home of the first night game in professional baseball had now turned out its lights for the last time.

Riverfront Stadium was a necessity as far as the city fathers were concerned. Paul Brown had wanted to locate an AFL franchise in the city. He had nowhere to play except at the University of Cincinnati's Nippert Stadium. This was workable for the short term but was not a long-term solution. New York had started a trend when it built Shea Stadium to replace the old Polo Grounds. Shea was a fairly new concept, a multipurpose stadium for use in baseball as well as football. Other stadiums, such as Wrigley Field in Chicago and Yankee Stadium in New York, had been used for baseball as well as football, but they had been designed for baseball and were used for football as an afterthought. The new multipurpose stadium was designed with multiple uses thought-out ahead of time, one size fits all for baseball, football, later soccer. Houston had followed Shea's lead, with the Astrodome housing the Astros as well as the Oilers of the AFL.

DeWitt had sold the Reds to the present ownership group because he didn't want to move downtown with the team. He wanted a suburban stadium out in the suburbs of Blue Ash where parking and land were plentiful and cheaper. The city fathers were banking that the stadium needed to be downtown to keep the city center vibrant. The downtown location is a model that many cities would copy in the ensuing decades.

A spot was chosen adjacent to the Suspension Bridge on the upriver side. John A. Roebling designed the bridge.[4] Opened in 1866, it was an early model for his subsequent and more famous project, the Brooklyn Bridge. His sons went on to fabricate the cables for the Golden Gate. The new stadium was to be right up against one of America's great inland waterways, the Ohio River, which starts upstream at the confluence of the Allegheny and Monongahela Rivers in Pittsburgh. From there it empties 981 miles downstream into the Mississippi.

Crosley Field was a cozy ballpark on the west side of town. It was home to the Reds from 1912 to 1970. The Reds' record slumped noticeably once they left Crosley's inviting dimensions and grass field (photograph courtesy the Cincinnati Reds).

Though it was nestled on the river bank, the fans wouldn't see the Ohio, or any other city landmark, from their seats. Up until this time, most baseball parks had bleachers in the outfield. They were the cheapest seats for the fans and generally did not rise as high as the seats around the infield and right- and left-field lines. Sluggers would occasionally hit the ball not only over the outfield wall but over the bleachers and out of the park and onto the street. In contrast, the stadium was to have the now familiar look of a circle with uniform sides rising skyward and high.

The symmetrical shape was chosen for two reasons. One was practicality. Heery & Heery and Finch, Alexander, Barnes, Rothschild & Paschal were the same architects that had designed Atlanta's symmetrical and multipurpose Fulton County Stadium.

The second reason was that city planners wanted the stadium to present a clean look on the river bank. It represented a crown for the Queen City. Indeed the stadium looked as though it almost hovered above the rectangular pad it sat upon. It was more appealing on the outside than the inside. Three Rivers Stadium in Pittsburgh and Veteran's Stadium in Philadelphia, would adopt similar looks, almost clones of the Cincinnati park. A fan participation contest was held to name the new stadium. "Riverside" and "Riverfront" were the frontrunners, and the latter was chosen.

The biggest change, however, was not the stadium's use, shape, or the

Riverfront Stadium opened in June 1970. It hovered like a crown above the plaza in the Queen City. It was more beautiful on the outside than the inside (photograph courtesy the Cincinnati Reds).

height of the stands. It was the substance on the field. The Reds had elected to go with AstroTurf. Inspired by Dr. Harold Gores to provide city kids with a substance to play on that would be similar to grass, it had been adopted by the Houston Astros out of necessity.[5] When the Astros moved from Colt Stadium to the "ultramodern" Astrodome in 1965, it was christened the Eighth Wonder of the World. To commemorate the move, the team had not only named the stadium but changed the team nickname from the frontier-sounding Colt .45s to one identified with the nearby Johnson Space Center: Astros.

The Astros planted grass in their new domed stadium, the first in the world. They found that it would indeed have to be the eighth wonder of the world to actually grow grass indoors. They tried everything — various watering schedules, different types of grasses, painting the glass ceiling different colors. Nothing worked: the grass didn't grow. A retractable roof like Toronto, Seattle, and Phoenix, would later employ was technologically years away. With a new stadium that they couldn't walk away from, unable to play baseball on dirt, the Astros then borrowed Gores and Monsanto's invention out of necessity more than desire.

The Reds also had a problem is search of a solution. The Reds historically draw fans from five or six states on any given night. With Cincinnati located at the junction of Ohio, Kentucky, and Indiana, you can be in all three states in a matter of minutes. Tennessee is about a three-hour drive south, and West Virginia is even closer to the east. Citizens of western Pennsylvania mostly follow the Pirates, but some are willing to drive several hours southwest to root for the Reds. When you draw fans from such a large region the last thing you want to do is disappoint them with a rainout. After driving a couple of hours from Columbus, Ohio, or Huntington, West Virginia, or Lexington, Kentucky, the last thing a family wants to do is turn around and drive back home after watching an umpire call a game before the first pitch.

The grassy field at Crosley had led to its fair share of rainouts every season. The Reds wanted to avoid that in the future. They decided to forego grass and put in AstroTurf, even though they were not in a dome. It was the first such move in all of professional sports.

AstroTurf does not prevent rain, though, it only prevents rainouts. You still have to deal with the rain once if falls. On a natural turf field you hope that the ground under the grass soaks up the rain. AstroTurf, on the other hand, is like a gigantic carpet. It doesn't allow the rain to soak down to the concrete below, rather it holds the water on top. Once it is lying there, something has to be done with it. The sun will evaporate the water, but waiting for the sun will not prevent a rainout either. The Reds came up with an invention to deal with the water that turned into a novelty for the fans.

It was similar to a Zamboni, the big machine that resurfaces an ice rink. It was a large machine with multiple rubber tubes or hoses that connected to a long vacuum board. The board was similar in shape to a two-by-four and was dragged behind the machine in a similar manner to a tractor pulling a board while grooming a dirt infield. The water was pulled up by the vacuum and through the tubes into a large tank inside the machine. Once the tank was full, the operator would drive the machine out to the outfield wall where the water was then sprayed over the wall. Fans nearby could get a little wet if they remained seated. The machine would continue its way back and forth across the outfield, while the infield lay covered with tarps, as long as the rain continued. Appropriately the machine was soon named the Big Red Machine. The fans loved it and so did Howsam and Wagner. Wagner quickly suggested they needed two of them and Howsam agreed. It was an entertaining show while waiting for the rain to break.

Howsam liked AstroTurf for another reason besides the ability to weather a rainout. He felt it leveled the field, figuratively and literally. He thought it provided each team equal conditions to play on regardless of the ballpark you were playing in. The AstroTurf in Pittsburgh would act the same as the Astro-Turf in Cincinnati. The ball would still bounce evenly even if a ground crew in one city was not as good as the crew in another. Previously, the teams without much speed would allow the natural grass to grow longer in their park in order to cut down on the opposition's ability to get on base via fast-skipping ground balls. Other teams could take the same route as the Orioles and shave the grass low to play to their strengths. Howsam didn't think this was fair. Ball-

A young fan looks out onto the field during Opening Night of the new Riverfront Stadium, June 30, 1970. Howsam's design of AstroTurf with base cut-outs is evident. Note that the scoreboard in center was not yet complete (photograph courtesy Roadwest Publishing [Jack Klumpe Collection]).

parks ought to have equivalent fields to the greatest degree possible. This would allow the best team to win.[6]

The Reds opened in their new ballpark against Henry Aaron and the Atlanta Braves on June 30, 1970. To get ready the Reds had worked out extensively in the Astrodome outfield during their previous road trip. That work would come in handy. Not only was the outfield covered with AstroTurf, but so was the infield. An outline of where the dirt portion would normally be located, where the infielders are stationed, was drawn in white paint on the green AstroTurf. Originally Howsam had thought of painting the AstroTurf infield area a brown color. The idea was nixed when the Monsanto Company, the makers of AstroTurf, would not guarantee that work.[7]

The only real dirt in the infield was on the pitcher's mound, a large circle around home plate where the umpire, catcher and batter were stationed, and a rectangular area around first, second and third. They were known as the sliding pits. AstroTurf can cause a nasty carpet burn; to spare the runner this, the dirt was added. Essentially the entire field was AstroTurf. It was another baseball first and quickly copied in other cities.

Bob Howsam did his homework before making the decision for Astro-Turf. He traveled to Portland State University in the late 1960s to check out their field. He asked a lot of questions. Portland State had an all–AstroTurf field, as well. In fact, they also had a synthetic surface on the pitcher's mound and around home plate. Howsam liked those features and wanted to incorporate them. However, he felt baseball wasn't ready for synthetic pitching mounds. In the end he decided on the all–AstroTurf field and got permission from baseball authorities for a five-year trial period.

Young Jim "Opie Taylor" McGlothlin drew the start in the inaugural game at Riverfront Stadium. His first pitch was a ball, followed by groans from the fans. Henry Aaron hit the first home run in the park and the Braves took the first game, 8–2.

The stadium was christened for a national audience a few weeks later when it hosted the 41st All-Star Game, a tremendous game played in the middle of the National League's dominant run of nineteen wins from 1963 to 1982. The NL had tied the game 4–4 with three runs in the bottom of the ninth. As the game went late into the night, Pete Rose singled with two out in the bottom of the twelfth inning. Rose advanced to second on a Billy Grabarkewitz single. Jim Hickman, a steady Chicago Cub outfielder, came to the plate to face Clyde Wright. Ray Fosse of the Indians was calling the pitches behind the plate.

Fosse was a promising young catcher. He had been chosen by Manager Earl Weaver to back up Bill Freehan, the perennial AL All-Star backstop. Fosse had entered the game in the fifth inning. Now he called for a fastball from Wright. Hickman lined the low pitch to center field and Rose broke with a fury for third. Approaching the corner he saw Leo Durocher, the Chicago manager, waving him home. Amos Otis fielded the ball cleanly in center and hurled it toward home.

Fosse, like all good catchers would do, had home plate blocked—feet on top of the third-base edge of the plate, shin guards and legs planted firmly, trunk and chest protector turned toward the outfield to receive the ball. All were waiting for Rose's slide and Otis's throw. Durocher clutched his fist like a mad gambler. There was no way to touch the plate. Rose was determined to do so. He lived for these moments. With the fury of a locomotive Rose barreled into Fosse as the throw arrived. Fosse buckled and flew backward in a heap. Rose landed on top of the plate. The ball came to rest near the backstop; Fosse lay writhing in pain. The National League won, 5–4.

It would prove to be one of several moments etched in the baseball psyche when the name Pete Rose is uttered. The event helped launch him onto the national stage. Meanwhile Fosse suffered a broken shoulder. It was a debilitating blow to a promising young career; he was never the same player again. In the baseball folklore, it would be his only moment in the spotlight.

Now a year later, in 1971, Rose was having another solid All-Star year in right field. Young boys in Little League were copying his barrel-into-the-catcher move on every occasion possible. The intentional collision became so rampantly repeated that eventually Little League rules would be changed in order to protect young Ray Fosses.

Besides Rose in right, McRae and Carbo were still platooning in left.

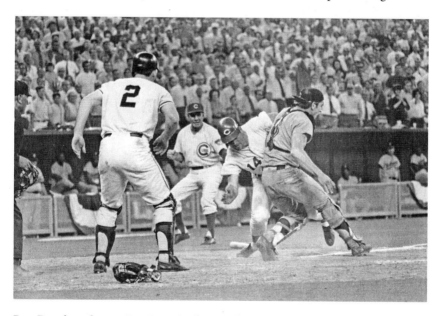

Pete Rose barrels over Ray Fosse in the twelfth inning of the 1970 All-Star Game as Cubs Manager Leo Durocher (facing camera) looks on like a mad gambler. Fosse was never the same. Rose's move was copied by so many young boys that it was banned in Little League play (photograph courtesy the Associated Press).

McRae was performing steadily again at the plate. Never a great fielder, with his bad legs, he was adequate defensively but ordinarily his shortcomings were compensated for by the team's strong fielding at shortstop and in center field. It was Howsam's way; balance was the key. You needed good hitting and good pitching. You needed good offense and good defense. You needed good starting and relief pitching. McRae's defense in left was normally balanced by Tolan's in center. In 1971 that balance would be gone.

While McRae marched on, albeit ploddingly, Carbo was struggling. His 1970 campaign had been wonderful, a .310 average, twenty-one home runs and the *Sporting News* Rookie of the Year honors, but nothing seemed to go right in his second campaign. It started with a salary holdout. To call his negotiations with Howsam, Wagner, and the Reds visceral, intense, and ugly would be an understatement. Carbo had made the league minimum of $10,000 in 1970. He wanted $32,000 after a great first season. The Reds offered $15,000. Carbo did not want to work in the off-season, plus his friend Billy Conigliaro was making more with the Red Sox with lower numbers. They grudgingly settled on $17,000.[8] Carbo finished the 1971 season at .219 with five home runs—call it the sophomore jinx if you will.

Looking under the surface, one discovers that it was more than simply a sophomore jinx. Carbo was having multiple struggles, some public and some private. The public ones bordered on the humorous. A superstitious man at the time, Carbo would try a variety of things to break out of a batting slump. He sometimes would leave his wallet with Al Michaels in the radio booth. If he hit well in that game, Michaels would get the wallet the next day and the next, as long as Carbo stayed "hot." Michaels would keep the wallet until Carbo's hitting went south again. At which point Carbo would put the wallet back in his locker or keep money in his pocket during games, in hopes that his hitting would return.

In further antics, Carbo kept a statue of Buddha in his locker. He said it looked like Baltimore manager Earl Weaver. Meanwhile Earl Weaver was in the dugout one game when the grounds crew carried a dummy across the field. He said it looked like Bernie Carbo.

Carbo's private struggles were not humorous in the least. He had grown up in a dysfunctional family where abuse was not uncommon. This had affected Carbo like it would any young man. Fame and success with the Reds had not soothed the pain. To cope he had turned to the bottle. When that didn't work he went on to stronger drugs, those of the illegal variety. It was a painful, torturous discomfort that he bottled inside, keeping it a secret from his teammates and others. What would they think if they found out? He began to struggle more on the field and in the batter's box.

One big question mark for the Reds in 1971 was how to fill in for Tolan in center. His Achilles tendon rupture had left a huge hole in center field, offensively and even more so defensively. In the spring, the Reds had considered moving Rose to center, Lee May to left field, Tony Perez to first, and Hal McRae to third. However, that plan was nixed early on. Rose started Opening Day in center field, flanked by Carbo and McRae, but for all his hustle, Pete simply was not a centerfielder. Rose returned to right and they tried McRae in center — not good. The hole had yet to be satisfactorily filled two months into the season. At the end of May, Howsam picked up the phone. He cut a deal with the San Francisco Giants. He traded a promising young shortstop, Frank Duffy, and a relief pitcher, Vern Geishert, for a twenty-two-year-old outfielder named George Foster. Foster was put in center field and proved to be at least adequate defensively. He would hit ten home runs but bat only .234 for the Reds that season.

Around the infield Lee May was having another fine year. Hitting for power, he would finish one of the finest seasons of his career with thirty-nine homers and ninety-eight RBIs. Tommy Helms was solid at second and Woody Woodward continued to platoon with Darrel Chaney and others at short while the Reds waited for the farm system to produce. Third base, on the other hand, had become a mixed bag.

Tony Perez was still steady at the plate. You could pencil him in for ninety-plus RBIs every season. He and May produced steady offensive numbers at the corners, but defense was another matter. In his fifth season since moving to third base to give May room at first, Perez was adequate but certainly not great.

The results seemed to be worse at Crosley Field. Perez would occasionally uncork a throw to first that was out of the reach of any living first baseman. The ball would carom against the wooden grandstand at Crosley with a tremendous crash that seemed to echo across the ballpark. One wondered how a major leaguer could throw that wide. The wild throws continued at Riverfront but the impact was not as significant, since the ball would squash against the padding of Riverfront's stands, not ricochet as far, and so was easier to gather up by the second baseman or right fielder backing up the play. Perez was last in the league in fielding percentage and first in errors, averaging more than thirty-three per year the previous two seasons. Though in 1971 he showed some improvement, he was never going to lead the league in fielding. The Reds tolerated this initially but became increasingly restless with it.

While Perez's defensive woes were hard to swallow, his offense was still steady and productive. The same could not be said at catcher. Johnny Bench was having a horrible year. Still suffering the lingering effects of his holdout, Bench's power production had fallen off 50 percent from his MVP year.

Trying to explain the drop in numbers is not easy. It could be that he became complacent after three consecutive years of putting up bigger and bigger numbers. He did spend a lot of time speaking on the banquet circuit, hosting a TV show, and venturing into other assorted business ventures, including buying a bowling alley. Perhaps he considered future success a given and stopped working as hard. Many believed it was due to the holdout. He was not the first, nor the last, to suffer after a holdout. Years later Washington Redskins quarterback Mark Rypien, the MVP of Super Bowl XXVI, held out the following summer. He finally reported to camp, weeks late. He had a horrible season and was released the following season by the Redskins, out of a job. Bench was not close to being out of a job but his holdout hadn't helped his numbers.

It was a microcosm of the Reds' entire year. The Big Red Machine never got rolling in 1971. They finished eleven games back of Willie Mays's San Francisco Giants. More troubling was the Reds record at Riverfront Stadium. They had been 28–8 at Crosley in 1970, before the move, and 29–16 afterward. That had been dismissed as a result of the pitching woes down the stretch[9] but now they had a full year at Riverfront and the results weren't any better. Granted, they were not at full strength but things didn't seem right in their new home.

Overall there were a few bright spots in the 1971 season. Al Michaels was excellent in the booth. Don Gullett emerged as a very good starter on the mound. Another lefty, Ross Grimsley, also arrived and had a good rookie year. His arrival was yet another tribute to the Reds scouting program under Howsam and the Bowen brothers. Howsam had increased the scouting staff from seven to seventeen in three years. The increase paid off. The Reds had four pitchers on the staff who had been drafted under Howsam: Simpson, Gullett, Wilcox, and now Grimsley. All were under twenty-three and very good. Not all of the promising young pitchers panned out, though. The Reds had an outstanding prospect in Class A by the name of Ken Hansen. In 1971, Hansen had 135 strikeouts in eighty-seven innings with an 8–3 record and a 1.76 ERA. He never made the majors, however.

The Reds watched as the Giants were disposed of in the playoffs by the Pittsburgh Pirates, who the Reds had bested the year before. Meanwhile the Minnesota Twins saw their two-year run as American League Western Division champions come to an end. They were replaced by a young and playful team from Oakland. But the Athletics were no match for Baltimore in the playoffs and the Orioles returned to the Fall Classic for the third year in a row.

Pittsburgh's Steve Blass pitched top-notch in the World Series. The pitcher looked more like an accountant than a professional athlete but he won two complete games as the Pirates upset the Orioles. While Blass's performance was excellent, Roberto Clemente's Series was the stuff of legends. Clemente seemed to excel everywhere in the series—in the field, at the plate, and on the base paths. He played with the joy and exuberance of a boy and was enchanting to watch as he glided around the field.

During Clemente's masterful Series, baseball tested an idea that would directly affect the Reds five years later and alter the World Series forever. To the young fan today, this idea may seem routine or blasé, a given. But in the 1971 World Series they played a night game, a World Series first. From 1903 to 1970 every single World Series game had been played during the day. Baseball was considered a day game. The Reds had revolutionized the sport by introducing night play in 1935 but daylight ball had been held sacred for the World Series.

If you had a nice school teacher, she would let you watch the Series during class. Games generally started about 1:00 P.M. EDT. When school ended, you would run or ride the bus to catch the tail end of the game. If anything, kids had the advantage over adults. Adults might sneak a radio into the office or factory and listen to the play by play.

With great fanfare there was a ceremony prior to the game. NBC interviewed Commissioner Bowie Kuhn who expected the largest television crowd in the history of all of professional sports. When asked about future plans for night games, Kuhn stated that the night game was the right thing to do and that the next season Saturday and Sunday games would be day games, but the weekday games would be at night. That way, he said, "the fans of America, the people that work, the kids in school can see the whole thing if they want to."

But World Series night games were not the concern of the Reds at this point. They knew that they had some problems to solve before they would return to the Series. It was to those problems that Howsam and his team turned their attention in late 1971.

9

THE TRADE
December 1971

Howsam gathered his inner circle. Wagner, Bender, and the Bowen brothers conferred in the large office overlooking home plate at Riverfront Stadium. There had been change at the strategic level. Riverfront was no Crosley Field. Much like Chicago's Wrigley Field, Crosley was considered a hitter's park, a place where a lot of home runs were hit.

Bench, Perez, and May had hit 119 home runs between them in 1970 while splitting time between Crosley and Riverfront. That total fell to ninety-one in 1971 while playing exclusively at Riverfront Stadium. To be sure, part of the dip was due to Bench's holdout but Perez had dropped off 37 percent as well. Riverfront's dimensions were more cavernous and the ball didn't carry as well as it had at Crosley.

Besides the drop in power, the Reds had another more insidious problem. To the trained eye, they appeared slow, a step or two short in the pinch. They seemed to drag. Part of this can be attributed to Tolan's health problems but "team speed" in 1971 was an oxymoron for the Reds. Rose led the club in stolen bases with just thirteen, compared with Tolan's fifty-seven the previous season.

The problem wasn't just on the base paths; the defense suffered as well. Rickey had taught Howsam that speed is the only thing that benefits you defensively as well as offensively. AstroTurf demands greater speed from your fielders, both infield and outfield. A ground ball hit on long natural grass, routinely fielded by the shortstop, would scoot into the outfield on AstroTurf. Likewise a line drive to the gap could be cut off after the hop on grass, while the ball seems to accelerate after hitting the artificial surface in the power alley. A single becomes a double or a triple.

Riverfront had strategically changed the rules of the game for the Reds, both with power and speed. It was a new paradigm, a new way of thinking, a new way of playing the game. An average leader might chalk up the Reds' season to the breaks of the game, figure it will get better, and press on. A great leader realizes that adaptation is necessary when the rules fundamentally change. Howsam was a great leader.

Once the problems had been clearly identified, an effective solution was needed. Most great executives apply the tried and true adage of "prior planning prevents poor performance" and Howsam was no exception. He believed in establishing detailed policies and procedures and then trusting quality people to make them work. In this case, Howsam's approach was to establish a new scouting paradigm and the man that would make it work was Ray Shore.

Shortly after Howsam arrived in Cincinnati from St. Louis, he got a call from a woman who worked at one of the local media outlets. She was wondering if Howsam could find a job for one of her relatives, Ray Shore. Shore had played in the big leagues and coached for Fred Hutchinson and the Reds in the mid 1960s. He was now a bullpen catcher for the Reds and running a sporting goods store in Cincinnati, trying to raise a family on $5,000 a year. That was not easy to do, even in the late 1960s.

Howsam told the woman that he would think about it. He looked into Shore's background. He was impressed with what he found, so he invited him in for a chat. As they talked Howsam became convinced that Shore could be what he was looking for. Howsam often uses the phrase "became convinced." It was often through a series of questions, ever more probing, and often over a period of time that he would arrive at what he thought was true and factual — and become convinced.

In this case, Howsam wanted a man to go ahead of the Reds to scout the opposition. At the time, major-league teams did this only twice a year. One such instance was during spring training, where they could get a look at prospects across the league in a small geographical area like Florida or Arizona. The other time advanced scouts were used was just prior to the World Series, in order to size up the opponent from the other league. Howsam had somewhat of a revolutionary idea; he wanted to employ an advanced scout all season long, full time. It is standard practice today but the Reds were the first to do it.[1]

He thought that Shore might be the man for the job. He decided to give him a test drive. He sent Shore out on the road for several trips. He brought him back for several face-to-face verbal reports. Howsam would ask a series of questions and after a while Shore picked up on what Howsam was really interested in knowing. Additionally, Howsam instructed Shore to bring a radio to all the games he scouted. He believed that radio announcers were open about communicating what was right and wrong with a team, making the scout's job even easier.

Shore took his scouting one step further. He became a regular at the hotel bar where teams were staying. He found out all sorts of useful information over a few drinks. It was amazing what players would reveal after having a few.

Advanced scouts actually serve two purposes for a ball club. As stated, their primary purpose is to scout the opposition (usually one road trip in advance) to size up the strengths and weaknesses of an upcoming opponent.

They relay back to the club who is hot and who is not; what part of the strike zone batters prefer to hit in; what kind of pitches the pitchers are throwing; and where their effectiveness lies. Finally, advanced scouts learn who is injured and what the likelihood is of their return.

Howsam had charged his scouts with another role, potential acquisitions. He had them identify which players they would like to see in a Reds uniform, who the players were that they respected, what their strengths were and how they could help the Reds. Specifically, where could they shore up some weaknesses on the Reds?

That was the subject of this 1971 meeting of the inner circle from the baseball side of the Reds' front office. Besides Chief Bender, Joe and Rex Bowen, Ray Shore, and Sal Artiaga, the secretary of the minor leagues was in attendance. Howsam had instituted a ritual that was carried out every September, the final month of the season.

Once the group was assembled they would discuss the needs for the upcoming season. They would review each position in turn. For example, "How are we in center field? If we lose Tolan who would we want to replace him?" "Who can we trade and not hurt the ball club too much?"

Then Howsam would begin dialing. He talked with every general manager from every team in both leagues. He had a standard set of questions he asked. "Who will be available on your club?" "What positions are you looking to fill?" "This is what we think we need; these are the positions we were looking for."

Ray Shore (pointing) chats with Sparky Anderson circa 1977. Shore became Bob Howsam's and the Reds' eyes and ears around the league (photograph courtesy Roadwest Publishing [Jack Klumpe Collection]).

Once he talked with all the clubs, Howsam would call his baseball council back into session. He would tell them what he had heard from the various clubs. He would then send them away with that information and tell them to come up with a list. Rate who we should have and who we shouldn't. They would go back and work on their task for as long as one week. They would then come back with a list with three groups labeled one, two and three. Howsam would look over the lists and ask questions. Why is he on the list? Why isn't he on the list? Additionally, he would ask how they thought Cincinnati could trade for the player. Who can we throw in the trade, not weaken our club, and still get the player we want?

Interestingly, the baseball council usually didn't think the Cincinnati players were worth as much as Howsam thought they were. Howsam acted as the safety valve to prevent a player from getting away "undervalued." After they came to an agreement on the players to pursue, it could be as few as four, but normally it was from six to eight players, those were the only ones that Howsam would pursue in that off-season. Once he had the council's input and buy-in, he began to work the phones trying to cut a deal for the players at the top of the list first. At the top of the list for that year was Joe Morgan of the Houston Astros.

Howsam had asked Sparky Anderson for his assessment of the club just days earlier. Anderson felt that the team needed pitching and better speed, and as a footnote added that he wanted Howsam to know that he sure admired Joe Morgan of the Houston Astros.

After discussions with the inner circle, they agreed that Joe Morgan was their man but how to get him was another question. In today's game a team that highly covets a player can simply wait until his contract expires and he becomes a free agent; then they throw a lot of money at him. The New York Yankees have built a franchise in current times doing this. Before the day of free agency, though, the only way to get a player you wanted was to trade for him. Additionally, Howsam still adhered to his adage, "to get value you have to trade value," keeping open the opportunity to do business in the future.

After more discussion, Howsam decided on a proposed deal, Lee May for Joe Morgan, straight up. On paper it looked like a steal, for the Astros that is. May had averaged .270, thirty-seven home runs, and 101 RBIs per season over the past three years. Morgan's numbers paled in comparison .253, twelve home runs, and fifty RBIs but he had averaged fifty stolen bases. However, there was an issue besides the numbers that mattered to Howsam.

For Howsam you had to be a good player on the field and off. You had to be willing to follow the rules, on the field and off. You needed to be a good teammate on the field, as well as in the clubhouse. There were some rumblings that Morgan might not meet those criteria. These rumblings drifted back to the same night that Chief Bender remembered when Sparky Anderson's name first came up. The manager who had ordered the late-inning bunt that set off the temper of the young Sparky Anderson in the minors was now the manager of the Houston Astros, Harry "The Hat" Walker. Walker had been a good hitter in his day, averaging nearly .300 lifetime and winning the NL batting title in 1947. Word was that he and Morgan did not see eye to eye and that Morgan had copped an attitude. As a result, further investigation was required. The Reds asked around. Back channels reported that the problem was more Walker's than Morgan's. It seems that Walker figured if he did things a certain way when he was a player and they had worked, then everybody should do it the same way he had done it. In other words, there was only one way to skin a cat and it was his.

While certainly there are some techniques that are better than others, no one style fits every baseball player. Various sized bats are an illustration of this. Two guys the same height and weight may each find success using different bat sizes. Some players follow their swings through with two hands, while others prefer the Mark McGuire one-hand approach. In the case with Walker and Morgan, Harry wanted Morgan to hit down or "chop" at the ball, as he himself had done, to utilize Morgan's speed on the Astro-Turf. Morgan preferred a more upward-arching swing and resisted. Each arched their back and refused to budge. Morgan resented his lack of freedom in the matter. Reports concluded that Morgan was a solid citizen and would thrive anywhere, even in Houston if he were out from under Walker.

That issue settled, Howsam set his sights on Morgan before considering the other players on the list. The playoffs were in San Francisco in 1971, and the National League general managers were in attendance. Howsam hooked up with Spec Richardson, the Houston GM, while in San Francisco. Howsam made him the May-Morgan offer and thought the deal was going to get done right there. It didn't happen.

Surprisingly Richardson hesitated. Howsam continued

Through the urging of Ray Shore, Joe Morgan became number one on the Reds' wish list after the 1971 season, once questions about his attitude were answered satisfactorily (photograph courtesy Roadwest Publishing [Jack Klumpe Collection]).

to press him. They talked often on the phone over the next two months. At one point, Richardson said, "Well, if we give you Morgan, then we won't have a second baseman." Howsam upped the ante with an offer to throw Tommy Helms, a former Rookie of the Year and All Star, into the deal. With the acquisition of Morgan, Helms was expendable at second. In exchange, Howsam wanted the Astros to include Jack Billingham, a starting pitcher, and Cesar Geronimo, a young outfielder with very little big-league playing time. Howsam had spotted Geronimo both in the Astrodome and at Riverfront by going early to the workouts. He was mightily impressed with his arm.

Still Houston hedged. Richardson always had some excuse for not pulling the trigger. He would say, "Well, the Hat is away" or "the Hat is hunting; I want to talk with him first." At the fall general manager's meeting, Howsam thought he was going to close the deal. "The Hat" then informed Richardson that he didn't want to do it. Weeks passed and the dialogue continued. Howsam and Richardson met again in late November at the Biltmore Hotel in Scottsdale, Arizona, site of baseball's winter meetings.

Howsam then asked Richardson to give Cincinnati Denis Menke because the Reds would need a third baseman with Perez moving to first to replace May. Richardson said okay but then he wanted Cincinnati's "super sub" Jimmy Stewart, if they were going to make a trade. Stewart could play any position on the field with the exception of pitcher and was a good switch-hitting pinch hitter. Additionally, he was a great player to have in the clubhouse, liked and respected by all. Howsam hated to give him up. "Well if I throw him in you have to give me another man." Houston gave Cincinnati a list of five players to choose from. Howsam took the list to Bender to ask whom he should choose. Bender circled Eddie Armbrister's name.

On the afternoon of November 29, 1971, Howsam called Wagner, Bender and others to his room at the Biltmore. He asked if any of them needed to make any phone calls, go to the bathroom, or had any other business to take care of. Several did. He told them to take care of those things and get back right away.

When they returned Howsam said, "Lock the doors; nobody use the phones in this room." Howsam had been stung in St. Louis with trades being leaked before they could be announced or the players notified. He didn't want that to happen again. He told the men gathered around that they would be going downstairs to announce a trade — and then he told them the details of the deal.

The management team then trooped downstairs and held a press conference announcing the trade. The Reds send Lee May, Tommy Helms, and Jimmy Stewart to Houston in exchange for Joe Morgan, Jack Billingham, Cesar Geronimo, Denis Menke, and Eddie Armbrister.

As they exited the pressroom, Howsam heard Dick Young, the legendary sportswriter, exclaim, "Now that's a trade." The trade exemplifies Howsam's leadership philosophy better than any other example in his tenure. He gathered good people around him, solicited their advice, asked lots of questions, got a game plan together, and then executed it. It took longer than expected, but he persevered until the job was done. Others did their jobs so he could do his, and he did it well.

"The trade," as it became known in Cincinnati, was announced on that November afternoon. The press and the fans of Cincinnati were at first shocked and then livid. What in the world was wrong with Howsam? How could he get fleeced like that? What in the world was he thinking? It was much of the same for the next few weeks, loud and prolonged. What had Howsam done? But Howsam wasn't fazed. He had been prepped for this event years earlier when he fired popular manager Mike Gazella of the Denver Bears. You try to do the right thing, the best thing. Some people will disagree but you can't let their anger dissuade you. You press on, knowing that you did what you thought was right. Howsam felt that one must be firm in making decisions and once they are made, don't look back.

In his mind, the trade was fair, even though he hated to see Lee May go. May was one of the Big Four, one of the big cylinders that powered the Big Red Machine. Additionally, he liked May. The Big Bopper had developed a very compact yet powerful swing, which is rare for a big man. Most big men take big swings, the most vivid example being Dave Kingman of the New York Mets. The problem with a big swing is that there are usually just two results — a home run or a strike out. May's more compact swing allowed him to wait a split second longer before committing to a swing. This allowed his average to hover around .280 while still hitting for power.

Howsam liked Morgan, too, though. In a way the trade represented the old philosophy: good proven talent for potentially great talent. It was the same principal he had used in the Leo Cardenas–for–Jim Merritt and the Vada Pinson–for–Bobby Tolan trades. Each had paid off handsomely for the Reds. Howsam thought it would again. Morgan would bring much needed speed and decent defense for Helm's great defense but lack of speed. He also thought that Morgan would hit for a higher average than Helms.

The trade also would accomplish another goal, it would move Perez back to first after a five-year hiatus at third. That, it was hoped, would fix the defensive problem they had lived with at the hot corner. Denis Menke would replace Perez there. Menke was a lot like a 1964 Rambler, not flashy but steady and dependable. He had a number of good years for Houston, making the All-Star team in 1969 and '70. He could play all infield positions but had mainly played second and short.

The trade also brought a workhorse to the mound. No one, not even the Baltimore Orioles of 1970, can have too much good starting pitching. Everyone is always looking for pitching. Pitching had been a big disappointment for the Reds in 1971. Jim Merritt and Wayne Simpson won five games between them. Gary Nolan had a decent year and the "young David," Don Gullett, had survived his encounter with Boog "the Goliath" Powell to become a bright spot in the starting rotation in 1971. Jack Billingham had averaged 208 innings and over eleven wins for Houston the previous two seasons and figured to be a guy who could go out every fourth day and throw multiple innings for the Reds. He would make a nice addition to Nolan and Gullett.

Howsam hated to lose a guy like Jimmy Stewart. Like the actor of the same name, Stewart was well liked in the clubhouse and was a steady guy. But Howsam wasn't going to give up the chance to acquire Morgan just to keep Stewart. He figured that he could find another good utility player to replace him. Besides, he figured that his lineup would be an everyday one and so, barring injury, his need for a utility man was low. Then there was the wildcard: you never know how a young player like Geronimo might pan out in the future.

Though by far the most well remembered, it was not the only significant deal of the off-season. At the same winter meetings, Howsam was working with the Minnesota Twins again, from whom he had obtained Merritt. He was offering Wayne Granger and the Twins accepted. In return they sent Tommy Hall to Cincinnati. Many Cincinnatians were perplexed by this deal, as well. Granger had set an all-time Major League record for appearances in 1969 with 90. He led not only the Reds but the league in saves during the 1970 World Series year. Along with Clay Carroll, they had been a formidable duo and now the Laurel and Hardy act was being broken up for a relative unknown. Tom Hall's record was only 4–7, but he was left-handed and Carroll and Granger were both right-handed. Granger and Carroll had been finesse and power. Again Howsam was searching for balance, a righty and a lefty for the bullpen. Plus, Tommy Hall was an exciting player who averaged more than one strikeout per inning pitched.

By spring training of 1972, Howsam was eager to see for himself and for the fans if the trades had been good ones.

10

ROLLING AGAIN
April–September 1972

There were other issues to be resolved during spring training of 1972. The outfield was a toss-up. It was in for a shake-up. Carbo's play had been sinking both in left and at the plate and the Reds still only partially knew the extent of his problems. His downward spiral had not reached the depths publicly, but inwardly it was deep, very deep.

Hal McRae was still pushing to play full time. Though they liked McRae's bat, the Reds couldn't stomach his defensive ability (or non-ability) enough to let him play left every day. So they decided to move Rose again, this time back to left after four seasons and two Gold Gloves in right, not bad for a former second baseman. Rose would be better defensively and offensively than McRae and Carbo. He also was his own platoon as a switch-hitter. Now the question was who would fill right field.

The Reds decided to try Cesar Geronimo. They weren't sure that he would have the bat to stay in the lineup but they sure loved his arm. It was a valuable weapon when making the long throw from right to third to gun down a runner. George Scherger was charged to keep that weapon loaded. Scherger was in charge of all the outfielders. Sparky instructed him to hit balls to Geronimo in the outfield daily and have him throw them back in. Anderson had seen too many outfielders come to the big leagues and totally focus on hitting to the detriment of their defensive skills. He wanted to ensure that one of Geronimo's biggest assets was not lost due to neglect. Use it or lose it. Besides Geronimo, Foster was another option in right field and McRae got a few starts as well. Tolan was back in center field, hoping that his Achilles tendon was repaired.

The Reds opened the season with Al Michaels and Joe Nuxhall in the radio booth. Perez was at first, Morgan at second, and Denis Menke was at third. Newcomer Jack Billingham drew the Opening Day start on the mound. Bench, a year removed from his holdout, was behind the plate. In 1972 he would rebound from his disastrous 1971 campaign and bat .270, with forty home runs and 125 RBIs. For his efforts he wound up on the cover of *Time Magazine* (as baseball's best catcher) and named MVP (as the league's top player).

It didn't take long to see that the trade had paid off, especially defensively.

Perez was a much better first baseman than third baseman. Anderson, who was a good teacher, helped further develop Joe Morgan's ability to turn the double play. Morgan didn't have the greatest arm, though it was a good one, but he had the smarts. He knew the game and he knew the hitters, so he put himself in position to make the play, which he did with regularity. He finished the season second in the league in fielding percentage with only eight errors.

Offensively Morgan's batting average increased significantly to .292, much better than Helms had been hitting. But Morgan's biggest contribution was on the base paths. He had very good speed, if not Bobby Tolan speed. What he also had that Tolan didn't was a keen eye for pitchers. He would study them like a doctor examining an X-ray. He looked for little hints as to whether the pitcher was going to attempt a pickoff. The sliding pits at Riverfront provided him with a barometer. His goal was to get a lead off the bag where the right, lead foot was on the artificial turf and the left, push-off foot, was in the sliding pit. His goal was to draw a throw. When he did so, his next goal was to extend his lead another half step to mess with the pitcher's psyche.

Morgan wanted a thought pattern to go through the pitcher's mind: "I throw over there and the guy extends his lead. What's the use, I shouldn't waste my time. It will only make matters worse." When the pitcher *did* throw over and Morgan had to dive back, barely safe, he knew that he had extended his lead as much as possible. No one in the league knew opposing pitchers' moves to first better. Morgan was rarely if ever picked off in his career. He and Tolan were partners in crime, garnering one hundred steals between them.

The other middle infield position was a question mark. Ever since the Cardenas trade at the end of 1968, the Reds had hoped that their farm system would produce a quality long-term shortstop. Woody Wood-

Woody Woodward was one of a trio of Reds to try to fill the shortstop position for the Reds. Woodward was not a threat to Babe Ruth: he hit only one home run in his career (photograph courtesy Roadwest Publishing [Jack Klumpe Collection]).

ward and Darrel Chaney had performed adequately while the Reds waited. Woodward, smart and baseball savvy, had decided to hang up his cleats at the end of the 1971 season. He would move into the television booth and then the front office after his playing days, eventually filling the general manager job for the Seattle Mariners in the Ken Griffey, Jr., era.[1]

Darrel Chaney was good defensively at short. He was also a good athlete; he had turned down a football scholarship offer to play quarterback for Notre Dame in order to sign with the Reds. Neither he nor Woodward were particularly good hitters. In fact they were poor — their gloves kept them in the big leagues. The duo was not going to challenge Babe Ruth's home run record either. They finished their careers with fifteen between them. Chaney was also a solid, respectable citizen off the diamond, busy with community endeavors on behalf of the Reds. He was a good and dependable speaker on the Reds speaker bureau. These were players who volunteered to speak to churches and civic groups about baseball in general, and the Reds in particular. Chaney had a great attitude regarding fans. He would tell his audience that fans pay good money to be able to boo him or any other player for poor play but "when they start attacking my wife or family with comments, that is a different matter."

What the Reds desired in a shortstop was someone who was more than just adequate. They wanted someone who was superior in the field and that could hit

Bob Howsam wanted fans to have fun at the ballpark, saying "You've got to give them a reason to come." Former quarterback Darrel Chaney cuts up with Denis Menke's wife during a wives' game. For a while it seemed that Chaney would be the answer at shortstop (photograph courtesy Roadwest Publishing [Jack Klumpe Collection]).

decently. They knew they had enough hitters in the lineup; the Big Four alone was enough to carry most of the offense. The shortstop didn't need to have All-Star slugging numbers but they wanted an All-Star caliber defensive player.

The two shortstops the Reds had been waiting for were both signed by Howsam in his first season as general manager. They both showed great defense but the question, as usual, was whether they could hit big-league pitching. One was a youngster from Stanford named Frank Duffy who had drawn the Opening Day start in 1971. The Reds liked his defense but finally determined that the offense wouldn't be there so he was dealt with Vern Geishert to the San Francisco Giants for George Foster. His .232 ten-year big-league average proved the Reds assessment of his offensive potential to be correct.

The other prospect was a young man named Dave Concepcion. By the beginning of 1972, the Reds were willing to take a gamble on him full-time. Duffy had been traded and Woodward had retired. Chaney was seemingly destined to be the back-up. If the farm system was going to produce like the Reds hoped it would, the Reds thought it would have to be Concepcion. Yet Concepcion failed to produce. He hit sporadically and his defense was too erratic. Darrel Chaney got most of the playing time at shortstop.

The farm system that groomed both Concepcion and Chaney was one that had the constant eye of Bob Howsam. It was important that the kind of players he wanted be developed by a specific system. To ensure that happened he had several procedures. First he had a rule that he talked to every manager at least once a month and those at Class AAA even more often. He looked at the reports that the managers sent in, so he could converse intelligently with his scouting staff. But most importantly he made it a habit to visit each minor league club at least once a year; that was six clubs in all. If the leader is going to put a personal stamp on an organization, he or she has to leave the office and communicate the message, and also inspect later to see that the message is being heeded.

Howsam had a specific procedure he followed during his surprise visits. He would fly into a city, rent a car, head over to the ballpark, and buy a ticket for the game so that no one would know he was there. He hoped no one spotted him as he sat in the stands and observed not only the players but even more so the manager and coaches. He would watch to see how the manager interacted with the players, how they ran the game, how they handled the early pitching, how they handled the infield, and all the moves they made. He was in leadership-evaluation mode as much as player-evaluation mode.

Following the game, he would drop into the dugout to visit the manager. "Their eyes would pop out," he later reported. He would then ask the manager to lunch the next day. Over lunch he went over every ballplayer on the roster, checking for progress and problems. He would help deal with the problems while in town. At the end of the meal, he would ask the manager, where is the best steak in town? Can you get a room there that will house all the players?

Howsam would then take the entire team to dinner at the steakhouse.

While having a dinner, Howsam would sit and watch how the guys interacted. Where they sat and how they talked. Specifically he would watch for cliques of any kind, particularly racial. If there were players off by themselves, he would call to the outsiders and say come sit with me, I want to visit with you. Howsam felt it was very important to break up cliques both in the minors and majors. He and Sparky depended on the Big Four to do that in Cincinnati.

As the season progressed, the 1972 outfield began to take shape. Rose was his consistent self, over the great hitter benchmark of 200-plus hits, with a .300 average for the eighth straight season. His move to left had not affected him in the least.

In right, Cesar Geronimo was a pleasant surprise. He played roughly two-thirds of the time, mostly in right, but sometimes spelling Tolan in center field. The question of his hitting seemed to be answered as he carried a .275 average through the season. Foster played some too, but was disappointing with a .200 average. Bench would sometimes get a rest for his knees by playing right field and then there was another member of the platoon, Hal McRae.

McRae was performing steadily again at the plate. Never a great fielder, with his bad legs he was a risk defensively. He had come up through the minors as a second baseman, but with a young Tommy Helms already at second the Reds had moved McRae to the outfield. The AstroTurf compounded his defensive problems. With little playing time, McRae's attitude was beginning to deteriorate. In a way, it was appropriate. McRae wanted to play every day—any player worth their salt does—but the Reds liked the platoon.

Meanwhile, Bernie Carbo had totally fallen out of favor with both Howsam and thus Anderson. The Reds did not completely realize his private problems but his on-the-field problems were readily apparent. By May he was hitting .192 in only twenty-one at-bats. He was gone by June when he was dealt to the St. Louis Cardinals for Joe Hague.

If Carbo was on a downward spiral, Tolan was on the way back up. After a year of rehab on the Achilles tendon, Tolan roared back to his old self. Still strong in the field, he rounded out the Reds outfield; Tolan, Rose, and Geronimo were a strong defensive unit. And Tolan's .283 average, eighty-two RBIs and forty-two stolen bases made him dangerous in the third spot in the lineup, known as the three hole. Rose would lead off, followed by Morgan, and then Tolan. With their combined hitting ability, and Tolan and Morgan's base-stealing acumen, the table was set, more so than it had been in 1970 for Bench and Perez. Granted, May was gone, but Morgan provided occasional power, hitting sixteen home runs in his first year with the club.

The final piece of the puzzle was Denis Menke at third base. He proved to be good in the field, certainly better than Perez at third, but his offensive numbers were not as good as they had been in Houston. It was a bit disappointing. Third base remained a problem but not one that needed to be addressed immediately.

Denis Menke (left) shakes hands with Clay Carroll after another save. Menke was thought to be the solution for the third-base situation but problems continued (photograph courtesy Roadwest Publishing [Jack Klumpe Collection]).

Overall the Reds were a lot better team than they had been in 1971 and probably better than the 1970 Big Red Machine. The team was more balanced and they had better speed on the base paths and in the field, which also led to better defense with Menke and Chaney or Concepcion on the left side of the infield.

The pitching was definitely better than it had been in 1971, with Gullett, Nolan, Billingham and Grimsley. Merritt was now gone from the 1970 club. After winning twenty games in 1970, he only won one in '71 and one in '72. Merritt was traded to the Texas Rangers for Hal King and Jim Driscoll at the end of the 1972 season. Wayne Simpson, "the next Bob Gibson," also was down, winning only four games in '71, but rebounded to win eight in 1972 before he was dealt to the Kansas City Royals. Merritt and Simpson are both evidence that fame is fleeting.

The bullpen again was very solid. The "Hawk," Clay Carroll, was steady as ever but Tommy Hall, the Granger pick-up, had a very bad habit for a relief pitcher. He had a tendency to walk the first batter he faced. Usually a relief pitcher is brought in when multiple bases are occupied. The last thing you want to do is aggravate the situation by putting another man on with a free pass. Occasionally Hall surprised. Summoned into one game in midsummer with men on second and third, Hall fell behind with three balls before striking the batter out with a full count to end the inning. He controlled his bad habit enough to notch a spectacular 10–1 record, as the Reds had the firepower to turn a losing game into a winning one in late innings.

Up in the booth, Michaels had proven to be the professional Wagner sensed he was. Before each game Michaels insisted on his quiet time. It lasted about fifteen minutes just before airtime. The young broadcaster would lay all his notes in front of himself, across the table in the radio booth. He would review each in turn, stopping to examine the sky, the park and the field, trying to get a feel for the circumstances. He preferred to be in the booth alone and undisturbed, and colleagues quickly learned to honor that desire. They wanted to do so out of respect. Michaels caught the attention of the networks as well and he was asked by NBC to help with postseason duties.

Once they were on the air, Al Michaels quickly coined the moniker "Little Joe" for the five foot seven Joe Morgan. Little Joe more than adequately replaced Big Lee May — the Big Four had a new member. The Big Red Machine was back. They won the National League West by ten and a half games over Houston. They didn't win a hundred games simply because the season was shortened to 154 games due to a player strike at the beginning of the year, something that would foreshadow labor unrest for the following decades. Houston's second-place finish was the best in team history and they too owed success to "the trade."

Now the Reds faced the defending World Series Champion Pittsburgh Pirates in the playoffs. The Pirates had remained strong, winning the NL East by eleven games over the Chicago Cubs. The Pirates' gritty week of work against the Orioles had won them a World Series few expected the previous year. They kept things rolling in 1972, winning one more game than the Reds during the regular season and entering the playoffs as a slight favorite over the Reds. Steve Blass, after several so-so years, had pitched two great games in the 1971 World Series. He kept it going in 1972, winning nineteen games and being voted runner-up for the Cy Young Award.

The Pirates took Games One and Three. This left the Reds with their backs against the wall in the five-game series. On the mound for Game Four, the Reds had a young pitcher who had emerged as a regular during the 1971 season. Ross Grimsley was twenty-two and a bit of a free spirit. He didn't particularly like the Reds long-standing rule against facial hair but when you are a sophomore you don't have much clout. The lefty was the son of Ross Sr., who had pitched briefly in the majors. Fortunately, Ross Jr. was a much better pitcher than his dad, with a variety of junk in his pitching arsenal. In other words he didn't have much velocity but instead relied on off-speed pitches, such as curveballs, screwballs and change-ups to get batters out. Junk pitchers don't sell as many tickets as strikeout specialists but when they have command of all their pitches they can be just as effective. Grimsley had command in Game Four. He threw a gem, a two-hit shutout, and had an RBI single, leading the Reds to a 7–1 victory. Grimsley became a local hero overnight. Children named their fish after him.

The stage was set for an epic Game Five. It was the clash of the titans and proved to be a hard-fought game, one of the greatest in playoff history. Don

Gullett faced Pirates ace Steve Blass. The Pirates got to Gullett early for three runs in the first four innings to go up 3–1 (Gullett was replaced by Pedro Borbon with none out in the fourth). It didn't look promising for the Reds. Nerves were on edge. Geronimo homered in the fifth to cut the lead to 3–2. During the regular season Geronimo had homered off of a Blass fastball and since that time Blass had fed him a steady diet of curveballs. Good pitchers adjust. After seeing a steady stream of curveballs, Geronimo hit one out of the park. Good hitters adjust, too. Before the series, Anderson had vowed to play Geronimo full time in the series after part-time duty during the season. It was the same baptism of fire he had used with Carbo, Gullett, and Wilcox in the 1970 postseason. The thirty-eight-year-old skipper proclaimed, "I will make a man out of him or else this series."

The Pirates continued to hold on to their 3–2 lead, failing to score in their half of the ninth. The Pirates brought in their closer then, Dave Giusti, following conventional wisdom. Giusti had racked up twenty-two saves and posted a 1.92 ERA during the year, and more importantly now he was a right-hander. The Reds had three right-handed batters due up: Bench, Perez, and Menke. On a 1–2 pitch to Bench, Giusti threw a palm ball[2] high and over the outside of the

"The Big Four" exit the field: left to right, Bench, Rose, Perez, and Morgan (photograph courtesy Roadwest Publishing [Jack Klumpe Collection]).

plate. A poor hitter would try to pull this pitch to get more power, but Bench went with the pitch and lined it to right, where it continued to carry and carry, as Clemente looked up. The ball cleared the wall by ten feet to make it a 3–3 game. The stadium erupted into a delirious but controlled pandemonium.

Next Perez followed with a single and Anderson sent George Foster to run for him. Menke followed with another single, sending Foster to second. With no outs the Reds were desperate to get Foster over to third where a sacrifice fly would score him and win the game. Grammas flashed the bunt sign to Geronimo. He pulled the bat back as Giusti threw high. Giusti was tightening; he threw another ball high. At this point the Pittsburgh manager, Bill Virdon, had seen enough. He called for Bob Moose out of the bullpen. Normally Moose was the number-two starter, a hard-throwing right-hander who had started game two and gotten rocked by the Reds three days earlier.

Moose stomped to the mound to try to stop the bleeding for the Pirates. His surname fit him well. He was similar in build to Clay Carroll, a big, stocky man with a barrel chest. Cesar Geronimo was waiting at the plate. Grammas went through his series of motions, again calling for the bunt. Geronimo missed for strike one. In an effort to fool the Pirates, Grammas did not signal for a bunt before the next pitch and Geronimo swung and missed. With two strikes they called off the bunt for good and Geronimo lifted a ball deep to right that Clemente gathered in at the base of the wall; Foster tagged and went to third.

The winning run was now ninety feet away with one out. Darrel Chaney only needed to hit a deep fly ball to score Foster. He hit the fly but it was only a pop to deep short. Gene Alley raced out and Rennie Stennett raced in; they collided as the crowd held their breath waiting for the ball to pop loose. Alley held on for the second out.

Clay Carroll was due up, so Anderson sent his ace pinch hitter, Hal McRae, to the plate. McRae worked the count to one ball and one strike. Manny Sanguillen flashed the sign to Moose for a slider. From the stretch Moose unleashed it. It bounced four feet left of the plate. Sanguillen sprang to block it but couldn't as it bounced extremely high and toward the backstop. Foster broke for home clapping during his last few steps. Moose ran to cover the plate while Sanguillen gave chase to the ball. It was too late, the play didn't even draw a throw before Foster stepped on home. The Reds were victorious. They had come back from the brink of elimination.

While the Reds were absolutely joyous with celebration on the field, Clemente gathered his beaten fellow warriors in the clubhouse. Batboys later reported being mesmerized by his speech, which turned out to be his last. Just as he had seemed to be everywhere and done everything on the field, he continued to be everywhere after the season as well. While flying relief goods from his native Puerto Rico to earthquake victims in Managua, Nicaragua, the 1971 World Series MVP's plane went down over the Atlantic. The world lost a true hero on New Year's Eve 1972. Clemente, who had notched the magical career

Pirate catcher Manny Sanguillen whirls to find Bob Moose's wild pitch as third base coach Alex Grammas urges pinch runner George Foster home with the winning run in the 1972 NLCS. It capped the wildest ninth inning ever in Riverfront and perhaps the greatest game in playoff history (photograph courtesy Roadwest Publishing [Jack Klumpe Collection]).

hit 3,000 on the last day of the 1972 season, was honored for his life's work by having a five-year waiting rule waived and was immediately enshrined in the Baseball Hall of Fame.

The Reds, not the Pirates, were off to the World Series again. After the game, Anderson pronounced the twenty-four-year-old Geronimo a man.

11

A SECOND SERIES
October 1972

After defeating the defending World Series champions, the Reds entered the Fall Classic as the odds-on favorites. The Reds faced a new opponent, the young Oakland Athletics, a team that had come of age and dispatched the Detroit Tigers 3–2 in a tightly contested playoff.

The A's were not only young, they were also a bit wacky. It started from the top. Charlie Finley was a maverick who seized opportunity when it arose. Stricken with tuberculosis in 1946, Finley underwent surgery. Upon his recovery the doctor offhandedly remarked how fortunate Finley was to have medical insurance; many patients did not and the physician himself didn't have any. Upon his recovery, Finley went on to become a multi-millionaire by writing medical insurance policies beginning with the American Medical Association. Now rich, he attempted to buy the Philadelphia Athletics in 1954 but failed. He tried again and this time successfully purchased the Athletics, now in Kansas City, Missouri, in 1960. Following the 1967 season, Finley was enticed by Oakland, California, city officials to come west and play in the Oakland Coliseum, which they would share with the Raiders.[1] Finley later called the move the biggest mistake he had ever made. To compensate citizens of Kansas City, the American League awarded the expansion Royals to them in 1969.

Finley was unconventional and loved to draw fans through marketing experiments. His opponents called them gimmicks. He had tried orange baseballs during warm-ups; he had introduced white baseball spikes to the club and the entire team was shod like Joe Namath. In 1972, Reggie Jackson had come to training camp with a mustache, which was against the rules. Finley sent word to Jackson to shave, but Jackson was reticent to pull out the razor. Finley wanted to avoid a confrontation with his superstar, so he eventually came up with another marketing scheme. He offered each player $300 to grow a mustache by Father's Day. On that day there would be a special promotion and a team photo would be taken. The vast majority of the players obliged.

Along the way, Finley inadvertently launched other careers. He decided "to be nice to umpires," so he had a local young lady bake them cookies. She took them out to the umpires in the fifth inning. Later she parlayed her recipe into a business, Mrs. Fields.

To the national media, Finley and his A's provided a contrast to the strait-laced Cincinnati Reds. The Reds were required to wear black spikes, meticulously polished, with red stir-up socks that were not pulled too high; the red needed to show below the uniform pants. They also had a longtime rule against growing any kind of facial hair; they certainly were not going to pay players to grow it. Outside of Cincinnati, it was billed as sort of a good-versus-evil, Ricky Nelson–versus–James Dean contest.

The A's were rebels—and their clubhouse was know to have some discord—while a high value was placed on harmony with the Reds. This is best illustrated by the incident between John "Blue Moon" Odom and Vida Blue just days before the Series. Blue Moon Odom had to be pulled from Game Five of the playoff series against Detroit after he began vomiting due to nerves. Afterward Vida Blue, upset that he had been relegated to the bullpen, asked Odom why the starters couldn't finish anything. Odom lurched at Blue and a scuffle ensued. Several players had to come in and break it up. In ensuing years other scuffles would break out between the A's players, causing black eyes, injuries, and sometimes a trip to the disabled list for players trying to break up the fight.

In contrast, the Reds had already shipped Alex Johnson to the California Angels for his attitude and others had been traded for being "clubhouse lawyers" or even excessive talkers. In essence the A's were willing to tolerate more turbulence in their stream than the Reds were in theirs. Turbulence's effect on performance in the short run doesn't make much difference; the turbulence can even seem exciting to a degree. But in the long term, your raft wears out a lot faster if you have to ride through lots of turbulence.

Clubhouse issues aside, what was going to make the difference in this Series was play on the field and that came down to the players. When it came to players, Reggie Jackson was Oakland's best. Jackson was a tough kid from just outside of Philadelphia. He sported a gold tooth early in his career, a memento from a run-in with a linebacker on the football field. After a stellar college career at Arizona State, he was drafted by the A's in 1966. He had a good start to his pro career, hitting twenty-nine home runs in his first full season with the A's. He emerged on the national stage at the 1971 All-Star Game, where he hit a ball that "just seemed to keep rising" according to legendary Detroit broadcaster Ernie Harwell. Harwell said he never saw a ball hit so far in his sixty-plus-year career. Jackson put Doc Ellis's pitch against the transformer at the base of Tiger Stadium's right-center-field light tower, on the roof in right field. Some calculate that the blast would have gone an estimated 650 feet had the tower not been there.[2]

Jackson was colorful and talented. His fame would continue to grow as his career progressed, reaching its zenith with his three home runs in three swings for the New York Yankees in the 1977 Fall Classic. But Jackson would not play in this, his first World Series. While sliding in for the first run in Game Five against Detroit, leading a double steal, Jackson had ripped his hamstring. Oakland had won 2–1, but now Jackson was lost for the Series. His leg was not going to heal in two days. The A's had lost their best player.

But Oakland had other weapons besides Jackson. Jackson was replaced in centerfield by a twenty-three-year-old named George Hendrick, who later sported what was arguably the best afro in baseball. In right field the former Pittsburgh Pirate and NL batting champion Matty Alou had come over in a mid-season trade. In left field, Joe Rudi was a great defensive player and a good hitter. It hadn't always been that way. Rudi had been an infielder through high school. When he was moved to the outfield he was scared to death and played very poorly. Enter Joe DiMaggio. Finley had hired DiMaggio to be a coach in 1968. DiMaggio tutored the youngster and taught him to turn on the ball and run hard after deep fly balls. Meanwhile legendary hitting coach Charley Lau taught Rudi not to try to pull every pitch he was thrown.

In the infield, Mike Epstein, whose refusal of a minor-league demotion had gotten him shipped out of Baltimore to Washington, now seemed to have found a home at first base for the A's.[3] Bert "Campy" Campaneris was slick at short and he was the answer to the Reds Morgan-Tolan combination on the base path. Sal Bando rounded out the infield with a good bat—fifteen home runs and 77 RBIs. Behind the plate, Dave Duncan handled most of the duties. Duncan was solid defensively but no Johnny Bench, and nowhere near Bench on offense.

What Duncan did do was handle the strength of the A's ball club. Oakland had the finest stable of starting pitchers outside of Baltimore. Jim "Catfish" Hunter, Ken Holtzman, John "Blue Moon" Odom, and Vida Blue were a terrific rotation. Once the game got near the ninth, the A's turned the ball over to a committee of relievers led by Rollie Fingers. Finley's mustache investment had gone further with Fingers than anyone; his handlebar mustache was the envy of barbershop quartets everywhere.

The mustachioed A's were managed by Dick Williams, the man who had been suggested by Howsam's inner circle to manage the Reds instead of Sparky Anderson two years earlier. Williams led the Boston Red Sox to the American League pennant in 1967. When the Red Sox didn't repeat and Williams became cross with Carl Yastrzemski, he was let go.

Finley had hired Williams to manage the Athletics in 1971. Ironically Williams was good pals with Anderson. They had both been in the Dodgers organization and played together for an entire year in Ft. Worth in 1955 and part of 1956 in Montreal. Williams had been a promising outfielder for the Dodgers until he dove for a shallow fly ball and stuck his right shoulder into the ground like a javelin. As he said, he "couldn't throw across the room" after that point and spent thirteen years in professional ball as a utility man.

Williams was known as a crafty manager. He didn't mind arguing with players and was often accused of overmanaging. That charge is laid at the feet of a skipper who sometimes makes too many moves.

All in all, the A's hitters were no match for the Red's offensive weapons but their relief pitching was just as good and their starting pitching was better. The old saying is that good pitching beats good hitting and this was about to be tested.

The Reds were confident, perhaps too confident, entering the World Series after having beaten the defending World Champions and the team with the best record in baseball, the Pirates. In the clubhouse after their playoff win, Bobby Tolan told reporters, "As far as I'm concerned the World Series is over. The best two teams have played." Rose echoed his comments. Delirious in their celebration, the Reds intimated that the Pirates were co-champions of the world. Imagine how Oakland players felt about that.

To add insult to injury, Sparky Anderson was open in his feeling that the National League was the better league. He asserted that one could stock four All-Star rosters with NL players, but the American League could not. As further evidence he pointed to that fact that Dick Allen went to the AL and was named the MVP but he was far from it in the National League. When the *Sporting News* listed the best players in baseball, more than 80 percent were from the National League. Oakland took all of this as a lack of respect.

The series opened in the NL park, Riverfront Stadium, on October 14. With four strong pitchers, Williams announced that his rotation would be Holtzman, Hunter, Odom and Blue. Holtzman got the nod due in large part to his last outing at Riverfront Stadium. As a member of the Chicago Cubs, Holtzman had no-hit the Reds sixteen months earlier. The lefty Holtzman had gone 19–11 in 1972, his first season with Oakland.

Ironically Holtzman's counterpart on the mound on the night of his no-hitter would also be his opponent in Game One of the Series. Holtzman had beaten Gary Nolan 1–0 in the no-hitter, when Nolan allowed one unearned run. Nolan had gone 15–5 during the 1972 regular season, tied for the best winning percentage in baseball, with a 1.99 ERA. He had been the first pitcher in the league to reach ten wins but had been slowed during the second half of the season with shoulder and neck problems, later blamed on an abscessed tooth.

Surprisingly, Dick Williams elected to go with a relatively unknown player named Gene Tenace at catcher instead of Duncan. He was put in the seventh spot in the lineup. His first time up he hit a fastball that barely cleared the left-field wall for a home run and a 2–0 lead. He returned to the batter's box in the fifth inning and hit a curveball — a pitch that hung "like a feather" according to Nolan — down the left-field line, just inside the foul pole, for a second home run. Thus Tenace became the first major-league player in history to hit home runs in his first two World Series at-bats. A day earlier he had been totally unknown outside of Oakland; by Saturday evening he was a household name across the nation.

After Reggie Jackson went down with the hamstring injury, the A's added young Allen Lewis to the roster. Lewis had stolen thirty-four bases for the Birmingham Class-AAA club that season and was impressed with his own base-stealing prowess. He claimed before the Series, "I'm not afraid of Johnny Bench. He should be worrying about me. If the pitcher doesn't keep me close, he could have a rifle with a bullet and couldn't hit me." Lewis got his chance to put his money where his mouth was in the ninth inning of Game One. Looking to extend the A's 3–2 lead, Lewis was inserted as a pinch runner for Mike Epstein after a walk. Lewis broke for second and Bench gunned him down. Williams speculated that Lewis must not have gotten a good jump because with his speed it would be difficult for Bench to stop him.

Bench had earlier thrown out Bert Campaneris back in the third inning on an attempted steal. Campaneris, Oakland's best base stealer, broke on a slow curve by Nolan and Bench still got him. Oakland's attempt to match Cincinnati's speed was off to a poor start.

Still, Gene Tenace had provided all the offense needed for the A's in their 3–2 Game One win. Rollie Fingers was brought in early in the sixth and a starter, Vida Blue, was brought in during the seventh to finish the job. After the game the Reds raved about Blue, comparing his fastball to Steve Carlton's, while pointing out that his breaking ball was not quite as good. Future pitching coach Wes Stock respected Blue's fastball and feared his streaks of wildness so much that he avoided catching for him in the bullpen. But more than Blue, the Reds were most frustrated by their own lack of offensive production. The top three batters in the order had failed to get on and stay on base. This caused clean-up hitter Bench to lead off the inning four times in the game. So far good pitching was beating good hitting, but it was still early.

It was the twenty-fifth-anniversary season of Jackie Robinson breaking baseball's color barrier, courtesy of Howsam's mentor Branch Rickey. Rickey had passed away in 1965, but Robinson was still active, having been the vice president of a restaurant chain and later the chairman of the board for Hamilton Life Insurance Company. He had the honor of throwing out the ceremonial first pitch for Game Two. Sadly, Robinson would pass away ten days later due to complications from diabetes. His visit to Riverfront on October 15 would be his last appearance at a ballpark.

The Reds did not want to get down two games as they had in 1970. Similar to Game One versus Baltimore two years earlier, Game Two largely turned on one play. Catfish Hunter started the game for Oakland. He had received his nickname from Finley but it had no basis in reality; it was a tall tale concocted for PR purposes. Hunter had encountered a Reds player before — in the night air of Anaheim five years earlier, a young Tony Perez had taken him deep to end the longest All-Star Game ever in fifteen innings. The right-hander was now Oakland's ace at 21–7 with a 2.04 ERA. He had been unable to start Game One because he had pitched Game Four in the playoffs against Detroit. The Reds countered with Ross Grimsley, the hero in Game Four of the NL playoffs, the man who had brought them back from the brink.

Both pitchers pitched well. Hunter helped himself with an RBI single in the second. He was a good hitter, having batted .350 the previous season. Joe Rudi added a solo homer in the third. Charley Lau's batting lessons had paid off.

In the sixth, the A's got a chance to see if the caught-stealing results of Game One had been a fluke. Mike Epstein drew a walk and was shocked and then furious when he saw action in the A's dugout. A pinch runner, the confident rookie Allen Lewis, emerged and trotted to first base. As the A's only left-handed power hitter, Epstein considered it a personal affront to be lifted in the sixth inning of a close ballgame. Meanwhile Lewis had another chance to test Bench. As Sal Bando struck out for the second out, Lewis broke for second base. Bench must have had the rifle and bullet that Allen alluded to because he shot Allen down. Bench: 2, Cocky Rookie: 0.

The Reds entered the bottom of the ninth down 2–0. Perez singled to open the inning. Denis Menke then launched a ball deep to left — which was going to be either a home run or a double off the wall, depending on the trajectory. It turned out to be neither. Joe Rudi knew it was trouble when it left the bat; he turned on the ball and ran hard after the deep fly. He leaped against the wall

The beauty of Joe Rudi's catch is belied by the height of Riverfront's walls. Rudi credited Joe DiMaggio after robbing Denis Menke and the Reds of victory in Game Two. Arrow indicates the beginning of the wall (photograph courtesy Roadwest Publishing [Jack Klumpe Collection]).

and came down clutching the ball in the H-web of his mitt. DiMaggio had taught him well.

The catch made all the highlight reels and deservedly so but its full beauty could not be appreciated due to the height of the Reds' outfield walls. They stood twelve feet high. In most parks today the walls are seven to eight feet high. That allows an athlete to jump and pull the ball down as it is about to go over the wall, a feat to behold. In the days of the high walls at Riverfront Stadium, an Olympic high jumper couldn't pull down a ball from on top of the wall. Twelve years later Reds fans would fully appreciate the beauty of the above-the-wall, home-run-robbing catch as the Reds finally lowered the outfield wall to eight feet. Aesthetics aside, Rudi's catch had robbed Menke of a double and the Reds of possible victory.

The next batter, Cesar Geronimo, smashed a liner to first. Mike Hegan, Epstein's defensive replacement, knocked the ball down, picked it up and crawled to first to get Geronimo. Dick Williams's maneuvering had paid off; Hegan was much better at first than Epstein. Perez, however, advanced to second on the play. A single by McRae then knocked Perez in; without Rudi's catch that would have made it at least 2–2. Instead pinch-hitting Julian Javier fouled out and the Reds lost 2–1 and were going to the opposition's park, down 2–0 again.

As both teams would publicly confess, both were flat in the first two games. Though both ballgames had been decided by one run, they lacked emotion and fervor. The Reds were emotionally exhausted from their epic playoff battle with the defending World Champion Pirates. Additionally some Reds confessed that they had relaxed a bit once they heard that Reggie Jackson would not be in the Series.

Likewise Oakland was exhausted from its five-game battle with Detroit. The playoff series had featured suspensions, extra innings, bad calls, and bad blood between Finley and Detroit Manager Billy Martin, who Finley claimed broke a verbal agreement the two had made for Martin to manage the A's in 1971.

What better way to pump emotion into the series than careless words. They came after Game Two—from both sides. When Rose heard Hunter say that he blew his fastball by the Reds, Rose was indignant. He felt Hunter was claiming to be a super pitcher and Rose was sure he was not one. Rose pointed out that Hunter had only six strikeouts and a super pitcher "who blows fastballs by batters" would have fourteen.

The A's reiterated that they felt disrespected by the Reds players' previous comments. Epstein and Bando felt that the biggest difference between the two opponents was not the league, but the AstroTurf. The AL had only one field (Chicago) with AstroTurf, and this was only on the infield, with regular dirt cut-outs. The depth the infielders had to play and how double-play balls became singles surprised the A's.

However, Oakland left it to Vida Blue to up the verbal ante. Blue said that playing the Reds was like playing the Rangers. The Texas club was widely considered the worst team in baseball. The Reds didn't miss the point. Sparky Anderson didn't miss it either. At the Monday workout in Oakland, Anderson gave the Reds a rare verbal tongue-lashing that he reported was not fit to print. He made it a point during the lashing to highlight Blue's Rangers comment.

The verbal jousting was not just between the two clubs. The A's were again quarrelling with each other. Epstein and Williams got in a shouting match on the flight back from Cincinnati about the pinch runner. Epstein said he didn't feel appreciated and Williams pointed out that he was the manager. Williams later attributed his comments to too much scotch. Dave Duncan jumped on the bandwagon, criticizing Finley and how he ran the club. Blue pointed out that Finley's now-and-then presentation of $5,000 to a team hero only built resentment among the players. It hardly sounded like a team with a 2–0 lead in a World Series.

When Dick Williams arrived in Oakland he made a surprise announcement. He was scrapping his planned rotation of Holtzman, Hunter, Odom, and Blue. Once he read the Reds' glowing comments on how tough Vida Blue was to hit, Williams decided to leave him in the bullpen where he could pitch more against the Reds. It also would help Oakland as star left-handed reliever Darold Knowles had broken his left thumb a few weeks earlier. The Reds tipped their hand in the press and Williams capitalized on it.

The Reds' primary problem in Games One and Two was a lack of offense. The top three hitters struggled, with only two hits in twenty-three at-bats. Perhaps to rub that statistic in their face, a flower arrangement was anonymously sent to the Reds clubhouse. A large arrangement of yellow flowers, shaped like a cross, was accompanied by a note that read, "Rest in Peace."

The Reds were encouraged by the fact that they had the best road record in baseball that year at 58–23, but Oakland had won more than fifty games on the road themselves. After reading the press clippings and hearing from their manager, the Reds were pumped for Game Three on Tuesday but they would be disappointed. Oakland experienced the rain of a decade, accompanied by hail. After less than an hour delay, and six inches of water in the outfield, the game was called off. Both teams were disappointed after being up for the game. Matty Alou took it best, "If my Lord wants it to rain, I am happy."

After the washout, Commissioner Bowie Kuhn announced that Game Three would be played on Wednesday, Game Four on Thursday, and Game Five on Friday, the normal travel day. The Friday game would start at 1:00 P.M. so the teams could fly back to Cincinnati that evening if necessary. There would be no travel day. NBC did not want to lose a Saturday afternoon World Series date. Television ratings were beginning to drive baseball decisions.

Helicopters were brought in to hover over the marshy Oakland Coliseum field in an attempt to dry it out for Game 3. The efforts were partially successful but the wet conditions would affect the next three games. Jack Billingham of the Reds got the ball in Game Three. After coming over from Houston in the trade, Billingham had gone 12–12. "Blue Moon" Odom was the A's pitcher, with a season record of 15–6. Like almost all of them, this was another nickname solely bestowed by Finley for PR purposes. Blue Moon was very fast and sometimes used by Dick Williams as a pinch runner.

The hitters complained about the 5:30 P.M. Pacific Time start time in order to accommodate an 8:30 P.M. Eastern start time for NBC. The low sun and long shadows made the ball difficult to see for both fielders and hitters. The hitters claimed it affected their performance. They had evidence to back their claim. Blue Moon Odom fanned 11 Reds through seven innings. However, as Bowie Kuhn noted, the hitting didn't get any better after sunset.

The game was a pitching gem and defensive nightmare on both sides. Billingham and Odom gave up only six hits between them but both teams recorded two errors. Bench and Morgan made rare errors on the same play in the sixth. However it was not the lowest point of the game for Bench. In the eighth inning, the Reds had Tolan at second and Morgan at third, with Bench at the plate facing Rollie Fingers. Fingers worked the count to three balls and two strikes. Williams sprang from the dugout, indicating that he had seen enough. He came to the mound to confer with Fingers and Tenace. He began pointing to first base, indi-

The envy of barbershop quartets everywhere, Rollie Fingers (right, posing with an unknown friend of the A's) proved to be the Reds' chief nemesis in the '72 series. Fingers humiliated Johnny Bench in Game Three. He and the little-known Gene Tenace were the A's heroes (photograph courtesy Roadwest Publishing [Jack Klumpe Collection]).

cating he was going to walk the power hitter rather than risk throwing him a strike down the middle of the plate that he could drive. All returned to their positions. Tenace stood and called for the intentional walk. Bench relaxed as Fingers leisurely reared back to make the toss to the outside. Morgan smelled something and yelled "watch out!" as Tenace deftly went back to his catching position and Fingers snapped a curveball over the outside of the plate for strike three. Bench initially felt absolutely humiliated. Snookered in front of eighty million television viewers, Bench was embarrassed and later angry at the A's trickery.

The water came into play in the third inning. With two outs, Rose drew a walk. He broke for second on the pitch to Morgan, and Tenace's throw to second was high and rolled to center field, which allowed Rose to hustle to third. Morgan then smacked a would-be single through the infield toward right, but the heavy, soggy grass slowed the ball. Dick Green dove to make the stop and threw to first in time to get the speedy Morgan and end the inning.

Rose had a chance to be a hero in the fifth. After Menke singled, Geronimo slapped the ball toward first on a hit-and-run play. Epstein fielded the ball and turned to throw to second and realized he had no chance for Menke, so he threw to first but nobody was on the bag. The Reds now had men on first and third with no outs. Darrel Chaney and then Jack Billingham struck out. It was now up to Rose. He worked the count to 2–2 when Odom threw very low. Home-plate umpire Mel Steiner hesitated for a moment and then called strike three. Rose went berserk.

The A's only threat came in the sixth inning, with the score tied 0–0. Campy Campaneris drew a walk to lead off the inning. Alou bunted him over and Bench's throw pulled Morgan off the first-base bag so both runners were safe. Meanwhile Campaneris began dancing around second base, unaware that Tolan was sneaking in behind him from center field. Morgan rifled the ball to Tolan who would easily have tagged Campaneris out but the throw was wild and rolled to the outfield. Oakland now had men on the corners with no outs. The pressure was squarely on Billingham. Rudi grounded out to third and Alou went to second base. Billingham intentionally walked Epstein to load the bases and then Bando made that move pay off for Cincinnati by bouncing into a double play. Billingham was out of a major jam.

The only run of the ballgame was scored by the Reds in the seventh. Perez singled and Menke bunted him over to second. Geronimo then lined a single to center with Perez flying from second base, rounding third and easily heading for home. Slipping on wet grass, Perez fell between third and the plate. Campaneris took the relay throw from center field but didn't see Perez lying on the ground. His lapse in attention cost the A's the game, as Perez got up and ran across home plate.

It is known as "little ball" or "small ball" and it is rarely seen in today's game of power-hitting long ball. Interestingly the great Big Red Machine, with all its power and offense, didn't find "little ball" beneath them when the situation called for it. They weren't above bunting a man over to put him in scoring position. It has become a lost art thirty years later. It was the final margin of victory in Game Three of the 1972 Series; the Reds were back in business, down two games to one.

The Reds played small ball again in Game Four. They found themselves down to Ken Holtzman 1–0, courtesy of Gene Tenace, who by now was playing every game in place of Duncan due to his Game One heroics. In the fifth inning Tenace homered for the third time in the Series to give Oakland the lead. The home run came at the expense of Don Gullett, who had experienced his first disappointing season in the majors. Hepatitis had limited the twenty-one-year-old to pitching just half the season and a 9–10 record. That fact, coupled with his having pitched Game Five of the playoffs, meant that he had not pitched in the Series until this point. He did pitch well in this game, giving up only the run to Tenace.

Entering the eighth, behind 1–0, the Reds decided to play small ball again. Concepcion, who started in place of Chaney, grounded a tough one to Campaneris and beat the throw to first. Again the infield hit by Concepcion highlights the value of speed, a Howsam trademark. Julian Javier batted for Gullett and bunted Concepcion over to second. Rose grounded out to second, moving Concepcion to third. Surprisingly Dick Williams emerged from the dugout. He asked Ken Holtzman for the ball. Holtzman was hopping mad, pulled from the game with two outs and a shutout in progress. To add fuel to the fire, he was being pulled for another lefty, Vida Blue.

Blue immediately made matters worse for Holtzman and Williams. Joe Morgan, known for his great eye, drew a walk. He led the National League in that department. That brought up Bobby Tolan.

Tolan had not hit well so far in the Series. Prior to the game, he got a call from an old friend offering help. Lou Brock, Tolan's roommate in St. Louis, had been watching the series on TV. A veteran of three World Series himself, Brock had some advice for Tolan. Teams sometimes forget their scouting reports when they get into the series. They may not pitch to you like you expect. That note struck a chord with Tolan. He was a very good fastball hitter. Most of the NL pitchers had learned that and Tolan saw a steady diet of off-speed pitches in the National League. He had grown so accustomed to the routine that he expected to see the same from the A's but he hadn't. They had been offering up plenty of fastballs but Tolan was behind them as he waited for the breaking pitch. He decided to change tactics. When Vida Blue offered up a fastball, Tolan smashed a double to right that scored both Concepcion and the speedy Morgan. After a scoreless A's bottom of the eighth against Pedro Borbon, the Reds failed to score in the top of the ninth but led 2–1 going into the bottom of the ninth.

The Reds' tremendous bullpen was set to finish the game. Mike Hegan grounded out and pinch hitter Gonzalo Marquez then singled to center. Anderson went to the mound to replace Pedro Borbon. He wanted his best for this situation and called on the Hawk, Clay Carroll. Carroll would face none other than Gene Tenace. For once, Tenace did not homer. He only singled.

In response Dick Williams inserted a left-handed pinch hitter, Don Mincher, to bat for the light-hitting, right-handed Dave Green. Anderson had Tommy Hall warmed up in the bullpen and Hall had been pitching well during the series. It was one of those difficult decisions for a manager. Do I bring in Hall, a good lefty to face a lefty? Or do I leave in my main guy, my go-to guy, who has done the job all year, but is a right-hander? Do I play the percentages or do I stick with my big gun? Anderson thought about going up the steps, but stayed put.

Mincher singled, followed with a game-winner by the A's Angel Mangual. In all of his six appearances against the Orioles and A's in the World Series, the Hawk had never given up more than one hit in an inning and had never given up a single run until that day. For once he had failed. Even the best fail at times. Not only did he give up a run, he'd allowed two to score as the A's won the game.[4] Anderson had stuck with Carroll thinking that he would end it; he was Anderson's best but he just couldn't do it this time. The Reds were devastated. They'd had the game in their hands, ready to tie the Series, and then they lost. They were down three games to one. It was the one that got away.

Sometimes fans don't know when to quit. As the Reds walked to their bus after the Game Four nightmare, a couple of fans were launching verbal assaults. The assaults were directed at Carroll. He looked over and saw someone who looked like the classic California hippie of the time. The hippie and his friend were looking for trouble. Carroll calmly and with polite words asked them to knock it off. The two increased the volume and language, challenging Carroll. Carroll took off for them but Johnny Bench and Big Klu restrained him. No one restrained utility man Ted Uhlaender, who got in a good pop to the heckler's ribs before someone pulled him away. The incident added fuel to the Reds' fire.[5]

Following Game Four, Gene Tenace kept up the war of words. Following Tenace's early Series performance with two home runs, Sparky Anderson offhandedly remarked, "You don't expect a guy like Tenace to beat you." Tenace felt slighted by the remark and later said all three home run balls had Sparky Anderson's name written all over them. Tenace shouldn't have felt slighted, as everyone felt that way about the .225 hitter. It had been that way all of Gene Tenace's professional baseball career. Finishing high school, the Reds had passed on the Lucasville, Ohio, product in the draft, ditto the New York Yankees (his favorite team) and the Houston Astros. Most everyone had overlooked the man who had grown up 110 miles from Cincinnati as a slightly above average high school outfielder. He wasn't being overlooked anymore.

Rose and Hunter kept up the verbal exchange as well. Hunter felt slighted by Rose's comments that he wasn't a super pitcher. He wondered how he had won twenty-one games without being super. Rose explained that a super pitcher blows pitches by hitters and that there weren't many around like that. He felt there was only one in the American League and that was young Nolan Ryan of the California Angels. Rose went on to predict that Cincinnati's hitting would get better now that they had seen all of Oakland's pitchers. He stated that he in particular would hit a lot better the second time around. Rose commented that a good hitter learns a pitcher's strengths and weaknesses after seeing him once. He would get his chance to prove it in Game Five.

When Rose stepped into the batter's box to open Game Five, sixty feet and six inches away stood his verbal jousting partner, Catfish Hunter. Rose made good on his words by depositing Hunter's first pitch into the bleachers. Rose seemed right, he was hitting better the second time around.

The Reds' backs were against the wall, three games to one, just as they had been in 1970. They had a surprise starter in Game Five, Jim "Opie Taylor" McGlothlin. Gary Nolan had been penciled in to start, but his shoulder had tightened after Game One and he couldn't go. After considering Wayne Simpson, Sparky Anderson tapped McGlothlin due to his previous American League and World Series experience. Both starters were ineffective, though; neither made it through the fifth. The tone had been set when Rose homered off Hunter to open the game. Then Gene Tenace had struck again, hitting a three-run shot in the second for this fourth home run of the series.

The Reds scored the final three runs of the game in different innings, all with singles, bunts, walks, errors and stolen bases—"little ball" again. Howsam's secret weapon, speed, allowed it to happen. In the fifth inning Morgan drew a walk and took off on the first pitch to Tolan, which Tolan knocked into right field. As Morgan approached third, Grammas waved him home — and he scored from first on a single.

Morgan and speed struck again in the eighth. Morgan drew a walk and on the first ball thrown to Tolan, Oakland called for a pitch out but Morgan wasn't running. On the second pitch he was—and stole second. Tolan then slapped another ball to right field, easily scoring Morgan. Morgan was a smart base runner and Tolan had been wise to listen to Brock.

Pete Rose loved to talk in a ballgame. Fans are often unaware of the many conversations that occur during the course of a major-league ball game. When Rose approached the plate in the seventh, he found Tenace arguing with the home plate umpire, Bob Engel, about how he was calling balls and strikes. Rose decided to lighten the mood and asked Tenace if he was building a garage in order to house the MVP car he might win if Oakland took the series. Tenace was not amused and continued arguing. Rose then suggested that Tenace bring an indicator with him if he wanted to call balls and strikes. At this point Tenace was incensed and told Rose to shut up, get in the batter's box, and swing. Rose smiled and obliged — end of conversation.[6]

Home plate was not the only spot where things were heating up for Rose. Left field was getting ugly. Oakland fans, unappreciative of Rose's assessment of Catfish Hunter's superiority, began to rain eggs down on the outfielder during Game Four. To his rescue came Karolyn, Rose's dedicated, loyal, and feisty wife. No one was going to treat her man that way. She marched right out to the left-field bleachers, plopped down in a seat, and began taking up for her husband. "You call yourself fans?" Someone pointed out that it was probably youngsters throwing the objects. She pointed out very clearly that they were grown adults. After apparently emptying the chicken coop for Thursday's game, the weapon turned to tomatoes on Friday. Rose attempted to settle the natives by throwing a few warm-up balls up to them.[7]

Back on the field, Rose continued the little ball in the ninth. With the score tied 4–4, Cesar Geronimo had led off the inning with a single. Ross Grimsley was ordered to sacrifice him over to second. His bunt attempt popped the ball into the air. Cincinnati's nemesis, Rollie Fingers, tried to trick the Reds again. He easily could have caught the ball, but let it drop, intending to then throw to first to get Grimsley. The A's then could easily throw to second to double-up Geronimo, who had held up at first, expecting the ball to be caught. Fingers turned out to be too clever for his own good. He let the ball drop but then fired wide to first; the A's were able to get to the bag and get Grimsley, but Geronimo was now on second.

Next Sal Bando bobbled Dave Concepcion's grounder to third, and the Reds had men on first and second. Pete Rose strode into the box, choosing to forego conversation with Tenace this time. He laced a pitch to center to knock Geronimo home for a one run Reds lead. It was his third hit of the game; he did hit better the second time around.

The key play of the ballgame occurred in the bottom of the ninth. The Reds were clinging to a 5–4 lead. Again it was up to the bullpen to save the game but it was two starters who came out of the pen this time: Grimsley and Billingham. Who else but Gene Tenace would lead off the bottom of the ninth? Grimsley was very careful with the newborn hitting star, walking him. True to his colors, Dick Williams inserted "Blue Moon" Odom to run for Tenace. Blue Moon made his way to third with only one out, after a single by Dave Duncan.

Campy Campaneris, the speedy shortstop, was at the plate. He popped a drifting fly ball into shallow right field. Geronimo charged in while Morgan sped back, settled under the ball, and caught it. Odom broke for home; Morgan slipped on the wet grass, jumped back on his feet, and fired the ball toward Bench. Bench had the plate blocked just as Elrod Hendricks had done in 1970. Odom went sprawling into a wild slide. There was no question that he was out — double play, end of ballgame. The Reds had staved off elimination.

After the game Oakland third-base coach Irv Noren didn't want to talk about the play. About an hour later he did. He reported that the runner was instructed to run if he thought he could make it. Noren's manner indicated that he disagreed on Odom's assessment of the situation. Had Morgan not fallen, the play wouldn't even have been close.

Williams was more whimsical about the play. "We took a gamble and lost" was his attitude. The fact that he was out was clear to Williams and everybody else, everyone except Blue Moon Odom, who had argued his case on the field and now in the clubhouse. No one was buying it. Reggie Jackson finally hobbled over on his crutches and said, "You were out."

The final two games would be played in Ohio. The Reds' backs were still against the wall. They had gone further than they had against Baltimore two years prior but that wasn't their goal. Their goal was to win the Series, not just get to Game Six. Additionally, the Orioles had been favored against the "new kid" Reds in 1970. Now the shoe was on the other foot; the Reds were the World Series veterans and favored against the less experienced A's, especially without Reggie Jackson.

The rainy weather in Oakland had not only affected the games but it foiled Dick Williams's pitching rotation plans. With no off day on Friday as originally planned, Game Six was finally Vida Blue's chance to start. Vida Blue was as talented as his name was colorful but for now, he was miffed at Williams and Finley—and everybody else for that matter. The trouble had begun the previous off-season. Blue had enjoyed a good rookie year, hurling a no-hitter against the Detroit Tigers. In 1971 he was a media darling, starting the year 10–1 and selected to start the 1971 All-Star Game. He finished the year as the Cy Young

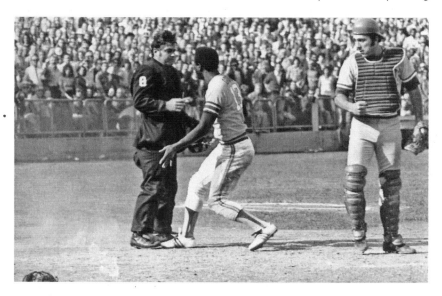

John "Blue Moon" Odom argues the out call that ended Game Five with a double play. His third base coach had not sent him and even his teammates thought he was out (photograph courtesy Roadwest Publishing [Jack Klumpe Collection]).

winner and AL MVP. After his fabulous '71 campaign, Blue expected a huge pay raise. In Blue's mind, Finley didn't offer one, though he did suggest that Blue legally change his first name to "True." When Blue asked him why Finley was not offering more money, Finley explained that Blue only used one arm while pitching.

Blue was blue the entire 1972 season, finishing 6–10. He was further incensed when Williams did not start him in any of the five playoff games against Detroit. Williams had initially promised to do so in the World Series but had changed his plans after reading in the newspaper how Bench and Rose raved about Blue after Game One. Blue had only been used in relief thus far and he was sulking. Williams granted Blue's wish for Game Six while the Reds countered with Game One starter Gary Nolan, who was finally able to loosen his shoulder. Williams likely regretted pacifying Blue, who gave up three runs in six innings, but the real damage came in the seventh against the relievers.

The seventh inning really tells the tale of the last half of the 1972 Series— speed, speed and more speed. With one out Concepcion singled to left. It put the young Venezuelan's batting average at .400 for the Series. He attributed it to Joe Morgan's bat. Concepcion borrowed it during the last regular-season series at Houston. It was working so well that he had no intention of giving it back. After Tommy Hall struck out, the A's decided to intentionally walk the switch-hitting Rose with lefty Dave Hamilton on the mound. While Hamilton threw the obligatory four balls, Rose decided to strike up another conversation with catcher Gene Tenace. He complemented Tenace on blocking some balls in the dirt and then added, "You know he's hitting .350 against lefties," referring to Joe Morgan, the next hitter.

"I know, but the boss is playing the percentages," Tenace solemnly replied. With that Rose was off to first.

Though Morgan hit well in the regular season, he was struggling — hitless in the World Series. He had drawn a number of walks to do some damage while waiting for his hitting to come around. Prior to the game, he had approached Ted Kluszewski for some help. Klu told him to stop opening his front shoulder on the swing. The advice paid off as Morgan had tripled in the first. It continued to pay off in the seventh as Morgan laced a single, scoring Concepcion, with Rose motoring to third and Morgan to second on the throw to try to nail Rose.

Tolan followed with a single to score Rose and Morgan. The A's brought in Joe Horlen to stop the bleeding. Tolan then stole second to raise the ire of the A's. It was another of those unwritten rules. You don't steal if ahead by four or more runs late in a game and the Reds were leading, 6–1. Meanwhile Horlen was having a terrible time on the mound. He was throwing balls in the dirt left and right, while Gene Tenace scrambled desperately to block the wild pitches. Finally one got through and Tolan broke for third.

That was the straw that broke the camel's back. Upon catching the next pitch, Tenace fired down to third in an effort to pick off Tolan, who got back easily. When Bando applied the tag, he also applied his arm and his leg — not gingerly — in an effort to shove Tolan off of the base. Bando said, "I tripped." No one believed him, especially when Williams was asked about it after the game. He said that the A's might try to do the same thing the next day.

There would be a next day, too. Game Six was the only blowout of the Series as the Reds pounded the A's 8–1, forcing a Game Seven. The Reds now had the momentum. Two straight victories, the latest being a total demolition job, while the Reds used all of their weapons at will.

The evening before the decisive game, Johnny Bench and Reggie Jackson met for dinner. They talked about the Series, baseball, and life. Bench offered a prophecy of how Game Seven would unfold. I will come up in the late innings with the game on the line, Bench said. Rollie Fingers will be on the mound. He has gotten me twice before in this series. This time I will get him.[8]

Heading into Game Seven, Dick Williams had a problem. The Reds had found the chink in Gene Tenace's armor. An unknown to them before the Series, they had expected to see Dave Duncan behind the plate and didn't know much about Tenace's game. It was always important to Howsam to know his enemy. After a few games the Reds figured it out; Tenace was not a good defensive catcher. Dave Duncan was, but Williams had been hesitant to pull Tenace from the lineup after his Game One fireworks. His subsequent offensive performance warranted that he stay with him. However Oakland's pitchers uncorked three wild pitches in Game Six that Tenace could not block and the Reds were running crazy. Once they figured out that Tenace had a weak arm, they took off. Ten steals in the last four games. Tolan himself had five with multiple-steal games, and he even stole third base in Game Five, the ultimate insult to a catcher. Meanwhile, Bench had detonated the A's running game: one successful steal (when Tommy Hall failed to hold the runner close), three caught stealing, zero steals for Campy Campaneris.

Williams thought he had the solution to stop the Reds from running in the pivotal Game Seven. He would insert Duncan behind the plate and put Tenace at first. The A's regular first baseman and clean-up hitter, big Mike Epstein, had been persona non grata in the Series, with no hits in sixteen at-bats. Epstein attributed the lack of hitting to the fact that Jackson was out of the lineup, allowing the Reds to pitch around him with no other power-hitting lefties in the lineup. Accurate assessment or not, Epstein was put on the bench. Williams had yet another tactic planned to stop the running, a tactic that the Reds would not learn until the game was on.

For the final game, the A's sent their ace pinch runner to the mound, Blue Moon Odom. The Reds countered with Jack Billingham, who had been the hero of Game Three. It would be a rematch of their epic Game Three 1–0 duel. This game would prove to be a classic as well. A weird kind of trouble started early for the Reds. After Campaneris flied to right to start the game, Angel Mangual hit a line drive to right center field. Tolan inexplicably ran in on the ball as it was going out. He leaped to try to snag it as it went overhead. It bounced off the top of his glove and rolled to the wall. Mangual easily made it to third.

Two men later, Gene Tenace, now batting clean-up in place of Epstein, came to bat. The last thing the Reds wanted was for Tenace to hit his fifth home run of the series. A very sick fan had also tried to stop Tenace from hitting another home run. "If Tenace homers again, he'll be shot," was the message received following Game Six. Fortunately, police were tipped off by an anonymous caller and a man from Louisville, Kentucky, was arrested a short time later, carrying a gun.[9] A man that confuses the consequences of a game with life and death is deranged to say the least.

Relieved after the arrest, Tenace came to the plate with Mangual still at third base. Anderson ordered Menke to take a step in defensively at third. The step would prove costly. Tenace hit a routine grounder toward Menke that would end the inning. The ball hit the seam where the artificial turf joined the dirt, right in front of Menke. Too close to adjust, with the ball veering oddly, it bounced off of Menke's glove and rolled into left field, scoring Mangual from third. With the error by Tolan and the ricochet off of Menke's glove, the A's had the early lead and regained the momentum. Menke had noticed the seam while Big Klu hit him practice grounders before the game. The seams were filled in pretty good but there was a little seam showing and that is where the ball hit. It is ironic that a field put in place by Howsam in order to allow fair play to all teams, hurt his own team by a feature unknown to natural fields.

The Reds threatened in the fourth. Joe Morgan walked with one out. The speed game was on again. Odom threw over to hold Morgan close. When Tenace applied the tag, he did it with some force. Odom then threw over again and Tenace again applied the tag, putting some weight on Morgan's ribs with the force of his mitt. Again Odom threw over, again Tenace applied the tag, pressing and holding it like a steam iron on a shirt. The drill was repeated again and again and again. The crowd grew restless and rained down boos. All in all, Odom threw over seven straight times. Tolan left the batter's box, went to the on-deck circle, put a doughnut on the bat, and took some practice swings in protest. Home-plate umpire Chris Pelekoudas invited him back to rejoin the inaction. Finally Odom threw to the plate and Morgan broke for second. Duncan sprang from his catcher's position and fired a rocket. Morgan, worn down and wearied from the constant dives back to first with Tenace's weight on him, was pegged out. Williams's two strategies for stopping the running had worked. He realized he was being burned by a weapon and set out to disable it. His decision to start Duncan was paying off.

Anderson's big decision came in the fifth inning with the Reds trailing 1–0. Jack Billingham was pitching a two-hitter. The bases were loaded with only one out. Catfish Hunter had been brought in to relieve Blue Moon. Billingham was due up to the plate. To say that Jack Billingham was a horrible hitter would be a gross understatement. He owned a .096 batting average to this point in his career. With the designated hitter in the American League, this would be a non-issue; Billingham would never have to lift a stick. However, this was before the DH was instituted and it made the game intriguing.

Do you send Billingham to the plate, hope he can hit a sacrifice fly and score Perez from third, or do you have him lay down a suicide squeeze bunt and hope to score Perez? In either case, do you take your chances with Billingham, figuring that if he makes an out you have a great hitter in Rose coming up next and hope he can get the job done? Do you risk letting Billingham hit, knowing that he is pitching well and figuring that the Reds will eventually generate at least one run, even if it is not in the fifth? Or do you call on your best pinch hitter, Hal McRae, to come to bat, who could easily make it a 4–1 game with one swing of the bat, and hope your fine bullpen can hold on from there? There was considerable consternation on the bench. It is one of those decisions that will be debated for years.

Anderson brought Billingham back to the dugout. McRae strode to the plate. McRae was a really, really good pinch hitter. The man could swing the bat. As has already been stated, he would have been in the lineup every day if he had been better defensively. Some good hitters aren't good pinch hitters but McRae was both. With the entire stadium on the edge of their seats, McRae took Catfish Hunter deep, very deep, but not quite deep enough. The ball settled into Mangual's glove at the base of the center-field wall, 400 feet away. Perez easily tagged and scored from third to tie the game. Rose flied to center to end the inning and the threat. Anderson's decision was still debatable.

The decision backfired the next inning. The A's jumped all over reliever Pedro Borbon. Tenace struck again, doubling in Campy Campaneris. Borbon then fell behind Sal Bando, three balls and no strikes, and offered up a fastball down the middle of the plate. Bando lined it to deep center, Tolan raced back, and as he approached the warning track he collapsed to the ground like a deer dropped by a hunter. The ball sailed over him and rolled to the wall. Tolan scrambled for the ball, threw it in, and collapsed to the ground again. Bando had an RBI double for a 3–1 Oakland lead. Jack Billingham watched helplessly from the bench. The Hawk, Clay Carroll, came in to stop the bleeding.

Bobby Tolan wasn't himself that day. His error in the first inning was unlike him. Larry Starr, the Reds trainer, ran to the outfield to attend to him, lying on his back after the Bando smash. Starr taped the pulled hamstring the best that he could. After getting his leg taped, Tolan finished the inning in the outfield. In the bottom of the sixth he struck out. Anderson pulled him after the inning. He moved Geronimo to center and put Foster in right.

Beginning in the pivotal fifth inning, the A's began bringing in starting pitchers like there was no tomorrow, because there was no tomorrow—this was the seventh game. Dick Williams was active, not only in replacing pitchers, but in visiting with them. All in all he made a total of seven trips to the mound during the game. He made several trips in one inning, seemingly one for each new batter. His multiple trips to the mound drove fans, TV audiences and opponents crazy. They were designed to do that. Baseball outlawed it shortly thereafter. Now a manager can only take one trip to the mound to see a pitcher in a given inning. If a manager makes a second trip to see the same pitcher in the same inning, he must be pulled from the game, courtesy of Dick Williams.

Besides visiting the mound, Williams was making other trips. He decided to coach first base during the fourth and fifth innings "because there must be something wrong with our television monitor in the dugout." He wanted to see what first-base umpire Jim Honochick was looking at on his calls because it was different than what the monitor showed. He also wandered over to Charlie Finley's box in the seventh inning to ensure that the champagne was on ice for the celebration.[10]

Rose singled to start the eighth inning. Morgan then smashed a liner right at Rose who had to dodge and hold his position in order to not be hit by the ball. If the ball hits the runner, the runner is out. Rose also had to avoid the diving Mike Hegan (a defensive substitution for Tenace) before he could really start running. At this point, Rose figured he would be lucky to make it to third, but the ball went into the corner and Matty Alou misplayed it. Third-base coach Alex Grammas held the stop sign and Rose began to put the brakes on as he rounded third. Grammas then changed his mind and encouraged Rose to head home as Morgan was ready and able to come to third. They then changed their minds again and Rose held at third. Ironically, he could have made it home as Alou threw toward third base instead of home plate.

The Reds had men at second and third now with no one out. George Foster, who had replaced Tolan, was due up. But Foster was pulled for Julian Javier, who was pulled for Joe Hague, while Ken Holtzman was pulled for Rollie Fingers, in a series of cat-and-mouse moves by Williams and Anderson. So instead of Tolan coming to bat in the situation, Sparky had Hague face the new pitcher Rollie Fingers. Hague popped out.

Johnny Bench then walked to the plate. It was just as he had prophesied at dinner the night before. He looked into the Oakland dugout and Reggie Jackson nodded and smiled. It was Bench's chance to get even with Fingers and put the Reds in the lead. Dick Williams had other ideas. He put an end to Bench's dreams by going against conventional baseball wisdom. It is said that you never put the winning run on base. If Rose and Morgan score, the game is tied. If Bench scores the Reds have the lead in the seventh game of the World Series. Williams had said publicly that he would never put the winning run on base via an intentional walk. However he had also said that he would not let Johnny Bench beat him. The latter trumped the former. Bench was given an intentional pass and the bases were loaded with one out.

Tony Perez hit a sacrifice fly to right field to cut the A's lead to 3–2. Denis Menke came up with men at second and third with two outs—and flew out to end the inning. It was a case of the same song, second verse. The Reds had threatened in the sixth with Bench at third and Perez at second but Denis Menke flew out to right to end that inning. It was a horrible day for Menke. He had struck out with Perez standing at second in the fifth inning. Not to mention the bad hop he could not control in the first inning.

In their last gasp, the Reds had Darrel Chaney on first with two outs in the bottom of the ninth. At the end Dick Williams was trying to decide if a lefty should come in to face Rose. It didn't matter; Rose was a switch hitter, he could go either way, though left-handed he was better. Like lots of natural right-handers, Rose had become a better left-handed batter after years of facing more righties than lefties. Practice may not make perfect but it does make better.

Rose was secretly hoping that they would pull Fingers and not because he feared Fingers. Vida Blue was warming up in the bullpen. He had started the previous game and would likely be tired. He also would be excited and Rose figured that with the adrenaline flowing the youngster might throw one in the dirt, allowing Chaney to get in scoring position. Blue had done just that, thrown a wild pitch, during Game One. Williams trudged to the mound for the umpteenth time. Dave Duncan, the catcher, intercepted him. He had a message: don't you dare take out Rollie Fingers. He's got good stuff. Williams agreed and Fingers stayed in the game. Rose belted a waist-high fastball to Joe Rudi in left to end the game and the Series.

Good pitching had beaten good hitting. The A's pitchers had done the job. Catfish Hunter won two games. Rollie Fingers was ubiquitous, appearing in every game except one, with two saves and a 1.74 ERA. The A's pitching staff had held the Reds to a .209 average. The Reds pitching had been pretty good, too. The A's also hit .209 as a team. It broke a record for the lowest combined batting average in a seven-game World Series. Only Gene Tenace really broke through, but he broke through in a big way.

Gene Tenace was clearly the hero of the series. He hit four home runs in the first five games, after hitting only five all season long. He knocked in nine of Oakland's sixteen runs, with a .348 average. While he was at it, he broke Babe Ruth's World Series record with a .913 slugging percentage.

When Tenace homered in Game Five for his fourth one of the series, he tied a World Series record also first set by the Babe. Sometimes when the star of an organization is out, someone else gets the chance to stand up and show what he or she is made of. In sports it has happened more than once. Given the opportunity, little-known guys can rise to the occasion. In 1999 the St. Louis Rams signed free agent Trent Green from the Redskins to be their star quarterback. He got hurt in the preseason, forcing the Rams to use Arena Football League veteran Kurt Warner in his place. Warner went on to lead the Rams to the Super Bowl title and to win league MVP honors.[11] Sometimes a star going down allows a new star to emerge.

World Series Hero Gene Tenace is greeted by Dick Green and George Hendrick after his first home run in Game 1. The heretofore unknown Tenace had a "Ruthian" series (photograph courtesy Roadwest Publishing [Jack Klumpe Collection]).

All along the way the 1972 World Series could have turned on one play. Six of the seven games, and all of the A's wins, were decided by one run, it was that close. The little things do matter. If Joe Rudi did not make that superb catch in Game Two, if Clay Carroll had held the one-run lead for an inning in Game Four — if only. Those things can be credited to the A's efforts. If the ball had not bounced over Denis Menke's head off of the artificial-turf seam in Game Seven — that could be chalked up to bad luck. If Bobby Tolan had cleanly played Angel Mangual's liner or Bando's blast in Game Seven — those could be chalked up to human error. The Reds were so close again but close only counts in horseshoes.

Following Game Seven, on the local Sunday evening news, WCPO sportscaster Jack Moran shared the contents of a Cincinnati housewife's letter. Sent to the station, postmarked before the World Series began, the letter contained the results of the entire series with the exact scores of each game. Moran and WCPO and all the viewers were left flabbergasted. In an interview the next night, the wife and mother recounted how she had asked God to give her a dream about the World Series. The prayer was answered clearly and when she awoke she quickly recorded the contents of the dream. When the Series began she started rooting for the A's, rooting against her family of Reds fans. Ironically, she was a Reds fan as well.[12] Her family was blown away by her rooting and then by the final scores as they unfolded, game by game. It was an extraordinary happening, perhaps more phenomenal than the phenomenal Series itself.

12

ADVERSITY

November 1972–August 1973

"I have some bad news for you — you have cancer." Those are among the most terrifying words a person can hear. It is not only terrifying but shocking when you are only twenty-four. For Johnny Bench those words were a very real possibility in fall of 1972. The doctors were hopeful but doctors aren't always correct.

A small spot or lesion on his right lung showed up on an X-ray during a routine medical examination performed for all the Reds in September. The Reds and Bench kept the lesion under wraps until after the season. Several months later it was determined that surgery would be required. The surgery was performed by Dr. Luis Gonzalez at Christ Hospital in Cincinnati on December 11.

During recuperation there was no doubt about Bench's popularity. The hospital received two thousand get-well letters per day. Bench was thankful for the letters but his real interest was in choosing the nurse required during his recuperation. The young bachelor had many offers; the sole male applicant was quickly rejected. Several days later the report came back from the laboratory. The lesion had been caused by a fungus-type inflammation: troublesome but not malignant. A sigh of relief was released by all. By Opening Day, Bench was given a clean bill of health.

There was one other issue to attend to in the off-season. Bobby Tolan's contract had expired at the end of the 1972 season. He'd had a wonderful year and had been named NL Comeback Player of the Year after missing all of 1971 with the ruptured Achilles heel. His 1972 campaign had been excellent from April all the way through Game Six of the World Series. Game Seven, however, was a disaster. The Mangual liner that Tolan definitely should have caught — and possibly the Bando smash he could have caught — sabotaged Cincinnati's chance for victory. The error cost them Game Seven and the Series.

Not long after the game, the Reds began picking up rumors from pretty reliable sources that Tolan had been out partying the Saturday night before Sunday's Game Seven. His drinking and carousing may well have cost the Reds the championship and had a definite effect on contract negotiations. The sides reached a standstill. The owners had agreed to salary arbitration early in 1973. When the two parties could not reach an agreement, an arbitrator was chosen to come in and hear arguments from both sides. Ownership and the player each submitted a salary figure and testimony was heard on behalf of both parties on why each sum was appropriate. Tolan admitted to the Saturday night partying. Nevertheless the arbitrator ruled in his favor and he was given his desired salary. The Reds were incensed. They felt they had been cheated twice.[1]

There was some positive news in the off-season. Sparky Anderson had achieved a great deal of success in only three years at the helm of the Reds. Only weeks after losing to Oakland, the success was acknowledged when Anderson was voted NL Manager of the Year.

Success is a two-edged sword. The legendary Dallas Cowboy Coach Tom Landry once said, "The hardest thing I have had to deal with in life is success." Success has ruined many a man. One antidote for the condition is to have people around to help keep us humble when success comes. Sparky Anderson was fortunate to have two such individuals in his life. The first was his wife, Carol. She telegrammed him in Baltimore during the 1970 World Series saying, "You're a celebrity now, all over America, but George is George is George. All my love, Carol."[2] The other was long-time Reds equipment manager Bernie Stowe. When Anderson first arrived in the Reds clubhouse Bernie Stowe introduced himself as only Bernie can. "Let's get one thing straight. I was here before you got here and I'll be here after you're gone, so don't give me any crap."[3] Such words from the equipment man tend to cut high-profile managers down to size.

Besides an overinflated ego, there is another danger that success offers: temptation to forget those who helped us get where we are. Sparky Anderson wasn't about to let that happen either. There were three such notable men in his life. The first was his mentor, Lefty Phillips. Phillips first spotted Sparky as a thirteen-

Bernie Stowe, the long time Reds equipment manager, made it his personal mission to keep Sparky humble. Stowe told Anderson, "I was here before you got here, and I'll be here after you're gone." Stowe was dead on the mark (photograph courtesy Roadwest Publishing [Jack Klumpe Collection]).

year-old youngster playing on the sandlots of Los Angeles. Phillips was doing some part-time scouting — bird dogging — for the Dodgers at the time. Bird doggers are almost like bounty hunters but in a positive sense. They beat the bushes looking for young, undiscovered talent. When they find it and recommend a player that latches on with an organization, they get paid a fee.

Lefty Phillips took young Anderson under his wing, eventually coaching some of his amateur teams. Phillips suggested that the Dodgers give Anderson a look and that is how George Anderson was signed to a professional contract. The relationship culminated when Manager Phillips offered Anderson the third-base coaching job with the California Angels. Anderson gladly accepted. The arrangement lasted exactly one day, then Bob Howsam hired Anderson to manage the Reds. Sparky was adamant throughout his tenure with the Reds that 75 percent of what he did as a manager came from Lefty Phillips. Anderson was devastated when Phillips died suddenly at age 62, just two years after Anderson came to the Reds.

While Anderson attributes his baseball knowledge to Lefty Phillips, he attributes his success in school to another man. More specifically, Anderson attributes the fact that he finished high school to Rod Dedeaux. Dedeaux was the legendary baseball coach at the University of Southern California (USC). When Anderson's parents moved the family from South Dakota when he was eight, they bought a house adjacent to the USC baseball field. Shortly thereafter a ball from the USC practice field rolled into the bushes of the Anderson's yard. The USC folks didn't bother to get the ball. Anderson burrowed into the bushes and emerged with it. He ran over to the practice and asked for "the man in charge." He was directed to Rod Dedeaux. Anderson handed him the ball and told him he had gotten it out of the bushes.

Impressed with the eager youngster, Dedeaux asked him if he would like to be the batboy. The stunned Anderson managed to stammer out a yes. Dedeaux said that if he wanted the job, George had to show him his report card every month. This kept Anderson at his books, though he was no threat for valedictorian.

The third man that Sparky Anderson was especially indebted to was Milton Blish. In the off-season, as a minor league player, Blish gave Anderson a job selling cars at his dealership. When Jack Kent Cooke fired him after the 1964 season, Anderson was completely out of work with no way to provide for his family through baseball. Blish hired Anderson full-time. Anderson found it was tougher to sell a Ford than it was to remove a pitcher from a game, and Blish began giving Anderson a commission on car sales that had no commissions. It allowed Anderson to make ends meet and feed his family. He never forgot it,[4] even after he was named the best manager in the National League.

After coming so close in 1972, many thought '73 would be the Reds year. There were many reasons to be positive. For one, the team's starting pitching seemed to be the best that it had been since the first half of the 1970 season with

Jim Merritt and Wayne Simpson, the "young Bob Gibson." The Reds felt that they had scored a coup when they made a deal with the Kansas City Royals in the off-season. The Reds were positive that Hal McRae would never be an every-day outfielder due to his arm and his lack of speed. They would have dearly loved to keep him as a pinch hitter, but McRae was tired of that. Simpson had rebounded somewhat with eight wins in 1971, but a recovery to his early 1970 form seemed unlikely. The pair was sent to the Kansas City Royals. The Reds seemed to get a lot in return. Starting pitcher Roger Nelson's 2.08 ERA was fifth best in the AL in 1972 and Richie Sheinblum had hit .300, sixth best in the league.

Again Howsam's goal was value for value. On paper it seemed that the Reds had gotten the better end of this deal, just as it had seemed at first that Houston had gotten the upper hand in the trade of 1971.

Jack Billingham, buoyed by his strong playoff performance against the Pittsburgh Pirates and strong series against the Oakland A's, gained newfound confidence. He soared in wins, coming one shy of being the first since Merritt to win twenty. Gullet was now a veteran at age twenty-two. The free spirit Ross Grimsley also had newfound confidence after his two-hit gem to keep the Reds alive in the 1972 playoffs. Nolan had led the NL in winning percentage in 1972 and hoped to repeat in 1973. With Roger Nelson, the Reds would have five dependable starters.

Again, however, things did not work out as planned. Nolan had begun suffering from shoulder problems in the last half of the 1972 season. After winning thirteen by the All-Star break, he'd won only two the rest of the way. The shoulder continued to bother him in both the playoffs and the World Series. He still wasn't healthy by 1973 and only pitched two games. Nelson didn't pan out either; he suffered a variety of injuries and started only eight games.

One of the few bright spots on the pitching staff was the continuing emergence of Pedro Borbon, the reliever acquired in the Alex Johnson deal along with Jim McGlothlin. McGlothlin was good but not great for the Reds. When Alex Johnson hit .329 for the Angels and won the 1970 batting title, it looked like the Angels had gotten the better end of the deal. However as time wore on, the tables began to turn. Johnson's attitude caught up with him again in California. He bounced from team to team and was out of baseball by the end of 1976. McGlothlin's finest season with the Reds was in 1970, when he won 14 games. He began to fade over the next three seasons, winning eight games in 1971, nine in 1972, and three in 1973 before he was dealt to the Chicago White Sox near the end of the season. Meanwhile, after initially struggling in the minors, Pedro Borbon came up to the Reds for good in 1972.

The year after Howsam traded Wayne Granger, Pedro Borbon filled his shoes. Like Granger, Borbon threw a sinker. The sinkerball is thrown in a similar fashion to a fastball. However the pitcher uses a downward and inward roll of the wrist as he releases the pitch, causing the ball to drop sharply as it approaches home plate. The nice thing about sinkerball pitchers is that their pitch sinks more when their arm is a bit tired. With a fresh arm, they have more velocity on the ball and it tends to stay up instead of sinking. Therefore a sinkerball pitcher who pitches frequently, coming out of the bullpen, can be very effective. Indeed Borbon's eighty appearances in 1973 were the most since Wayne Granger's ninety in 1969. Borbon would win eleven games and save fourteen in 1973. So Borbon's emergence softened the loss of Wayne Granger. Plus, Tommy Hall, the man Howsam got for Granger, turned out to be an exciting left-handed strike-out pitcher. The bullpen was better than ever.

Although it initially appeared that the Angels had gotten the best of the Alex Johnson trade, in the end it was clear that the Reds had gotten the better end of the deal. It sometimes takes years to realize the full impact and results of a trade. In 1987 the Detroit Tigers sent a young right-hander named John Smoltz to the Braves for seasoned veteran Doyle Alexander. Alexander pitched two more so-so seasons for the Tigers, while Smoltz has been phenomenal for the Braves for more than a decade.

In the field, Tony Perez continued to feel at home at first base. He again had more than ninety RBIs and notched a contact-hitter-like average of .314. Joe Morgan proved that '72 was no flash in the pan: he hit .290 and stole sixty-seven bases but he had more than just a higher average than Helms. His bat had some pop. His newfound power surprised even Anderson and Howsam,

"Little Joe" Morgan was slight of stature, but big on desire, talent, and smarts. A member of the Big Four, he is greeted by Pete Rose after one of his many home runs as a Red (photograph courtesy Roadwest Publishing [Jack Klumpe Collection]).

though it shouldn't have. The dense air inside the Astrodome did not allow many round-trippers. Morgan averaged ten a year in Houston, but by the 1973 season's end he had twenty-six in Cincinnati, one less than Perez and one more than Bench, Cincinnati's power hitters.

Denis Menke was becoming more of a problem. It was clear that his best offensive years were left behind in Houston. Though a 1964 Rambler is steady and dependable, it begins to break down with high mileage. Menke's mileage was getting high. The Reds still had problems at third base.

Bench had rebounded completely from his 1971 holdout to win the NL MVP award again in '72. He was poised for a great 1973 but the MVP award would go to a teammate. Pete Rose enjoyed perhaps his finest season as a Red in 1973. He hit .338 and broke Cy Seymour's club record for hits with 230. The league MVP is usually reserved for a power hitter with many home runs and RBIs, as well as a decent average. The other type of player who may occasion- ally garner the award is a pitcher who has pitched better than anyone could imagine. Sandy Koufax and Bob Gibson in their greatest years wrestled the MVP from the sluggers (once each), but no NL pitcher had done it since them.

As a singles hitter, Rose broke though the glass ceiling in 1973. His 230 hits and 680 at-bats were among all-time highs in the National League. He was aided by the fact that no player put up big home-run numbers. Willie Mays, Willie McCovey, and Hank Aaron were in their declining years and certainly there were no Koufaxes or Gibsons around shutting down the entire league. Competition aside, Rose's year could not be ignored. He was named the league MVP.

Sparky Anderson enjoyed the competitive advantage of having his closest associates still with the team. The staff he assembled prior to 1970 was still intact. Many a manger has uttered the words, "if we can stay healthy, we will be a factor." The Reds didn't stay healthy in 1973. Who would start at short- stop was still a question mark. Way back in 1968 Howsam felt that Leo Carde- nas was not as good as advertised at short. He was good but Howsam wanted someone who was great.

Woody Woodward and Darrel Chaney had also been good but not great. The Reds had their eye on a youngster coming up through the minors. He had been drafted out of Venezuela in 1967. It was clear from the beginning that his arm strength and range were superb. He also had good speed; the big question was his bat.

The Reds had started scouting internationally soon after Howsam arrived in 1967. He had begun tapping into the international pipeline twenty years ear- lier, through a series of fortunate events. Back in 1947, the United States had an Air Force base in Balboa, Panama. The local government decided to build a new school and, with what can only be described as poor planning, located the new school at the end of a runway. When the school children had difficulty hearing the teacher over the airplane noise, the local officials demanded that the United States close the base. Due to his aviation background, Howsam's father-in-law, Senator Johnson, asked him to take a team to Balboa to investigate the problem. While there, Howsam met Carlos Elit-A who owned a local team called Marlboro (named after the cigarette distributorship he owned). They struck up an immediate friendship, and Elit-A routinely gave Howsam information on promising Panamanian talent. Several of the players played for Howsam on the Denver Bears.[5]

Latin American players, from Central and South America as well as the Caribbean (particularly the Dominican Republic and Puerto Rico), had begun to make a splash in U.S. baseball. Roberto Clemente of the Pirates and Orlando Cepeda of the San Francisco Giants and St. Louis Cardinals were among the first. The Reds' eyes were on a product of Venezuela, Dave Concepcion. He would be their first from that country.

The Reds signed Concepcion as an amateur near the end of Howsam's first season in Cincinnati in 1967. There was never any question about his ability to field but like most players the question was whether he could hit major-league pitching. Actually the first question was whether he could endure a season at shortstop. At six foot one and roughly 150 pounds, Concepcion, when he first arrived with the Reds in 1970, looked like a newborn colt trying to stand. His legs were so thin that one might wonder how they could support his torso. Anderson was first tipped off on Concepcion's potential by long-time Chicago White Sox second baseman and fellow Venezuelan, Luis Aparicio, during 1970 spring training. Aparicio told Anderson that Concepcion could play baseball and hit at least .250. Anderson replied that maybe that could happen in the American League but he would be happy if Concepcion could hit .200 in the National League.[6]

Alex Grammas took him on as a special project and Tony Perez mentored and shepherded the twenty-one-year-old. Concepcion platooned with Woody Woodward in 1970 and played surprisingly well offensively against the Baltimore Orioles in the World Series. His 1971 season also was good defensively, but his offensive numbers barely exceeded Anderson's minimum hope of a .200 average. By the beginning of 1972, the Reds were willing to take a gamble on him full-time. Frank Duffy had been traded and Woodward had retired. Chaney was seemingly destined to be the back-up.

By the end of 1972 the jury was still out. During the regular season Concepcion had hit only .209, while the switch-hitting Darrel Chaney played much more than hoped for and hit .250, getting most of the starts in the postseason. But Chaney then had a dreadful playoff and World Series, hampering his chances to win the job full-time.

Chaney had good defense. Concepcion's defense was, at times, spectacular, but also inconsistent. His youth and eagerness sometimes led to ill-advised throws but he was growing. Entering spring training of 1973, the question of who would fill the shortstop position for the Reds was still unanswered.

Early in the 1973 season, Dave Concepcion finally broke through. Not only could he field better (he would go on to win five Gold Gloves in the late seventies), he began to hit decently — .287 compared to his peers' combined .234 average the previous three seasons. He was also a threat on the bases, with twenty-two stolen bases by July when he went from part-time shortstop to NL All-Star. Alex Grammas, third-base coach and appointed by Anderson to work on the development of infielders, was particularly proud of his pet project. He spent many hours working with Concepcion and like a proud papa wanted to see the young Venezuelan succeed. Meanwhile Perez had nurtured the youngster in the clubhouse, befriending him like an older brother or uncle. Concepcion had two proud individuals cheering him on, a big help to a youngster in a strange land. Young people in any organization would benefit from such tutelage, challenge, and support.

On the day before the All-Star break, the Reds were cruising along to an easy 6–0 win over the Montreal Expos. Concepcion was having another good day, three hits and a stolen base, and was feeling his oats. He had a huge lead-off from first base and a good jump when Menke grounded to the infield. As

Promised nipped in the bud: Davey Concepcion is carried from the field with a broken ankle just as he was blooming. It was the day before the All-Star break in 1973. Left to right: Don Gullett, Bobby Tolan, Equipment Manager Bernie Stowe, Bill Plummer, Trainer Larry Starr, Joe Morgan, and Tony Perez, with Johnny Bench looking on (photograph courtesy Roadwest Publishing [Jack Klumpe Collection]).

the throw went to first, Concepcion decided to try to stretch his advance to third. He went into his slide but it was too late. His spike caught and he was too close to the base. Before he could get all the way down, his left ankle jammed into the base with all his weight forcing behind it. Snap.

This is a problem at the major-league level. Fans know that in Little League the bases are not anchored. When the runner slides into a base, it often moves away from him on contact. In the majors, the bases are anchored by a metal spike roughly twelve inches long and two inches in diameter. Therefore, a metal spike two inches in diameter sometimes meets a leg bone with a diameter of an inch or so. The latter will generally reach its breaking point before the fortified metal. Such was the case with Dave Concepcion. His left ankle was broken badly. He lay writhing in pain, asking someone to put him to sleep to take away the pain. Dr. Richard Jolson, an orthopedic surgeon, jumped out of the stands to reset the bone, which eased the pain considerably. His coach and mentor Alex Grammas huddled over him.[7] Dave Concepcion would miss not only the All-Star Game in Kansas City but the entire rest of the season. At the time of his injury it was finally clear that he belonged in the majors.

In a way one has to admire Concepcion's grit and desire but in retrospect his decision was a bad one. The team was leading the lowly Expos in the seventh inning by a 6–0 score. Jack Billingham was cruising on the mound with thirteen wins and yet Concepcion tried to get an extra base. The older and wiser Joe Morgan called the move dangerous and one he had learned not to do. But Concepcion was still young and youth can bring excitement and mistakes. He was heartbroken, as this was to have been his first All-Star Game.

Besides Concepcion, there was another player with an injury to contend with, this one a bit more mysterious. In the second half of the season, Tolan began to complain of back troubles but they were hard to pinpoint. In retrospect the entire year had been an ailment. It began in spring training. He wasn't the same Bobby Tolan. He felt conspicuous upon his arrival after his highly publicized arbitration hearing. He was standoffish during those weeks in the Grapefruit League in Florida. He felt his teammates looked at him differently after the horrors of Game Seven. He wasn't his smiling, social self anymore. He felt like an outsider.

His on-the-field performance was very different as well. His average was mired around the .200 level through the first part of the season. It was the first prolonged slump of his entire career and he didn't deal with it well. He sometimes showed flashes of his old self. Maybe recovery was on its way. He began to lay down some drag bunts, his signature, in May and early June. The drag bunt was a barometer for how Tolan was doing. When he was doing that well, he was on. If he couldn't get the drag bunt down, it was an indicator that his game wasn't right.

The drag bunt has all but disappeared from the game but when executed correctly it is a beautiful thing to watch. The way it works is fairly simple. Tolan would lower the bat from his clean-the-ceiling-of-a-spider-web stance as if he were going to swing but instead of cocking he would stick the bat out parallel to the ground across home plate. Tolan would keep both hands still on the handle rather than use a normal bunting grip of one hand on the handle and the other behind the bat. Simultaneously he would begin to leave the batter's box, rotating toward first with his body, while compensating with the arms and hands to leave the bat over the plate. Just as the ball approached the bat, he would turn it slightly, as if catching the ball with the bat, and rotate the barrel of the bat toward first base, the direction his body was now going. It almost looked as if the ball were stuck to the bat like a ball in a lacrosse stick. He would then pull the ball downward in order to roll it along the first-base line. When the ball would first leave the bat it would dribble out in front of him temporarily but as he began accelerating out of the batter's box it looked as if he were racing the ball toward first. With Tolan's speed, he quickly overtook the ball, which slowly rolled along in the turf just as the surprised pitcher or first baseman was approaching the ball in order to field it.

There was always a moment of hesitation from both the pitcher and the first baseman, as if each was thinking, "Am I going to cover first base and he's going to go get the ball or is he covering and I'm going to get it?" While all this was going on in their minds, Tolan was crossing first base with an infield single. It was pure poetry in motion. When Tolan was on, it was an almost unstoppable weapon. It was like a basketball player with a hot hand — the only way to stop him is hope he goes to the bench.

Tolan's slump continued into August. Everyone tried to talk with him: Howsam, Sparky, his teammates. Rose, as the team captain, pulled up a chair one day to clear the air with Bobby. What was the problem? "The team is doing me wrong," Tolan told him. Rose pointed out that the main thing was for the team to win. Rose reminded Tolan he was hitting .200 and needed to face up to that. It didn't do any good. Tolan began to grow a beard. Larry Shepard, the pitching coach, talked to him, and he shaved it off. When the Los Angeles Dodgers and Reds faced off for a series, Dodger Willie Crawford, an old high school friend, approached him at the batting cage. He tried to encourage his old friend and in response Tolan tried to pick a fight with him. Crawford was emotionally crushed. Tolan began to get surly, sullen, and withdrawn — nothing worked.

Things reached a head in August. In the middle of the month Tolan began complaining of a sore back. A week and a half later, Howsam received a phone call from the team physician. Tolan had missed a couple of doctor's appointments. Howsam was livid; he had reached the end of his rope. He called Chief Bender to his office: "You go down there immediately and tell Tolan he has an appointment with the doctor in the morning."

Bender immediately marched down with the orders. Entering the Reds' clubhouse, he saw Tolan sitting. Bender told him he had a doctor's appointment in the morning and had better be there. Tolan said it was too early for an appointment. Bender told him he better show up if he wanted to be a Red the next day. Tolan erupted. Curses spewed from his mouth. He shoved Bender and Bender shoved back — a mini melee erupted. Big Jack Billingham jumped in between them to break things up. It was ugly. Bender returned upstairs to report to Howsam.[8] Tolan was immediately called into Anderson's office, where Sparky told him he was not welcome until he apologized to Chief. Tolan refused to do so and began to clean out his locker until his teammates talked him out of it. Tolan then stormed out of the clubhouse.

This was the straw that broke the camel's back. If you don't deal with an ailment, the whole body suffers. In order for an organ in the body, such as the liver or the stomach, to stay healthy, the cells that make up that organ must reproduce themselves through cell division. When those cells divide in an unregulated and unhealthy way, they begin to produce damaged cells. We call these damaged cells malignant and we call this process cancer. When an organ has many of these unhealthy cells, we say that a person has cancer of the liver or cancer of the stomach. The malignant cells can then sometimes spread and invade other organs. So if the organ becomes cancerous, it sometimes has to be removed for the good of the rest of the body. Tolan had become a cancer.

Why or how these things happen are somewhat mysterious. Usually it is a gradual process; some kind of disappointment comes into a relationship. There had been strong rumors that Tolan was out partying the night before the

After the 1972 Game Seven debacle, Tolan became withdrawn and distant. The apple of Bob Howsam's eye had gone sour (photograph courtesy Roadwest Publishing [Jack Klumpe Collection]).

1972 finale. His muffed catch in Game Seven had likely cost the Reds the title. One side feels betrayed; the other feels guilty. Instead of dealing with the guilt, one lashes out, and the other party gets defensive and reacts, adding the fuel of justification to the burning embers. The situation spirals downward. The hurting individual can usually find a sympathetic ear. The ear in turn begins to whisper. The whispers get to the player. "You don't deserve to be treated like this, you are better than this." The offender then feels like the victim, and things continue to roll downhill. For Howsam they had hit rock bottom; there was no further to tumble.

He started working the phones. Maybe a change of scenery would help Bobby. It was clear that the scenery in Cincinnati wasn't conducive to healing. After the season Howsam found a taker. Tolan would go to the cellar-dwelling San Diego Padres on the coast. In exchange for the sullen falling star, San Diego sent the Reds starter Clay Kirby. The Reds were lucky to get that. Perhaps San Diego hoped that Tolan could become the player he once was. It would depend on his attitude and the Padres were willing to take the chance.

Bobby Tolan is in many ways a tragic figure. Immensely talented and merely reaching his prime, the apple of Bob Howsam's eye had become a prodigal son who never returned. After a sub-par season in San Diego, Tolan's career trickled on for a few more years and then he was out of baseball as a player forever.

13

TRYING AGAIN
August 1973–October 1973

The Reds now had an unforeseen problem midway through the season. Sparky had a gaping hole to fill. Who would play center field now that Tolan was gone?

This was a tactical as well as a strategic decision. Tactics help achieve strategy. All organizations face the same questions. The strategy is often easier to discover than the tactics. The devil is often in the details.

In the Reds' case, the strategy was twofold. Balance was the primary strategy: good pitching and good hitting, good starters and good relievers, good power and good speed, good average and good power, and good offense and good defense. With strong defense as a strategy, the tactic was to be strong up the middle. Bench, Morgan, the emergence of Concepcion and Tolan had provided that in spades. Tolan's problems jeopardized the strategy.

When Tolan was out during the 1971 season with the Achilles injury, Foster had filled in decently. However, Foster was more of a left- or right-fielder and he had failed to hit above .234 as a regular. While Rose was steady and dependable in left, he did not posses great range or speed. The Reds had enough power and hitting in the lineup. The new centerfielder didn't have to be great at the plate. Their offensive speed had deteriorated with Tolan's demise but they still had Morgan as a threat to steal. More importantly, they needed defensive speed. The centerfielder has a huge territory to cover. While right- and left-fielders have foul lines and grandstands to diminish their turf, the centerfielder has no such luxury. His only friend is the deep center-field wall and that is not much of a friend. If the ball is hit that far, it is trouble. In the power alleys between center and right and left fields, and with the increased area due to the fences reaching their farthest distance in center, there is a lot of territory to cover. That makes speed and the ability to get a good jump on the ball paramount. Certain players are able to break for the ball with the crack of the bat; they instinctively know where it is going. Willie Mays was the master, just ask Vic Wertz about Willie's famous back-to-home-plate catch. That is called getting a good jump on the ball. Bobby Tolan had the speed and the ability to get a good jump.

Since he came over in the trade in the winter of 1971, Cesar Geronimo had spent most of his time in right field. His name conjures up images of the great Apache warrior but Geronimo was not from the American Southwest, he was from the Caribbean. Born in the Dominican Republic, he was blessed with a tremendous arm. He was first signed by the New York Yankees as an amateur free agent in February 1967. Later he was drafted by Houston from New York in the 1968 first-year draft.

Geronimo had an amazingly strong arm, developed by throwing softballs as a youth, so the Yankees set out to make him a pitcher. As a pitcher in the Yankees' farm system, Geronimo couldn't get batters out consistently; his control left something to be desired. Deemed to still have something to offer, the Yankees moved him to the outfield, hoping his arm strength would prove handy from the deep hollows of the outfield. He was sitting on the Astros' bench when Howsam requested he be part of the deal if Tommy Helms was to go to Houston.

Much like Concepcion, the Reds knew Geronimo had the defense. The question was whether he had a major-league bat. Most pitchers have lost their ability to hit, due to all the time and effort focused on pitching. Though a former pitcher, Geronimo had a decent swing, and it was hoped that his average would hold high enough to reap his outstanding defense in the outfield. You can sacrifice some hitting for a good defensive outfielder, but nobody is going to play a .230 singles-hitting outfielder for his defense. He'd hit .275 in 1972, his first year in the Reds organization.

Howsam, Bender and Anderson wanted to give Geronimo a shot at the center-field job. Several specific plays had suggested possible success. One opponent hit a ground ball up the middle and the runner on second broke for third, and then the third-base coach waved him around as Geronimo glided to the ball. Fielding it cleanly, he threw a strike to the awaiting Bench at the plate. The runner was out. It wouldn't have even been a play for an ordinary centerfielder but turns out that Geronimo wasn't ordinary. He didn't simply have a gun, he had a cannon. He also got a couple of hits in that game. He had been almost an afterthought in the Morgan deal, but the Reds had found their replacement for Bobby Tolan.

Even with Tolan's troubles, Richie Scheinblum was unable to crack the Reds lineup. He hit only .222 in fifty-four at-bats off of the bench and was traded to the California Angels on June 15. Nelson wasn't contributing much on the mound either, with just three wins. Meanwhile, Hal McRae led the Royals in batting the next year. Eventually it was clear that the Reds may have gotten the better of the big 1971 Astros deal but the Royals got the best end of the McRae trade.

The Tolan issue and pitching woes had gotten the Reds into a big hole by late June of 1973. The Los Angeles Dodgers had finally overcome the loss of Koufax and later Drysdale to threaten in the NL West again. With Nolan out and Nelson not performing, Howsam got on the phone again. He called the San Diego Padres to get some pitching help. He was interested in a little man with a big screwball, a pitcher named Fred Norman. His screwball was almost on par with Mike Cuellar's. The Padres were not too attached to the five foot eight lefty. He had won only one game for them all season, unremarkable even on a last-place club. The Dodgers had not been impressed with Norman either; they had waived him at the end of the 1970 season but Reds' advanced scout Ray Shore saw something he liked. Howsam offered back-up outfielder Gene Locklear, minor-league pitcher Mike Johnson, and some cash. The Padres snatched the deal. The Padres were in desperate financial straits, with their continual losing and low attendance. The reported $150,000 the Reds sent for Norman would help them keep afloat. Again Howsam was banking on his philosophy of spending money to make money, but spending it wisely.

Norman was rejuvenated by the trade. In his first two starts he pitched shutouts. The second was sweet indeed, against the Dodgers, the team that had

cut him three years earlier. At the end of that game Norman pumped his arms in the air triumphantly. He went on to win three of his first four starts. He finished the year with twelve wins for the Reds but nobody called him Fred Norman. He was always referred to as Little Fredie Norman. It kind of sounds like the poor boy down the street.

Howsam got on the phone again. This time he was calling Indianapolis. Did they have anybody that could help the Reds? In the 1970s Cincinnatians and others referred to Indianapolis as "Indian No Place." In the days before Indianapolis made themselves into an amateur athletic capital of sorts, it had the Indianapolis 500 and little else. But it did have something important to the Reds, it was the home of their Class-AAA ball club that had moved from Buffalo in 1968, the last stop before the big time.

Super scout Ray Shore saw something in Little Fredie Norman (pictured here) that no one else saw. Norman was a pleasant addition to the Reds in 1973. His excellent screwball propelled him to twelve wins for the Reds after arriving in June (photograph courtesy Roadwest Publishing [Jack Klumpe Collection]).

In Howsam's mind he had

the perfect man as the field general of the Indianapolis Indians, Vern Rapp. Howsam hired Rapp the same week that he hired Sparky Anderson. Rapp was a known commodity back to Howsam's days in Denver. Rapp's charge was very clear: prepare men for the majors both on the field and off. He was the finisher, the last craftsman to get his hands on the commodity before it hit the consumer. Without someone to find quality personnel or develop people, the organization is in trouble.

For Howsam a good Class-AAA manager did more than finish baseball-playing skills. He also groomed players to handle the lights and stage of the majors, taught them how to conduct themselves on road trips, public appearances, in the clubhouse and before the microphone and cameras. To Howsam this was just as important as their ability to play. If you couldn't follow the rules, if you couldn't conduct yourself properly, you weren't going to play for the Cincinnati Reds. Rapp was serious and task-oriented. Both Howsam and Bender had the utmost faith in Rapp as a master craftsman.

Howsam called or visited on a regular basis to keep abreast of the club. During this June phone call, he had a specific question. Did Rapp have anybody who could hit the ball a little that could help the Reds right now? Rapp said he had just the player. He told him that this man could really hit the ball.

Hal King was a twenty-nine-year-old journeyman catcher, which is a nice way to say that he had bounced from club to club and didn't play a lot. He had come over from the Texas Rangers in the Merritt trade. The Reds really didn't have a need for a back-up catcher. Bench caught 130 or more games every year. Bill Plummer ably filled in during the second game of a doubleheader or whenever Bench needed a breather. However, Hal King had the potential to be an excellent pinch hitter, a commodity that is always in demand in major-league baseball. He was hitting the ball really hard at Indianapolis and the Reds called him up.

The ability to respond to a manager telling a guy sitting on a long wooden bench to get up, grab a bat, loosen up, go up to the batter's box sixty feet and six inches

Vern Rapp was the Indianapolis manager and Bob Howsam's "finisher." His primary job was to prepare talent both on and off the field for Howsam (photograph courtesy Roadwest Publishing [Jack Klumpe Collection]).

away from a guy with a ball in hand who is going to hurl it toward him at around ninety mph, and to hit the ball is not an easy job. Ted Williams once said that hitting a baseball was the hardest thing in all of sports. If so, the hardest thing about the hardest thing in all of sports is to pinch-hit. Yet as a pinch hitter, the stakes are usually high. There is usually someone in scoring position that needs to be knocked in or else the manager would not remove a pitcher that is performing well, as in Sparky Anderson's decision to bat Hal McRae for Jack Billingham in Game Seven of the 1972 World Series.

Hal King got such a call while sitting on the bench on July 1, 1973. Los Angeles had come to Cincinnati for a doubleheader. The Reds trailed the Dodgers by eleven games in the NL West and were on the verge of falling twelve back when King was called on to pinch hit with two outs in the bottom of the ninth inning. Perez was on second and Johnny Bench had been intentionally walked to first. Dodgers ace Don Sutton was on the mound. Sutton had King down with a two-ball, two-strike count. In fact he had made King look foolish on the second strike when King swung like a Little Leaguer at a fastball over his head. Then Sutton offered up a screwball and King swung so hard that he ripped the leather from his spikes.[1] The ball sailed high and deep into the stands for a three-run homer and a 4–3 Cincinnati win. Al Michaels said from the booth that if the Reds were able to overtake the Dodgers, this would likely be consid-

Hal King is greeted by jubilant teammates after his blast off of Don Sutton in the bottom of the ninth on July 1, 1973. Al Michaels declared King's homer the turning point of the season. Lightning struck not twice but three times for the little-used King that summer (photograph courtesy Roadwest Publishing [Jack Klumpe Collection]).

ered the turning point of the season. The Reds won the second game of the doubleheader on a Perez RBI single in the tenth and the Dodgers' lead was down to nine games.

King struck again eight days later with a pinch hit grand-slam home run against the Montreal Expos. In an almost unbelievable sequence, King turned the trick again on August 17. The Reds trailed the Mets and George Stone at Shea Stadium 1–0 in the top of the ninth inning but scored a run to tie the game on three consecutive singles. After a scoreless bottom of the ninth, Anderson called on King to pinch hit to open the tenth inning. King responded by launching one deep into the right-field seats for a 2–1 Reds lead that held up for a victory. Al Michaels again echoed his earlier words, saying that King's work might have turned the season around. Michaels proved to be a prophet.

Another reason the Reds' season turned around, springing up roughly at the same time as Hal King's heroics, was the emergence of Danny Driessen. Denis Menke's hitting woes at third base continued unabated as the season wore on. By June 1973, he was hitting less than .200. The tires had fallen off.

It is difficult for a potential big fish to escape the wide net of the professional baseball scouting system. Rarely does it happen but every once in a while it does. Danny Driessen never played high school baseball. He was only able to play in the weekend leagues after he graduated. He wrote the Reds a letter from his home in Hilton Head, South Carolina. He wondered if the Reds would give him a chance. Bender and Howsam talked about it. The word was that the

Danny Driessen seemed to finally be the solution at third base. After his call up from Indianapolis, he hit .301 in the second half of the season (photograph courtesy Roadwest Publishing [Jack Klumpe Collection]).

kid could hit. They decided to give him a shot; it was a low-risk wager. Bender sent him a Reds yearbook and a ticket to Tampa, Florida. This was 1970 and Driessen's first season of minor league ball was dismal. He returned to Tampa in 1971 and this time won the Florida State League batting title. He spent the next year at Class-AA Three Rivers. After spring training of 1973 the Reds assigned him to Rapp at Indianapolis with an order: make the first baseman a third baseman.[2]

With Menke's woes at third, Anderson decided to give Driessen a shot. They called him up from Indianapolis, where he had caught their attention by hitting over .400, and he was an immediate hit. He batted over .310 in his first two months on the job, the best offensive production from a Reds' third-baseman since Perez had played third. Driessen hit .301 in his rookie season. Folks around Cincinnati swore that if Driessen had been in the lineup in '72, the Reds would have won it all.

While Tolan's problems festered and Geronimo moved to center, the Reds manned right field by committee. Any successful organization has people that can fill in for short periods of time when the big hitters are indisposed. McRae and Carbo would likely have been committee members but they had moved on. Howsam had a knack for picking up guys at the end of their careers who could help out for a while before they went out to stud. Previously Jimmy Stewart had been wonderful and was able to fill many positions, which is why Houston wanted him so badly. In the past, Ty Cline had filled the bill as well. This time Richie Scheinblum did some spot duty before he was traded. George Foster played some center and some right. Larry Stahl, who the Reds had purchased from San Diego in the off-season, hit left-handed and filled in some, and, finally, the big surprise was thirty-six-year-old right-hander Andy Kosco. Howsam had picked up the veteran in a trade for seldom-used Mel Behney at the beginning of the year. Kosco ended up playing twenty-eight games in right and batting .280, seventy-four points higher than Tolan.

When the committee couldn't do the job, some of the more regular players chipped in. Some big help in right came from Johnny Bench. Anderson put him out there twenty-three times, which helped rest his knees and helped his bat to stay sharp.

Despite the loss of Tolan and Concepcion to attitude and injury, the Reds ended up winning the NL West by three and a half games over the Dodgers. With the emergence of Geronimo and Driessen, they were heavy favorites heading into the playoffs against the mediocre Mets. The Mets had overcome the Pirates due more to a slide in Pittsburgh than strength in New York. Roberto Clemente had been lost to a plane crash and Steve Blass had been lost to his mind.

Blass, with a completely healthy arm, had totally lost his ability to pitch. He no longer could throw strikes consistently. For a while, coaches thought it was his pitching motion and they tinkered with that. Maybe it was a problem with is body but medical exams revealed that he was physically healthy. His body was fine. His pitching confidence was not. In the end they determined that it was all mental. Blass simply lost his confidence and thus his ability to throw the ball accurately. He began to think about it too much. No matter what he tried, and he tried it all—counseling, Transcendental Meditation, rest, coaches analyzing his motion, demotion to the minors—he could not regain his control. He would sometimes be so far off that he threw behind batters. After being the Cy Young Award runner-up in 1972, he won only three games in 1973. He pitched one game in 1974 and was out of baseball in 1975. It was similar in a way to what happened to Johnny Bench's predecessor Johnny Edwards in 1967. This time the condition earned a name, Steve Blass disease.[3] It isn't a real disease at all, it is a state of mind. In fact the case seemed to take the old adage "baseball is a mental game" to a whole new level. Confidence is a funny thing.

It was a familiar sight. The Mets had entered the 1969 playoffs on what was considered a fluke. They were underdogs to the powerful Atlanta Braves. In 1973 they were again heavy underdogs, this time to the Reds who had won ninety-nine games during the regular season, while the Mets finished a mere one game above .500.

Some of the 1969 hitting stars were gone by now, Tommy Agee, Art Shamsky and Ron Swoboda. Gone as well was the Mets stoic manager, Gil Hodges, who had died unexpectedly of a heart attack just days before the 1972 season began. He was only forty-seven. He was replaced by the oft-quoted Yankee great, Yogi Berra. However Berra wasn't the only baseball legend on the club. The Mets had forty-two-year-old Willie Mays. He had come to play his last year in the city where he had spent his best days. He was in the twilight of his career, so his numbers were down, but his leadership, love for the game, and presence alone were inspiring.

While the Mets' offense wasn't good, their pitching remained just as great as in 1969. Tom Seaver was still young and still the ace. Jerry Koosman was still a solid number-two guy, with fourteen wins, and another left-hander had emerged to complement Koosman, 1972 Rookie of the Year Jon Matlack. Matlack had a low ERA and also fourteen wins. George Stone closed out the rotation with twelve wins. When the starters were through, the Mets had one of the best relievers in the game to call on, fiery lefty Tug McGraw.

The Reds had fans in high and powerful places. They had Potter Stewart sitting on the bench — of the Supreme Court of the United States. A native of Cincinnati, his father had once served as mayor. After graduating from Yale, Stewart practiced law in Cincinnati and served as a judge until appointed to the high court by President Eisenhower in 1958. Hearings were being held on a Wednesday afternoon in October 1973. Stewart was intent on following his Reds, regardless of the fact that court was in session. He arranged for a young clerk to shuttle notes to him about each batter while he heard oral arguments. The most humorous one read, "Kranepool flies to left, Agnew resigns."[4]

Tom Seaver and Jack Billingham hooked up in a classic pitching duel in Game One. Seaver handcuffed the Reds in the game with thirteen strikeouts, a playoff record. It looked very bleak until Rose homered in the eighth to tie the game, 1–1. Bench then hit a walk-off home run in the ninth for a 2–1 win. The Reds had cleared a big obstacle in beating Seaver, one of the very best pitchers in the National League.

The next day the Reds were not as fortunate, as Jon Matlack pitched a complete game shutout. It took a bit of the wind out of the Reds' sails and set the tone for the rest of the series. Koosman beat them in another complete game in Game Three. The Reds then squeaked out a Game Four victory, 2–1, when Rose homered in the twelfth. Seaver and Billingham hooked up again for Game Five and Seaver was again outstanding. The Mets won the game and the series. They say that good pitching beats good hitting, especially in a short series. Years later, in 2001, the Arizona Diamondbacks demonstrated what a couple of strong arms could do, the arms of Randy Johnson and Curt Schilling. The Mets showed the Reds in 1973 with the arms of Seaver, Koosman and Matlack. The Mets had surprised the Braves with a three-game playoff sweep in 1969. This time they surprised the Reds, 3–2, though the Reds had finished seventeen games better during the regular season.

Game Three had featured an ugly scene that unfortunately was symbolic of the era. From the late 1960s to the late 1970s, some people, especially young people, decided that many rules of common decency were old-fashioned and didn't apply to them anymore. The entire series at New York showed obnoxious examples of that thinking.

In Game Three Rose went into second base hard to break up a double play. It is common practice during the postseason with more on the line. Bud Harrelson, the Mets shortstop, took offense and the two got into it. It wasn't the first time — the two had also tangled in 1970. When the Reds returned to the field in the bottom of the inning, the New York fans began raining debris toward the players. Bottles came flying, mostly in Rose's direction, but at other players as well. It was pitiful. Anderson pulled his team from the field for their own protection. The Mets might have had to forfeit the game, which they had well in hand, but Yogi Berra saved the day. He and several players went to the outfield and tried to reason with the fans. The game was able to resume. When Rose hit his game-winning home run in the twelfth the next day, he raised a clenched fist and held it as he rounded second. The fans went berserk.

An ugly situation unfolded a day later when a group of fans who entered the game late headed for the Reds contingent. For many years it was common practice to throw the gates open after the seventh inning. Non-paying spectators could then take in the last few innings for free. These spectators were not interested in the game at all. They spied an entourage of Reds fans by the third-base dugout, many clad in red jackets. They began to curse at them, call them the enemy, spit on them and pull the women's hair. The Reds rooters had to climb over the fence and onto the field to get away. Once on the field they asked police for protection. Conforming to the disengaged-cop stereotype, the police informed them that they were on duty only to ensure that no bats would be stolen from the dugout. So the entourage escaped through the dugout and out through the clubhouse to a bus where they hoped to find safe harbor. The mob followed them out and rocked the bus, while spitting obscenities.[5] It was a nasty scene and a horrible conclusion to the Series and the season.

About the only consolation for Potter Stewart and other Reds fans was that Willie Mays would be returning to the World Series in his last year of professional baseball after being traded to the Mets from cash-strapped San Francisco in May 1972 for $50,000. The Reds were not returning and that was disappointing after hopes had been so high.

14

THE NL WEST
October 1973–September 1974

The loss to the Mets wasn't the only one the Reds suffered in the fall of 1973. Al Michaels was leaving for California from whence he came. He had a better offer. KSFO out of San Francisco offered him the chance to call the San Francisco Giants action as well as John Wooden's UCLA basketball games. Year-round employment for a sports broadcaster in those days was very attractive. Outside of ABC's *Wide World of Sports* team of Jim McKay and company, many broadcasters found only seasonal work in the booth. Michaels aspired for more; he wanted to call a variety of sports. He had spent his boyhood dreaming of being a sports announcer.

The Reds hated to see him go. They recognized that he was a boy wonder and had hoped to have him behind the microphone for decades alongside Joe Nuxhall. Michaels said he wouldn't have left if it weren't for the dual-sport opportunity but the Reds couldn't match the offer. The Cincinnati Royals basketball team had bolted for Kansas City and Omaha after the 1972 season. The Bengals had their inaugural broadcaster Phil Samp behind the mike and he wasn't going anywhere. Wagner and the Reds sent Michaels off with their best wishes.

During the baseball winter meetings in Houston, Texas, late that year, Dick Wagner bumped into Dave Rosenfield on his way to a session. Rosenfield asked if Wagner had found a replacement for Michaels yet. Wagner told him no. Rosenfield, who was the general manager of the Tidewater Tides, the Mets Class-AAA affiliate, said that he had a guy he wanted Wagner to hear. He had called the games for the Tides that past season. Rosenfield sent a demo tape shortly thereafter. Wagner thought it was okay, but he certainly wasn't blown away. Later he agreed to have the thirty-one-year-old broadcaster come for a visit to Cincinnati. Into his office walked a short man with a mound of brown hair, parted at the side. They talked for a while. Wagner sent him over to WLW to do some test radio spots and demos, ads for local breweries like Burger, Wei-demann, and Hudepohl, as well as a simulated game. Wagner was much more impressed with the demos than he had been with the earlier tapes.[1] After some thought, he offered Franchester "Marty" Brennaman the position — and Brennaman took the job.

With a new broadcaster signed, the Reds were also looking at new players who might help them get over the hump. They had fallen short in 1970, '72 and '73. What — or who — would it take to reach that next level? It was to that task that Howsam turned his attention.

At the same time that Al Michaels was exiting, Howsam gathered his inner circle as he always had. He looked over the scouts' wish list, they talked about the club, and Anderson contributed his two cents. Right field was a problem. With Tolan's demise and subsequent trade to San Diego, the Reds had manned right field by committee. That had worked well for part of a season but was not a full-season solution. Now the question was who would fill right field.

There were three possibilities and one was a newcomer from Baltimore. The Orioles had thought enough of him to trade Frank Robinson in order to make room in their outfield but after showing great promise as a part-time player and pinch hitter, Merv Rettenmund had disappointed them in full-time duty, hitting only .248 in the two seasons after Robinson's departure. To get Rettenmund from Baltimore the Reds paid a high price. Ross Grimsley's insidious rebellion was reaching annoying proportions. With each succeeding season and increased success he became more vocal about guidelines he felt were oppressive. The Reds, tired of his moaning, decided that he had to go.

Franchester Brennaman, a.k.a. "Marty," became the voice of the Reds in 1974. The Reds were heard on flagship station WLW and over one hundred other stations from West Virginia to Nebraska (photograph courtesy the Cincinnati Reds).

If you weren't going to follow the rules, you weren't going to play for the Reds, it didn't matter who you were. The rules were not just important for their own sake. It was what they represented. They represented a willingness to subordinate one's self to established authority for the good of the team. In a nutshell, the rules were a barometer of whether you were willing to put the good of the team ahead of yourself. For example, Howsam and Anderson preferred short hair, but more importantly, they viewed it as an outward sign of an inward reality. It was display of self-discipline. Tolan starting a beard was one of several signals that he sent the club that he didn't want to be part of the team. Actions often speak louder than words. Ross Grimsley was now off to Baltimore where he could grow the facial hair that was so important to him.

Another possible solution to the right-field puzzle came from within. George Foster was a candidate. He had filled in for the injured Tolan in 1971 and played sporadically since then, but the Reds were hoping that another man they had kept their eye on for quite a while would pan out. Since Bender's visit to see him in 1971 in Sioux Falls, Ken Griffey had continued to develop. Griffey had actually been part of the committee that filled in for the disenchanted Tolan in late 1973. He even played a bit against the Mets in the 1973 playoffs. He hit .384 over that span, but since he had less than a hundred at-bats, he still qualified as a rookie. Like Concepcion and Geronimo before him, his defense and speed were never a question. Both were very attractive. His speed was one of the primary attractions to scouts in 1969, though he was not an attraction for a lot of scouts. The Reds got him in the 29th round of the 1969 amateur draft. Could he hit in the big leagues?

Griffey could certainly hit in spring training. He caught the fancy of fans that flocked to spring training to escape the gray of winter for sunshine. He attracted quite a following that spring. He had an infectious smile and was a primary target of autograph and photo hounds at Al Lopez Field. He signed and smiled gladly. By the end of March, the Reds fans practically held a pep rally around the young player, demanding that he be brought up to the parent club. By the time April rolled around, Sparky Anderson thought that he might have found his right fielder; Griffey came north with the club. He stayed there and became part of a platoon similar to the one Anderson had employed in 1971. Griffey as a lefty and Foster as a righty split time in right field. Merv Rettenmund was relegated mostly to pinch hitting duties.

Griffey was just the latest in a long line of Cincinnati players who served as a tribute to the Reds scouting and player development departments. Most of the Reds regulars were home-grown, drafted and developed by the Reds. The only exceptions were Morgan, Geronimo, and Foster, who had been obtained in trades by Howsam for other Reds products: Lee May, Tommy Helms, and Frank Duffy. Of the Reds regulars, all had been acquired under Howsam's watch, except for Rose, Perez, and Bench.

One of the reasons that so many regulars were developed within the Cincinnati organization was the excellent scouting done by the Reds. Scouts are the lifeblood of an organization but among the least appreciated cogs in the machinery. They often work for years in obscurity. Think for a moment; how many scouts do you know by name? Yet they are responsible for discovering the household names we all know and love. Bench, Rose, and Perez were all discovered by some virtually anonymous scout.

Bob Howsam worked hard to increase the size of the scouting department. When he arrived in Cincinnati in 1967, there were seven full-time scouts. By 1970, he had increased the number to seventeen, plus thirty part-time summer

Former army private, muscular Ken Griffey stretches during spring training. Writers and fans lobbied for his promotion to the majors in 1974 (photograph courtesy Roadwest Publishing [Jack Klumpe Collection]).

scouts. He wanted his scouts to be able to cover the entire country, including the small towns that are often overlooked. That is how the Reds found Don Gullett. He also increased the Reds' international exposure. As mentioned earlier, he began scouting Latin America in the late 1940s, beginning with Panama. The efforts in Latin America were ahead of their time; more than 30 percent of major leaguers now come from south of the border. While with the Reds, Howsam even began scouting efforts in Europe, which had picked up baseball from American GIs. Those efforts never panned out, mainly due to a lack of competition in Europe that hampered the youngsters' efforts to improve.

Howsam looked not only to Europe but to the Pacific, with scouting in Australia and Taiwan. The Taiwanese efforts were particularly promising. Many will remember the Taiwanese youngsters dominating the Little League World Series in Williamsport, Pennsylvania, during the 1970s. Unfortunately those scouting efforts were short-circuited when Jimmy Carter decided to normalize relations with the Chinese Communists. As a result, the Chinese who escaped Communist rule and fled to Taiwan broke off many relations with the United States, including the Cincinnati Reds connection.[2]

Ross Grimsley was a talented lefty and a hero of the '72 playoffs. His free spirit and obsession with facial hair got him shipped off to Baltimore despite his talent. If you didn't follow the rules, you didn't play for the Reds (photograph courtesy Roadwest Publishing [Jack Klumpe Collection]).

Scouting is a tough job. A scout may view a game one evening, jump into his car and drive 200 miles to the next town late into the night, check into a hotel, and get up in the morning to run a camp. It is hard work, with many lonely hours. Bob Howsam wanted the scouts to know that he appreciated and valued them. When he was visiting a town, he would contact the scout in that area. He would take the scout and his wife out for a nice dinner, then bring them to the ballgame and give them very good seats right next to him. Over dinner and the game he would visit with the duo and get to know them. He also would share some of his philosophies and say what he was looking for in a ball player. In turn he also would get the pulse of what the scout was seeing in his area. Howsam also had a rule that he would speak with each scout by phone at least once a month. Those scouting the major leagues were spoken with more frequently.

Chief Bender (left) and Bob Howsam (right) assemble with the key members of the Reds minor league system. Standing left to right: Vern Rapp, Russ Nixon, Jim Snyder, Ron Plaza, unknown, Sal Artiaga, Scott Breeden. These gentlemen fed a steady stream of talent to the parent club (photograph courtesy Sheldon Bender).

Furthermore Howsam would gather all the scouts in September of each year for a meeting in Cincinnati. He would have them attend a game against one of the Reds' biggest rivals, the Dodgers, for example. He wanted the scouts to see firsthand what the Reds were up against, what the competition looked like, what the Reds were trying to do.

In addition to having scouts converge in Cincinnati, he wanted to increase cross-pollination among scouts in other ways. After spring training each year he would have his scouts work south to north. Baseball begins earlier in the year in the Sun Belt. Howsam had scouts from the northern region stay with the southern men and scout with them until the weather got warmer. Slowly they would migrate northward as the spring thaw arrived. As a result, scouts got a better idea of what players from other regions looked like. This in turn gave them a better gauge of talent in their own areas. The gauge was important. Historically much big-league talent comes from Florida, Texas, Arizona, and California. Scouts from other areas saw these players early in the spring and could size up prospects in other states against this standard.

Because scouting was such a tough job, Howsam wanted to do other things for the scouts. He tried to give them a big enough car to get around comfortably. The car was always an automatic with cruise control so that the scout didn't have to keep a foot on the gas pedal on long trips. He wanted the car to have a large enough trunk to put their gear into easily. He wanted the scouts to know that he was thinking of them, that they were important to him. These may seem like small things but Howsam believed it was the small things, not the large things, that make an organization successful.[3]

The 1974 Cincinnati home season was about ten miles away from not happening at all. On April 3, 1974, a tornado watch and then a tornado warning were issued by local weather authorities. No one paid much attention, since these warnings and watches were fairly common at that time of year. A tornado watch is announced when conditions are right for the creation of a tornado, while a tornado warning is issued when a tornado has actually been spotted, regardless of whether it has touched the ground. Folks soon learned to take heed and to know the difference. A tornado formed over some farmland just west of the Greater Cincinnati Airport in northern Kentucky and began to sweep across the land. It hit just north of the small town of Hebron, Kentucky, then descended a steep bank down into and across the Ohio River, ripping apart a section of the Saylor Park community. Saylor Park, near Pete Rose's boyhood home, lies ten miles downriver from Riverfront Stadium in downtown Cincinnati. A tornado in the city would have had devastating consequences. Residents of Xenia, Ohio, know that all too well. Another tornado almost completely destroyed the entire town that same day. It was a close call and a reminder that cities and ballparks are not exempt from natural disasters.[4]

The community was shaken but a sellout crowd still gathered the next day, most wearing red, to see the traditional baseball opener against the Atlanta

Hammerin' Hank Aaron swings for number 714 against Jack Billingham in the opener of the 1974 season, a season almost wiped out by a tornado (photograph courtesy Roadwest Publishing [Jack Klumpe Collection]).

Braves. Henry Aaron had finished the 1973 season tantalizingly close to Babe Ruth's all-time home run record. Babe Ruth had set the mark at 714 when he finished playing ball in 1935. Aaron was at 713 going into the 1974 season.

Jack Billingham was awarded the honor of the Opening Day start. Billingham had finished the 1973 season at 19–10 and pitched well in the playoffs. He retired the side in order in the first inning. Henry Aaron, batting clean-up, was the first batter of the second inning. On a 3–1 pitch from Billingham, Aaron's wrists snapped with their trademark strength and quickness. The ball was not hit high but it was hit hard. A liner to left, it had little arc, almost parallel to the AstroTurf. It cleared the wall by less than three feet. Aaron had tied the Babe.

The crowd rose in appreciation, a standing ovation. It was warm and heartfelt, a recognition of a lifetime's work, but it certainly was not thunderous and passionate. Aaron seemed to evoke that same feeling across the league, outside of Atlanta and Milwaukee where he had played as a Brave. There was nothing majestic about the home run. In fact it was more prose than poetry. A workmanlike hit, not a grand shot. It certainly wouldn't be called "Ruthian." That was typical of many of Aaron's home runs. They were not deep, deep shots. They cleared the wall and some were deep, but not many made fans say "wow, can you believe he hit the ball that far?"

In fairness to Aaron, a home run is a home run. No matter how deep it is hit, if it clears the wall it is a round tripper. You don't get an extra run because the ball lands in the upper deck. There were other reasons that Aaron did not seem to be embraced by the American psyche. First and foremost is that when you are trying to overcome a popular legend, and Babe Ruth certainly is among the biggest of all legends, you have an uphill battle. When Jack Nicklaus came along and threatened Arnold Palmer's kingship, he got similar treatment. Nobody likes their icons torn down or replaced.

Another reason for the lukewarm reception that leaps to most people's minds is racism. Ruth was white and Aaron was black. "No one wants a black man to overtake a white man" was the conventional thought at the time, and to a degree is today, but I don't think it is as simple as that. To be sure there were far too many back in 1974, and still are today, who can't get past the pigment of a person's skin. As has become known since that time, Aaron received many a threatening and racist letter during his record chase. Death threats were not uncommon. He withstood them with grace and dignity, which is inspiring. He suffered many humiliating comments and remarks throughout his life and career and never made a fuss or big deal about them, even though he had the right to do so. His grace under fire has garnered perhaps even more respect than his breaking of the record itself.

I think there was something more to the fact that America never really embraced Aaron. It was his personality. We all have one, and some are more charming than others. Aaron did not come across as a warm person. Some people just attract you by who they are. Those types of folks are in the minority. Most of us don't have that advantage and Aaron didn't either. He was nice enough and is probably very warm with his family but that warmth certainly didn't come across on television or in the newspapers. He seemed serious and distant. Unfortunately for Aaron he had a contemporary in New York and later in San Francisco, who was bubbly, warm, charming and had an infectious smile and obvious love of the game. America embraced the "Say Hey Kid," Willie Mays, more than they ever did Aaron, even though their skin pigment was the same.

Had Mays and not Aaron been nipping at Ruth's heels, I dare say the reaction would have been different, not from the racists out there but from the average baseball fans. I think there would have been more passion and enthusiasm for Mays. Many thought Mays would have been on Ruth's heels if his circumstances had been the same as Aaron's. Willie Mays played about a dozen seasons at Candlestick Park, notorious for winds holding balls in play. Aaron spent nine seasons at Fulton County Stadium, a home run hitter's dream park, with friendly breezes. Give Mays five or ten more home runs a year at Fulton County and take five or ten from Aaron and it is Mays who is the all-time home run king, not Aaron. That doesn't even count Willie's two years of service in the army early in his career but Aaron can't help who was drafted. My point is that there was more to the home run race than race. When Henry Aaron tied the Babe at Riverfront he earned the record and our respect, if not our adoration. He would be joined by two young men from the grandstands during his home run trot four days later when he broke the Babe's record off Al Downing and the Los Angeles Dodgers.

There is an old adage in baseball that you have to be strong up the middle. That refers to the middle defensive players on the field anchored by the catcher, and Johnny Bench was the best in the league when it came to defense. Cat-quick, he could spring like a puma from behind the plate. With his strong arm and confidence, Bench essentially shut down the opposition's running game when it came to steals. As the Reds knew and the rest of the league was finding out, Joe Morgan was really good at second, due to his mind if not his arm. He had the ability to cut a runner down at any base due to his anticipation. Meanwhile Dave Concepcion had enjoyed a breakout year in 1973. His shattered ankle was healed and in 1974 he picked up where he had left off. His defensive plays, featuring range, grace, and a powerful arm, sometimes left one breathless. Finally, Cesar Geronimo had settled in at center. His speed and cannon arm made him valuable, but his speed had a deceptive quality to it. Rarely did he make a spectacular play but he made many plays and almost all of them seemed routine and effortless. He felt that if a player made a catch diving, he should have caught it running. Geronimo knew where the ball was going by where the ball was pitched. He also had a trait that belied his quickness. His

Cesar Geronimo came over from Houston in the trade of 1971. The former pitcher possessed a cannon for an arm. "The Chief" seemed to glide effortlessly across center field. His deceptive speed made the spectacular seem routine. His secret was a nine-foot stride, noted by Branch Rickey (photograph courtesy Roadwest Publishing [Jack Klumpe Collection]).

stride was amazing. It was so long that it seemed that Geronimo was just gliding across the AstroTurf when in fact he was moving at great speed. When they measured it, the Reds found that Geronimo had a nine-foot stride, the exact stride length that Howsam had heard Rickey recommend all those years ago.[5]

Bench, Morgan, Concepcion and Geronimo hardened into the defensive core for the Reds up the middle. The foursome all earned Gold Gloves in 1974. The Gold Glove has been awarded since 1957 to the most outstanding defensive players at their respective position in each league. The sweep of all four Gold Gloves would be repeated three more times. It was a defense Howsam had wanted since 1967; it took eight seasons to get it but it was worth the wait and beautiful to watch.

While the defense up the middle was inspiring, there was a problem elsewhere. Danny Driessen was a big hit, but he was also a poor fielder, though it hadn't been evident right away. Time tends to reveal such details. Like Perez, he was more of a first basemen. For now the glow of his bat barely hid the gloom of his glove.

Johnny Bench was not only great behind the plate in 1974, he was having another fine offensive season. He led the league in RBIs with 129, his third time as the league leader. He also topped the circuit with 315 total bases, making him the only catcher in baseball history to lead the league in that department. He seemed to be best in the even-numbered years, winning the MVP in 1970 and 1972. He was defeated for the award in 1974 by a player on the Reds archrival team, Steve Garvey of the Dodgers.

The previous season the Los Angeles Dodgers had replaced Houston and San Francisco as the Reds' chief competition in the Western Division of the National League. Their manager, Walter Alston, was on his twenty-first consecutive one-year contract going into 1974. Alston didn't need the security of a long-term contract. Unlike so many owner-manager relationships you read about today, Alston trusted the O'Malley family to take care of him and to do the right thing. Ever since they shortchanged the fans in Brooklyn, they pretty much had. After Walter O'Malley broke the fans' hearts in Brooklyn, he had won them over in L.A. O'Malley bought all the homes in the community of Chavez Ravine, moved many to Universal Studios[6] and then built a beautiful ballpark, served lots of Dodger Dogs, and kept ticket prices low.

Walter and his son Peter O'Malley were two of only a few full-time baseball owners in the game. Running the Dodgers was the O'Malleys' full-time job and only business. This was as rare in 1974 as it is today. There were the Yawkeys in Boston but pretty much every other club was a side business for the owner. The Brewers' Bud Selig owned a car business. The Yankees' George Steinbrenner was a shipping magnate. The Reds had a number of owners, with businesses ranging from newspapers to insurance and household goods. So if the Dodgers made money, the O'Malleys made money. If they lost money, then the O'Malleys ate tuna. Well, not exactly, but you get the idea.

As opposed to some modern managers and head coaches, Alston did not go around demanding "total control," "full authority," or the "ability to buy the groceries if he was going to cook."[7] Peter O'Malley and others ran the front office. Walter Alston took care of things on the field. Alston never complained about security and O'Malley never complained about trust. They had a mutual respect and did their jobs; it was refreshing.

It had taken Alston and the Dodgers nearly a decade to get over the loss of Sandy Koufax. When they did, it was primarily because of pitching. They had a great rotation. Don Sutton had been a rookie in Koufax's last World Series, the 1966 debacle against the Baltimore Orioles. He was now the ace, crafty and confident, some would say cocky, a right hander and the de facto team spokesman. Andy Messersmith was a twenty-game winner. Tommy John, Doug Rau, and Al Downing were three pretty good left-handers.

But the Dodgers were also strong in the field and in the batter's box. In center field, Cincinnati native Jimmy Wynn, like Morgan, prospered once he left Houston, the Astrodome, and Harry "The Hat" Walker during the previous off-season. Their other offensive star was a clean-cut former Dodger batboy, Steve Garvey, who played first. Their infield was young and poised to jell for years to come. Davey Lopes was at second, Bill Russell was at short. At third base was Ron Cey, the pride of Tacoma, Washington. Cey had a squatty gait to his walk and swayed side to side as he moved. As a result he was tabbed "the Penguin."

The 1974 All-Star Game at Three Rivers Stadium in Pittsburgh would be typical of all the All-Star Games in the mid–1970s. The starting lineups were comprised almost entirely of Reds and Dodgers, sprinkled with a player or two from every other club. Perez or Garvey at first; Morgan and Lopes at second; Concepcion and Russell at short; Ron Cey at third; and Wynn and Rose in the outfield. Bench was always behind the plate. One would start through fan voting and the other was selected a reserve through performance and manager recognition. Seven of the nine NL starters were either Reds or Dodgers that year.

Near the All-Star break, Tommy John was posting his finest season to date—he was 13–3—when a tendon in his pitching elbow was torn. Most figured his career was over at age thirty. Dr. Frank Jobe wanted to try a revolutionary procedure where he would take a tendon from John's right (non-pitching) forearm and replace the torn tendon in the left elbow. The surgery worked better than anyone ever dreamed and John returned to baseball in 1976. As John would later recall, before the surgery he asked Jobe to put in a Koufax fastball. Jobe did, but it was Mrs. Koufax's.[8]

At the All-Star break the Dodgers led the West by five and a half games. When they met the Reds for a series in Los Angeles one month later, the lead was six and a half games. The series was a microcosm of the entire season. The first game was slated for Monday night, August 5. NBC was on hand for *Monday Night Baseball*. They had borrowed ABC's wildly successful *Monday Night*

Football concept but fortunately without Howard Cosell. Besides the *Game of the Week* broadcast on Saturday afternoon, this was most baseball fans' only opportunity to see a game other than pay for a seat at the ballpark. Cable was practically unheard of and ESPN was five years from birth. Curt Gowdy and Tony Kubek were in the booth; Doug Rau and Don Gullett dueled on the mound.

Leading 6–2 late in the game, the Dodgers called on their ace relief man, their closer, to finish off the game. Mike Marshall was a man before his time, or, better put, a man out of his time. Marshall was a medical marvel of knowledge. He had studied kinesiology (the science of muscles), earning a PhD. He was convinced that pitchers' problems in general, but especially relief pitchers' problems, primarily stemmed from the fact that they failed to warm up their muscles properly. Before he began to throw in the bullpen he would do a series of arm calisthenics in order to loosen his pitching muscles. He would then make a few tosses and he was ready to go. He believed that arm stretches would allow himself — and any pitcher, for that matter — to pitch far more than common without injury. It was hard to argue with the man. He appeared in 106 games that year, still a record.

Marshall entered the game in the eighth, arm muscles limbered. Pete Rose stepped into the left-handed batter's box. Besides an array of cardiovascular knowledge, Marshall possessed a wicked screwball, like Cueller and Norman. Rose was ready for the challenge. The count rose to a few balls and two strikes. As is well known, once a hitter gets a second strike, he must protect the plate. This simply means that any pitch near the strike zone must be swung at. The batter doesn't want to leave his fate in the umpire's hands (or eyes). Against a good pitcher like Marshall the hitter may get a pitch near the strike zone that he doesn't feel he can hit but he can't afford to let it go by. So the great hitters forego trying to hit the ball into fair play but rather try to "get a piece" — hit it into foul territory. If successful, he remains at two strikes and stays alive.

Watch the video clip between Marshall and Rose — it is a baseball hitting clinic. The broadcasters were gushing about it in the booth and justifiably so. After nearly five minutes, over one dozen pitches, and multiple foul balls, Rose finally slapped a single to center off Marshall. It was baseball at its finest, a purist's dream — two professionals going head-to-head, each practicing their trade with their utmost being, with the game in the balance. It was like admiring fine art, you had to know what you were looking at to appreciate it fully, to appreciate the subtleties. The novice fan sees only the opportunity to eat a second hot dog in the same at-bat, figuring that Rose can't hit Marshall a lick. Baseball connoisseurs realize just the opposite; they have witnessed two masters at work. Most of us are somewhere in between.

The Marshall-Rose battle went Rose's way but the war went to the Dodgers as they won this particular game, 6–3. The Reds returned the favor with a 6–3 victory the next night. In part three of the trilogy the Reds prevailed again, 2–0.

It showed just how close the teams were in 1974. The series was typical of the era; the Reds and Dodgers were clearly the class of the league. The Reds took the series and left Los Angeles trailing by five and a half games in the race but they couldn't get over the hump. The Dodgers won the West by three and a half games.

For the Reds it was a hard pill to swallow. They won ninety-eight ballgames that year, the most since 1970, and yet they came up short. The Dodgers had a spectacular year and earned the division title by winning 102 games. The Reds had overtaken the Dodgers in 1973 but they couldn't do it in '74. The Dodgers simply earned it.

The Dodgers beat the Pirates in the playoffs that season and faced the Reds' 1972 opponent, Oakland, in the World Series. The A's had beaten the Baltimore Orioles in the playoffs and were now in the Series for the third straight year — and they would earn their third straight victory. They are the only team since the Yankees in 1951 to win three straight World Series titles.

Bob Howsam and many others were baffled. How could a team with seemingly so little discipline win three straight World Series? Obviously you must have talent but Howsam felt that discipline was essential. Yet Oakland seemed to defy this principle. It would be years before he would discover the answer but he had a more pressing mystery to solve right now, a question that haunted Howsam and gnawed at Reds fans. After five straight seasons of high hopes and lots of talent, why was there still no title? Maybe the answer lay somewhere other than the field.

15

THE MISSING PIECE
October 1974–September 1975

Two guys sat talking on the steps of the old Cincinnati Law School, then part of the historic Ninth Street Baptist Church. The middle-aged man said, "If Sparky doesn't win it all this year, he's gone."

The 13-year-old boy was flabbergasted; he couldn't believe what he had just heard. "You can't be serious. The Reds have been to the World Series and playoffs several years; you can't do that. The Reds are first or second every year. Why would you fire Sparky?"

"First or second in the division is fine, but there comes a time when you've got to win it all. Everything else seems good, so maybe the problem is at the top. If he can't get them there, maybe somebody else can. There probably is someone else who can."

This thought was not isolated to Ninth Street. It was a conversation that was occurring all over the city that spring. Howsam swears he wasn't thinking it but Sparky Anderson says it had entered his mind. I need to win this year or else. Since he had taken the helm, they had averaged ninety-five wins per year, ninety-nine if you didn't count the 1971 injury year, plus three division titles and two World Series appearances. Not bad for a club that had been averaging a World Series appearance every other decade but everyone was beginning to get a bit restless. The Reds boasted two MVPs on the club and eleven different All-Stars over that period, eight of whom were still on the club, but still they had a second-place finish to the Dodgers in 1974. Anderson felt it would be now or never, not for the ball club but for him.

Anderson always addressed Howsam as "Mr. Howsam" or "the boss." The boss is the one with authority, so there is some wisdom in recognizing that reality by addressing him or her politely. It reinforces the idea of who the boss is. Howsam practiced that in his own life, always referring to his mentors as "mister" and also addressing August Busch this way.

Howsam and Anderson did not feel that the general manager and manager could be friends. It was impossible. They are good friends now and talk on the phone frequently but in those days it was a friendly working relationship, not a friendship. That helped organizational effectiveness. Howsam often asked Anderson what he thought about matters, but rarely shared his own opinions with Sparky. Howsam tried not to tip his hand about his own opinion with any of his employees until it was time to make a decision. That way he got input from his people without influencing what they said. Howsam used the tact effectively with Sparky, letting Anderson vent. If Sparky was having trouble with a player, he would sometimes rant and rave about it to let off some steam. Howsam would listen patiently but say little. Usually within a few weeks that player was the greatest guy on the team. However, when Sparky continued to vent about a player over a several-month period that is when Howsam knew he had a real problem.[1]

The use of honorifics was not isolated to Sparky Anderson. There also was a protocol in the Reds' front office. All who worked for the general manager called him "Mr. Howsam." This included Chief Bender, the Bowen brothers and Ray Shore. The only exception was Dick Wagner, Howsam's closest associate. Even Wagner sometimes called him "Mr. Howsam," if often, "Boss." Bender sometimes called him "Big Bear," a title of respect for Howsam's work with the Denver Bears.

In most organizations nowadays it is fashionable for all employees to be on a first-name basis with all the other employees, including the boss. That certainly has its advantages; it allows people to feel comfortable and it can encourage them to speak up with ideas and suggestions but it also has its pitfalls. It sometimes sends the wrong message, that we are all on the same footing, when in reality that is not the case. It can lead to the false impression that no one has to take any direction from anybody else because we are all just friends. It can also detract from the professionalism required to run an organization properly. This was to be a first-class organization. Professionalism in the front office and on the field was very important to Bob Howsam and all of the Reds.

Some of the biggest news of the season became known the day before spring training began in February. Cincinnati's most eligible bachelor was not eligible any more. Johnny Bench was head over heals in love and he was getting married. Bench's dating and social life had always been of intense interest around the city. The bride-to-be was Vickie Chesser. She had been Miss South Carolina in 1970 and runner-up for Miss USA. Following the Miss USA pageant she moved to New York to begin a modeling career; there she was best known as the Ultrabrite toothpaste girl. Bench had been attracted to her in part because she didn't know who he was when they started dating. She was not a baseball fan.

Vickie was blonde, blue-eyed, and quite attractive. The wedding was the biggest thing to hit Cincinnati social circles in decades. It was a gala event with invitations sent to President and Mrs. Ford (who had to decline due to previous commitments). More than 900 guests did attend that evening at Christ Church in downtown Cincinnati. The attendees included a senator and a governor, as well as two former beauty queens as the bridesmaids. The cake was five feet high and weighed more than one hundred pounds.[2] The event provoked the excitement and buzz of the Prince Charles–Lady Diana wedding six years later. Charles and Diana had the attention of all of England; Johnny and Vickie had the attention of all of the Queen City. Quite a few women were heartbroken. Most Reds fans saw it as a good thing — it would keep Johnny's mind on baseball.

The Reds still had a sticky problem — third base. Perez had not worked out there, Menke had not worked out, and finally the Reds had decided that Danny Driessen had not worked out. Good with the bat and with decent speed, Driessen's defensive shortcomings at the corner could no longer be overlooked. As much as the Reds hated to take his bat out of the lineup, they had to.

Balance was an overriding principle. Good defense, good offense, good hitting, good pitching, good starting, good relief. The Reds were so potent on offense with the Big Four plus Griffey and Concepcion that they didn't need Driessen's bat. They needed someone who could field consistently at third — routine plays, bunts, difficult plays, everything. Driessen's defense had actually gotten worse after a year in the position. Driessen had twenty-four errors and was last in fielding percentage, by a wide margin, in 1974.

The solution in 1975 was John Vukovich. Howsam picked him up in a trade with Milwaukee in the off-season. The twenty-seven-year-old was a good defender but like Concepcion, Geronimo and Griffey, the question was whether he could he learn to hit major-league pitching. He had a decent spring and was

Danny's Driessen's fielding woes finally forced the Reds to pull him from third base and his bat from the lineup. Third base was still a problem for the Reds (photograph courtesy Roadwest Publishing [Jack Klumpe Collection]).

the Opening Day starter on a fifty-degree sunny April afternoon in 1975. In his first game, Vukovich looked like he was there to stay. In the sixth inning he snared a hot liner off the bat of Joe Ferguson that practically took his hand off. He was even better in the eighth, when he dove to stab a Davey Lopes liner and was rewarded with a standing ovation. Batting eighth in the order, he doubled in the fifth inning. Great defense and 1 for 3 in the game: the Reds could live with that.

Unfortunately he was a flash in the pan. Within two weeks he was out of the lineup and Darrel Chaney came back in. Chaney defensively could play short, second, and third, but offensively he never got going. The Reds put in Doug Flynn, a young rookie. He couldn't get it going offensively either. After the first month of the season the trio of third basemen was hitting a combined .151. The Reds couldn't put Denis Menke back in either. After his dismal 1973 season and Driessen's emergence, Menke had been traded back to the Houston Astros for Pat Darcy and cash. Danny Driessen was out of the question; he was too much of a defensive liability.

The Reds were sputtering. By May 3 they trailed the Dodgers by four games. The previous evening they were scheduled to play the Atlanta Braves. Rose was at the park early as usual. He trotted out to first base to take some grounders. He was trying to break in a new first baseman's glove for his child. Sparky ambled over Pete's way. "I wish you played on the other side," he said. "I do, in left field," Rose replied.

Anderson began musing out loud. "I sure would love to get George Foster and Danny Driessen in the lineup more often. Would you be willing to try third base to make that happen?"

"If you don't think I'll hurt the team, I'll try it," Rose said, and with that he was off for the clubhouse to get an infielder's glove.[3] He took grounders for the next forty-five minutes. Rose was good to his word. When Anderson had arrived five years earlier Pete told him, "I make the most money on this team and I will do whatever you want me to."

Since 1889, the third-base position has been known as the hot corner.[4] This is because the ball can be hit so hard that it travels to the third baseman standing approximately ninety-five feet from home plate at over 110 miles an hour.[5] The balls are sometimes too hot to handle due to their sheer speed. The position demands hair-trigger reaction time as it is often the third baseman who must swoop in to field a bunt. The sacrifice is the most familiar bunt — when a batter sacrifices himself by bunting in order to advance a runner currently on base. Fielders often know that this type of bunt is about to occur by the circumstances of the game — the score, the batter, the runners, how many outs there are, who is up next, etc. The pitcher, first baseman, catcher, and third baseman all know what they are going to do depending on the situation and how well the batter executes the bunt. Depending on where the bunt rolls, each player executes their role in turn. The situations are practiced all during spring

training. A much more challenging bunt for fielders is when the batter is trying to get on base through a surprise bunt. The situation does not call for a
bunt; in fact a runner is rarely on base at this point. The batter senses that the
fielders are not expecting the bunt, perhaps they are playing a bit too deep, and
he surprisingly lays down a bunt and breaks for first. In this situation the third
baseman must often charge in from third, especially if the ball is rolling down
the third-base foul line, a favorite place for bunts, grab the ball with a bare hand
as it trickles along the ground, and fire the ball across his body on the run. The
play requires speed, agility, balance, throwing power and accuracy — all combined in seconds. From a biomechanical aspect, it is amazing. There is no
machine built that can execute this play; it requires a human being, a talented
one.

Minutes before the game on May 3, Sparky Anderson penciled in Rose at
third and Foster in left. Some of the Braves noticed that Rose had been taking
some infield balls. When Anderson turned his lineup card in to the home-plate
umpire before the game, Atlanta manager Clyde King's suspicions were
confirmed.[6] Rose was playing third that night. King had been around the game
for more than three decades. He immediately devised a plan.

He sent leadoff man Ralph Garr to the plate with a mission: test Rose. It
had been eight and one-half seasons since Rose's move from second to the
outfield. He had been an All-Star in right and left. Now he was back in the
infield, but this time at third at age thirty-four. Garr, the defending NL batting champion, could fly. On the pitch, Garr lowered the bat and smashed one
to Rose's left and broke for first. Rose was no dummy; he had been around the
game a long time. He knew how it was played, knew you had to find the weak
point in your opponent and expose it. He was expecting the test. Without batting an eye, Rose stepped to his left, snagged the ball and threw a bullet to the
awaiting Perez at first. Garr was out by several steps. In later games Rose would
be bunted on and he defended well. If third tests a fielder's talent, Rose had
passed the test.

Imagine asking most superstars to switch positions at age thirty-four,
especially in the middle of the season. Granted some longtime All-Star outfielders make the move to first in their later years as their legs begin to give way.
Mickey Mantle was among those. But to ask a superstar to go to third after
eight seasons as an All-Star outfielder is another matter. Most could not fathom
making the move or even suggesting it as Anderson had done. It is a testament
to Sparky's leadership that he would air a concern and allow one of his players
to give him input but this was Sparky's way. In Rose's case, Anderson made it
clear that if Rose didn't feel it was working out, he would be moved back to
left field.

When it came to the Big Four, Sparky expected them to lead in the clubhouse. In return they had greater access to his office and his ear. If they came
in and shared something with him, he took it to heart. In return they were to

take care of most of the clubhouse matters. He expected them to keep every-body in line. He didn't have to worry about things like that. This relationship required trust from both Sparky and the Big Four.

Sparky had his own internal test for whether this understanding was violated. He had both a dress code and an appearance code. Players were to wear a jacket and tie on road trips while traveling by air. No jeans allowed. And of course there was the no-facial-hair rule. Anderson once said if one of the Big Four came in with facial hair or inappropriate traveling attire he would have immediately resigned as skipper. He would have known instantly through that superstar's actions that he had lost his authority and the star's trust and respect. With no authority, you have no hope of leading. As long as the Big Four went along with the rules, everyone else would to. He never lost their trust.

Another concern with the Rose move was the possibility that preoccupation with his fielding would affect Pete's hitting. He went 1-for-4 that first night with a double and a run scored. After a week, his offense showed no effects of the move and his defense was still solid, fifteen chances handled with no errors. He hit .317 that year, .320 before the move and .316 afterwards.

The other half of the equation was George Foster. Acquired from the San Francisco Giants in 1971, he had played sparingly through the years. His highlight was the Series-winning score on the Bob Moose wild pitch in the tumultuous Game Five of the 1972 playoffs against the Pittsburgh Pirates. Foster helped man the outfield by committee during Tolan's year of demise but was used the most sparingly of all the committee members. The Reds saw fit to give him only thirty-nine at-bats. Limited to mostly pinch hitting and fill-in work for short-term injuries or guys who needed a day off, he had platooned with Griffey in right in 1974, but hit only .264 with seven home runs. Foster's best year had been 1971, when he hit thirteen home runs, yet hit only .241 for the year. For some reason, though there was little concrete evidence on the field, Anderson saw something. He thought Foster would produce if given the chance to play every day. Now he had the chance.

Foster was six foot one and 180 pounds, with strong, quick wrists, like Hank Aaron's. After ten weeks of starting in left he was hitting .290 with fifteen home runs and thirty-nine RBIs.

The original plan was to have Foster platoon with Danny Driessen in left. Foster would face left-handers and Driessen would get the call against righties. When Foster immediately hit the ball so well, Driessen again found himself out of the mix. Foster played so well that Driessen ended up getting only spot duty in left, occasionally in right, and he also relieved Perez at first.

Like a miracle drug, the Rose-to-third experiment was successful and produced breakthrough results. The Big Red Machine began to get traction and gain ground on the Dodgers. Within a month they caught them. By July they were on cruise control and Foster was comfortable in his new role.

Another very positive event occurred the evening of May 3, 1975, which would make the day the watershed mark in the Reds' season and in the life of the Big Red Machine. Gary Nolan won a game. In the 1972 season Nolan had been the major's leader in winning percentage but he finished the season nursing a sore shoulder. The shoulder did not respond in 1973, as he pitched in only two games. The next season was worse; Nolan sat out all of 1974 trying to get the arm well. Many thought that his career was over. On May 3 he beat the Atlanta Braves, 6–1, in a complete game, his first victory in twenty months. It was as nice a present as Rose's willingness to move to third.

The lineup was now as strong as it had ever been or as strong as it had been since the first half of 1970. Rose and Morgan set the table. Bench, Perez and Foster did the big damage, and Concepcion, Griffey and Geronimo cleaned up the leftovers before the pitcher came to bat.

The defense was superb. The middle of the defense all won Gold Gloves again. The Reds set a major-league record of fifteen consecutive games without an error in late June. The streak was broken by Danny Driessen, who bobbled a single in left on July 1.

The pitching also was in good, if not happy, hands. By this time the starters had almost come to despise Sparky. It wasn't disrespect, it was dislike. Jack Billingham was the ringleader. His distaste for Anderson was so strong, that it bordered on hatred.

Sparky's trusted assistant Larry Shepard shares a light-hearted moment in his Kangaroo Court with the pitchers in 1970. Such moments grew few and far between by 1975 as the Reds starters resented being pulled by Sparky Anderson, a.k.a. Captain Hook (photograph courtesy Roadwest Publishing [Jack Klumpe Collection]).

Unlike many managers, especially young ones, Sparky avoided a cardinal sin. Sparky played to his strengths, regardless of what the players thought. He wasn't afraid of the players, and didn't mind being unpopular with some of them. The pitchers' dislike boiled down to one fact, they wanted to pitch more, just as Hal McRae several seasons earlier had wanted to play every day. Any player worth his salt wants to play every day. The pitchers wanted to pitch more, not every day, of course, but more innings than they did pitch. They thought they were getting pulled too early by "Captain Hook," as Anderson was being called. The pitchers felt that they were too frequently being pulled offstage in the middle of a good performance. The Reds would set a major-league record in 1975 by going forty-five consecutive contests without a complete game by a starting pitcher.

Anderson was no-nonsense about the approach. Asked once after a game what he said to a pitcher when he went to the mound to pull him even when the pitcher was doing well, Anderson replied, "'Gimme the ball'; that's all I ever say."

Anderson liked his staff of Billingham, Gullett, Nolan, and Norman, but he had two simple philosophies when it came to his pitchers. First he wasn't going to listen to them; he was only going to listen to the expert and the expert wasn't the pitcher, it was pitching coach Larry Shepard. What his pitchers tried to tell him didn't hold any weight. In fact he didn't care what they thought. What he did want to hear was what "Shep" had to say. He trusted Shepard

Clay Carroll, "The Hawk," arrives for yet another outing. Sparky's words were brief when he yanked a pitcher, "Gimme the ball" (photograph courtesy Roadwest Publishing [Jack Klumpe Collection]).

completely. As Lou Piniella would later say, "The pitching coach is a manger's best friend. He handles twelve of the twenty-five guys on the team, and there are not many managers out there who can teach a player to throw a curveball, slider or change-up." You hate to lose a good pitching coach. When it came to his pitchers, Anderson followed Shepard's advice.

Anderson's second philosophy when it came to pitching emanated from the cards he was dealt. He didn't consider his starters the strength of his ball club — they weren't. He considered his relievers one of the strengths of his ball club and he was going to play to his strengths. While he thought his starters were good, he didn't think they were great. Therefore, he wasn't going to let them dictate the outcome of a ballgame. And when it came to relievers there wasn't a better set of them out there than what was found in Cincinnati.

The Hawk, Clay Carroll, was still as big and strong as he had been in 1970 and was still itching to get the ball. Pedro Borbon was from the Dominican Republic but you might think he was from Akron, Ohio, home of Firestone and Goodyear — the man's arm seemed to be made of rubber. He pitched more than

any other Reds pitcher. He never seemed to tire.[7] His specialty was middle relief. If a starter was struggling and had to come out in the fourth, fifth or sixth inning, Borbon would come in and take the Reds into the late innings when he would turn it over to Carroll or one of the Gold Dust Twins.

The Gold Dust Twins were another product of Rapp's work in Indianapolis. When Howsam needed help for the bullpen, Rapp sent him Rawly Eastwick and Will McEnaney. Eastwick and McEnaney were just the next in a long line of pitchers that had been drafted and developed under Howsam. Don Gullett, Wayne Simpson and Milt Wilcox had all been drafted on Howsam's watch. Howsam also acquired Jack Billingham and Fredie Nor-

Rubber-armed Pedro Borbon was a mainstay of the relief corps after coming over in a trade that at first seemed disastrous (photograph courtesy Roadwest Publishing [Jack Klumpe Collection]).

man via trades with Cincinnati-grown talent in return.

Rawly Eastwick was a thin right-hander from New Jersey. He was drafted by the Reds in the third round of the 1969 draft. After five years in the minors he found his way to the Reds late in 1974. Unlike many baseball players, Eastwick had a love and a talent for art. He gave Vickie and Johnny Bench one of his own paintings for a wedding present. By the next season he had assumed the closer's role from the aging Carroll.

Will McEnaney was a slender left-hander from Springfield, Ohio. His attitude had almost kept McEnaney from playing professional baseball at all. Like too many high schoolers, McEnaney thought he knew more than his coach. Sometimes that actually is the case but it is rare. When he and the

Right hander Rawly Eastwick, one half of "the Gold Dust Twins," arrived in May and went on to lead the team in saves (photograph courtesy Roadwest Publishing [Jack Klumpe Collection]).

coach did not see eye-to-eye after his sophomore year, the coach invited him not to be on the team. McEnaney's talent had garnered the interest of almost every professional team. Once word got out about McEnaney's dismissal, the scouts and their interest scattered. Professional ballplayers' attitudes can be hard enough to handle when they make the major leagues. No one wants an attitude problem from someone still in high school. It is likely to get worse, not better, in the professional ranks.

With no high school team, McEnaney was left with American Legion and Babe Ruth baseball. Warren Bennett, a Springfield area amateur coach, wrote the Reds to tell them about McEnaney. The Bowen brothers sent Cliff Alexander to check out the youngster. They decided to take a chance on him and drafted him in the eighth round of the 1970 draft.[8] Without the attitude, he would have gone much higher. He was lucky to go at all.

Drafted the year after Eastwick, McEnaney was a starter in the minors but once he arrived with the Reds he went to the bullpen. He actually shared the closer role with Eastwick, in particular when the opposition had several left-handed hitters due up. They had a great 1975 season, notching thirty-seven saves between them.

Generally it was not Sparky Anderson's style to stick with just one guy as the closer. As he had done in filling in for Tolan, he often used the committee approach. He preferred to spread the wealth around and look for the hot hand. In today's game it is common for one man to have almost all his team's saves. Normally Anderson had several players with double-digit saves in the same year. Remarkably, even with such an approach the Reds had two men lead the league in saves: Granger in 1970 and Carroll in 1972. This demonstrates the degree to which Sparky relied on his bullpen. In 1970 it was Granger and Carroll. In 1971 it was Carroll, Granger, and Joe Gibbon. In 1972 and 1973 it was Carroll, Borbon, and Tommy Hall. This 1975 season was probably the best year ever, with Eastwick, McEnaney, Borbon and Carroll recording forty-nine saves between them.

Foster's newfound comfort and the relievers' ubiquitous presence merged on one warm summer evening in 1975. Telecasters Curt Gowdy and Tony Kubek were on hand for a Monday night baseball game against the Houston Astros. The Reds starter, Tom Carroll, had been pulled by Captain Hook in the second inning. Borbon came on in the third inning and uncharacteristically struggled.

He was getting hit pretty hard yet Sparky never made a move to go and pull him. The Astros continued to pound hits, inning after inning, while the Reds barely escaped and Reds fans began to grow restless and yell. "Pull him!" "Yank him!" "Get him out of there, Sparky!" Uncharacteristically, Anderson never made a move. Finally another Astros hitting spree came to a merciful end and the Reds trotted back to the dugout for the bottom of the inning.

Foster was kneeling in the on-deck circle waiting for his next at-bat. The fans were still irritated about Captain Hook's uncharacteristic inaction. Sparky had allowed Borbon to give the Astros the opportunity to put the game out of reach. The fans were still hot about it.

Lefty Will McEnaney rounded out perhaps the greatest bullpen in history in 1975 (photograph courtesy Roadwest Publishing [Jack Klumpe Collection]).

The blue seats at Riverfront were the best in the house. They occupied the area closest to the field, around the dugout and behind home plate. Fans in that area could easily be heard on the field, especially by players in the dugout, and those waiting in the on-deck circle. A man in the second row sitting with his son yelled, "Hey, George, what's wrong with Sparky? Is he asleep in there or what?" Foster turned around and glanced slyly into the dugout and then slowly looked up at the man and, with a wry smile, nodded his head affirmatively, then turned back to the action. The man roared with laughter. The Reds came back to win the game 9–6 in the twelfth inning.

The Reds won a lot of games that year, 108 to be exact — an all-time franchise record. The Dodgers finished twenty games back. With their strong bullpen and great offensive lineup, the Reds were never really out of any game. If they were down three or four runs in the seventh, very few left for the exits at Riverfront Stadium. If they left they may have missed one of the twenty-five regular-season games that the Reds won batting in the ninth inning. The Big Red Machine was rolling toward the postseason but they had done that before and come away disappointed. Would this year be any different?

The first test would be in the playoffs against an old nemesis, the Pittsburgh Pirates. The Bucs had pretty much dominated the Eastern Division since 1970, winning the division every year except 1973 when they stumbled and the Mets surprised them and the Reds. This year Pittsburgh had beaten their cross-state rivals, the Philadelphia Phillies, by six and a half games. Though they weren't the same team since losing Clemente, the Bucs were still very good. Willie Stargell was their big hitter and leader. Besides Clemente, the Pirates had lost Steve Blass since their 1971 World Series victory over the Orioles. Despite the loss of Clemente and Blass, the Pirates were expected to offer stiff competition to the Reds. They didn't, though. The Big Red Machine ran right into the World Series with a three-game sweep, stealing seven bases in Game Two alone. The Reds had never looked stronger. Maybe things would be different this time.

16

THE GREATEST SERIES EVER PLAYED
October 1975

The Boston Red Sox had replaced the Orioles and A's as the Reds' World Series opponent. The tumultuous reign of the A's had come to an end at the hands of the Red Sox. The Athletics had been the only team outside of the Yankees to win three consecutive World Series titles. They had bested the Reds, Mets, and Dodgers in turn.

The bubbling turmoil in the A's clubhouse finally took its toil. Reggie Jackson and centerfielder Billy North got into a fight. Ray Fosse rushed in to break up the brawl and received a crushed disk in his neck — and four months on the disabled list for his efforts. Dick Williams had resigned at the end of the 1973 season. He was replaced by Alvin Dark, a man known for his solid character. He was as strong a Christian as one could find in baseball. He was an unlikely figure to head a bunch of "bad boys" but led them to the World Series title in 1974. He tried to bring some tranquility to the club and had succeeded in getting the team to have no fights and make it to the playoffs in 1975 but the Red Sox were waiting with both young and old talent. Surprisingly the Red Sox swept the A's in three straight games.

The Red Sox patriarch was Carl Yastrzemski, better known as "Yaz." In 1967, managed by Dick Williams, he had carried Boston to the World Series against Howsam's old Cardinals on the back of his Triple Crown year. He is the last man to lead the league in average, home runs and RBIs. In the 1969 All-Star Game, he robbed a young Johnny Bench of a second home run by climbing the chain-link fence in RFK Stadium. Yaz was still very productive in 1975 and one of those guys with the intangibles; he had the respect of everybody in the clubhouse, just by the type of man he was. In New England he was a legend.

Yastrzemski had been moved out of his left-field position where he had himself replaced a bigger legend, Ted Williams. The Red Sox had two young rookie outfielders they needed to get into the lineup. Jim Rice was one and he replaced Yaz in left. However Rice had broken his hand with a few weeks remaining in the season, so Yaz returned to left.

The rookie in center field was almost too good to be true. A star for Rod

Dedeaux's three-time College World Series Champion Southern California Trojans, Freddie Lynn was handsome, polite, well-spoken and talented. He was good with the bat and the glove. He hit .331, with twenty-one home runs and 105 RBIs while winning AL Rookie of the Year and MVP honors.[1] Rice was third in the MVP voting. Dwight Evans provided great defense and steady offense in the tricky right-field sector of Fenway Park.

The Red Sox catcher resembled a model out of an LL Bean catalog. Carlton Fisk looked at home in a flannel shirt with a couple of hunting dogs at his feet, something central casting would send over for a film about New England. He not only hunted, he also had a rifle arm. Unlike most good defensive catchers, Fisk also could hit the ball well, a trait he shared with Bench. They were among the top three catchers in all of baseball. It was Fisk's battery mates that were the question entering the series against the Reds.

Lots of players can hit in Fenway Park; few can pitch there. Fenway is a hurler's nightmare. The problems start in right, where Dwight Evans played, and get worse as you come around the outfield. The right-field wall is only 302 feet from home and between three and a half and five feet in height as it slopes. The park then goes out to center, which is not the deepest part of the park. From center, the wall juts out and back toward right field, into a corner, an area known as "the triangle," which ends at 420 feet from the plate. That was the reason Lynn was so valuable. He covered a lot of ground and played the triangle very well. Left field is the most distinctive feature of Fenway and one of the most distinctive in all of sports. It is also the primary source of pitchers' pain in Fenway. The left-field wall is just a shade over thirty-seven feet high, and painted green, aptly called "the Green Monster."

The large wall is constructed of wooden railroad ties covered with tin and concrete. It houses a scoreboard and holes for TV cameras. Behind the scoreboard is a room in which operators walk around to post scores on the manual scoreboard. The wall separates left field from Lansdowne Street. Because the wall is only 310 feet from home (though it was posted 315 in 1975) it was built that high when the park was renovated after a fire in 1934 to prevent easy home runs. It succeeds in that regard, but allows a savvy hitter to bounce balls off of it for easy doubles, which instantly puts a man in scoring position.

How many great Boston Red Sox pitchers come to mind? The only pitchers with any real success in Fenway are pitchers who can keep the ball down low, which makes it difficult for batters to hit the ball in the air, either over the shallow right-field wall, deep into center field, or off the large left-field wall. The only other pitchers who have enjoyed success are power pitchers with a blazing fastball. Most power pitchers don't consistently throw the ball low; they like to throw some "high heat" to keep the batters salivating. Outside of Babe Ruth—before he left the mound—and Roger Clemens, there haven't been a lot of great Boston pitchers. Both Ruth and Clemens could pitch with power and keep the ball down low.

The 1975 World Series was slated to open in the AL park, so Cincinnati pitchers would get a quick taste of what it takes to pitch in Fenway. Don Gullett was the first to get a crack at it. He fit the profile of someone who could have success at Fenway. He had a good low fastball. He also had begun to develop a forkball or what later became known as a split-finger fastball. For this pitch the ball is gripped by the pitcher with fingers spread like a peace sign, without touching the seams. The ball is thrown like a fastball but has less rotation and dips dramatically just as it approaches the plate.[2] Gullet's opponent had mastered Fenway that season — Luis Tiant had been splendid.

The Reds seemed to have all the advantages going into the series. They were experienced and hungry. The bulk of the team had been through the close calls in the 1973 playoffs and the '72 World Series, and many had been in the '70 Series, as well. They had four solid starters in Gullett, Billingham, Nolan, and Norman. Their relief pitching was the best in the game. The Big Four all had big years. Morgan had been named MVP with a .327 average, seventeen home runs, ninety-four RBIs and sixty-seven stolen bases. Additionally Concepcion, with thirty-three stolen bases, and Griffey, hitting .305, had been solid. Most importantly, thanks to Sparky's pondering and Rose's reaction, the Reds had solved the third-base problem that had plagued them ever since Howsam had arrived.

Outside of Yaz, all but two of the Red Sox were new to the club since 1967. They were good but they were young and inexperienced. Beating the A's three straight in the playoffs had boosted their confidence but they were underdogs entering the series with Cincinnati. Boston was managed by Darrell Johnson, who had spent six years in the big leagues as a reserve catcher. He was a backup backstop for the Reds' 1961 pennant winner. After years in the Red Sox minor league system as a manager, he was finally given the senior ball club in 1974.

Game One's first pitch was thrown on Saturday, October 11, 1975, by Luis Tiant. Everyone talks about the Reds' offense and justifiably so; their entire infield plus Bench had gone to the All-Star Game but their defense also was there. In Game One both Concepcion and Geronimo cut down runners at the plate. The game was tied going into the bottom of the seventh inning when Tiant led off with a single. To add injury to insult, Yaz eventually singled him in with the game's first run and five more followed that inning. Gullett pitched well for Cincinnati but Tiant pitched even better for Boston.

A former Cleveland Indian, Tiant had a variety of windups he would use. In his most colorful one, he would rotate his body so that his face pointed to center and his back was to the batter. His eyes looked skyward and he would then pause, sharply rotate and fling the ball toward home. It not only was hard to pick the ball up coming out of his hand, because his arm came from so many angles, it was unnerving to the batter. "Does this guy even know where he is throwing it? Is it going to hit me?" It usually hit the catcher's mitt somewhere in the strike zone. Tiant shut the Reds down the rest of the way on a five-hitter. Boston won Game One, 6–0. Tiant loved to smoke cigars, the large fat kind, and he lit up a big stogy in the clubhouse to celebrate the victory. Back in Cincinnati, things seemed all too familiar in the World Series. Folks were wondering, "Close but no cigar again?"

The Reds felt considerable pressure to win Game Two. They didn't want to dig another hole for themselves as they had in 1970 and '72. They would face Bill Lee. In the world of wacky pitchers, Bill Lee was a certified nut case. How much was real and how much was show was anyone's guess, but Lee knew that the press was always looking for a story, especially around World Series time. Lee knew that the only way for an average pitcher to draw the media's attention was to be different. He was, and as a result he drew the press like hungry bears to honey. He was outspoken and known for his off-the-wall mutterings. That's how he earned his moniker "Spaceman." He was actually a pretty decent pitcher, good but not great. His 1975 record was 17–9, no small feat for pitching half his games at Fenway but he drew far more attention than his talent deserved.

Now Lee had a sore arm. He hadn't started a game in a month and hadn't won in nearly two months. However he was a ground-ball pitcher who could win at Fenway and he had also picked off eleven runners during the regular season. Reds scout Ray Shore was sure that the Red Sox would start Lee for the latter reason despite the injury. Anderson had learned to listen to Shore. Sparky thought the Reds had lost the '72 Series because he had neglected to follow Ray's scouting reports.[3] Meanwhile, Manager Darrell Johnson just hoped that Bill Lee could hold the Reds close.

The "Spaceman" went back into history to pull out one of his off-the-wall tricks. Rip Sewell had been a twenty-game winner for the Pirates in the 1940s. When he lost part of his left foot in a hunting accident, he developed a blooper pitch, which his teammates called the "eephus" pitch. Sewell would arc the ball up to twenty-five feet in the air; the pitch would then descend down across the strike zone and was very difficult to hit. An exception occurred when Sewell threw one to Ted Williams in the 1946 All-Star Game and Ted hit it into the right-field seats for a home run. However it was the only "eephus" pitch ever hit for a homer against Sewell. Lee had developed his own blooper pitch. It did not arc as high as Sewell's eephus pitch but it was definitely a lob. Lee called it a slow curve, or a "leephus." He used it on Tony Perez and struck him out in the second inning, making Perez look bad in the process.

Lee's opponent on the mound would be Jack Billingham. Though he had done poorly down the stretch, Billingham got the nod because he was a sinker-ball pitcher, which increased the chance for success in Fenway. The Reds played Game Two like the seasoned veterans they were. The Red Sox got one earned and one unearned run off Billingham before the stable of relief pitchers entered and shut them down the rest of the way. Trailing 2–1 in the ninth, Bench came to the plate. He took one look at how the Red Sox outfield was playing him and figured what the heck, I am going to try to hit the ball to the opposite field. He did and doubled to start the inning. With the double, Darrell Johnson pulled the Spaceman. Perez moved Bench to third on a grounder. Two batters later Concepcion atoned for an earlier error and got an infield hit to score Bench, tying the game.

On the bench Merv Rettenmund and Terry Crowley, both ex–American Leaguers, told Ken Griffey that Dick Drago, the Red Sox reliever, threw mostly fastballs. Griffey went to the plate looking for one. Third-base coach Alex Grammas flashed the steal sign and Concepcion stole second. Soon thereafter Griffey got the fastball he was looking for and knocked Concepcion home with a double for a 3–2 lead that held up for a victory. After the game Sparky said Jack Billingham had taught the Reds something that they would be able to use for the rest of the Series but Anderson wouldn't say what it was. Billingham didn't know either, so he went to Sparky to ask him. Upon learning what he had taught Anderson, Billingham was sworn to secrecy by Anderson as well.[4]

Speed (evidenced by infield hits, stolen bases, and doubles) had served the Reds well. It was a weapon Howsam had always valued. It was a weapon the Red Sox did not have in their arsenal. The Red Sox had stolen sixty-six bases all year, one less than Joe Morgan had done all by himself. After the Game Two victory in Boston, Sparky said, "We were lucky to get out of here with our lives."[5]

The series rotated to Cincinnati for Games Three through Five. The Reds were looking forward to returning home where they had been a phenomenal 64–17 on the year, setting a National League record for best winning percentage at home. The Reds started Gary Nolan in Game Three. After returning on that big day, May 3, he had notched a 15–9 record. The Reds watched as Nolan continued to develop into a crafty pitcher after arm trouble had robbed him of the amazing fastball he'd had as a teenager. It was a testament to Nolan that he had adjusted his style and persevered over an eighteen-month rehabilitation to stay in baseball.

His opponent on the mound was a strong right-hander, Rick Wise, an old nemesis of the Reds. While with Philadelphia in 1971, Wise had pitched a no-hitter against the Reds, hitting two home runs himself in the game. The following off-season the Phillies traded him to the St. Louis Cardinals for a lefty named Steve Carlton. Almost two years from the day after he'd no-hit them, Wise almost no-hit the Reds again, the no-hitter broken up by a Joe Morgan single in the ninth. Wise had led the Red Sox in victories in 1975 with nineteen.

There wouldn't be a no-hitter against the Reds this night. As in Game Two, the Red Sox jumped to a 1–0 lead, this time on a Fisk home run. Bench returned the favor in the fourth with a two-run shot and the Reds added three more runs in the fifth to take a 5–1 lead. Nolan then came out, complaining of a stiff neck, and the relief corps was uncustomarily shaky, as the Red Sox scored runs off four different relievers, sending the game into extra innings. After no home runs in the first two games, a World Series–tying record of six were hit in this game.

In the bottom of the tenth the most controversial play of the entire Series unfolded. Cesar Geronimo led off the inning with a single that rolled just past a diving Denny Doyle's outstretched glove into centerfield. Sparky Anderson sent Eddie Armbrister up to bat for reliever Rawly Eastwick. Armbrister was the last man thrown into the 1971 trade for his speed and potential bat. He had been a sparsely used back-up for the Reds for the past three seasons, with a little more than one hundred total at-bats. His assignment: drop a sacrifice bunt to move Geronimo into scoring position at second. It is a fundamental in baseball and practiced over and over again in spring training. Pitchers are well-versed in the drill, as it is a staple in their batting arsenal. Armbrister as a back-up outfielder, way at the end of the bench, was not well drilled in the procedure, having accomplished only one all season and two in his career. Armbrister made it exciting.

What exactly occurred depends on whom you ask. Fisk says the ball was a pop-up in front of the plate. Armbrister says the bunt went down, hit the plate and bounced up into the air. Unsure of what to do, Armbrister started to leave the batter's box and then paused. Fisk bounded up to field the ball. They collided. Fisk pushed Armbrister aside, grabbed the ball and fired to second base to get the speedy Geronimo. The ball sailed high off of Rick Burleson's glove and rolled into shallow right-center as Geronimo continued to third and Armbrister sprinted all the way around first to second base.

Fisk and the entire Red Sox team were livid. They claimed that when a runner interferes with a fielder it is an automatic out. Fisk argued that it should have been called a double play. The home plate umpire, Larry Barnett, who presided over the play, ruled it was simply a collision. According to Barnett, for interference to be called, a runner must intentionally interfere with a fielder. If the contact is unintentional, or incidental as they say in football, then it is simply a collision and play continues.

Probably too much is made of this play. As for Armbrister, he seemed to be merely a deer in the headlights. To suggest that he somehow thought it through to intentionally interfere with Fisk is absurd. The pictures are clear — he looked much more like a tourist from off the boat in the Bahamas (where he was from) than some scheming player trying to short-circuit the Red Sox. He was simply lost. Armbrister bumped into the catcher, the catcher bumped into the runner, and the umpire made a call, which was certainly reasonable. The call was much more reasonable than the one Ken Burkhart made with Bernie Carbo and Elrod Hendricks in 1970. This time the controversial play went the Reds' way. In fact the Burkhart-Carbo call provides a good barometer for the later World Series controversy. Baseball experts were unanimous in declaring Burkhart's call in the 1970 World Series incorrect. This time the

Barnett-Armbrister-Fisk play got mixed reviews from baseball experts, some siding with Barnett and some with Fisk. In that case one must concede that it was a reasonable judgment call by Barnett.

Back to the game, Darrell Johnson then brought in Roger Moret who walked Rose intentionally to load the bases in order to set up a possible force out at home with no one out. Moret was a lefty and due to face the left-handed Griffey so Anderson countered and brought in his best right-handed pinch hitter, Merv Rettenmund. That strategy backfired as Rettenmund struck out. Morgan then lined a single into left-center and the Reds had won Game Three. In the dugout the Red Sox could only think about Barnett's call, just as the Reds had fumed over Burkhart's five years earlier. They knew how the Red Sox felt.

With so much talk about the Barnett call, there was an overlooked dimension in Game Three. Again, speed was a primary weapon instrumental in the Cincinnati victory. The Reds stole three bases. Foster took off in the second inning and Fisk threw wildly to second base, allowing Foster to go to third. Perez, not normally a base-stealing threat, drew a walk in the fourth. When the first baseman played behind Perez, Anderson flashed a sign to Alex Grammas, who flashed the steal sign and Perez took off for second, making it successfully. Griffey got into the act in the fifth, stealing after his walk. Advanced scout Ray Shore had told the Reds that Fisk's arm was strong but that his accuracy was questionable. The throws on the Armbrister bunt and Foster steal confirmed the report. The Red Sox never made an attempt on Bench. The speed factor was definitely in Cincinnati's favor.

The momentum had turned Cincinnati's way. They had beaten the Red Sox in close contests in Games Two and Three. Now it was Boston who desperately did not want to get down three games to one, so Darrell Johnson sent Luis Tiant back to the mound. The Reds countered with Little Fredie Norman who had won ten of eleven decisions down the stretch. The five eight Norman was in the limelight. At the beginning of the Series, Anderson had announced that Norman would not be in the rotation but later changed his mind. This ran counter to his catcher's advice. Bench lobbied unsuccessfully to have Gullett work Game 4, so that the Reds could bring him back for Game 7 if necessary.

Norman would need his good screwball to shut down the Red Sox. Fortunately for Fredie, the Reds got off to a 2–0 lead when, for the first time in the Series, they scored first. However Tiant was getting better as the game progressed. It was a long way from Marianao, Cuba, where Luis Tiant was born.

Luis Tiant's father had been a great pitcher in Cuba. The younger Tiant signed a contract with the Mexican League in 1959. When Castro declared his communist affiliation in 1961, Luis Tiant's father advised him not to return to Cuba. The younger Tiant was heartbroken. Since Fidel Castro overthrew the Cuban government in 1959, many Cubans had fled the island ninety miles from Key West and had come to Miami. John F. Kennedy's mishandling of the Bay of Pigs invasion had caused hundreds of deaths and raised tensions even higher.

Thousands of Cubans were desperate to leave Castro's Cuba. Tiant's parents were among them. Luis Tiant had not seen them in fourteen years. Fellow Cuban Tony Perez could sympathize; Perez had only been allowed to see his father once, when he was very ill in 1973.[6] One wonders how many of Tiant's teammates and fans thought even twice about their ability to visit relatives.

Tiant's fine pitching in the Red Sox's victorious 1975 campaign had thrust him into the national spotlight and given new notice to the plight of his parents. Senators Edward Brooke (R-MA) and George McGovern (D-SD) took up his case, writing to Castro asking for Tiant's parents to be allowed to join their son in the United States. Diplomatic efforts through the Ford administration and Senate worked. Tiant's parents arrived in the United States in August and were in attendance when Tiant opened Game One.[7]

Buoyed by the presence of his parents, Tiant was shutting down the Reds again. In the fourth inning he even reached base on a single to center, his second hit of the Series. What made this even more remarkable was that Tiant had rarely batted in more than three seasons. In 1973, the American League had adopted the designated hitter (DH) rule. The fact that the DH was proposed by Oakland's Charley Finley speaks volumes. Television audiences like offense, so the thinking was that since most pitchers can't hit, why not fill the pitcher's spot in the batting order with someone who *can* hit, while allowing the pitcher to just pitch. To many baseball fans this was—and still is—ridiculous. At the time of the introduction of the DH, many shortstops couldn't hit either; they were defensive specialists. So why not replace them in the lineup with a better hitter and just allow them to play in the field?

Since the game had been played for more than one hundred years with the pitcher batting, it was decided that the World Series would be played the way the game was invented—all players would bat. When Tiant reached on the fourth-inning single, he took a very wide turn as he rounded first. He had walked in the third inning and nearly was hit on the base paths by the ball before he took another wide turn at second. Joe Garagiola chuckled from the booth after he got a hit in Game One, saying that the Red Sox ought to give him "a jacket and a road map." He needed a map. When scoring in Game One he missed home plate and had to go back to touch it. He didn't seem to know where he was on the base paths. But when he was on the mound, coming from every conceivable angle, he, and not the batters, knew exactly where he was. When it was over he had a complete game 5–4 victory and the Series was tied, two games all.

One of the keys to the Game Four win was the fact that Tiant was able to hold runners close. It was something he worked hard at and had the umpires watching closely, since he had been called for a balk in Game One. The Reds did not steal a base. Furthermore, Griffey tried unsuccessfully to stretch a double into a triple in the first inning, costing the Reds a run.

The most ironic point of the night was when Geronimo singled late in the game again. In a moment of déjà vu, Eddie Armbrister was sent to pinch hit and was assigned to lay down a sacrifice bunt. This time there was no hitch from either Armbrister or Fisk, and Armbrister was thrown out at first. After Rose walked, Griffey smashed a deep ball to center field that Freddie Lynn caught over his shoulder to save two runs. It was redemption for Lynn, who was unable to gather in a blast by Rose in Game Three. His catch this time saved the game.

The Reds' bullpen, as wonderful as it was, had been stretched to its limit. They had logged nineteen innings in the first four games and twelve innings in the last two days alone. Entering Game Five in Cincinnati, Anderson announced that his starter Don Gullett needed to go deep into the game to give his bullpen a break. If he didn't, the Reds would be in trouble. Johnson meanwhile elected to go with a fresh pitcher, thirteen-game winner Reggie Cleveland.

The Reds were facing a new phenomenon in the series, a plethora of night games. All their Series games in 1970 had been in the afternoons. The majority of the 1972 World Series had also been played in the afternoon, with all four weekend games plus a Friday game that had kicked off just after lunch. Two of the weekday games in Oakland had been played during prime time for East Coast watchers, late afternoon in Oakland. Essentially the Reds had not played a World Series game at night. Neither had Boston, for that matter, who hadn't been in the Series since 1967, four years before Bowie Kuhn announced weekday night games would be played.

Over the last two months of the season, Tony Perez had been the Reds' hottest slugger. As a result he was batting clean-up in place of Bench, the spot reserved for a team's best power-hitting threat. Perez had been dismal against the Orioles in 1970, hitting .085 in the five-game Series. He had come back like a man on a mission in the 1972 series, leading the Reds with a .435 average. But in this Series, in games one through four, he had returned to his "Oriole Series" ways, batting 0-for-15. Anderson did what any good skipper would do and made an adjustment. Bench was returned to clean-up, while Perez dropped to fifth in the order. It could be coincidence but the move got results. Perez belted home runs in consecutive at-bats in the fourth and sixth innings, driving in four runs. The Reds also got the speed game going again; Morgan and Concepcion swiped bases.

Don Gullett managed to do just what Sparky wished. He went almost a complete game and he had good heat on his fastball. Eastwick came on with two out in the ninth to close it. The Reds fans, very knowledgeable about the game but also reserved, saving their enthusiasm for the appropriate moments, broke into a rare chant in the bottom of the ninth. "Reds in Six! Reds in Six! Reds in Six!" They had no idea of what the sixth game would bring.

17

THE GREATEST GAME EVER PLAYED
October 1975

The Reds were chomping at the bit to get back to Boston to finish off the series. They had won big in Game Five and if Boston hadn't had Luis Tiant, the Reds felt the Series would have been over already. Sparky Anderson was confident; he had Jack Billingham who had pitched decently in Game Two ready to go on five days of rest. Darrell Johnson was not shaken. He had Billingham's opponent, Bill Lee, ready to go with five days of rest as well.

What the teams found in Boston was an old-fashioned New England downpour. Fenway Park was drenched and Saturday's game was canceled. Ditto Sunday's game. Having packed lightly for the weekend trip, the Reds players and their wives began doing laundry in the hotel room sinks and calling back to relatives asking them to stay with their kids back in Cincinnati a while longer. Meanwhile many of the Red Sox battled the flu, having caught it during the cold, rainy Game Two the previous Sunday.[1] The entire weekend series was rained out and with it the managers' tactics.

Johnson had the most difficult dilemma. "Do I go with Luis Tiant, who has proven that he can beat the Reds and get myself to Game Seven where I can take my chances with another pitcher, or do I hold out Tiant and give him another day to get ready for the final game?" At this point Tiant had four days of rest. (In baseball the last day the pitcher pitched and the current day the pitcher is pitching are not counted in the rest total; so Tiant more accurately had five days of rest, counting hours strictly.) Another factor in the decision was that Tiant had shut the Reds down when he was fresh in Game One. He didn't exactly do that in Game Four. The Reds had scored four runs and were threatening again in the ninth when Tiant finished the job. He had pitched eighteen innings in a four-day span and thrown 163 pitches in getting the victory in Game Four. Managers are paid to weigh the options and make the best decision possible but it is an uncertain science.

Darrell Johnson finally decided that getting to the seventh game was the top priority and the best man to get him there was Tiant. When informed about Johnson's decision, the Spaceman went nuts. Never one to hold back his thoughts or feelings, Lee pronounced that Johnson had been falling out of the tree all year long and landing on his feet.[2] Lee wasn't complimenting Johnson's balance. It's striking that Lee, with his team at the pinnacle of his profession, would publicly embarrass his leader with such a remark. It certainly didn't increase the Red Sox's chances of winning. A similar remark made by a Reds player would likely have led to a fine, a suspension or just plain bench time.

Anderson's dilemma was not as drastic; he had to choose between Jack Billingham and Gary Nolan. After the Saturday rainout, it was still a non-issue, Jack Billingham would start Game Six. When the Sunday rainout occurred, Sparky changed his mind. Gary Nolan would start Game Six. Billingham was angry and many of the Reds were perplexed. Hadn't Billingham taught Sparky and the Reds something that they would use the rest of the Series in Game Two? Yet Sparky was pulling the sinkerball-pitching Billingham for Nolan, a pitcher known to give up a lot of fly balls, which was dangerous at Fenway. Additionally, Gary Nolan had pitched in five previous World Series games and had won exactly none of them. It was one of Sparky's most perplexing tactical decisions of his entire tenure with the Reds.

The pitchers' reactions to their managers' decisions provide a striking contrast into the fabric of each team. Both were angry and were very clear about that with the press. When Sparky called Billingham and Nolan into his office to break the news to them, Billingham made it very clear that he disagreed with the decision and was angry about it. When asked about it later in the press, Billingham again said he was upset and disagreed with the decision. Once he made that clear, he also added that he would now support Sparky, move on, and be ready to pitch when called upon.[3] Meanwhile, Bill Lee was angry and said his manager had fallen out of a tree. Nine years of Howsam and six seasons of Sparky's discipline had once again paid off for the Reds. It also was a credit to Jack Billingham's character that he conducted himself as a professional even after a questionable decision that affected him personally, choosing the good of the team over his personal ego.

Bowie Kuhn, the commissioner of baseball, also had a big dilemma. The World Series was supposed to end on a weekend. For several years the series had followed a Saturday, Sunday, Tuesday–Thursday, Saturday, Sunday schedule. This allowed two weekends of television coverage if the Series went more than five games, always a bonus. Monday and Friday were travel days. It also avoided a confrontation Kuhn didn't really want to have. NBC had long been the network of both the National and American Leagues. A rival network, ABC, aired *Monday Night Football* in the fall. On that Monday in 1975, O.J. Simpson and his Buffalo Bills were scheduled to play the New York Giants, promising a big TV audience. So Kuhn had to decide to play the game either in the afternoon when it would be warmer, which is what traditional fans wanted, or to play at night for the additional TV network revenue. Dollars won again, and an evening telecast was selected.

Kuhn was saved the tension of competing against *Monday Night Football* when weather again caused a postponement of Game Six. It was now set for Tuesday and again Kuhn selected the TV dollars, scheduling the game at night. With another twenty-four-hour slip, Anderson now had the chance to go with Don Gullett, who now had four days rest, his normal allotment. It was a chance to finish off the Series with his best pitcher. He decided to stay with Gary Nolan, who now had five days of rest. The decision again was perplexing. When Anderson publicly announced the Nolan decision, some of the Reds were disappointed and privately felt he was playing for a seven-game Series.

Nolan had only gone four innings the previous Tuesday but had pitched well until he left. Sparky had a back-up plan. If things did not go well with Nolan, he would immediately bring in Jack Billingham. Billingham had come out of the bullpen before, Nolan had not. He felt that Billingham could warm up quickly. Anderson reasoned that if he did not start Nolan he would not be able to use him at all.[4] Essentially, Sparky felt he had two starters ready for the game. Meanwhile, the postponement further reinforced Johnson's view that Tiant was the man for the job in Game 6, as he now had five days of rest.

"El Tiante," as he was now being referred to by the NBC crew, had the opportunity to psych out the Reds. He had beaten them two times with his flair and pinpoint control of a variety of pitches coming from all different directions. His Fu Manchu mustache and husky, large-waisted build added to his mystique but the Reds were not going to be intimidated. They knew that they had gotten to Tiant in Game Four and were ready to do further damage this time.

The decision to start Gary Nolan quickly seemed to be a poor one. In the first inning the sensational rookie, Freddie Lynn, hit a three-run shot off of Nolan driving in Yaz and Fisk. Nolan never got past the second inning, as he was lifted for a pinch hitter in the top of the third.

As the game proceeded into the fourth inning, Reds fans were beginning to think about Game Seven. Only some great pitching from Jack Billingham, the would-be starter of Game Six, kept matters from getting worse. After three days of rain delays, plus the travel day, the Reds had every pitcher available and it looked as though Anderson would use them all. In the end he used eight. Norman started the third and gave up a double to Doyle and eventually walked Fisk intentionally with two outs. He then unintentionally walked Lynn to load the bases. The Reds were in danger of being down by six runs or more. That's where Billingham came in. Facing Rico Petrocelli, who had hit as many as forty home runs in a season, Billingham struck him out. Billingham kept the Red Sox off the scoreboard the next inning using his sinkerball to get harmless ground balls after allowing runners to second and third, leaving Anderson's decision not to start him in question.

Meanwhile, El Tiante was spinning his magic again. The Reds barely threatened through four innings but finally started rolling in the fifth. An unknown before the series, Eddie Armbrister was sent to pinch hit for Billingham and drew a walk. Pete Rose then singled and Ken Griffey came to the plate and drove a ball to deep left-center. Freddie Lynn gave chase and Lynn, who had been shaded toward right, had a long way to go after it. He and the ball arrived at the wall, Lynn slamming into the concrete and the ball ricocheting off and rolling back across the outfield as Lynn lay motionless on the ground. Griffey eased into third, his speed easily securing a triple. After two and a half games, Griffey was the first man from either team to hit a ball off the Green Monster.

Lynn would lie on the field for five minutes. Fenway was an old park and its walls were not protected by pads. The Green Monster was covered by tin and concrete. Dazed and sore, Lynn returned to his feet and his position, ready for further battle after his gallant effort. After Morgan popped out, Bench, who had remained in the clean-up spot even after Perez's Game Five heroics, singled off the Green Monster to bring Griffey home. It was a whole new ball game, tied 3–3.

After Billingham left, the Reds began a parade of relievers, substituted for by pinch hitters. First out of the bullpen was the Hawk. Carroll was followed by Pedro Borbon. Both shut down the Red Sox. Meanwhile the Reds felt they were getting to Tiant with the big fifth inning but Tiant regained control in the sixth, keeping the Reds scoreless while giving up two hits. The Reds got three hits in the seventh as the big man on the mound further tired. Griffey and Morgan singled and the Reds' new left fielder of five months, George Foster, doubled them in, with Lynn again giving chase. The Red Sox were on the ropes.

In the eighth, down 5–3 the Red Sox sent Tiant back out to the mound and Geronimo greeted him by sending a pitch out of the park. Johnson came out to get his warrior; Tiant had just thrown too many pitches. The Red Sox were no longer on the ropes, they were getting a standing eight count. The Reds had knocked out their best pitcher and led by three runs with six outs remaining. They had the best bullpen in baseball and the Gold Dust Twins hadn't even been used. The World Series title was in the Reds' grasp, as El Tiante went to the dugout.

Anderson was so confident of victory that he left Pedro Borbon in the game to bat for himself. After pitching two scoreless innings and possessing a three-run lead, Sparky wanted to keep Borbon in the game. Tiant's replacement, Roger Moret, retired Borbon, Rose and Griffey to end the inning.

No one dreamed that the game was just beginning. Lynn singled to begin the bottom of the eighth. Borbon then walked Petrocelli. Anderson immediately emerged from the dugout. He called for closer Rawly Eastwick, who immediately struck out Dwight Evans. He then got Burleson to line out to Foster. The Reds were now four outs away from the title. Moret was due up, but Johnson wisely called him back to the dugout. Bernie Carbo, the Reds' former Rookie of the Year, emerged from the dugout.

Though he was still struggling deep inside and slowly being sucked down the drain of alcoholism and drug abuse, Carbo was desperate to prove his old team wrong. As a left-handed batter, he knew he wouldn't be facing Eastwick, a right-hander. Sparky played the odds and with southpaw Will McEnaney warming up in the bullpen, Carbo was mentally preparing for McEnaney. Anderson was going through his own internal struggle on the bench. He almost always played the percentages, which called for him to pull Eastwick for McEnaney. But he really liked Eastwick; he had become his go-to guy. His mind went one way and then another. For some reason his feet never went up the dugout steps. Carbo was shocked. Eastwick began pitching. Even as Eastwick began throwing strikes and balls, Anderson's mind was saying, "Maybe I should go get him." Still his feet did not move. On a 2–2 count, Carbo swung and the ball arched high toward center and over the wall. The game was tied. Anderson began to kick himself. The expression on Carbo's face as he rounded third on his home-run trot reflected temporary peace, relief, and satisfaction at what he had done.

This wasn't the first time Carbo had exacted some revenge on his old teammates. He had hit a pinch hit homer in Game 3.[5] He wasn't exactly happy with his current team, feeling he should have gotten some playing time in the outfield during the Series, with Rice being down. He got the playing time now, being inserted into left after the pinch hit home run, with Yaz going to first and Cecil Cooper leaving the game.

Meanwhile in the press box they began to tear up the MVP ballots. In anticipation of the Reds impending victory, Rawly Eastwick, with two wins and one save to this point in the Series, had been voted the series MVP. Balloting was tabled for now; there was a game to watch.[6] Eastwick retired Cooper to end the inning, but the damage was done.

The Reds were retired in order in the top of the ninth by Dick Drago. Now the momentum had swung to the Red Sox. They went from a standing eight count to counterpunching toe to toe with the Reds, and knocking them back on their heels. In the bottom of the ninth, Eastwick returned and immediately was greeted by a Denny Doyle single. Yaz singled to right, moving Doyle to third. This time Anderson's feet took him up the dugout steps. McEnaney came in for Eastwick and walked Fisk intentionally to enable a force at home. Bases were loaded with no outs. Freddie Lynn, who had already done great damage with his bat and glove, strode to the plate. The Red Sox needed only a sacrifice fly for the win. Lynn obliged. He lifted a fly to left toward Foster, drifting toward the left-field line and stands, not too deep but deep enough. Foster caught the ball for out number one. With third base coach Don Zimmer yelling "No! No! No!" Denny Doyle tagged and broke for home anyway. Foster's throw was on a rope and one hopped to Bench, who dove to get the head-first-sliding Doyle. Doyle was out, tagged on the shoulder, double play. The air left the Fenway crowd as Petrocelli then grounded out to third.

Denny Doyle's disregard for his coach had cost Boston dearly, just as Carbo breaking for home in 1970 had cost the Reds dearly. Sometimes professionals feel they don't need to listen to a coach. Sometimes they are wrong. We never get to the place where we are above coaching.

Now the Reds were reinvigorated. Concepcion singled to center and stole second to get into scoring position with one out in the tenth. Geronimo left him there with a strikeout for out number two. Anderson now had his last reliever, McEnaney, due up to bat with a runner in scoring position and two outs. He felt this was his moment. His best-hitting non-starter was sitting on the bench. Danny Driessen was told to grab a bat. It was a perfect set up, Driessen a lefty to face Dick Drago a righty. It could force Johnson to pull the effective Drago and increase the Reds' chances of winning. Anderson was again playing the percentages. Surprisingly, Johnson did not reciprocate and left Drago out to pitch. Driessen failed to deliver, lofting a fly ball to Carbo in left.

The Reds now had to return to starting pitchers. Pat Darcy, the rookie the Reds had gotten for Denis Menke, was sent to the mound as the Reds' eighth pitcher of the night. Darcy was normally a starting pitcher, the Reds' fifth, but during the postseason, they had stuck to their top four starters, as most clubs do. The Reds' deep bullpen, the best in the game and arguably among the best in the history of the game, was worn thin. Don Gullett had offered a reprieve with his strong outing in Game Five, but by the twelfth inning Carroll, Borbon, Eastwick and McEnaney had all been used. With the game going late it was a tactical move by Sparky to put Darcy in. As a starting pitcher who was well rested, he could potentially go nine innings if needed. At this point the Reds needed someone to go indefinitely; they had only one available pitcher left, Clay Kirby. The Red Sox were in slightly better shape. Dick Drago was on the mound but they had already used Moret since El Tiante had departed in the eighth. It was a war of attrition. Like a heavyweight title fight, it looked like this one might go fifteen rounds or more.

Darcy got the job done, retiring the Red Sox in order in the tenth. He finished the inning by striking out Carbo, no small feat at this point. Meanwhile, Carlton Fisk was slowly drifting into a kind of never-never land. Fatigued from days of competition and the mental stress of getting up all day for a game only to come down for another rain delay at night, his body was getting too tired for his mind to think. It was late and dark and cold as he trotted off the field in tenth inning. Pete Rose went past with all the enthusiasm of a twelve-year-old boy at the Little League World Series. "This is some kind of game isn't it?" and off he skipped. The comment was a jolt to Fisk's system. It indeed was a great game. Fisk was reinvigorated by Rose's comment and boyish enthusiasm.

Drago came back out for the eleventh. He had now gone three innings himself. He hit Rose to start the inning. Griffey tried to bunt him over but Fisk made a fine play by fielding the bunt and throwing to second to get Rose. Griffey was now at first with one out. The NL MVP and Reds' triple threat, Joe Morgan, came to the plate. Morgan was simply spectacular in every respect in 1975. Power, speed, defense — he had it all. Bench and Perez were due up after him. The Reds had the Red Sox on the ropes again.

Morgan smashed a ball toward what is known as "Williamsburg" at Fenway Park. It is an area where the right-field bullpens were added in 1940, which moved the right-field wall in twenty-three feet and aided Ted Williams's home run totals, thus "Williamsburg." The ball was sailing toward the lowest part of the wall, near where the bullpen meets the stands. It was going to be a double or a home run, and Griffey wasn't taking any chances on the home run. He was intent on scoring on the double. Like a bolt of light, Dwight Evans came out of nowhere in the New England night to catch Morgan's drive just as it was to clear the wall. He turned and fired a bullet back to the infield to double up Griffey, who had zero chance of returning safely. He was well past second, frozen now in his tracks. Evans had saved the series. It was the first notice to the baseball world of his defensive prowess. It would be recognized with eight Gold Gloves over his career. Boston was off the ropes again, regaining the momentum.

But Darcy again retired the Red Sox in order, including Rick Miller who pinch hit for Drago. Rick Wise, the Reds no-hit nemesis, took the mound for the twelfth and the Reds immediately jumped on him. After Bench popped out, Perez and Foster singled to put men at first and second with one out. Concepcion had singled in the tenth and sparkled in the field. He was ready to strike again. Instead he lofted a fly that Evans easily gathered in. That left Geronimo, who had homered in the eighth. He watched a called strike three go by with men in scoring position to end the inning.

Darcy returned for the bottom of the twelfth. Bench called the signals from behind home. Darcy's first pitch was high and inside for ball one. Bench dropped the sign for a sinker and set up outside. Darcy did the wind-up and the pitch. The ball sailed slightly and headed down for the inside part of the plate. Carlton Fisk's bat left its position above his right shoulder.

The crack of the bat resulted in a massive roar that shook NBC cameraman Lou Gerard whose job was to follow the flight of a batted ball with his camera from inside the Green Monster in left. Gerard missed — distracted by a huge rat — but through his camera lens he picked up Fisk, now out of the batter's box and slightly up the first-base line, waving and hopping and motioning frantically, almost begging the ball to go right; he waved as if trying to push an object away.

The ball reached its apex and began to descend downward near the left-field line. It was still so high that it was unclear whether it was a long foul ball or would clear the top of the Green Monster in fair territory. It would be a matter of inches either way. In the end it did neither: it hit high on the foul pole atop the left side of the Green Monster, an automatic home run, game over.

The television shots of the ball actually hitting the foul pole are grainy and difficult to see. It was a dark night in New England. You can barely make out the ball hitting the pole in the grainy films. But the enduring image captured would be that of Fisk "waving the ball fair." Baseball fans around the country would have never seen that lasting image of Fisk waving frantically in that greatest of all Series games had Lou Gerard not seen the biggest rat of his life.

The Red Sox and the fans in Fenway, in Boston and across New England were delirious. They had snatched victory from the jaws of defeat thanks to a troubled outfielder settling a score with his old team and a catcher who personified all that is New England.

The shame of it all was that so many kids missed it. Four years earlier, Bowie Kuhn had said that he was moving weekday games to night so "kids in school can see the whole thing if they want to." But conscientious parents had their children in bed hours before this game ended, at least in the eastern time zone on a school night. The World Series had once been an event enjoyed by children during and after school. Now it was not seen by many of them. Baseball was damaging its pipeline and future fans, all for the TV dollar.

A familiar sick feeling took root deep in the pit of Reds' fans' stomachs. "Not again," they thought. Another gallant effort and close call was almost too much to fathom. It would almost have been better to have not come at all. It would have been easier on the mind. They had this game and the Series in their grasp and it had gotten away. Perhaps it was their fate to always finish second: the "Almost Big Red Machine." Maybe they were still not quite there. Maybe there was still a missing piece. Maybe it was at the top.

On the Boston side, fans were thinking that perhaps they would finally break the curse of the Bambino and win a World Series. Babe Ruth had been sold by the Boston Red Sox to the New York Yankees after the 1919 season. A prodigious talent on both the mound and at bat for the Red Sox, he had led them to the World Series title in 1918. Legend has it that the Babe, also known as the Bambino, had pronounced a curse on the Red Sox for the trade and had doomed the Red Sox to futility in all future Fall Classics. The curse of the Bambino had never been broken by the greatest of all Red Sox and one of the game's top players, Ted Williams, though he had tried for nineteen seasons. Yaz had been on the brink of breaking the curse in 1967, only to fall one game short. Perhaps this was the year. It seemed the perfect storybook ending: the underdog Red Sox turn the trick against the heavily favored Big Red Machine, who are destined to fall just short again.

It would come down to Game Seven, as it had for the Reds in 1972 and the Red Sox in '67, on Wednesday, October 22, 1975. The Red Sox were riding high. After his very adamant protest about Johnson's Game Six decision, the Spaceman had his chance to go back to the mound.

The Reds were a bit dejected, discouraged, and wondering. However, one encouraging note for them was that Don Gullett would be on the mound.

Johnny Bench would prefer no other. Gullett had been superb in Game Five. Fisk intimated that Gullett's heat had almost been unhittable. Due to the New England monsoons, Gullett was pitching on five days rest. He had the chance to be really sharp. The only question was his stamina. He had missed two months of the season with a broken thumb and he had already pitched three games in the postseason. Could his body hold up to the strain?

Anderson again made a slight adjustment to his batting order. With the lefty Bill Lee on the mound, Sparky decided to drop Griffey from the two hole down to the seven hole, hitting just before Geronimo. It was the lineup he had been using the last half of the season. Griffey would bat second against righties and seventh against lefties. This put Bench, Perez, and Foster at three, four and five.

Johnson made a few minor adjustments himself. He inserted series hero Bernie Carbo into left and had him lead off, even though Gullett was a lefty and Carbo batted from the left side. He sat the young Cecil Cooper and put Yaz at first. The strategy looked good as Carbo doubled to left to start the game. He was now 4-for-5 in the series with two home runs and four RBIs. Gullett settled down, however, and retired the next three batters, stranding Carbo.

The Reds meanwhile were intent on using their speed. Foster singled to left in the second inning but was thrown out trying to stretch it into a double, gunned down by Carbo, who had always been knocked for his defense. Carbo continued to make his presence felt in the bottom of the third. After the Spaceman struck out, Carbo got aboard with a walk and then scored the game's first run on singles by Doyle and Yaz. Gullett intentionally walked the previous night's hero Fisk to prevent further heroics, loading the bases. The strategy seemed to work, as Lynn struck out, but then Gullett began slitting his own wrists. He walked Petrocelli to score Doyle and then did a repeat with Evans, scoring Yaz. He finally put the razor away by striking out Rick Burleson. The Reds were down again, 3–0.

Joe Morgan tried to get the Reds jump-started in the fourth inning with a bunt single and a steal. Even though the Red Sox expected him to go, they couldn't stop him, but Perez and Foster stranded him at second.

Through the fifth the Spaceman was pitching a five-hit shutout. Sparky Anderson pulled Don Gullett for pinch hitter Merv Rettenmund, who grounded into a double play. Stomachs in Cincinnati were churning. Jack Billingham replaced Gullett and got into and out of a bases-loaded jam in the bottom of the fifth without allowing any runs.

The Red Sox were nine outs away from the title. Into the sixth inning they were seven outs away with Bench standing at second. The inning would have been over already, if it hadn't been for a hustling Rose. With Pete Rose at first, Bench hit a tailor-made double-play ball to Burleson at short; he flipped to Denny Doyle at second. Rose came barreling into second base — high, hard and clean. With his high slide, Rose took out Doyle's feet as he threw the ball toward first. The ball went ten feet over Yaz's glove and into the Reds dugout, advancing Bench to second. Hustle kept the inning alive.

Tony Perez strode into the box. On the second pitch Lee again uncorked a leephus. There is an expression in sports, "going to the well one too many times." Lee had just done it. After seeing the pitch in Game Two, and in the second inning of this game, Perez was waiting for it and simply hammered it to deep left, over the Green Monster and the net above it, as a whistle of admiration and disbelief emanated from the NBC booth. It was 3–2 and the Reds had life again. Why Lee thought he could embarrass a six-time All-Star twice with the same gimmick can only be understood by someone from outer space. It was sweet revenge for the thirty-four-year-old Cuban.

Billingham held the Red Sox at bay in the sixth. Among his victims was Bernie Carbo, finally retired to a groundout. Darrell Johnson then replaced him in left field for defense; defense was still his Achilles heel. Bernie Carbo was finally unable to do further damage to his old machine.

Ken Griffey walked in the Reds' seventh. While pitching to Griffey, Bill Lee popped a blister on his left thumb. Darrell Johnson had to replace the Spaceman and called for the lefty Roger Moret, who had been sensational all Series long. The suddenly omnipresent Eddie Armbrister was sent to bat for Billingham. Griffey took a chance and stole second with two outs. He was in scoring position. Armbrister again drew a walk. Rose then belted a single up the middle to the charging Freddie Lynn. He scooped the ball and threw home, trying to get the flying Griffey, but the throw didn't arrive in time and the game was tied 3–3. Morgan then walked to load the bases and the Reds had a chance to blow the game wide open. The Red Sox brought in Jim Willoughby, who got Bench to pop up toward the stands. Fisk reached into the box seats to grab it for out number three.

The Hawk shut down the Red Sox one, two, three in the bottom of the seventh and then Jim Willoughby returned the favor for Boston in the top of the eighth. Carroll again faced the minimum three batters in the bottom half of the eighth. The game was 3–3, entering the ninth.

Rookie pitcher Jim Burton was sent out for the ninth for the Red Sox. Sparky Anderson's decision to slide Ken Griffey to the seven hole turned out to be a good move. He walked to open the inning. Geronimo moved him over to second with a bunt. He was in scoring position again. Driessen pinch hit for Carroll and grounded to Doyle at second base for an out but Griffey was able to advance to third. He was standing ninety feet from home with two outs and Pete Rose at the plate. Rose bore down; he had made the last out for the Reds against the A's three years prior and didn't want to repeat that mistake again. It was just like his first at-bat twelve and a half years earlier, as he watched every Burton pitch into the mitt. Eventually he watched four balls go past and took first.

Joe Morgan now came to bat. "Little Joe" had an odd habit he had picked up in Houston years earlier. It was actually courtesy of the manager he hadn't seen eye to eye with, Harry Walker. Morgan had a tendency while batting to keep his back arm (in his case the left arm) too close to his body while in his batting stance. Walker had tried and tried to break him of that bad habit. Finally, in disgust, Walker suggested that Morgan flap his back arm like a one-winged chicken and slap the elbow against the rib cage to remind himself to keep the elbow and arm away from the body. Except for a brief span a season or two after arriving with the Reds, it had worked. The one exception was a slump Morgan went through. Upon reflection he realized that even after he had done his by now habitual flapping, the arm was returning too close to the body. As a result, the flapping had ceased to work. After rectifying the problem, the slump ended.

With Burton on the mound, Morgan began flapping in the batter's box. The Reds in the dugout were yelling encouragement; the fans were yelling for a strikeout. Burton threw three pitches. Then on the 1–2 count the lefty threw a slider, a dart moving down and toward the outside of the plate. Good pitchers get good hitters out by pitching in this location and Burton had the ball on the spot. Morgan swung, trying to stay alive with a foul or get it into fair play to advance Griffey. He made contact off the end of the bat and the ball was lofted softly into the shallow center-field grass about ten feet in front of a charging Freddie Lynn. Griffey took off with the crack of the bat and made his way toward home. He didn't even draw a throw. The Reds had the lead for the first time all night.

Now it was up to the strength of the pitching staff, the relief pitchers. Sparky sent one of the Gold Dust Twins, Will McEnaney, out to face the three left-handers due up for the Red Sox in the bottom of the ninth. Bernie Carbo would have been due to lead off the ninth. The Reds were relieved that he had been replaced. Juan Benitez, who had replaced Carbo, flew to Griffey in right. Then Bob Montgomery pinch-hit for Doyle and grounded to Concepcion. The Reds were one out away as Yaz strode to the plate.

Carl Yastrzemski had experienced some big at-bats in his life. He had hit a game-winning home run on the final weekend of the regular reason to propel the Red Sox into the 1967 World Series and then homered three times against the St. Louis Cardinals in that series. He was hitting better than .310 in this series, after hitting .400 in the '67 Classic. Ray Shore's scouting report said that if the Red Sox could have anyone up to tie the game, they would choose Yaz.[7]

The 23-year-old McEnaney had a good sinker and he planned to use it. Yastrzemski took a mighty cut and lofted the ball to center. Cesar Geronimo gathered underneath it. Nine years of Howsam's work, six years of Sparky Anderson's, a lifetime of practice by the players, and thirty-five years of fans' expectations gathered as the ball descended. Geronimo closed the mitt—and the Series. McEnaney bounded and jumped into Johnny Bench's arms, utter ecstasy bursting from every nerve ending in his face. His countenance mirrored the emotion of every Big Red Machine fan across the country. The Cincinnati Reds were the champions of the world.

The Reds celebrated in a relatively quiet Fenway Park. Red Sox fans who had waited for sixty-seven years would have to wait at least another year. But the Red Sox fans had much to be pleased about. The next day the headlines read, "Reds win, but Red Sox don't lose." It was very apropos. It had been a valiantly contested contest. Five games had been decided by one run. In seven games the total score was 30–29, Red Sox favor. Both teams had played unbelievable defense, with dazzling catches by the Red Sox and runners cut down at home by the Reds. Hitting had been timely on both sides. World Series television ratings and interest in the game in general had been on the wane for more than a decade but this series rejuvenated American interest in baseball. The sheer drama had fans on the edge of their seats like a movie thriller. The ups and downs for each team were like an emotional roller coaster. The drama left fans drained but satisfied. As *Sports Illustrated* said, it was "a Series to shout about."

What was that thing that Jack Billingham had taught the Reds in Game Two that they would be able to use the rest of the series? A day or so after the series, Sparky Anderson finally shared it with the press. Jack Billingham had shown the Reds that Boston hitters did not hit breaking balls well. It doesn't sound earth shattering but it affected Sparky's decisions the rest of the series. It was something the Reds had been told about but didn't believe. Reds' scouts Ray Shore and Rex Bowen had been tracking the Red Sox for the last twenty days of the season. What they saw convinced them that the Red Sox were not good at hitting breaking balls. As a result they suggested that Reds pitchers throw a steady diet of curveballs, change-ups, screwballs, and sinkerballs. Don Gullett was a fastball pitcher and that is what he used in Game One. When Billingham used his sinker and other breaking-ball pitches in Game Two to stymie the Red Sox, Sparky finally believed the scouting reports. Seeing was believing. This helps explain somewhat the choice of Gary Nolan in Game Six. Nolan had been a good breaking-ball pitcher but his World Series record and history of giving up fly balls still makes one wonder about his selection. Meanwhile Billingham had already been proven effective with his sinker in Game Two and seemed to be the logical choice for Game Six. It also explains the decision to hold Gullett out until Game Seven. Gullett was a power pitcher; his breaking ball was not his strength.[8] As the Reds had learned, you must play to your strengths.

Why had the Reds finally been able to get over the hump? There are probably three major reasons. One was that for the first time since the Big Red Machine went to the World Series, their starting pitching was as good as the opponent's starters, or maybe just a tad inferior, considering Tiant. Maturity was another big factor. The Reds had been in the bright lights on two other occasions. It is probably what allowed them to come back when a lesser team would have quit. In all four of the Reds victories they had come from behind. Speed also made a difference. Ken Griffey's speed allowed him to move to third on Driessen's grounder in the ninth inning of Game Seven without being challenged. Over the course of the entire Series, both teams had two runners thrown out stealing, but Cincinnati had nine steals for the series, while Boston had zero, a decided advantage in the Reds favor.

In the end though, the win was probably due to small things. The little things seemed to make a difference all along the way: the variety of Tiant's motions and then his fatigue; Armbrister's bump on the way to first; Rose's comment, lifting Fisk's spirits and game; two blooper pitches from Bill Lee with two drastically different results. The final little thing was Joe Morgan's ability to hit an excellent pitch by Jim Burton to drive in Ken Griffey with the Series-winning run. One month from being voted the National League's MVP, Joe Morgan was a man on top of his game. After the contest he shared, "A couple of years ago, I would have struck out on that pitch," showing that even the very best strive to improve their game in order to reach greater levels of excellence.[9] Morgan could have rested on his laurels as one of the best second baseman in the game but instead he chose to continue to improve even after reaching the top.

Finally, a passing comment between Sparky Anderson and Pete Rose five months and nineteen days prior seemed to make all the difference in the world. Third base had been a problem for Howsam for all nine of his seasons in Cincinnati. Perez, Menke, Driessen and a host of others were not the solution. The solution was within the organization the whole time, it just hadn't been discovered. Sometimes we don't see the solution to our problem within our own organization. We get too busy looking for it elsewhere.

Furthermore, the man who was the solution didn't see it himself. Pete Rose would do practically anything he could to make his team successful. He knew third base was a problem but he didn't realize that he was the solution. It wasn't his lack of interest in the club that caused his blindness. He just didn't realize that he, more than anyone else on the team, possessed what the position required. Someone had to point it out to him. Better put, they had to suggest it to him and encourage him to try it out.

Sparky Anderson didn't see the solution for a long time either. What gave him the sudden insight? Years of studying the problem? Months of mulling over the situation? Creative people often report sudden insight with a novel solution but this insight is usually preceded by a lengthy incubation period of thought. What brought the insight to Sparky was when he began to consider the other men in the league that played third base, men like Bill Madlock, Richie Hebner, and Joe Torre. When he looked at those men, he realized that they didn't possess anything that Pete Rose didn't possess.[10] The only difference was that those men were considered third basemen. Pete Rose was considered a left fielder. Rose had the skills to play third, they just weren't recognized because he had another label — outfielder. Looking past the labels, Sparky suspected that the knowledge, skills and abilities found in other third basemen also were found in his leftfielder. So he asked him to move.

Sparky's other genius was how he communicated the idea to Rose. He ran it by him, let him think about it, gave him an out. He said, I sure would appreciate you trying it out and if it doesn't work out, I will move you back. It was presented as a favor from Sparky for the team, not an order from the manager.

Rose's response was also admirable. Even as a superstar with "veto power," he was willing to do it if Sparky thought it would help the team. As long as he was playing, he was happy to do whatever was necessary to make the team better.

Once that solution was found, it created the breakthrough for the organization after years of knocking on the door. The problem was not at the top after all. Rose at third and Foster in left were the missing pieces; the puzzle was now complete and it was something to behold.

18

A MACHINE IN MOTION
December 1975–October 1976

Most baseball fans have heard the terms "antitrust exemption" and "reserve clause," but few really know what they mean. The terms began to make all the difference in the baseball world just two months after the Reds and Red Sox completed their magnificent World Series struggle.

In 1922 the Supreme Court and Chief Justice Oliver Wendell Holmes ruled that the playing of baseball games did not constitute interstate commerce. Since baseball was ruled not to be a form of interstate commerce, baseball could therefore not be regulated by Congress through antitrust legislation. In essence, the Supreme Court ruled that the antitrust legislation passed by Congress did not apply to baseball. A trust is an organization or small number of organizations that unite to reduce competition and control prices for an industry, as Rockefeller and Standard once did with oil, and Carnegie and U.S. Steel with steel. Antitrust legislation was passed in order to prevent one individual or company from monopolizing an industry. Essentially the Supreme Court decision left the National and American Leagues with legalized monopolies.

The most practical implication of baseball's antitrust exemption is that there can be no rival leagues. Recall in the 1960s and '70s when it seemed that every time one turned around a young businessman, Gary Davidson, started a new professional sports league. First it was the American Basketball Association (ABA), with its red, white and blue basketball in 1967. Then he formed the WHA (World Hockey Association), which lured such hockey immortals as Bobby Hull and Gordie Howe from the NHL. Davidson's final brainchild was the WFL (World Football League) with such teams as the Shreveport Steam. Notice that he didn't form the WBL (World Baseball League). The antitrust exemption is the reason. Davidson, a man with no shortage of ambition, never tried it. Bob Howsam and Branch Rickey did in 1959 with the Continental League, but the Senate failed to over turn the antitrust exemption on a 73–12 vote.

In essence, Congress and the U.S. Supreme Court granted both the National and American Leagues the exclusive rights to run what we now call Major League Baseball. They have a legal monopoly, being the only ones allowed

to have major league teams. The justification is simple: without these monopoly rights, the minor-league farm system would collapse. Why would Indianapolis field the Reds' Class-AAA farm club when they could have their own
big-league team? They wouldn't, nor would many cities. Major League Baseball would then lose its pipeline of developing talent and many small cities
would lose their teams.

Baseball's reserve clause is the other issue closely related to its antitrust
exemption. The reserve clause stipulates that once a player signs with a team,
he is property of that team and can only go to another team through a trade
or sale by the owning club. In other words, the player is not free to seek a contract on his own with another club. The reserve clause was enacted by baseball
in 1887. For several seasons prior to then players would go from team to team
each year and there was no stability for the clubs or the fans.

In 1922 the Supreme Court ruled not only that baseball's antitrust exemption was legal but also that the reserve clause was constitutional. The court
considered the reserve clause part and parcel of baseball's antitrust exemption.
Both were considered good for baseball by the courts. In 1953 the reserve clause
was challenged again — and again it was ruled to be legal by the Supreme Court.
The court also made it clear that if the antitrust exemption and reserve clause
were to be changed, it should be done by Congress not by the courts.

Ownership often argued that the reserve clause was necessary to preserve
effective competition among teams and to retain fan interest. Congress and the
Supreme Court agreed. The Supreme Court quoted hearings in the House of
Representatives stating, "Baseball's history shows that chaotic conditions prevailed when there was no reserve clause. Experience points to no feasible sub-
stitute to protect the integrity of the game or to guarantee a comparatively even
competitive struggle."[1]

The Supreme Court in 1972 acknowledged that baseball was indeed a form
of interstate commerce (contrary to the 1922 ruling) but restated that the long-
standing antitrust exemption should not be overturned by the courts. It was a
matter for the legislature to decide, the Court said, and pointed out again that
Congress had clearly felt that the antitrust exemption and the reserve clause
were best for baseball. In addition, a lower court had earlier suggested that the
players and owners could negotiate the topic of the reserve clause during collective bargaining.

Congress had chosen to let the antitrust exemption remain in place to this
present point. That is why during recent hearings on steroid use on baseball,
Congress has threatened to remove the antitrust exemption if baseball and the
players union fail to get tougher on steroid use. The threat of losing the exemption has been a tool Congress has used to get baseball's attention.

In addition to the ability to maintain extensive farm teams (most major-
league teams have six — two rookie, two Class-A, one Class-AA, and one Class-
AAA) the reserve clause gave clubs the ability to keep players once they had

developed them. It takes the average player four years to make it through the farm system to the big league. For every member of the Big Red Machine in 1975, there were five players in the minors, roughly 125 players total in the minor leagues. Most would never see the majors.

Once a player was drafted by a team and signed, the only way for that player to leave the team was to be traded or released. If he was released he was free to sign with another club but few clubs wanted a player who had been released by another team. Essentially the reserve clause allowed baseball teams to keep the talent they scouted, drafted and worked very hard to develop at a high cost.

The downside for the player, of course, was that they were stuck with the team they signed with. This also gave them very little negotiating power with ownership. They could not threaten to leave the team if the team did not offer what the player considered a fair contract. The player's only recourse was "to hold out." This meant the player did not report to spring training and refused to play until he was offered more money. Koufax and Drysdale held a somewhat famous tandem hold out in 1966, refusing to play unless both were paid more than $100,000 each. Rose had held out in the past, Bench and Carbo did in 1971, and others on the Reds had as well.

This ability to switch teams was challenged by one of Howsam's old players, Curt Flood. The St. Louis Cardinals traded Flood, along with Tim McCarver, to the Philadelphia Phillies for Richie Allen and Cookie Rojas. Flood didn't want to go and protested the move. Flood stated that he wasn't a slave to be sold or traded like property. The case reached the Supreme Court. In Flood vs. Kuhn (1972) the Court sided with baseball, reaffirmed the reserve clause, and informed Mr. Flood that indeed he would play for his new team if he wanted to play at all. A club had the right to trade a player.

This did not derail the players from further challenges to the reigning system. They had a leader in Marvin Miller. Marvin Miller is not a person on which opinion rides the fence. You either love him or despise him. If you are pro-union, Marvin is your guy; if you prefer that a third party stay out of the player-owner relationship, Miller is the enemy.

Miller was a union guy through and through. He earned his pedigree as the vice chief of the steelworkers union, in an industry known for labor troubles, an industry in decline when Miller jumped ship to head the baseball players' union in 1966.

Miller showed the players early on that it was his way or the highway when it came to the way the union operated. Ironically this is what the players had accused ownership of for so many years, dictatorship — and not of the benevolent variety. Miller appeared sophisticated, charming, suave, and likeable, but he was as tough as steel when it came to his methods. Miller threatened a strike in 1969 if the owners did not offer increases in minimum pensions and eligibility benefits that they had increased previously. Furthermore, he threatened to resign if the players didn't go along with his strike threat.

In 1970 Miller negotiated the right to have grievances be heard by an "impartial arbitrator." In 1972 he led the first strike in baseball and sports history over the players' pension plan and health-care benefits. The strike lasted for thirteen days at the beginning of the season. In 1973 owners agreed that a player with at least two years of experience and an expired contract would be offered salary arbitration. If the player and ownership were unable to reach a new agreement, each side would present a figure to an impartial arbitrator. The arbitrator would then choose the figure he considered the fairest between the two. There was no requirement that the arbitrator have any baseball knowledge.

Miller's biggest blow to the owners occurred in 1975. Knowing full well that the Supreme Court had ruled in favor of the reserve clause and owners' rights to control the talent they had developed and that the Supreme Court had gone on to state that only Congress should change that ruling, Miller tried another tactic.

The Uniform Playing Contract (UPC) is the general agreement that covers all players' contracts with baseball management. Miller inserted a section (10A) into the UPC that stated that a team could unilaterally extend an unsigned player's contract for one year.[2] Miller's insertion of this section was absolutely key to the future course of baseball. Marvin Miller interpreted this section to mean that after one year without a signed contract the player would be free to

Marvin Miller, head of the player's union, was suave and sophisticated. His cunning maneuvering overturned nearly a century of practice, stability, and legal precedent. The result was greater freedom for players and higher prices for fans (photograph courtesy Roadwest Publishing [Jack Klumpe Collection]).

negotiate with any club for his services. He would be a "free agent." The owners had a very different interpretation. The owners understood this section to mean that they could pay the unsigned player his previous salary for the unsigned year as clearly specified by the UPC. Then after that unsigned year, the player was still bound to them as specified in the reserve clause. So in the owners' interpretation, the next step would be that the contract could either be extended yet another year (due to the reserve clause), or at the very least, the player would have to negotiate a new contract with only that owner, again due to the reserve clause. That was the legal precedent. Armed with two very different assumptions, both Miller's union and the owners signed the UPC.

Miller then had two of the better players in the league, Andy Messersmith of the Los Angeles Dodgers and the Montreal Expos' Dave McNally (the former Oriole) test the system. Both played the 1975 baseball season without signing a contract and their teams allowed it.[3] At the end of that season, Miller declared that the players should be free to negotiate with any club since they had played without contract for a year. In essence they were free agents who should be free to offer their talents to the highest bidder without regard to their former team.

The owners went to arbitration which they had agreed to in 1970. They had legal precedent on their side; however they did not face a judge. Rather, at the table before them was a three-member panel. Two of the members were Marvin Miller, appointed by the union, and John Gaherin (head of the Player Relations Council), appointed by the owners. It was clear how they would vote. Peter Seitz, hired to be the impartial arbitrator, was the chair and the wild card. Amazingly, Seitz ignored the legal precedent established by the Supreme Court as late as 1972 and ruled in favor of Marvin Miller and the players' union.[4] Messersmith and McNally were free to bargain with any club they wished and the reserve clause was deemed illegal without regard to legal precedent.

The Supreme Court had directed that if the reserve clause was to be changed, it was to be through Congressional action. In the end it was changed by the actions of a lone arbitrator. The owners appealed to the federal court feeling that both legal precedent and Supreme Court direction were on their side. Surprisingly, when the decision was challenged in federal court, two separate courts also pushed aside the Supreme Court's legal precedent and ruled in favor of the players' union. A new age had dawned in baseball. It was a new framework, a new paradigm. All the rules were about to change. The game and how it was run was again going to change at the strategic level.

Though spring training was initially delayed as the owners determined their next move, this issue was not the primary concern of the Reds as they gathered in Tampa, Florida, that year. They were the defending World Champions for the first time since 1941, before most of the current Reds had been born. They also were World Champions for the first time in the Big Red Machine era. *Sports Illustrated* said the Reds were "off and running as usual." Actually that was not quite accurate. The Reds were traditionally slow starters. In Sparky's first year they had gotten out of the blocks quickly and were in first to stay by April 12. But in all the years since, the Reds had taken their time getting their traction; big runners rarely start quickly. The 1971 season was a total flop. In the division-winning years of 1972 and '73 they had not taken first until June 9 and Sept. 3 respectively. When Sparky made the Rose-Foster move in May of '75, the Reds were 12–12 and four games in back of the Dodgers. It wasn't until June 8 that they took first place and stayed there.

The Reds brought back the 1975 team almost completely intact, almost unheard of these days and actually fairly rare in the bicentennial year of 1976. Perez, Morgan, Concepcion, and Rose were in the infield. Foster, Geronimo, and Griffey were stationed left to right in the outfield. Bench was behind the plate, and the starting rotation of Gullett, Billingham, Nolan, and Norman remained. The bullpen returned Pedro Borbon and his rubber arm, and the Gold Dust Twins, Eastwick and McEnaney, were in their sophomore and junior years.

The Reds were one of the most stable franchises in all of sports. Seven of the eight regulars in 1976 had been with the club during the 1972 World Series against Oakland. Griffey was still in the minors during that Oakland series. Only Tolan and Menke were gone from the 1972 club. Contrast that with Cincinnati's championship team of 1990. Four seasons after that club won the championship, only two of the starters were in the everyday lineup.

There was one important person missing and thus one big hole to fill. The Hawk, Clay Carroll, had been traded to the Chicago White Sox by Howsam two months after the World Series. It was like having your old dependable neighbor move away.

In return for Carroll the Reds received Rich Hinton. Hinton was a left-hander, which would help McEnaney, who was the only other southpaw in the bullpen. He was six years Carroll's junior. He also was a flop. Howsam always liked to stay young and Carroll had completed twelve years in the majors and was perhaps past his prime, or so was the thinking. Some trades work out well for both teams, which was Howsam's goal. Sometimes the Reds got the advantage and sometimes the other guy got it. This time Chicago got it. Hinton had no saves and an atrocious 7.64 ERA for the Reds. He was gone after one year.

There was one other loss. Sparky Anderson suffered what successful, title-winning managers and head coaches inevitably do, a fleecing of their brain trust. After six full seasons of having Grammas, Shepherd, Scherger and Kluszewski at his side, Grammas was picked by the Milwaukee Brewers to be their field general.

When managers and coaches win championships or enjoy sustained success, inevitably other franchises look to capture some of that magic. Bill Belichek of the New England Patriots has had several of his coaches leave for head coaching jobs in recent years. It is beginning to take its toll on the Patriots. Bob

Stoops of the University of Oklahoma and Bobby Bowden of Florida State have lost key assistants over the past several years, and as a result, both Oklahoma and Florida State's performance has taken a dip over the past few seasons.

Grammas would finally have a shot at being the head man but he was going to a franchise that had been in existence for a total of seven seasons (one as the Seattle Pilots) and had little chance of championship success. It would be a big step down in performance expectations but managerial opportunities are hard to come by and Grammas didn't let it pass. As a consolation he would be managing the great Henry Aaron who had been dealt back to Milwaukee, where he had once starred for the Milwaukee Braves, to play out his final two seasons as a designated hitter for the Brewers.

The loss was a big one. Sparky Anderson thought so much of Alex Grammas. Dick Wagner called Grammas "Sparky's alter ego." Sparky said that Grammas was good for an extra five to seven wins a year. "I'll be honest, I learned from him. You have to be calm. But I'm an up and down person. When I'm getting ready to talk to a player sometimes he'll say, 'Do me a favor, wait until tomorrow.' He knows players. He'd make an outstanding manager."[5]

Grammas had coached third base steadily. Sparky called coaching third base the hardest job in the business. Aside from minor league managing, Sparky felt that coaching third base best prepared a man to be a major-league manager. Grammas had Sparky's trust and confidence and his permission to disregard the skipper's signals. Sparky often directed the bunt and steal signs from the dugout. Grammas had the green light to modify them. He also had the green light to call for a play when he saw the opportunity, either after being tipped by an opposing player's mannerisms, from seeing something in the dugout, or by simply being out in the action, getting a feel for the game.[6] Grammas would be sorely missed.

Anderson now had to replace one of

Alex Grammas (right), Sparky Anderson's alter ego, was lured to Milwaukee for a chance to manage. His departure was the first and only by one of Sparky's coaching staff (photograph courtesy Roadwest Publishing [Jack Klumpe Collection]).

his confidants for the first time. It was a decision he had considered in advance. He knew that eventually he would lose one of his assistants, likely due to promotion. Therefore he kept an eye on the Cincinnati system in order to have a replacement ready. Good leaders anticipate personnel moves and prepare for them.

Sparky had met Russ Nixon through spring training and the Reds organization. Nixon was a native of Cincinnati and had graduated from Western Hills High School, the same school that produced Pete Rose. Nixon spent twelve seasons as a major-league catcher with the Cleveland Indians, Boston Red Sox and Minnesota Twins until he was cut in spring training of 1969. At the following winter meetings, Chief Bender asked Nixon to manage for him. Chief was always looking for good baseball men to manage in his farm system. He wanted men who could teach younger players and work with them well. He thought Nixon would be perfect. He was right. He became one of Chief's top three men for developing talent in Chief's thirty-nine-year history with the Reds.'

Nixon started at Class-A Sioux Falls in 1970, where he managed Ken Griffey. The next year he was given the Class-A Tampa club. It was in Tampa that he really got to know Sparky Anderson. The minor-league managers help conduct spring training each year. After watching Nixon work with the players in camp, Sparky pulled him aside. He told Nixon that if he ever lost anybody from his staff, he would bring him up. He wanted men who could teach, had people skills, and could get along with others. Four years later Anderson was good to his word.

Aside from losing Grammas in the third-base coaching box, the Reds were intact in the front office. Howsam's Big Four — Wagner, Bender and the Bowen brothers— helped him run the ship. Ray Shore continued to do the advance scouting duties. With the Big Four on the field and upstairs, the Reds were ready to roll again.

The nine seasons of tinkering by Howsam had resulted in a machine that could really roll. Sparky was brilliant in pulling the levers. Filling out the lineup card every day with the starters was the easy part. His most difficult task was knowing when to sprinkle in the reserves to keep them motivated, sharp, and improving, while resting the veterans. Rose was oldest of the group at age thirty-five but he was more capable and durable than anyone playing every day. He played all 162 games that year.

Rose still had his zest for the game. One evening he made it on base and eventually wound up at third. George Scherger was coaching third base now that Grammas was in Milwaukee. "Let's run the butcher-boy play," Rose begged.

The butcher-boy play was called with less than two outs. At the crack of the bat the runner was to take off. It was a dangerous play as the runner could easily get caught off base if the batter hit a line drive to an infielder. Scherger replied, "Sparky's not going to run the butcher play, we are up by five runs."

"I want to score, let's run it," cried Rose.[8]

A typical night for the Reds began with "the old left-hander," Joe Nuxhall, throwing batting practice to the Reds. Nuxhall holds the distinction of being the youngest man ever to play in a major-league game. In 1944, the major-league ranks depleted by World War II, Nuxhall was still a student at Hamilton High School when he was signed by the Reds. On June 10, Nuxhall was brought in to face the St. Louis Cardinals at fifteen years, ten months and eleven days of age. He was sent to the minors for the rest of the season and the six years after that. He rejoined the Reds in 1952. He pitched for them from 1952–1966, with a brief stint with the Kansas City Athletics in 1961 and Los Angeles Angels for part of 1962. After retiring, Dick Wagner hired him to be the color commentator on Reds radio broadcasts beginning in 1967. His folksy language, knowledge of the game, great stories, and occasional botching of pronunciations and words immediately endeared him to Reds radio fans. As an added bonus, he was a staple as a batting practice pitcher. The Reds even voted him part of a World Series share for those duties in 1970.

Following each contest Joe hosted a "The Star of the Game" segment on the radio. He would spend five to ten minutes with the star of that night's game, whether it was a Red or an opponent. As often as the Reds won, it was usually a Cincinnati player. He signed off each segment with the phrase that became beloved by every Reds radio fan, "This is the old left-hander, rounding third and heading for home."[9]

Joe Nuxhall (right) began his broadcasting stint with the Reds in 1967 working with Jim McIntyre (not shown). He later worked with Al Michaels (center). The radio technician (left) is unidentified (photograph courtesy Roadwest Publishing [Jack Klumpe Collection]).

One of Joe's classic interviews occurred with Tony Perez — or "Doggie," as his teammates called him. Tony Perez was a humble man. He also struggled a bit with his English, having spoken only Spanish in his native Cuba. On July 7, 1975, Perez blasted a ball from Steve Carlton more than five hundred feet into Riverfront's upper-deck red seats. Afterward, on "The Star of the Game," Nuxhall was gushing about the home run. "Tony, you hit a ball tonight into the red seats for the second time in your career. What do you think about that?"

"I hit it pretty good, Joe."

"But Tony, you are only one of two men to ever even hit one in the red seats."

With a nervous chuckle, Perez replied, "Yeah, I hit it pretty good, Joe."

While Joe Nuxhall pitched batting practice, Bob Howsam and/or Dick Wagner would personally make the rounds of the stadium. They wanted it presentable each evening. They would tour aisles, checking for debris, and especially the bathrooms. Bathrooms are notoriously dirty at public facilities. Smart organizations, such as McDonald's, go the extra mile to ensure that they are clean. A dirty restroom can ruin a visit to a ballpark or any other public venue. Howsam and Wagner felt the same way. Restrooms were checked daily before the crowd entered the stadium. It was part of their detailed policies and procedures.

Howsam's principle of establishing detailed procedures and policies and

"The Old Lefthander" Nuxhall (left) later teamed with the young Marty Brennaman (right) (photograph courtesy the Cincinnati Reds).

adhering to them posed a hidden danger, the pitfall of being resistant to change when it is called for. Policies and procedures ensure efficiency and curb chaos. They allow things to be done decently and in order but detailed policies and procedures, if dogmatically adhered to, can stifle creativity and forward momentum. Howsam avoided this problem by being open to change if a case could be made for it. Again, there was a policy and procedure for change. One had to come to Howsam and present a case. If one made one's case well and could show him why the change was good, he could be persuaded. If one didn't persuade him, one could tell by the way he set his jaw. At least Dick Wagner could tell. Dick Wagner knew when he saw Howsam's jaw go a certain way, it was time to shut up. There was no use in arguing further.

Bob Howsam was an idea man but you had to sell him on the idea. The idea was sold by showing him how it would make money, be quicker, be cleaner, or accomplish more. If you could do that, Howsam would agree to the suggestion. Dick Wagner wanted to acquire a computer to track payroll and cut checks. It was one of those great big computers of the 1970s with punch cards and would take up a good portion of a room. Dick Wagner made the case on how the "high-tech" computer would make the front office more efficient and Bob Howsam signed off on it. The Reds had their first computer by the mid 1970s.[10]

During the games, Howsam was often found in his box, dining with one of the Reds employees. It was his habit to have each employee of the front office once a year to his private box for dinner to watch a game. When Howsam arrived in 1967 there were five full-time front office employees but, like the game, the front office had grown since then. By 1976 there were more than fifty full-time employees. It was an opportunity for him to get to know his people better and vice versa. Suggestions about the Reds or the way things were run were welcome. However, topics usually revolved around the game or the person's family, hobbies, and background. Bob Howsam genuinely wanted you to feel that you worked with him, not for him.

While Howsam dined with employees or Reds' guests in the box, the "red seats" were often occupied by junior or senior high school students from around Greater Cincinnati. Howsam had instituted a program that he had first tried with the Denver Bears and later the St. Louis Cardinals. Every student with straight A's qualified for "straight-A tickets," receiving two tickets for each of three different games. Schools identified the students, congratulated them for their excellent work, and passed out vouchers. Students and their parents would then select the three games they wanted to attend from a list and mail in the voucher; their tickets would come by mail a few weeks later. In 1976 more than 600,000 fans came into the stadium on straight-A tickets. This total was not counted toward official attendance.[11] The red seats were the ones farthest from home plate in Riverfront Stadium, but when the tickets are free, who can complain?

Howsam, like his mentor Branch Rickey, believed it was essential to continually prime the next generation's interest in baseball. It is the lifeline for the future. The recent television deals had hurt baseball's efforts to reach kids, with many World Series games going past ten or eleven and some even past midnight, well after many children in the East had gone to bed. Things would continue to decline for kids wanting to watch baseball games on television, as sporadic games televised by the local NBC affiliate, WLWT, eventually moved to pay-for-view cable packages in the late 1990s.

Rickey had done his part to interest the next generation by starting Knothole Baseball. Most have heard of Little League. Knothole is a similar concept played in certain pockets of the country. It was big in Cincinnati. It is a program to allow boys (and later girls) to play the game. Rules are similar to Little League, with some minor differences. For example, the distance between bases and between the pitching rubber and home plate differ in the two organizations. A Howsam initiative helped Knothole Baseball continue in Cincinnati. Every year the Reds hosted "the Kid Glove Game," an exhibition game against the Detroit Tigers in May or June. The regulars might play an inning or two and then the substitutes played most of the duration. All proceeds from the game went to the local Knothole organization to buy gloves, batting helmets, and other equipment for the youngsters.

The starters were still not enthralled with pitching for Sparky Anderson. His policy remained in place; he conferred only with Shepard on the pitching, he wasn't going to let his starters dictate the outcome of the game, and he still played to his strength — the bullpen. Reds starters pitched only thirty-three complete games in 1976. There was one change for the starters. Jack Billingham decided to learn to hit. His highest batting average in the big leagues had been a paltry .123. He realized he was hurting only himself by having become essentially an automatic out every time he came to the plate. His efforts to improve paid off; he hit .237 that year, higher than Dave Concepcion hit early in his career.

Billingham had made another adjustment to help his teammates a few years prior. A notoriously slow worker on the mound, he took what seemed like an eternity between pitches. It was difficult for fielders and fans to focus their attention when the opposition batted. Innings seemed to drag on forever. But when he began to work faster, results were better. He won nineteen games and had many thankful defensive players behind him.

Johnny Bench would need the most rest from Sparky in 1976, even though he was just twenty-eight. Catching is hard on a man's body. Bench had caught the standard load for a catcher, around 130 games a season, every year he had been in the majors. By 1976 it was beginning to show. Bench was struggling at the plate.

Bill Plummer was Bench's backup. He was adequate behind that plate and with the bat but he was no Bench. When the guy in front of you is considered the game's best catcher and is a future Hall of Famer, your role is pretty clear — spot relief. But Plummer got more of an opportunity that year. It was routine to give Bench the afternoon off if a day game followed a night game. Bench would also catch only one of two doubleheader games but there were only eight of those all season. This season, Sparky began to pull Bench in the late innings if the Reds were comfortably in the lead, and often they were. Plummer would then finish up the game. Anderson thought that the additional rest might shake Bench from his season-long hitting slump.

Ballplayers tend to be superstitious. Though academicians like Stanford's Daniel Kahneman and Amos Tversky can show statistically that "streaks" are really random events, you will never get a ballplayer to believe that. There are certain times when a player sees the ball better. It looks bigger and they just know they are going to hit it. At other times they feel like they are swinging at an aspirin with a pencil.

Most good hitters take some extra batting practice or review videos, searching for the solution to a hitting slump. Smart hitters also consult their batting coach to help find the answers. That was Ted Kluszewski's department but he told Sparky, "I can't help anybody with their hitting unless they want help." Big Klu realized the secret of helping. The first thing a person must do is admit they need help. Secondly, they must realize they need your help.

Joe Morgan and the Reds had been big beneficiaries of Big Klu's help. Mor-

Ted Kluszewski, "Big Klu" (left), shown here with Sparky Anderson, was the hitting coach, with arms too big for his sleeves and a heart to match. Kluszewski's pupils won batting and home run titles as well as multiple MVPs. But he knew he could only help those who wanted his help (photograph courtesy Roadwest Publishing [Jack Klumpe Collection]).

gan described in-depth what he meant by his comments concerning his World Series game-winning hit in the ninth inning of Game Seven. It was all about his approach to the pitch. "Three years ago ... I'd have missed that pitch I hit for the game-winning single because I'd been pulling away from that ball.... Thanks to Big Klu that's a habit I've been able to break."[12] Morgan had few bad habits left to break. He had another sensational year in 1976. He was awarded his second consecutive MVP for his efforts, only the second National Leaguer in history to repeat.

Meanwhile, nothing Johnny Bench tried seemed to work that year. He did have injuries to his shoulders and to his head but he had been injured before and was still able to hit. He was used to an occasional two-week slump but not one lasting all season long. The beauty of a Bench at-bat was to watch his hands. They were enormous—he could hold seven baseballs in one hand—but they also were strong. In one game in the sixties he was having a who's-in-control contest with a pitching teammate named Gerry Arrigo. Getting fed up with the hurler, Bench set out to teach him a lesson. To show Arrigo that his fastball wasn't that great, Bench flashed his index finger, indicating fastball. Arrigo delivered one and Bench caught it barehanded.[13] Yet when those big strong hands gripped a baseball bat, a look at the fingers revealed a relaxed, controlled grip. Great hitters know you can't hold a bat like you are trying to choke a snake. You have to get the feel of the bat and hold it firmly but relaxed. Bench was a master. Despite the great grip, nothing was working for Bench. He hit .234 with sixteen home runs for the year.

Bench's sub-par year aside, the rest of the Reds' picture was rosy. Seven of the players gathered under Sparky Anderson's managing for the All-Star Game in Philadelphia. It was the nation's 200th birthday and a really big deal. Those who are old enough remember all the celebrations associated with what was referred to as "the Bicentennial." As the place where the founding fathers inked the Declaration of Independence on July 4, 1776, Philadelphia hosted a lot of events this year. College basketball's Final Four was played in the Spectrum, for example. The forty-seventh All-Star Game was played in Philadelphia's round, multipurpose Veterans Stadium, which had opened in 1971. The 63,974 in attendance made it the third highest attendance in All-Star Game history.

It was a typical National League team, with Reds and Dodgers at most positions and the token appearance by one player from several teams. Seven of the Reds' eight position players were there, with five starting; only Geronimo stayed home. The National League had come to dominate the Midsummer Classic. With the exception of the 1971 Reggie Jackson tower-hitting game, the National League had won every All-Star Game for thirteen years. Three things explain this dominance: talent, confidence, and camaraderie.

A clue to these components lies in a TV promotion that Major League Baseball was running at the time. The tag line was "Baseball Fever, Catch It." The scene was an All-Star game. Joe Morgan was at the plate. The camera panned to the dugout where Pete Rose said, "C'mon Joe, let's go." The rest of the team was up on the steps pulling for him, as well. Technically the All-Star Game is an exhibition game, but the National League didn't treat it that way. They were pulling for each other like it was the World Series. It helps to explain why from 1963–82 the National League won nineteen of twenty games. Clearly they had talent, but so did the American League. The wins each year bred an increasing confidence, an attitude that "you can't beat us and we will show you that," and that talent and confidence resulted in a strong camaraderie, as the commercial showcased.

Camaraderie was not only strong in the NL All-Star dugout. The Reds clubhouse was a fun place to be. Joe Morgan heard the batboy talking about his upcoming prom. Morgan flipped him his car keys and told him he could use the car for the evening. Sparky continued to trust the Big Four with running things and making sure everyone followed the rules. But the rules did not mean that there were no pranks, as the young Davey Concepcion found out one afternoon. Snatched by some conniving teammates, Concepcion found himself tumbling — inside a gigantic dryer. The tumble did no damage, he went on to play well that night. As George Scherger said, "We'd go to the ballpark laughing and leave the ballpark laughing."

Alex Grammas in particular loved to laugh and cut up with other people, especially Johnny Bench. Bench was notoriously difficult to get an autograph from. Kids would send balls into the clubhouse for Bench to sign. Alex Grammas got to where he could imitate Johnny's signature pretty well. He'd tell the clubhouse guys, "You bring those balls in to me, I'll sign 'em." After a while he decided to have real Johnny Bench signatures ready for the kids. He'd go up to Bench and say, "Johnny, this is for a kid in the hospital with a broken leg, would you sign this ball for him?" Bench would give Grammas that look. He knew he wasn't serious but he'd still take the ball, sign it and give it back to Grammas. Grammas would then keep it until he found a deserving youngster. This continued for months.

One day he and Bench were sitting in the dugout, alone, about thirty minutes prior to a game. Grammas handed Bench a ball and said, "Johnny would you sign this, it's for a blind kid." Without saying a word, Bench reached over and took the ball. Pen in hand, he began to punch out letters in Braille. Grammas fell off the bench with laughter.

The Reds as a whole got along very well. However there was some tension between Bench and Pete Rose. At first the two had been very close, on and off the field, including some joint business ventures. That relationship fizzled when Sparky named Pete the Reds captain shortly after being appointed the manager of the Reds.

Bench felt that as the catcher it was his job to run things on the field. It also happened to be the captain's job, thus Bench's desire for the title. Called "the Little General" early on by his teammates, Bench didn't mind the label even if it wasn't meant in a complimentary fashion by teammates. He clearly felt that the catcher ran the show and if that was resisted, so be it. He was still going to do it. He was twenty-one and a two-year veteran when Sparky came along. Rose had seven years under his belt at age twenty-eight. Sparky wasn't about to make a twenty-one-year-old the team captain but for Bench age and experience were non-issues. The captain should be the leader on the field and he unabashedly felt he was the leader.

This tension did not keep the players from pulling for each other on the field. After Bench's playoff-tying home run off of Dave Giusti in 1972, Rose was the first out to celebrate, even before Bench reached first base. Rose also was at the top of the steps leading the cheers after Bench's World Series home runs. They were able to put petty jealousy aside when it came to play on the field.

The Reds had a curious way of communicating. They loved to dig at one another. An error or leaving a runner in scoring position during a loss made you fair game for some good-natured ribbing. The practice had two effects: it inspired better play, as no one wanted to be the target, and it also provided entertainment in the clubhouse. Only once did it have a negative side effect. Tolan could not tolerate the ribbing after his Oakland Game Seven disaster and it was one of many factors that led to his demise. Once in 1975, Sparky felt the digs were beginning to adversely affect the Reds play. The Reds were on a los-

Bench's hands were enormous. Here he answers a fan's letter by holding seven baseballs at one time. Though the hands were big and strong, they were also soft (photograph courtesy Roadwest Publishing [Jack Klumpe Collection]).

ing streak and Sparky outlawed the digs. After several days, the losing streak continued. An angry Joe Morgan entered the clubhouse and declared that the digs were to start again and they did. The losing streak ended shortly thereafter.

A typical pregame scene found players sitting around the clubhouse working on a crossword puzzle or playing cards. When they didn't know an answer to a crossword clue, they would call over to Klu, who would inevitably bark out the answer and return to whatever had his attention at the time. About the only time Klu showed much emotion is when the jokes started to fly. "Polack jokes" were a big fad at the time. Most people didn't really picture people from Poland when they told the jokes; they pictured a generic moron. Klu, though, pictured Poles—his family had immigrated from Poland. He would never say anything but his face would get red and the nerve on the side of his massive neck would pop up. That's about as excited as Big Klu got.

Unbeknownst to the Reds, they were eliciting another kind of emotion in their opposition—fear. George Foster would later relate that he had no idea until he joined the New York Mets how much other teams feared the Reds. Conversations with his new teammates brought him this insight. This was best exemplified in a late summer game on *Monday Night Baseball*. After four years of NBC borrowing the "Monday Night" concept for baseball, ABC wrestled their concept back and now had both the football and baseball versions of the broadcast. Their number-two announcing team was a good

The Reds' clubhouse was generally a happy place. Most of the Big Red Machine had young kids. Janet Howsam made sure that the moms had a playroom for them outside the clubhouse. Here Pete Rose, Jr., snuggles with Dad (photograph courtesy Roadwest Publishing [Jack Klumpe Collection]).

one; Bob Gibson, the old St. Louis Cardinals ace, and Norm Cash, the former Detroit Tigers first baseman, offered color commentary. The play-by-play man was an old friend of the Reds, Al Michaels. The Reds were playing Howsam's old club, the Cardinals. The Cardinals had a decent club and were trying to climb back into the Eastern Division race. On at least three occasions Michaels mentioned that if the Cardinals could just get by the remaining games with the Reds that they had a shot at the division crown. As the game wore on and the Cardinals continued to lead, he expounded on the point with more passion. Gibson and Cash agreed: how the Cardinals and their division rivals survived the Reds games were key to their own fortunes. The Reds were clearly the class of the league and other teams didn't like seeing them come to town.

Volumes could and have been written on how good the Reds were offensively in 1976. They led the league in all twelve offensive categories. Two numbers really stand out. The first was batting average. Five of the eight regulars hit higher than .300, including the eighth hitter in the lineup, Cesar Geronimo. Ostensibly the weakest offensive link, Geronimo hit .307. The other statistic was steals. Every starter stole at least ten bases except Rose, who stole nine. Danny Driessen made up for him off the bench with fourteen steals, as the team had 210 steals as a whole.

By the end of August, the Reds were up on the Dodgers by eight and a half games. Anderson continued to explore ways to get Driessen in the lineup, so that his skills would not rust on the bench. He played some first base, especially in the late innings, some left field, and he pinch-hit. The traditional September stretch was more of a test drive as Sparky fine-tuned the engine and tried out September minor league call-ups, keeping the veterans fresh for the playoffs.

The biggest decision on the last day of the season was whether to play Ken Griffey in right. Going into the game, Griffey had a slight lead over Bill Madlock of the Chicago Cubs for the league batting title. Griffey was hitting .337, an average that greatly benefited from his speed — he'd garnered thirty-nine infield hits during the season. The question was whether to sit Griffey, so that his average would not fall, or to play him, in hopes that it would stay the same or rise. It is one of those decisions that is a big deal at the time, with a man's reputation at stake, but later no one considers it as they look at the record book.

Ted Williams had faced the decision in 1941 when he was trying to hit .400. He had a .400 average going into the last day, a double-header. His manager wanted to sit him down so as not to jeopardize the magic mark but left the decision up to Ted. Williams balked, insisting on playing. You have to admire that kind of boldness but it is risky. It worked for Williams, as he went 6-for-8, playing in both games and raising his average to .406.

Griffey took the other tact. Actually, Anderson took the decision out of Griffey's hands and sat him down, forcing Madlock to hit well in order to overtake him. Griffey chose not to fight the decision. Madlock got a couple of hits early against the Braves, threatening to raise his average above Griffey's. The

Reds, who were monitoring the Cubs-Braves game, quickly hurried Griffey into the lineup as a pinch hitter. The move backfired, as Griffey struck out, dropping his average further. When all was said and done, Madlock had gone 4-for-4 and Griffey 0-for-2 with two strikeouts. Madlock shaded him for the batting title .338 to .336.

When asked what he would have done if the shoe had been on the other foot, Madlock said he would not have let his manager sit him down. That was easy for him to say. More telling was the fact that Madlock himself was removed from the game once he had gone 4-for-4 and taken the batting lead. An additional irony was that over in the American League, George Brett beat his teammate and former Reds left fielder Hal McRae for the AL batting title on his last at-bat of the season.

The October 11 issue of *Sports Illustrated* featured George Foster on the cover. "An Explosive Playoff," the cover read. It was explosive but only for one team. After six years of pretty much having their way in the NL East, Pittsburgh had given way to the other Pennsylvania team, the Phillies. The Phillies had hit rock bottom in 1972 when they won only fifty-nine games; Steve Carl-

The 1976 Big Red Machine led the league in every offensive category. Here the eight starters are positioned where they played on the field. Bench (C), Rose (3B), Concepcion (SS), Morgan (2B), Perez (1B), Foster (LF), Geronimo (CF), Griffey (RF).

ton had won twenty-seven of those on his way to the Cy Young Award. Then he was the entire show but he now had help.

The converted shortstop that Chief Bender had coveted years earlier had arrived at third base for the Phillies. Mike Schmidt had a banner year. He was young, tall and strong and hit thirty-eight home runs that year. Greg "The Bull" Luzinski resided in left and had twenty-one home runs and ninety-five RBIs. Garry Maddox hit .330 while stealing twenty-nine bases. The Phillies' starting pitching was strong as well, featuring three different award winning hurlers: Steve Carlton, Jim Lonborg and Jim Kaat. The Phillies won the East by nine games.

Appropriately, given the bicentennial, the playoffs opened in Philadelphia. There was no doubt who the Phillies pitcher would be — lefty and ace Steve Carlton. The Reds countered with Don Gullett, who had lost only three times all season against eleven wins, after a pinched nerve in his neck limited his action. Gullett shut down the Phillies on two hits through eight innings, with Eastwick giving up two runs in the ninth. Meanwhile, the Reds roughed up Carlton, winning 6–3.

Jim Lonborg, who had won the 1967 Cy Young Award in Boston's "Impossible Dream Season," was the Reds opponent the next day. The Reds continued to cruise in Game Two with their number-five starter, Pat Zachry. Zachry was a tall right-hander from Texas whom the Reds had drafted in 1970. He had a face and build similar to Abraham Lincoln's but, playing on the Reds, he couldn't have Lincoln's beard. Texas seems to produce tall right-handers in spades, Nolan Ryan and Roger Clemens among them. After six seasons in the minors Pat Zachry had finally made it to the parent club and he won NL Rookie of the Year honors after going 14–7. He showed that it was no fluke, combining with Pedro Borbon to limit the powerful Phillies to two runs and a 6–2 victory.

Jim Kaat was tapped to start Game Three for the Phillies. He had been the *Sporting News* Pitcher of the Year in 1966.[14] The game provided the only real excitement of the entire playoffs. Trying to stave off elimination, the Phillies had taken a 6–4 lead into the bottom of the ninth inning. George Foster, who had by now replaced Bench in the five hole, led off the inning. On a one-ball, two-strike count, reliever Ron Reed threw the ball over the center of the plate and Foster took it deep for a home run. Next up, Bench also had a one-ball, two-strike count when he got a fat pitch from Reed and homered to tie the game at 6–6. Gene Garber was brought in to close the barn door even though the horses had already gotten out. Concepcion greeted him with a single. The Phillies brought in Tom Underwood who walked Geronimo. Eddie Armbrister came in to pinch hit for Eastwick and was called on to bunt, just as he had been in the 1975 World Series. He successfully moved Concepcion over to third with a sacrifice. Rose was walked intentionally to load the bases. Griffey ended it by hitting a high chopper off both the artificial turf and the first baseman's glove as Concepcion scooted home. The Reds were NL champs for the fourth time in seven seasons. An old reemerging dynasty waited for them in the World Series.

19

COMPLETE AND TOTAL DOMINATION
October 1976

The New York Yankees dominated baseball from the time Babe Ruth first put on the pinstripes in 1919 until Mickey Mantle retired in the 1960s. In between, Lou Gehrig and the Yankee clipper, Joe DiMaggio, carried the Yankees to twenty World Series titles over a forty-year span. They were the marquee team of baseball, the Rolls Royce.

However, as Mantle's career declined so did the fortunes of the Yankees. Since their last World Series appearance against Devine and Howsam's Cardinals in 1964, the Yankees had experienced five losing seasons. The ownership (CBS) sensed the dynasty fading and sold the club to a young shipbuilding magnate named George Steinbrenner in 1973. Steinbrenner had sporting ambitions from a young age, buying his first club, the Cleveland Pipers of the short-lived National Industrial Basketball League in 1960 at the age of thirty. He tried unsuccessfully to buy the Cleveland Indians the next year. Steinbrenner wanted the glory back in the Bronx. Under his ownership the Yankees fought their way back to respectability. In 1976, just before free agency would explode and Steinbrenner's deep pockets would control the game, the Yankees had developed enough talent to return to the World Series. Steinbrenner had built a well-balanced team.

For his skipper, George Steinbrenner had tapped Billy Martin after firing Bill Virdon in August 1975. Martin had grown up with the Yankees, with Casey Stengel treating him like a son. He had been traded from the Yankees as a result of a barroom brawl he'd participated in during the 1957 season. His fiery temperament had cooled little since his playing days. He had managed four teams in seven years, getting pink slips more for his behavior than his results. Before the Series, he compared players between the two teams. He said only two of the Reds could start for his Yankees. Upon hearing that quote Joe Morgan snorted, "He's snapped; no wonder he can't hold a job."[1]

The Yankees had assembled a fine pitching staff, with three players familiar to the Reds. The first was Jim "Catfish" Hunter, the former Oakland ace who had beaten the Reds twice in the 1972 Fall Classic. Hunter had been a member of Finley's A's through 1974. During that campaign Finley had failed to fund a

life insurance annuity as stipulated by Hunter's contract. Catfish filed a griev-
ance and federal arbitrator Peter Seitz ruled that due to the breech of contract
Hunter was a "free agent" able to negotiate with any club. Steinbrenner saw an
opportunity to immediately improve his pitching staff and signed Hunter to a
record $750,000 annual contract. In an era when the game's best players were
making just more than $100,000 per year, the salary kicked off a spiral in salaries
that has continued unabated until this time.

Through a trade, the Yankees brought over one of Hunter's old teammates
from Oakland, left-hander Ken Holtzman. It wasn't only Oakland talent that
Steinbrenner acquired. Doc Ellis, who had faced the Reds many times in the
playoffs with the Pittsburgh Pirates, had come over to the Yankees in a trade.
The fine staff was rounded out by Ed Figueroa, a nineteen-game winner. The
fifth starter was Doyle Alexander who would get the call in Game One after
the Yankees had spread their pitching thin in a five-game playoff series with
the Kansas City Royals. Billy Martin felt that Alexander had the kind of stuff
that could get the Reds out. When the starters got tired, the Yankees called on
Sparky Lyle, who sported a Fu Manchu but not as nice a one as Tiant's.

Surprisingly not one of the Yankees' key starters had come up through
their minor league system. In fact the assembly of the two teams was a contrast
in styles. Three of the Reds five starting pitchers had come through the farm
system. Five of the eight position players had been drafted and developed by
the Reds, while the Yankees had only two. Furthermore there were only four
members of the entire Yankees twenty-five-man roster who had come through
the Yankee farm system. You have to hand it to Steinbrenner for the many
trades that had made the Yankees competitive. He had only one free agent, but
that would change in the future.

Catching the fine crop of pitchers was Thurman Munson. Like Bench, he
was good offensively and defensively. He'd hit .302 with seventeen home runs
and 105 RBIs. At the corners the Yanks had two fine sluggers, Greg Nettles at
third and Chris Chambliss at first. The two combined for forty-nine homers.
Roy White in left and Willie Randolph at second provided speed with more
than thirty steals each.

But the man who made the Yankees go was a young center fielder named
Mickey, who was very different from his predecessor. The most obvious difference between Mickey Mantle and Mickey Rivers was the color of their skin but
the real difference was how they played the game. Mantle was fast but powerful and strong — a clean-up hitter. Rivers was fast but not a slugger — a leadoff
hitter. The Yankees had hoped a converted shortstop named Bobby Murcer
would replace Mantle in center field — they even gave him Mantle's uniform
number (7) for a few years, but, unhappy with Murcer after six seasons, the
Yankees had traded him to Oakland and opted for speed on the base paths and
on defense. Mickey Rivers could fly — from home to first in 3.1 seconds. He had
forty-three stolen bases that year, more than any Red except Morgan. When he

settled into the batter's box for the opening pitch of the 1976 World Series, the game was on.

As the Reds' starting pitcher Don Gullett began to toe the pitching rubber, Rose began to creep in at third. He didn't stop creeping until he was well inside the third-base bag — ninety, then eighty, then seventy, then sixty feet from home plate. Rivers looked to the area where he would sometimes drop a sneak bunt before flying to first. Rose was there, waiting. It blew Mickey Rivers's mind.

Third base is located ninety feet from home plate. Most third basemen play about even with the bag or a few steps back. When the opposition has runners on base and a sacrifice bunt is suspected, the third baseman will usually move inside the bag a few feet and begin to trot toward home as the batter squares to bunt. This was not a sacrifice situation and Rose was in even closer than a sacrifice bunt would call for. He was staring Rivers down. Rivers had never seen anything like it.

One of the most powerful weapons in sports is getting into your opponent's head. It takes them out of their routine, their rhythm, their comfort zone. They begin to question the situation and then themselves. Taken out of their routine, their performance often slips, and then the confidence slides. Rose had just opened the door to Mickey Rivers's head.

Gullett struck Rivers out and Mickey headed back to the dugout, thinking. He managed to get his bat on the ball in the third inning, grounding out to Morgan as Rose again peered in twenty yards away. In the sixth, Gullett walked Fred Stanley, the first batter. When Rivers came to bat, Rose again crept in. Rivers laid down a sacrifice bunt away from Rose and toward the pitcher. Gullett fielded it cleanly, turned and fired to second to get Stanley. Rivers's sacrifice attempt was foiled.

Bench crouched behind the plate expecting Rivers to take off. When he did, Bench fired to second and nailed him. The Reds were intent on sending a message to Mickey Rivers. Nothing is going to be easy for you; we are going to shut you down this series. With Rose creeping in again, Rivers popped out to Bench in foul territory in the eighth.

While Gullett was working to Rivers in that eighth inning, he stepped into a pitch and into a hole, twisting his ankle. He was upset with himself because he had seen the hole after the previous pitch and failed to cover it. The ankle got sore and tender in a hurry. Intending to rest the ankle, he removed himself from the game after surrendering a single to Roy White. It was going to need a lot of rest. Two and one-half hours after the game, X-rays revealed a dislocated peroneus longus tendon in his right ankle. That is the tendon on the outside of the ankle that helps you go up on your toes. Gullett would be in a cast for the next six weeks and was lost for the series.

As Rivers had been about to step into the batter's box back in the first inning, three Yankee staffers were being ordered out of the press box by Commissioner Bowie Kuhn. George Steinbrenner and the Yankees' fiery skipper

Billy Martin had stationed three men in the press box with binoculars, walkie-talkies and a TV monitor in order to send messages down to the dugout for the purpose of "positioning the defensive players." Kuhn had given permission for one man to be in the stands with binoculars and a walkie-talkie for that purpose. When Howsam learned of the situation, he complained to Kuhn, sitting nearby, that the Yankees could use the television monitors to steal Johnny Bench's pitching signals and have them relayed to the batter via coach in the dugout. Kuhn ordered the men out of the box. Interestingly two of the three had previous ties to the Reds.

Clyde King had been the Atlanta manager who had ordered Ralph Garr to test Rose in his first game at third base. He was now the Yankees advance scout and he had been shadowing the Reds for weeks. Birdie Tebbetts was alongside. He had managed the Reds in the 1950s and also was now scouting for the Yankees.

When Martin lost his walkie-talkie connection, he was livid and accused Kuhn of bowing to Howsam. He mused that Howsam must have threatened to take Kuhn's job. Howsam had a lot of credibility and power with the commissioner but not *that* much power. Additionally, Martin was livid that anyone would accuse him of cheating, though his past behavior wasn't exactly above reproof. The Reds got word from the Kansas City Royals that they'd had to change their signs four times during their five-game series with the Yankees.

After Game One, a mediation meeting would be held with Kuhn, Howsam, Dick Wagner, Steinbrenner and Yankee president Gabe Paul. Kuhn agreed to let King sit in the stands with another man and his walkie-talkie as originally agreed upon. The Reds would provide two red seats for their comfort.

While the walkie-talkie affair provided the only controversy of the game, Gullett's injury was the only bad news of the day for the Reds. They got rolling in a hurry, with Morgan homering in the first. Perez attempted a steal of second base in the first inning as well, sending a clear message that the Reds intended to run again, just as they had against the Red Sox the previous October. To emphasize the point, Griffey scored run number three on an RBI single by Perez after stealing second.

The Yankees' lone run in the game was scored by designated hitter Lou Piniella, the former Kansas City Royals Rookie of the Year, who had come over in a trade to the Yanks. The Reds dominated Game One, 5–1. Following the whipping, the Yankees claimed that they had come in flat after an exhausting five-game playoff against the Kansas City Royals.

Prior to the Series, Commissioner Bowie Kuhn had made an interesting decision. He called it "an experiment." Sunday's Game Two would be moved from the afternoon and played at night. Five years prior, Bowie Kuhn had said that nighttime World Series games would be limited to the weekdays. He had now changed his tune. The 1975 World Series had been the first to have every weekday game at night. Now a weekend game was being moved.

The impending opening of free agency had the owners scrambling for money to pay for outside talent. In the past they simply had to grow their own or trade for it. The biggest source of revenue for the increased free-agent pay would not be the paying customers at the ballpark but fans watching for free at home. Television promised to be the cash cow the owners coveted. Television was happy to pay more money to the owners to broadcast their games but there was a catch. NBC wanted to move the games to prime viewing time, where they could command top dollar from advertisers and increase their revenue substantially. In this case, NBC paid the owners $700,000 ($35,000 to each team) to move the game to Sunday night.

The World Series had traditionally been played the first week of October, a nice time of year, with some of the most comfortable weather in the afternoon from coast to coast. With the introduction of the five-game playoff in 1969, the World Series had been bumped back to the second week of October, still not much of a problem, weather-wise, for afternoon baseball, but the evenings can be chilly. Such was the case on October 17, 1975. It was fifty-one degrees Fahrenheit that afternoon in Cincinnati. With sunset the temperature began dropping, falling to forty-three degrees by game time.

It was another change that would alter how the game was played. Uneasy about his previous statements and present decisions, Kuhn decided to pretend it was no big deal. It was baseball as usual, let the game begin. He refused to wear an overcoat and sat with a suit coat and no hat in the stands. It is a wonder that he didn't freeze solid. Later it was revealed that under the fall afternoon apparel had been layered thermal underwear. Instead of a competition in decent weather to find the best team, it became a competition against the weather to see who could survive.

By the middle innings it had fallen to thirty-eight degrees. Joe Morgan said it felt colder than that. It was all he could do to concentrate on anything except how cold he was. He wasn't alone. Yankee batters left their bats in the clubhouse to stay warm. Billy Martin called playing in this weather "ridiculous" and the Yankee players passed their issued blankets to their wives in the stands.

Baseball-wise, Game Two was the same song, second verse. Ray Shore had recommended that the Reds throw left-handers against the Yankees; therefore, Fredie Norman had gotten the nod to start. Mickey Rivers opened the game facing Norman and in came Rose. Rivers lofted a fly to Geronimo in center. The Yankees countered with Catfish Hunter who had never lost a game in three World Series with Oakland. The weather did affect the game; Hunter said the ground was so cold this night that he had a hard time digging a hole on the mound to get his footing and was unable to do so until the fifth inning. The Reds jumped on him early with three runs in the bottom of the second, with a series of hits, walks, and steals. They again were intent on running. Munson was doing a better job than Fisk in holding them at bay; George Foster was thrown out stealing but Morgan and Concepcion succeeded. Jack Billingham came in for Norman who'd gotten into a jam in the seventh. Billingham had injured his arm on the last day of the season. He was then relegated to relief work in the postseason and on this night would get the win, retiring all eight batters he faced. He'd allowed no earned runs in twenty-five innings of World Series games.

With two outs in the bottom of the ninth and the score tied 3–3, Catfish Hunter was still on the mound for the Yankees. Ken Griffey smashed a ball into the hole at short. Fred Stanley, very aware of Griffey's blazing speed, knew that he had to get the ball off quickly to have any chance of getting him. The ball ended up in the Reds dugout and Griffey was awarded second base.

Martin then played the percentages and had Hunter walk Morgan intentionally to set up a force at second. This brought up the right-handed Perez to face the right-handed Hunter. Anderson had put Perez behind Morgan in the lineup, figuring Morgan would get a lot of walks against the Yankees. Tony Perez was Sparky's best RBI man.

Perez was upset with himself. Hunter had gotten him on a fastball the previous three times to the plate. Perez decided to look for the fastball this time, as he figured Hunter would want to start with one to get a strike. Smart players learn from previous mistakes. On the first pitch, Hunter threw a fastball over the plate and Perez drilled it into left field scoring Griffey, winning the game for the Reds, 4–3. Game Two had been no better for Mickey Rivers. He went 0 for 5.

Under-appreciated Jack Billingham came over in "the trade." Shown here after a victorious Game 3 in the 1972 Series, he was the Reds' best pitcher in the postseason and most intense in his dislike for Sparky Anderson (photograph courtesy Roadwest Publishing [Jack Klumpe Collection]).

The Series had all the makings of a complete blowout. As the Series switched from the Midwest to the Bronx, the press was looking for a storyline. They found one: "How would the Reds handle the pressure of Yankee Stadium?" As the press repeatedly noted, only one Red had ever set foot in Yankee Stadium. Johnny Bench had filmed a commercial there. In the days before the controversial interleague play, the only time the Reds played in New York was in Queens at Shea Stadium against the Mets. Over in the neighboring borough of the Bronx, Yankee Stadium had recently been renovated and the "House that Ruth Built" housed his memory as well as that of Gehrig, DiMaggio, Whitey Ford and the M & M boys. Could the Reds deal with that legacy? The simple answer was yes.

They were aided by an unexpected source. Ever since the Reds decided after 1974 that they could not live with Danny Driessen's defense at third, Driessen had been relegated to spot duty for Perez or others. He was Sparky's pinch hitter of choice. He had gotten only 219 at-bats this year.

The American League had begun the ill-advised designated hitter (DH) rule in 1973 but baseball had opted to keep World Series games as they had been designed, so the pitchers always hit. The American League agreed, at first. After three complete World Series with baseball under the agreement, the AL began to complain that the system was not fair. Their pitchers had no experience hitting all year and then were forced to bat in the biggest games of the year, the World Series. Of course the NL could make a similar argument. All year

Kuhn's decision to play Game Two at night in near-freezing conditions affected the play on the field in the 1976 Series. His willingness to switch games to late at night meant low temperatures and a sharp decrease in the ability of kids to watch the Series on television (photograph courtesy Roadwest Publishing [Jack Klumpe Collection]).

long they had no one that was used to simply batting every day but not fielding. It takes a certain mindset to just sit on the bench and only hit. However, Commissioner Bowie Kuhn wanted to see the DH used to generate more offense.

After initial resistance baseball changed its stance and it was decided that the designated hitter would be rotated by even and odd years, just like the host team. In even number years, the designated hitter would be used in all World Series games and the National League team would host Games One, Two and Six and Seven if needed. The situation would be reversed in the odd-numbered years. This was the first year of the new system.[2]

As Sparky's ace pinch hitter, Driessen was the natural selection to be the first ever National League designated hitter. Sparky had a consistent answer for what he thought of the DH rule — "it stinks" — and was close to not using the DH at all, just to make a statement. In the end he used Driessen.

Meanwhile, Steinbrenner called Mickey Rivers in for a chat in order to help break him out of his slump. Steinbrenner reported that the meeting had been a good one for both sides. Rivers had a different version. He said that the meeting might backfire; he was on the edge. It wouldn't be the first or last time that "the boss" got involved in running the Yankees fortunes on the field.

Game Three temperatures for the 8:30 P.M. start plunged toward the forties and dipped into the thirties again during the game. Once again it had been fifty degrees that afternoon. Players were issued thermal underwear and portable heaters were brought into the dugouts and the bullpens. NBC tried to console everyone by reporting that television ratings for Sunday night's Game Two were 49 percent higher than they had been for the Sunday afternoon Game 2 in 1975. That was little consolation to the players on the field or to the fans who paid good money ($15) to shiver in the stands. NBC also didn't mention that a percentage of the increase could be explained by the fact that the Yankees are from the largest TV market in America.

Billy Martin announced that his Game Three starter would be Doc Ellis. The Reds had a history with Ellis. They had seen him many times when he was with the Pittsburgh Pirates and Ellis had a bone to pick with them. In one of his last outings against the Reds, on May 1, 1974, Ellis began the game by hitting Pete Rose with a pitch. He followed that by hitting Morgan and then Driessen with the first pitch. He then tried unsuccessfully to hit Perez with four pitches and then threw two at Bench before Danny Murtaugh pulled him out of the game. When asked about the incident, Ellis said he was upset because the Reds were real friendly when they talked with the Pirates in person but would later say that they were "dumb" after a series was over. It sounded like the explanation of an elementary-school child.

It also could have been a way for Ellis to get back at the Reds for his old friend from high school, Bobby Tolan, or perhaps it was induced by drugs. Ellis had admitted to using marijuana just prior to the 1971 All-Star Game.

Whatever his reason in 1974, and there were probably several, Ellis promised that he wouldn't waste a game on the Reds by intentionally hitting them during the World Series but he still wasn't happy with them.

The Reds didn't treat him too nicely during this game. Driessen got things going in the second with a single. He stole second base and scored the game's first run. Geronimo later successfully stole second, despite a pitchout, as the speed game was still on. Driessen added a home run in the fourth and a double in the sixth and was intentionally walked in the eighth. Game Three would show that the Reds benefited more from Driessen than the Yankees did from their year-long DH trio of Elliot Maddox, Carlos May,[3] and Lou Piniella.

The Reds pitcher, Pat Zachry, had followed the Yankees and idolized Mickey Mantle as a boy in Texas. He pitched many games against them in his backyard in Waco, Texas, and now he was on for the real thing at Yankee Stadium. He and Will McEnaney combined to limit the Yanks to two runs. The Yanks felt they'd let themselves down, as they stranded eleven base runners against Zachry alone.

Meanwhile, Rose continued to stalk Rivers. Perhaps his talk with Steinbrenner would help. Unable to get on base with a hit so far in the Series, Rivers laid down a bunt away from Rose and toward Zachry in the first inning. Zachry made an error on the play and Rivers was on first, briefly. Moments later Zachry picked him off. His fortunes continued to fall as Rivers struck out in the third.

Finally, in the fifth inning, Rivers got his first hit of the series, a single to left. He went to second on a Roy White walk. The Yankees had two men on with no outs, trailing 4–1, but Munson lined the ball to Perez who fired to Concepcion at second base where Rivers had left too soon for third and couldn't get back—double play. Rivers managed to draw a walk in the seventh but was forced out on a White grounder. He singled in the ninth only to be stranded on second as the game ended. He had reached base but still could do no damage.

The Reds had identified what they considered to be the key component of the Yankees and determined that they would shut it down and thereby cripple the entire system. Put another way, they went for the Yankees jugular vein and bit hard.

The Yankees' backs were against the wall. No team in the World Series had ever come back from a 3–0 deficit to win the Series. Yankee coach Yogi Berra correctly pointed out that this gave the Yankees the opportunity to be the first. At this point the Yankees just wanted to get their first win, which would be the one hundredth win for the club in all their World Series combined. They would have to wait another day, though, as would the Reds and their chance to sweep. The weather did not cooperate and buckets of water fell on hallowed Yankee Stadium.

This pushed Game Four to Thursday evening. If the Series were to go to Game Five, Bowie Kuhn announced that it would be played on Friday evening.

This presented two problems. If the Yanks were to win Game Five on Friday, then Game Six would start at 1:00 P.M. on Saturday afternoon in Cincinnati. That would give the teams only sixteen hours to pack their bags, get to the airport, fly to Cincinnati, get to the hotel, sleep a few hours, get up, eat, and get to the stadium in time to warm up for the game.

The other problem was a scheduled debate on Friday evening between two gentlemen named Ford and Carter. They happened to be running for president. Kuhn said that the game would begin at 6:00 P.M., so it would end before the 9:30 P.M. debate. When asked what would happen if the game went into extra innings, Ford didn't seem to be too concerned. "We'll work something out," he told Kuhn. Maybe he didn't expect the Series to still be going on Friday night. Perhaps he sensed a sweep.

Sparky Anderson began publicly stating that he wanted a sweep badly, to show that the Reds were among history's greats. For Game Four the Reds had their leading winner from the season, Gary Nolan, on the mound. He had just completed his second consecutive 15–9 season. Troubled by shoulder and neck problems through his career, he had consistently given the Reds good innings in the World Series, but not a lot of them. He had never gotten a World Series win and he was eager to erase the memory of his controversial and lousy start in Game Six of the 1975 World Series.

The Yankees countered with right-hander Ed Figueroa, who was their top winner. In making the choice Martin bypassed Ken Holtzman, who had plenty of rest and eight games of experience pitching in the World Series. Figueroa had none. Additionally, the lefty Holtzman had an 8–3 lifetime record against the Reds, including a no-hitter, and the Reds had more trouble with lefties than righties.

The decision caused some controversy among the Yankees. Thurman Munson publicly, but politely, questioned Martin on the Holtzman decision. Munson suggested that Ken Holtzman was not Billy Martin's favorite person. Sometimes feelings about personality shade our decisions about who the best person is for the task when they shouldn't. Martin said he was holding Holtzman out for Game Five and Holtzman was none too happy about it. Martin was a little testy himself when a reporter from Boston, asked him in the press conference after Game Three, "How do you spell 'Holtzman?'" implying that he should have pitched by now.

The night started promising enough for the Yankees. Rose doubled to lead off the game and tried to go to third on Griffey's grounder to short. The Reds challenged the Yankee defense with their speed at every opportunity, just as Ray Shore had recommended. Rose was picked off at third, though, and Griffey was caught trying to sneak into second. Morgan then grounded out harmlessly to first.

When the Yankees came to bat, Rivers popped to short with Rose staring down at him. After Roy White was retired, Thurman Munson singled. Chris

Chambliss knocked him in with a double and the Yankees led for the first time in twenty-eight innings. New York was back in business but the excitement didn't last long. The Reds roughed up Figueroa in the fourth with a Morgan walk and steal, a Foster RBI single, and a two-run blast by Johnny Bench.

Mickey Rivers fought off Rose's stares and singled to right in the fifth. He then broke for second and beat Johnny Bench's throw. The Yankees and Rivers had their first steal of the series. Bench had thwarted the only other attempt, also by Rivers, in Game One. Munson then knocked Rivers in with a single and they were playing Yankee ball for the first time in the series. It was 3–2, Reds.

It remained that way until the top of the ninth when Perez and Driessen walked. Dick Tidrow relieved Figueroa and Bench greeted him with a three-run blast. Geronimo and Concepcion doubled to add the icing on the cake for a 7–2 lead.

While Rose had continued to haunt Rivers, Bench and Munson had been facing off like two gladiators in the Coliseum. With Bench's counterpart behind the plate in 1975, Carlton Fisk, they were the best catchers in the game. Bench, with that soft grip, made up in this Series for a season of frustration. He homered twice in Game Four and hit .533 for the Series. Munson meanwhile had hit .529. Couple their hitting with their tremendous defense (five men thrown out stealing in the Series) and there has never been a finer collective performance by catchers in a Fall Classic.

By Game Four Rivers was 2-for-13. NBC broadcasters Joe Gariagola and Tony Kubek were now practically screaming, "Why is he not gunning for Rose at third?" Rose was taunting him, as if to say "Take my dare, smack one this way, see if I can handle it." Rivers finally did. With one out in the ninth inning he smashed one right at Rose, sixty feet away. Playing at normal depth, a third baseman has less than six-tenths of a second to react to a line drive. At sixty feet it is even less, .372 seconds to be exact.[4] Rose didn't blink as he snared the line drive like snaring a dart flying from a blowgun. Game Four had been no better for Rivers, 1-for-5 — three hits in the entire Series. He was on base just six times, picked off one of those, doubled up another, and thrown out stealing in a third. The man who made New York go had one run scored in four games. Rivers had a complete meltdown.

Will McEnaney, who'd come on in the seventh, closed the game and the Series just like in 1975. It was apropos. Like Bench, McEnaney hadn't had the season he would like to have had, only two wins and six losses with seven saves, after having fifteen saves in 1975. More troublesome yet was the fact that he'd had the second highest ERA on the team. After Mickey Rivers's shot at Rose, McEnaney enticed Roy White to loft a fly ball to Foster in left and the Reds had wrapped up the series.

It had been complete and total domination not seen before or since, as if professional champions had played a college all-star team. The Reds' pitching had shut down all but Munson and the Reds' bats and base running had been timely and consistent. Their defense was strong. The Reds won 102 games that season. They then swept a powerful Philadelphia team by a combined score of 19–11, three games straight. Now they had swept the AL champion four games straight, by a combined score of 22–8.

It had been the first World Series sweep since 1966. Additionally, the Reds became only the fifth National League team in history to sweep the series. They were the first National League team to win back-to-back titles since 1921–22. From the beginning of the playoffs in 1969 until the present, only one team has ever swept the entire playoffs and World Series in one year, going undefeated in the postseason: the 1976 Cincinnati Reds. *Sports Illustrated* asked, "How good are the Reds?" At this point it seemed to be anyone's guess.

How much confidence a person has in regard to their ability to do a certain task is known as self-efficacy. Perhaps the most powerful means to build self-efficacy is through practice and previous experience until a task is mastered. This gives increased confidence to continue to perform well. Past performance reinforces present performance in a reinforcing cycle.[5]

The Reds had high self-efficacy when it came to playing baseball in the 1976 postseason. Their 108 wins the previous season, their ability to beat a very determined Boston club in the World Series, their machine-like domination of the National League in the 1976 regular season, and their sweep of the Phillies in the playoffs had them brimming with confidence as they faced the Yankees. As Sparky Anderson said, "Now we know ourselves. We know we can win. We believe we can win. But we never lose sight of the fact we can also lose. It keeps us from getting a false high."[6]

NBC came back from a commercial break and switched down to the visiting locker room in Yankee Stadium to find a joyous celebration. A championship validated with a repeat is sweet indeed. The celebration was not as wild and raucous as the previous year's affair. The Reds expected to win this time. It wasn't a hold-your-breath-until-the-last-moment type of Series. The Reds came into the Series with high expectations and met them. They were happy, but more than that, they were satisfied by what they had accomplished.

There were several interviews with the players but the most interesting were with those with the men at the top. Tony Kubek pointed the microphone at the Reds' majority owner Louis Nippert and Bob Howsam, clad in business suits and raincoats. At this point owners and general managers generally gush about what a great manager, coaches and players they have and how they worked really hard and had to overcome difficult odds to reach the championship. They also mention that they have the greatest fans in the world and that this championship is for them. However Nippert was brief, sharing what a satisfaction this was for the team and how happy they were for the show they had put on; he also graciously commended the Yankees for the competition.

The microphone and attention then turned to Bob Howsam. It was a sublimely pleasing moment for Howsam — his dynasty had been validated against baseball's most storied team. At first he appeared satisfied in his comments to Kubek. "This is the one I wanted more than anything," but then he turned surprisingly somber as he continued, saying, "I think you may have seen the last balanced teams in baseball." As he spoke he became more serious and introspective. There was even sorrow in his tone and his countenance. Howsam turned to a local reporter, Walt Maher, and appeared sad, deeply sad. Baseball was changing. Howsam spoke slowly and philosophically about the state of the game. After such a resounding validation of his club and his life's work, it was an intensely ironic moment. "This may be the last time you see a club win that has been built this way," he said.[7] We may never see such a team again.

20

Two Trades, One Year
December 1976–September 1977

The phone rang in California at Sparky Anderson's off-season home in Thousand Oaks. It was Bob Howsam; he had a question for Sparky, a question that was remarkably similar to a proposition eleven years earlier.

Déjà vu is French for "already seen." In 1965 Reds owner and general manager Bill DeWitt had asked the question to himself. Frank Robinson was the first player of color to make an impact for the Cincinnati Reds. Frankie Robinson, as he was then known, arrived at the Reds in 1956. He had a stellar rookie year, hitting .290 with thirty-eight home runs on his way to Rookie of the Year honors. He became a fixture in the outfield and the Reds' star player through 1965. As he neared the end of the third decade of his life, Robinson's attitude began to sour, at least in the eyes of Reds ownership. Reality or not, that was the perception. Things began to deteriorate when Robinson was arrested for possessing a gun at a local nightclub. At times he was surly in attitude. DeWitt dealt him months later with the infamous statement, "Robinson is an old thirty."

The fact that a star player was traded is not as surprising as what the Reds received in return. Milt Pappas was a twenty-six-year-old right-handed pitcher for the Baltimore Orioles who had won thirteen games in 1965. The Orioles also threw in Jack Baldschun (a journeyman reliever) and Dick Simpson (a light-hitting, seldom-used outfielder). So that was essentially the trade: Frank Robinson for Milt Pappas.

Robinson's career was reenergized in Baltimore. He won the Triple Crown on his way to the AL MVP Award in his first year with the team. He also led the Orioles to their first world championship in 1966. He went on to make three more World Series appearances with the Orioles, winning the '70 Classic against his former team. In 1975 he became the player-manager of the Cleveland Indians, the first black man to hold such a position. He finished his career with 586 home runs, fourth on the career list at the time, and was inducted into the Baseball Hall of Fame in 1982.

On the other hand, Milt Pappas went 12–11 for the Reds in his first season. He was mediocre on the mound and a clubhouse lawyer off it. By the time the Reds reached the World Series against Frank Robinson in 1970, Pappas had already been traded to Atlanta after chalking up thirty wins for the Reds in two-plus years.

Now Howsam had a deal on the table: Tony Perez for Woodie Fryman. Howsam was torn inside. On the one hand there was increasing pressure to get Danny Driessen into the lineup on a regular basis. He was just too good to sit on the bench every day. They had tried third base and Driessen had hit well but they just couldn't live with his defense. He was a first baseman but that is where Perez resided and Perez had already been tried at third. The Reds couldn't live with *his* defense there either, especially now that he was thirty-four. That was the other rub, Perez was nine years senior to Driessen. Perez was on the backside of his career, while Driessen's best years lay ahead.

Howsam and others sensed the pressure mounting after Driessen's performance in the 1976 World Series. It is amazing what a four-game series can do to change minds. It can have too much influence. His .357 average with a home run and RBI over four games promised bigger things over an entire season. He didn't have the power that Perez did but he was faster and the Reds valued speed. If Perez's power departed, they still had Bench at age twenty-eight and Foster whose power seemed to grow each year at age twenty-seven.

There was something else nagging at Howsam, something he usually didn't let get involved in baseball decisions—his feelings and his emotions. He had long held to the adage, "I love the game but I am not in love with the game." The same thing held with his players. He liked them but did not want to get emotionally attached to them. The problem was that he really liked Tony Perez and he liked his family. The thought of Perez sitting on the bench didn't sit well emotionally with Howsam. He liked Perez and he wanted to have him play everyday. With the emergence of Driessen that was looking increasingly unlikely in Cincinnati.

So Howsam worked the phones. Teams liked Perez but were leery of his age. The Montreal Expos seemed to be offering the best deal, Fryman for Perez. Woodie Fryman was at age thirty-six an eleven-year veteran who had won thirteen games the previous season, the same total as Pappas. Howsam wanted to know what Sparky thought.

Anderson had many of the same thoughts that Howsam had. He hated to see Driessen waste away on the bench. At the same time he was a big Tony Perez fan. He also had felt the urgency to get Driessen into the lineup after his performance against the Yankees. He remembered how badly he had wanted to get Foster's talent on the field every day and what big dividends that had paid. In the end, he okayed the deal.

There was another part of the deal that made it slightly easier for Howsam to stomach. The Reds would send one of the Gold Dust Twins, Will McEnaney, to Montreal with Perez. McEnaney had been a big disappointment in 1976 and the Reds were not sure he would return to his 1975 form. In exchange the Expos would send a big right-handed relief pitcher, Dale Murray, to the Reds. Murray had come off two workhorse seasons. He won fifteen games in relief in 1975 and then saved thirteen games while working in eighty-one for the lowly Expos in 1976. Murray promised to have many bright years ahead as he was only twenty-six. Howsam was very excited about him.

Opening Day 1977 found the two-time defending World Champion Cincinnati Reds facing the perennial cellar-dwelling San Diego Padres. All the position players were the same except for Driessen in Perez's slot at first: Foster, Geronimo, and Griffey were stationed from left to right field; Rose, Concepcion, and Morgan were left to right in the infield; Bench was again behind the plate; and Woodie Fryman was on the mound. Fryman was not the man the Reds would have preferred as the Opening Day starter but Don Gullett was now in New York where the Reds had won the Series seven months earlier.

Marvin Miller's work had now affected Cincinnati's team directly. Miller professed to be a baseball fan and said it was one factor in his decision to leave the steel industry for baseball. But make no mistake, regardless of his affinity for baseball, Marvin Miller's first and foremost allegiance was to the union. Miller was very savvy. When arbitrator Pete Seitz announced that the reserve clause was not legally binding, Miller realized that the decision could actually be harmful to his players' salaries and thus to his salary and job security. If hundreds of players decided to become free agents each year, it would flood the market with talent. Following the rules of supply and demand, supply would outstrip demand and salaries could actually drop. So Miller approached own-

What do to with Danny Driessen and Tony Perez (pictured here with Howsam, in the early 1970s) was a question that gnawed at Bob Howsam in the off-season of 1976–77 (photograph courtesy Roadwest Publishing [Jack Klumpe Collection]).

ership with the offer to limit free agent availability. His initial offer was that players could only become free agents after six years of minor- and major-league experience combined. The owners countered with ten years of major-league service. After poor negotiating by owners, the two parties settled on six years of major-league service, an agreement reached in July 1976. The first free agents would go on the market after the 1976 season.

Don Gullett became eligible for free agency after the 1976 season. When Gullett's future came up in NBC post-game World Series clubhouse interviews the previous October, Sparky had confidently predicted, "Donnie will be back with us." He was wrong. Gullet had arrived with the Reds as a nineteen-year-old in 1970. By the mid–1970s he was their best pitcher. His good fastball and the forkball he developed in later years made him one of the best pitchers in the game. He was Johnny Bench's first choice to be on the mound. His .686 winning percentage was the best lifetime of any pitcher in the 1970s and is fourth best in the game's history.[1]

The Yankees had been impressed with Gullett's performance in the Series. Their owner, George Steinbrenner, eager to upgrade the club after its disgraceful Series performance against the Reds, wanted Gullett. He offered Gullett two million dollars for six years; pretty good for a kid from Lynn, Kentucky.

The offer was ironic in many ways. Gullett's experience in contract negotiations had not been pleasant. Bob Howsam and Dick Wagner handled negotiations for the Reds. Both were experienced business men. They were interested in paying players for their services, while being very mindful of keeping the balance sheets in the black. They wanted to pay the players fairly. The players also wanted to be paid fairly, knowing that they were one injury away from being out of baseball on any given day. Even injury-free they knew their playing days would likely last only ten to fifteen years in the big leagues. What they considered fair and what ownership considered fair were two different things.

Initially it was the player sitting across the desk from Howsam or Wagner, eyeball to eyeball. Gullett said he would have rather faced Henry Aaron with the bases loaded. In Gullett's case he was in his young twenties, a few years removed from high school. Both Wagner and Howsam had been in baseball longer than Gullett had been alive. The match-up didn't seem very even, at least not in the players' minds.

To help even the playing field, the players began to hire agents. This generally was not well received by the public at large or by ownership in particular. A great story is told about Vince Lombardi, the legendary Green Bay Packer coach and general manager. Jim Ringo, the Packer center and team captain, had hired an agent to represent him during contract talks. Ringo had been a Pro Bowl center for seven years. The agent walked in and introduced himself to Lombardi. He said, "Hello, I am here to represent my client, Jim Ringo." Lombardi said hello and excused himself for a moment. Lombardi went to another room and came back several minutes later. "Mr. Agent, your client is now a Philadelphia Eagle." That certainly reduced the number of agents employed by the rest of the Packers.

The practice, however, was catching on with other teams and other sports. Many of the Reds had hired agents by this point. Gullett's agent was Jerry Kapstein, a man who represented nine of the twenty-six free agents available. When he didn't get the terms he wanted from the Reds, he went to the team with the biggest pockets, which happened to be Mr. Steinbrenner's team. It was a scenario that would repeat itself that same year. Reggie Jackson was signed by the Yankees as well as Gullett. The trend would continue over the subsequent years with increasing regularity. In 2004 Steinbrenner was one of only a few owners who could afford to pick up Alex Rodriguez's ludicrous ten-year, $252 million contract from the Texas Rangers. Reggie Jackson signed with the Yankees for $2.96 million at the end of 1976. George Steinbrenner bought the Yankees for $10 million from CBS in 1972. Four years later he was paying two players half of that sum.

Gullett's main issue was not so much the money but the length of the contract. He wanted a five-year deal. The Reds hesitated on that request. Gullett had completed only one full season of work since becoming a starter in 1971. He'd had an assortment of injuries, including a broken thumb and a sore neck, as well as hepatitis. The Reds offered a two-year deal. There were two reasons that Howsam offered two years. One was Gullett's history of injury, the other was out of principle. Bob Howsam strongly felt that players with long-term contracts relaxed and did not play as well. It was and is human nature. The evidence certainly backed up Howsam's claim. In the end, the length of the contract and the big bucks of New York were the deal breaker. Gullett went to the Yankees.

With Gullett gone to New York, the Reds' best remaining pitcher was Jack Billingham. Don Gullett had been the best pitcher; he also happened to be a lefty. That was one attraction to Woodie Fryman, he was left-handed. Fryman, though, was more like the third starter, not the number one. Starters are generally listed as one through four or five (depending on the size of the rotation); the lower number indicating greater value. Woodie Fryman was no spring chicken either, having just turned thirty-seven. Like Billingham, Fryman was not enthralled to be pitching for Sparky, except it was even worse. As the 1977 season wore on, Fryman and Anderson separated like oil and water. Increasingly disgruntled, Fryman ended the season with five wins and five losses.

Jack Billingham was beginning to show his age as well. Now thirty-four, his win total had gone from nineteen to fifteen to twelve over the previous three years. Even more indicative was his ERA, which was now hovering above five runs per game. A good starting pitcher at the time would have an ERA in the mid threes. An average in that range gives the team a chance to win on a regular basis. His number of innings pitched dropped from a high of 293 in 1973 to only 161 in 1977. He no longer had the strong back to carry a heavy pitching load.

Little Fredie Norman was still plugging along, with fourteen wins in 1977 and a good ERA; however, Gary Nolan was again having injury worries. After missing most of 1973 and all of 1974, Nolan was having problems with his arm again. He was only twenty-nine and was fresh off of consecutive fifteen-win seasons but he just couldn't get going. He was 4–4 and the front office and coaches felt like he wasn't going to recover a second time. Howsam dealt him to the California Angels for Craig Hendrickson, a minor league player. Using Howsam's value-for-value yardstick, one can tell what the Reds saw for Gary Nolan's future.

In the bullpen there was a problem. Rawly Eastwick won the inaugural Rolaids Relief Award in 1976. This was one of the first awards to be commercially sponsored with the name of a commercial product. The Rolaids Relief Award is given to the player with the most saves and wins combined. Eastwick's total was 37 in 1976. Considering himself the league's top reliever, Eastwick was looking for lots of money and a long-term deal with the Reds. If he didn't get it, he declared that he would become a free agent. Howsam did not want to get burned again. He was not going to give any player, especially a pitcher, a long-term contract. He believed that the player's performance would dip if he did so. He also knew that if he gave it to one player, he would be opening the floodgates to giving it to many players. Negotiations reached a standstill.

In Howsam's mind there were too many similarities between the Eastwick and Gullett cases for his comfort. Rawly Eastwick was represented by Jerry Kapstein, who also was Don Gullett's agent. Kapstein was not the Reds, or any club's, favorite agent. Fool me once, shame on you; fool me twice, shame on me. Howsam picked up the phone. Eastwick was traded to the St. Louis Cardinals for left-handed pitcher Doug Capilla. The trade was made on the trade deadline of June 15, 1977.[2]

By June, seven games behind the Los Angeles Dodgers, Howsam realized the Reds needed some pitching help. After twenty-three one-year contracts, Walter Alston, the Dodgers manager, had decided to retire. He was replaced by his energetic third-base coach, Tommy Lasorda. Lasorda had long been considered managerial material. He was the heir apparent to Alston but the Montreal Expos had wanted him while he was waiting for Alston to call it quits. They aggressively went after him after the 1975 season. Lasorda was tempted but he had a line he used often with the Dodgers. He would refer to "that Big Dodger in the Sky." He couldn't imagine telling an Expo pitcher to look to "that Big Expo in the Sky." So he turned the job down. Peter O'Malley was impressed with the loyalty. He thanked Lasorda but made him no promises. One year later he gave Lasorda the job he really wanted—Dodgers manager.

Lasorda's energy and positive outlook was absorbed by the Dodgers. Sixteen years junior to Alston, he was refreshing for the Dodgers. If Alston was the wise and calm grandfather, Lasorda was the fun-loving, energetic and suc-

Woodie Fryman's girth is suggestive of the size of bust he was with the Reds. He won five games in 1977. The Perez-Fryman trade was the worst of the Howsam era. The Big Red Machine was never the same (photograph courtesy Roadwest Publishing [Jack Klumpe Collection]).

Sparky pegged Don Gullett for the Hall of Fame. The precocious young talent was often plagued by injury. When he was healthy there was no one better in the 1970s (photograph courtesy Roadwest Publishing [Jack Klumpe Collection]).

cessful uncle, the one you love to be around at family reunions. Besides Lasorda's youth and vigor, the Dodgers had something the Reds did not, good starting pitching. Don Sutton, Doug Rau, Burt Hooten, Rick Rhoden and Tommy John (back from surgery), made a great starting rotation. Mike Marshall, who had boasted of the efficacy of his arm calisthenics, had been beset by arm troubles and shipped to Atlanta. He had been replaced in the bullpen by knuckleballer Charlie Hough. The everyday players were very good and continued to populate the All-Star lineup with the Reds.

Howsam could sense that his club was in trouble. A midseason solution needed to be found and Howsam was looking for it. Winds starting blowing around the league that Tom Seaver, the Reds nemesis in the 1973 playoffs, was unhappy in New York. Howsam picked up the scent. Seaver was feeling unappreciated in New York. He was not happy with the contract he had signed prior to the 1976 season, $225,000 a year for three years, which was full of incentives and penalties depending on performance. He was even more unhappy with the New York Mets front office's seeming contentment to have mediocre hitters and fielders around him. Seaver wanted the club to improve.

Seaver had rebounded from a shoulder and pelvis injury in 1974 to notch twenty-two wins in '75 and his third Cy Young Award. Though he dipped a bit in '76, he had averaged nineteen wins each year since 1969. His disgruntlement reached a peak during a June road trip. He picked up the New York paper and read an article written by veteran sports writer Dick Young. Seaver considered Young to be the mouthpiece for Mets Chairman of the Board M. Donald Grant. He couldn't believe what he read. Young reported that Seaver was pushing for a raise because Seaver's wife, Nancy, was jealous that their friend Nolan Ryan made more than Tom did. Seaver called back to the Mets and told Grant he wanted out of New York.[3]

Howsam returned to a ritual he had perfected over the years. He went alone into the Reds' conference room with a phone. He loved to work the phone. On the large conference table he had his papers of information and statistics on various players with other organizations spread out in a systematic way. He was alone at these times, always alone. As a negotiating tactic he would often name players he wasn't really interested in trading for or trading. By working trades alone Howsam didn't need to worry about explaining his methods or being interrupted by a well-meaning colleague.

When Howsam called the Mets General Manager Joe McDonald that day, he brought Seaver's name up gingerly. He discussed several different players before he got around to Seaver. When he did, the Mets were ready to listen. The Reds weren't really willing to part with an everyday talent. They liked what they had in place. They did, however, have an abundance of talent seemingly ready for good everyday play but with nowhere to move up to in an already crowded field of established All-Stars. After postseason births in 1969 and '73, the Mets had begun to age and were looking to rebuild with young talent. The Reds had what the Mets were shopping for — value-for-value was the principle again.

In the end the Reds offered Pat Zachry, who had been the team's fifth Rookie of the Year the previous season. They also included infielder Doug Flynn, promising Class-AAA outfielder Steve Henderson, and minor-league outfielder Dan Norman. The Mets would give Tom Seaver in return. Howsam cut the deal on June 15, the same day he dealt Gary Nolan.

When it hit the press, the Mets fans were incensed. They felt they had been fleeced, just as Reds fans had felt they had been fleeced over the Lee May deal. How could you get zero established talent for an All-Star pitcher? Zachry and Seaver had both been Rookies of the Year, but that is where the similarities ended. The Mets justifiably explained that they had been caught between a rock and a hard place. It was no secret that Seaver wasn't happy, so teams knew the Mets had to deal him. There also was a short list of teams that Seaver was willing to go to: Cincinnati, Los Angeles, Pittsburgh and Philadelphia — the National League powerhouses. As a ten-year veteran with at least five years on the same team, Seaver had the right to veto any trade. The Mets also feared that if they didn't trade Seaver, he could have an adverse affect on the ball club. Disgruntled players can be divisive, though that didn't seem to be in Seaver's character. The Mets also knew that in a year and a half Seaver could leave to free agency, perhaps even to crosstown rival George Steinbrenner. Getting young, promising talent, and lots of it, was about the best the Mets could hope for and was really what they needed for a guy like Seaver. They weren't planning to win the title any time soon.

"Look Who's In Cincy" said the *Sports Illustrated* cover that week. Reds fans' hopes were buoyed. Much-needed pitching help had arrived and it was among the best in the game. Seaver was excited as well; he had a good shot at another World Series title. His excitement showed in his first outing with the Reds, a complete game, three-hit shutout of the Montreal Expos. Not even in his World Championship year of 1969 had Seaver been surrounded by so much talent.

Fans, Howsam and Sparky Anderson also were excited that the acquisition of Seaver had not cost the Reds an everyday player, especially a Big Four player. Technically, it was now the Big Three with the departure of Perez, but Foster filled the fourth spot nicely. He was having a season that Perez, and for that matter Bench and Morgan, had never had. Foster hit the ball harder than any man in baseball. His strong arms and wrists were pounding out home runs on a pace not seen since the days of Maris and Mantle. He had twenty-nine home runs by the All-Star break in mid–July, nearly the total of the league leader for all of 1974.

Foster's power was awe-inspiring but sometimes it got him in trouble as it had once during the previous season. The center-field wall was 404 feet from home plate at Riverfront. One night he hit a towering blast to dead center. He paused at home plate to admire his work and then realized with its trajectory that the ball might not clear the fence. He was right and, with good speed for a power hitter, he broke quickly for first. He barely managed a double after the ball hit the top of the wall. It was a good reminder to admire your work after it is done. Foster had plenty to admire at season's end, fifty-two homers to break Big Klu's club record of forty-nine, and the most in baseball since Mantle's fifty-four and Maris's sixty-one in 1961. His work also was admired by the sports writers who voted him National League MVP, the fourth Red to be chosen in eight years, with six MVPs among them.[4]

Johnny Bench also rebounded nicely from his sub-par 1976 season. Perhaps he was buoyed by his World Series performance. More likely he was able to concentrate on baseball again. Ballplayers have personal lives too. If life at home isn't going well, it can affect play on the field. Johnny Bench's personal life was going very poorly. His marriage was, at best, rocky. It was over by the end of 1976. It ended almost as quickly as it started, less than two years. With his marriage woes temporarily behind him, Bench had another good offensive year with thirty-one home runs and 109 RBIs.

Howsam got a surprise call from his secretary one day. He had some guests who wanted to see him. He opened the door to find Johnny Bench and Joe Morgan. They wanted to talk. Howsam invited them in. They exchanged pleasantries. What was it they wanted to see him about? They had a question.

"Mr. Howsam, how come you never come down to the clubhouse to visit the team?"

Howsam knew the answer immediately; it was a long-standing principle of his and he figured the players appreciated it. He told them that he considered the clubhouse the player's second home. They were away from their own homes so much during the season that he wanted them to view the clubhouse as their own. A place they could relax and be themselves. He felt that the last thing the players wanted was for the front office staff to be hanging around, looking over their shoulders. He felt that this would change their behavior and they would feel like they had to act a certain way, much like a teenager when his or her parents are around.

Bench and Morgan appreciated the sentiment but didn't completely agree with the policy. They thought that Howsam's presence would show his personal interest in the players as individuals. In essence it would show that he cared. They told him so and asked that he reconsider his position.

After they talked, Howsam thought about it and decided to compromise. Howsam would visit the clubhouse on a regular basis. He would come by at a set time before game time and visit with players. He would then leave and not return until before the next game. The solution proved to be satisfactory to both parties, value-for-value. Howsam got to know his team and players better. The Reds saw firsthand that he cared about them as people, not just players.

While changing his longtime philosophy on not visiting the clubhouse,

Quiet George Foster got a shot in left field when Rose moved to third base. His wrists were not big, but they were strong and quick like Hank Aaron's. Foster's 1977 season was the most monstrous hitting year of the Big Red Machine era. He hit the ball harder than any man in baseball (photograph courtesy Roadwest Publishing [Jack Klumpe Collection]).

Howsam developed another to fit his new tradition. He decided he would treat every player equally during his visits, regardless of status. This simply meant that a utility player would get the same amount of time and attention that a Big Four member got. He would chit-chat with each player equally, no one "earned" more of this time or attention than others. This bothered a few of the better-known players. They were use to the press and fans making a fuss over them. The Big Four even had greater access and input to Sparky Anderson in exchange for their clubhouse leadership. Some didn't particularly like it that they weren't getting the same treatment from Howsam. Even though it bothered them to a degree, overall they were still glad he visited. The change in policy was a good one.

A policy that was not going to change was personal dress and appearance. Sparky still demanded coat and tie with slacks (not jeans) on all road trips. Facial hair and excessively long hair, were forbidden. No one was going to have the type of afro sported by George Hendrick nor were they going to rival the Beatles in their length of hair. On the field they were still going to wear only black polished spikes without sponsor endorsement and conservative stirrups on the socks.

While players on other teams were receiving thousands of dollars from sponsors for wearing a shoe logo on the side of the shoe, the Reds simply removed the logos and the players received nothing. That was fine with the players. They more than made up for it in postseason money. In the days from 1970 to 1976, the Reds received approximately $80,000 in World Series and postseason shares. Teams reaching the playoffs and World Series received bonus money from the television contracts and other money generated from the Fall Classic. The teams divvied it up amongst themselves. They would give the batboys a small share and perhaps give a portion to a player who had been traded in midseason but the rest went to the current team members. For some of the players the shares amounted to 150 percent of their regular salary. For example, in 1970 the league's minimum salary was $10,000 and several Reds were paid that much. Their 1970 World Series share was $15,000, far more than they would receive from a shoe sponsor. The shares don't seem much compared to today's salaries but in the 1970s and prior, they were a huge incentive.

In a world where some profess to be good role models but don't live up to it, Tom Seaver was genuine. In a game known for swingers, Tom Seaver was a dedicated family man. He was the real thing. Often his family would be at the Greater Cincinnati Airport to greet the star upon his return from the road. He would meet his family at the airport after a road trip and walk from the plane with his little girl, Annie, in his arms and his devoted wife, Nancy, at his side. He was refreshingly unlike the stereotype of a professional ballplayer. He also was refreshing on the mound. He won all six games he pitched in August.

Upon the Seaver trade on June 15, the Reds were seven games behind the

Dodgers. At the end of July, they were playing only .500 ball and were fourteen games back. Despite Seaver's unbelievable August, the Reds gained only five and a half games on the Dodgers. They desperately wanted to overtake the team in September. In the end they couldn't do it. The Dodgers finished ten games ahead of the Reds; a complete turn around from 1976 when they had finished ten games in back of the Reds.

Howsam sat down in September to reevaluate the season, as was his habit. Why had the Reds come up short after being so dominant the previous year? One had to admit that the Dodgers pitching had been outstanding all year long. As the old adage goes, "good pitching beats good hitting," and it seemed to hold. The Dodgers had both great pitching and good hitting all year long. The Reds had great hitting but poor pitching, at least until Seaver came along. Gullett was gone and Fryman was lousy. Billingham was showing his age.

The relief corps were not what they used to be, either. Borbon was still consistent, with his rubber arm, logging 127 innings, but the Gold Dust Twins

didn't sparkle like they had. Eastwick was solid but locked in a salary dispute with the front office. The New York Mets initially wanted Eastwick instead of Zachry in the Seaver deal but Eastwick's contract difficulties squelched that, thus the Eastwick for Capilla deal in the last of the June 15 trades. As a result, Borbon became the leader of the committee of closer. McEnaney had been shipped to Montreal for Dale Murray, who was a big disappointment in Cincinnati. With Clay Carroll's departure for Chicago the previous season, the bullpen didn't have the depth it had enjoyed for so many years.

Another reason for the Reds' dip seemed to be physical conditioning. It's true that they were a year older but the Reds didn't seem to be in as good a shape as they had been physically. They seemed a step

Tom Seaver was a genuine family man. His arrival in 1977 gave the Reds hope of resurgence, but they were unable to overcome the deficit and the Dodgers. It was the last of Howsam's great trades (photograph courtesy Roadwest Publishing [Jack Klumpe Collection]).

slow, a pound or two heavy, a half second too late.[5] Professional athletes usually train year-round, especially in today's free-agent world where salaries allow them the luxury of no off-season job. However, when you win a world championship, an already high demand for speaking engagements begins to soar. The "rubber chicken" circuit beckons and pays well, a guest dinner here, a banquet there, some off-season income, but also less time to work out. You arrive at spring training, not quite in the shape you had hoped to be, but you plan to make up for it. You don't quite get there and then the season and the grind starts. That seemed to be another factor.

The most obtuse factor to reflect on was the Perez trade. On paper it seemed to be even. Perez hit .283 with nineteen home runs and ninety-one RBIs for Montreal, while Danny Driessen had almost identical numbers for the Reds— .300, seventeen home runs and ninety-one RBIs. One has to keep in mind that Driessen had many more opportunities than did Perez to drive in runs with a talented lineup around him. There weren't as many targets of opportunity for Perez in Montreal, which make his numbers all the more impressive. His streak of eleven years with ninety-plus RBIs continued in sparser grazing land.

There was, however, something more than statistics to consider regarding the trade. Howsam didn't realize it until he changed his no visiting philosophy and began getting to know the culture and the feel of the clubhouse. Perez's biggest contribution to the Big Red Machine was not at third base or first base or at the plate or anywhere on the field for that matter. Perez's biggest contribution was in the clubhouse and in the dugout. It was the kind of person that he was and is.

Rose and Morgan had sensed the trade coming even in the middle of the 1976 World Series and the thought saddened them. Joe Morgan said of Perez, "He's the one guy you look at and say, 'He's a man.' He's the one you want your little boy to be like."[6]

Some have said that Sparky Anderson was fortunate to have leaders on the ball club from different ethnic groups. That is a true statement but it tends to obscure an important fact. Yes, the white players would perhaps be drawn to Bench and Rose while the black ballplayers could perhaps relate better to Joe Morgan. The Latin ballplayers, especially with the language barrier, could communicate more effectively with Perez. But the danger in the statement is to infer that Perez was only the leader of the Latin players. As Sparky said, "that is a big misconception." Perez was a leader for everybody. He was the only player who had everybody's ear, including Bench, Morgan and Rose. He was a leader's leader. Anderson would later say he never saw a leader like Tony Perez. "What a leader."

Intangibles, those things that we can never quite put our finger on, are hard to define. They sometimes make all the difference in the world. They sometimes make World Championship differences. If Carroll's departure had been like losing a longtime neighbor, Perez's had been like losing the heart of the family. The Reds had lost part of the essence of who they were; it was not the same machine anymore.

Bob Howsam doesn't like to look back. He doesn't second guess himself; he makes the very best decision he can make at the time, weighing all the facts and inputs of his advisors. He then pulls the trigger and moves on. But this one he looked back on, especially as the years wore on. He had let his emotions, his desire for Tony Perez to play everyday, get in the way. With 20/20 hindsight, he wishes he would have directed Sparky Anderson to declare an open competition for first base and let the seasoned veteran Perez battle it out with the young-gun Driessen. But he didn't; his heart won out, and he made the trade, influenced by feelings.[7] He regrets it. Reds players would later say that there was one reason they finished second that year: Tony Perez was in Montreal.

The disgruntled Fryman was shipped to the Chicago Cubs at season's end. He went on to win thirty-one games in six seasons. Perez would play nine more seasons and end up at Cooperstown, New York. To quote the legendary Yogi Berra, "It was déjà vu all over again."

21

TIME TO MOVE ON
December 1977–February 1978

As Howsam looked back upon the 1977 season he began to try to figure out how to remedy the problems. One of the primary areas he targeted was pitching. Fryman was obviously not the replacement for Gullett, so Howsam set out to find someone else. He seemed to find the answer by the San Francisco Bay.

After the Reds were defeated by the Oakland A's in the great Series of 1972, the A's fortunes continued to increase and then plummeted rapidly. After three straight World Series titles, the A's were swept in the 1975 playoffs by Boston. That was the point when the wheels began to fall off. As the years progressed, things continued to unravel. The most bizarre episode was when Finley named sixteen-year-old batboy Stanley Burrell the club's executive vice president. Burrell was famous for entertaining players in the clubhouse with his dance moves. His other credentials for being named executive vice president were unknown.[1]

With Peter Seitz's ruling that players could become free agents, Finley could see the handwriting on the wall. Finley realized what other small market owners would later learn: he couldn't hold on to his talent. He had lost Catfish Hunter in a contract blunder. He knew that Ken Holtzman and Reggie Jackson were due to be free agents, so he traded them to Baltimore at the beginning of the 1976 season. In the small market of Oakland there was no way he was going to be able to keep his stable of superstars. He would be cleaned out by the 1978 season. He decided that if he couldn't afford to re-sign them, he would at least get money for them before they left.

Finley began a fire sale in June of 1976. First on the block were Joe Rudi and Rollie Fingers, who could become free agents at the end of 1976. Finley sold them to the Boston Red Sox. Just to keep things even between bitter rivals, Finley sold Vida Blue to the New York Yankees. Finley was to receive $3.5 million for the three players combined. Commissioner Bowie Kuhn voided both deals declaring they were not in the best interest of baseball. Sure enough Finley lost both Rudi and Fingers at the end of the year and received nothing in return.

Vida Blue was not eligible for free agency yet and he was left-handed. Like so many power pitchers in the 1970s, Blue relied heavily upon a great fastball. Invariably, a few years later those type of pitchers were heard saying, "I finally learned how to pitch," after their strong young arms began to give way. Howsam contacted his old foe Finley to see if they could work out a deal for Blue. After negotiations in Honolulu, Hawaii, at the December 1977 baseball winter meetings, Howsam offered Finley $1 million and Dave Revering for Blue's services. Finley agreed. Kuhn stepped in again, voiding the deal as "not in the best interest of baseball."

Howsam was furious. He and Kuhn had a good relationship; they were friends and Howsam admired the job Kuhn had done under difficult circumstances. However, Howsam felt that Kuhn was dead wrong in this case when he imposed an arbitrary $400,000 maximum price that could be paid for another player. Meanwhile a club could lose a player with no compensation whatsoever. Undaunted Finley traded Blue to San Francisco for seven players and $390,000 three months after the deal with Cincinnati. Fight as he might, Howsam respected the authority of the commissioner and tried to fight the decision through official baseball channels. When that failed, he let the matter drop.[2]

Bob Howsam's handling of the aborted Vida Blue deal says a lot about who he is. He felt the commissioner's decision was both incorrect and arbitrary. He did not view the decision as right or legal. He possibly could have sued in court and won, yet he chose another path. He wrote to the other owners of baseball clubs asking for their help in fighting to overturn this policy and stated the reasons for it. Though the legal option was there, he did not take it. He did not feel that the courts were the place to settle baseball disputes.

Being the general manager of a baseball team is hard work but the work was not Howsam's alone; the work was shared by all. Bob Howsam had a philosophy: work your people hard and reward them for it. Wagner and all the others who worked for Howsam had no doubt that he expected hard work. He poured it on but it was work they enjoyed, so they didn't mind.[3] The long hours and the determination required to work for a major-league club are best exemplified by Greg Park. Park represents the hundreds of employees that work for major-league clubs who are never mentioned on TV or the radio. They don't show up in the box scores or anywhere in the sports page but without their efforts, the games would not go on.

Park graduated from Wittenberg University with a business degree and then got an MBA from Bowling Green State University in 1972. He went into the banking industry but he really wanted to be in baseball. After eighteen months he was miserable. His wife, Pam, advised him, "Why don't you follow your dreams?"

So Greg Park went upstairs and typed a letter to every one of the twenty-four major-league baseball teams. This was before the era of word processors. He typed all twenty-four letters by hand on his Sears portable typewriter. He received twenty-four "no thank you" letters in return. Several months later he was still frustrated at the bank and his wife encouraged him again to follow his dreams. He pulled out the typewriter again. He mailed off twenty-four more letters to major-league clubs. He received another twenty-four rejections. The cycle was repeated every few months for three years. He even mailed letters to minor-league teams, hoping that they would be a steppingstone to the majors. He actually got an offer from the Evansville Triplets but the salary was too low. Greg and Pam were committed to having Pam stay home to raise the children. At the salary Evansville could offer, Greg couldn't feed Pam or the kids.

Several years went by; all in all 304 "no thank you" letters were received. Then one day, he got a different letter. "You are invited for an interview with the Cincinnati Reds." The invitation came after his seventh letter to the Reds. After a day-long interview, Greg Park's dream was fulfilled; the Cincinnati Reds offered him a job in the accounting department. Now the hard work really began.

During the season Park reported to work around 8:00 A.M. He would eat lunch at work. At dinner he ate with other front-office staff and the broadcasters. He would stay for the evening's game, accounting for ticket sales and revenues. He would usually finish up around the seventh-inning stretch, by 9:30 P.M. or 10:00 P.M. He would then drive home and go to bed. Since they were still committed to Pam being at home for the kids, he would get up at 6:00 A.M. in order to spend two hours with Pam and the children. Breakfast time was the family mealtime. He would jump in the car and repeat the procedure while Pam cared for the kids. They occasionally would join him at a ballgame.

Weekends were no different, except during afternoon games when he got home at 6:00 P.M. Long homestands were the worst and made the job the most difficult. There would be stretches of twenty-five days with no days off. It was long hours from April to September each season. The off-season was a lot better; then he only put in 8–5 days.[4] Greg Park is not an isolated case. Some people work longer hours, some work shorter. It is the life of front-office staff in the big leagues. You won't last long if you are looking at your watch.

As a result of this hard work, the Reds ran a huge operation with a little more than fifty people. They were dedicated, loyal, and very good. Both Bob Howsam and Dick Wagner made sure staff were rewarded for it. They treated their staff as professionals and recognized their skills. Each December the head of a department would deliver a letter by hand from Dick Wagner informing the employee of their pay increase for the year. The raises were fair and depended on the Reds fortunes that year, a first- or second-place finish was much more profitable than finishing last.

Many of the rewards were family-oriented. One Sunday each summer all employees and their families were invited for a picnic on the field of Riverfront Stadium while the team was out of town. Each family was sent a turkey at Thanksgiving. There was a luncheon for the wives once a year hosted by Janet

Howsam and Gloria Wagner. Employees and their spouses were taken on a riverboat cruise every summer and invited to a formal dinner at the Reds annual Hall of Fame Induction Dinner.

During the playoffs the Reds received tickets to other playoff games in both leagues. An employee could get the ticket for free and pay their way to the game where they had very nice seats. The best perk of all was the World Series. When the Reds were in the series, full-time employees and their spouses were flown out for at least one game in the visiting park.[5] Hard work was expected but the rewards were there as well.

Shortly after the Vida Blue affair, Bob Howsam was having his weekly lunch with Louis Nippert. They dined at the Queen City Club on East Fourth Street most of the time. Sometimes they would have lunch at Mr. Nippert's home. Nippert was part of the eleven-member group (originally known as the "617 Group") that bought the Reds from Bill DeWitt prior to the 1967 season. After the first six seasons, Nippert decided he wanted a bigger share of the team. He had the wealth to acquire it. He was from the Gamble family, as in Proctor and Gamble, the household-goods empire headquartered in Cincinnati.

Though he was a man of considerable means, he was not overly impressed with himself. He certainly wasn't spoiled. He cut his own grass at his home in Indian Hill, a wealthy Cincinnati suburb, and often packed his own lunch for work. He was a tremendous benefactor of the people of Cincinnati. Some of his family's donations were well known; the University of Cincinnati's (and for a short time the Bengals') football stadium is named in honor of the family. Most of his philanthropic work, however, was of the anonymous variety. When someone would approach him with a need that he felt was worthy, he would respond with a question. "How much does it take to go over the top?" Then he would often pull out a pen and write a check for the entire sum, without a word uttered on TV or in the newspaper about it.[6] Every town needs a man like Louis Nippert.

Before Nippert would agree to increase his shares with the team, he wanted an assurance from Bob Howsam. He wanted Howsam to stay on with the Reds for at least five years. Howsam agreed. Nippert then acquired more than 90 percent of the team. Over the years Nippert and Howsam became good friends. They met weekly for lunch, except when one of them was on the road. The topic was rarely baseball. Howsam would fill him in on the important baseball news and then they talked about life, family, politics, business, and local, national and international affairs. Nippert was a very interesting man to talk with, a great conversationalist.[7]

Nippert trusted Howsam completely in all baseball matters. Nippert had to approve financial matters but that was essentially a rubber stamp of Howsam's decision. Both Nippert and the other owners had kept their word when they hired Howsam away from St. Louis, Howsam was free to run the ball club as he saw fit. Howsam represented the Reds at all official baseball meetings. Bob Howsam came to the Reds as general manager, was later promoted to vice president, and became president of the Reds in 1973. Even though they were friends, Howsam always called him "Mr. Nippert." Howsam had been taught to always use the honorific "mister" with older men, out of respect. He had the greatest respect for Mr. Nippert.

The past season, the commissioner, and Vida Blue were not all that Bob Howsam was thinking about in that off-season. True, he had been disappointed with the 1977 effort, but he was confident that the situation could be turned around in 1978. There were other things he was not so confident of. He was concerned about the state of the game as a

Bob Howsam (left) viewed Reds majority owner Mister Nippert (right) as a second father. They had the utmost respect for one another (photograph courtesy Roadwest Publishing [Jack Klumpe Collection]).

whole. Throughout the history of the United States the pendulum has swung back and forth between the power of management and the power of workers. In the case of baseball, ownership had enjoyed the upper hand for decades. The players had made great strides toward equilibrium but now the pendulum had begun to swing past the center and toward the players' side. Howsam and others felt it was swinging too far. He sensed trouble for baseball.

Howsam had always been a bit of a visionary or perhaps even a prophet. He had foreseen good things for the family honey business and helped get it off the ground and profitable after World War II. He had seen opportunity in going to work for Senator Johnson in Washington, D.C. Once Johnson asked him to run the Western League and help with the Denver Bears, he sensed opportunity and bought the ball club, essentially risking the family nest egg. He sensed the need for a better stadium and built Bears (Mile High) Stadium. He sensed waning fan interest and moved the Bears from Class-A to Class-AAA baseball. He sensed Denver was ripe for major-league baseball and tried to start the Continental League with Branch Rickey. The present day Rockies' popularity and attendance showed that he was right.

The Denver Broncos also showed that his vision was often prescient. The

Broncos went on to become one of the foundational franchises in the AFL. Once the team and league merged with the NFL, they became one of the most successful in all of football. Unfortunately Howsam didn't have the deep pockets to ride it out for the long term.

When he came to the St. Louis Cardinals, he sensed the need to replace some aging veterans with younger players and the Cards went on to win two World Series. In Cincinnati he saw how AstroTurf and the configuration of Riverfront Stadium had changed baseball. He adjusted accordingly and emphasized speed on artificial turf. Over and over his sense of what was coming in the future proved to be correct. What he saw in baseball's future troubled him.

He had watched as Charlie Finley was forced to dismantle the team he had built, unable to afford to keep his players. Teams from big markets like New York, Chicago and Los Angeles had always had an advantage when it came to generating revenues but costs (mainly salaries) had been fairly even before the advent of free agency. Now players could go to the highest bidder. The owner with the most money could obviously bid the most. The owners with the most money were generally in the biggest markets.

The situation was exacerbated when the owners agreed to Miller and the players' demands that a player be eligible for free agency after six years of major-league experience. Considering that it takes an average of one to two years for a player to become established in the majors and then a couple more seasons before the player hits his prime years, that gives a small-market team maybe only a year or two before they are at risk of losing a good player.

The Big Red Machine is illustrative of this problem. Had free agency been available starting in the 1960s, Pete Rose could have left after the '68 season, before the Reds reached the World Series the first time. Perez could have left after the first World Series in 1970. Morgan also could have left in 1970 but he would have left Houston; he hadn't been traded to the Reds yet. Johnny Bench would have gone after the 1973 season. In other words, the Reds would not have had time to jell into the great team they became in the mid–1970s had free agency been around. The Reds would likely have been split apart by that point. This illustrates how difficult it is to build a long-term contender under the six-year free-agent rule.

More than the state of the game pained Howsam, his back was killing him. It had been bothering him for years and was growing worse with time. The fact that one of his legs was slightly shorter than the other, by about one-half inch, was the start of the problem. Things were really exacerbated during his years with the Denver Bears. Long car trips with infrequent stops through the night to see the next game or upcoming talent had taken their toll. Those in the long-distance transportation industry know what hours of sitting at the wheel with no breaks can do to the back.

The advent of passenger flight didn't help remedy the situation either. While trips may be shorter on an airplane, airline seats are not exactly known for their ergonomic value. If you have ever flown with a backache, you know you don't feel better at the end of the flight, except you get to get up and move again.

By this time the pain was mounting. A baseball general manager is busy throughout the season with the parent club, as well as out visiting the five or six minor-league clubs. The off-season is filled with baseball's winter meetings, committee work, working trades, and maybe a few weeks off with one's family. It isn't a March to October job. Howsam had been going nonstop in baseball since he had left his financial advising job in Denver in August 1964, thirteen straight years of intense work.

Howsam's body and mind were telling him that it was time to take a break. Nippert, a kind and thoughtful man, thought the world of his friend and wanted the best for him and his wife Janet but he also cared greatly for the city of Cincinnati and their Reds. He didn't want to lose Howsam. He agreed to let him step down from his general manager duties but asked him to stay on and represent the Reds' interests as their official spokesman and ambassador at all baseball meetings.

When word got around the front office that Howsam was leaving, rumors began to fly. Perhaps he was leaving to join Marvin Davis. Davis was a wealthy oilman who had made a name for himself in the 1970s as a man in search of a pro franchise. It seemed that every six months brought yet another story that Davis was about to buy one franchise or another and move it to Denver. Knowing Bob Howsam's Colorado connection, some feared Howsam was going to lead a Marvin Davis franchise to Denver.

Separately, emissaries from both the baseball side and business side of the Reds approached Bob Howsam. If he was going to another franchise there was a group of people that wanted to go with him.[8] It was similar to a situation encountered by Meriwether Lewis during the Lewis and Clark Expedition. There was a fork in the river. All two dozen men thought the river to the right was the correct river to take. Lewis felt it was the river to the left. The men finally said we believe you are choosing the incorrect river but we choose to cheerfully follow you because we trust your leadership. It was much the same with the front office. They didn't particularly want to leave Cincinnati and they didn't want Bob Howsam to leave but if he was going somewhere else, they wanted to go with him. Perhaps no greater compliment can be paid to a leader.

Alas, there was no truth in the rumors. Davis had consulted Howsam seeking some advice and made Bob Howsam an offer of employment. Howsam had no intention of taking it. He was under contract to Louis Nippert and intended to honor the contract, especially for a man that he loved and respected so much. However, his employees' show of loyalty deeply touched him. (Marvin Davis never did get a professional franchise of any kind.)

Who would replace Bob Howsam as the GM? Once they discussed Howsam's situation and future, that was a question from Louis Nippert. Who would Howsam recommend as his successor? Dick Wagner was the likely choice. An old baseball man himself, Wagner had been named Minor League Executive of the Year by the *Sporting News* in 1958. He had been Howsam's right-hand man for his entire tenure in Cincinnati. He also had served that role in St. Louis. Nippert agreed with Howsam. He always went along with his recommendation.

Howsam called Dick Wagner into his office, told him the news, and asked if he'd like the job. Wagner said yes and it was done. The Reds had lost a member of the Big Four on the field when Perez went to Montreal the previous year. Now they were losing the head of the Big Four in the front office. Things were changing.

The announcement hit the papers on February 17, 1978. In his eleven seasons at the helm, Howsam had built an organization that was a model for all of baseball. Early on in Cincinnati, Howsam had stated that his goal was to build "the No. 1 organization in baseball."[9] Again note that his goal was not to win world championships but to build a great organization. By building a great organization, the world championships came. He had reached his goal.

22

A New Sheriff in Town
March 1978–September 1978

With the well-known Howsam stepping down, everyone in town began scrambling to figure out the guy who was stepping up. At this point Dick Wagner was primarily known as Howsam's chief lieutenant, his right-hand man. Wagner was the guy who ran the business side of the Reds and ran it very efficiently. Dick Wagner's best days with the Reds were when the ballpark was absolutely full and the Reds won the game.[1] That happened several times in the 1970s. But there was much more to Dick Wagner.

Dick Wagner was born in Central City, Nebraska, a railroad town. The town was built around the Union Pacific Railroad, its lifeblood, as it was in many towns across the Great Plains in the 1930s. Growing up, Wagner played football and basketball. His leadership potential was recognized early. At age sixteen he was asked to go to a nearby school in Hordville and coach the basketball team. He did it. Some of the boys were his age and some were older. The team photo is memorable, roughly one dozen boys in uniform, with another boy, Wagner, in a suit and tie, shepherding his team.

Like Howsam, he was part of the Greatest Generation. Fresh out of high school, he joined the navy and served in the Pacific. First aboard the troop attack transport USS *Pitt* and then on a new hospital ship, the USS *Haven*, after the war he was docked in San Diego, with one hundred thousand other sailors. He went over to the local minor-league club and talked with its publicity director, Steve Gardner, about getting a job in baseball. Wagner had watched some games and loved the sport but he had never played it. His hometown didn't have the resources to purchase equipment for baseball during the Depression and the war. Gardner pulled down "the blue book" and gave Wagner eight to ten addresses and some encouragement. Wagner returned to the ship and wrote letters to every single address, asking for a job. He heard back from almost every team he wrote. One of his letters was answered by Eddie Gilliland, the farm director of the Detroit Tigers. He offered Wagner the vice president and general manager position at Thomasville, Georgia, a Class-D club of the Tigers. At age nineteen Dick Wagner assumed his duties.[2]

The 1947 season went well and Wagner was promoted to run the Tigers'

Bob Howsam (left) confers with his hand-picked successor, the tough-talking Dick Wagner. No one in the Reds organization was closer to Howsam; Wagner was the only Reds organization member who addressed him by first name (photograph courtesy Roadwest Publishing [Jack Klumpe Collection]).

new Class-A league club, the Flint Arrows. Since it was the Arrows inaugural season, they needed everything. Wagner learned several new business necessities, including how to acquire transportation, in this case a bus. He went to an Ohio bus factory and picked up a new one off of the assembly line. The Arrows were successful on the field, winning the Central League title.

In 1949 Gilliland took Wagner to Miami, Florida, to help run a new minor-league club for a wealthy Cuban by the name of Manuel Alemau. While there, he helped Gilliland build Miami Stadium near the Orange Bowl. It was his first taste of what would influence the rest of his career, building stadiums. They ran the Class-B franchise for the Brooklyn Dodgers and played to a sold-out crowd when Jackie Robinson came to town to play in an exhibition against the Braves.

At the end of World War II, the military was drastically downsizing. Since Wagner had not served his entire military commitment, he was put on inactive reserve for several years. Exactly one day before the reserve duty was to come to an end, one day before he would be officially discharged, President Harry Truman called Wagner back to active duty. Not happy, Wagner reported for duty at the Naval Training Center in San Diego. The chief petty officer looked over Wagner's papers and said, "We haven't got any bleepin' baseball clubs to run here."[3] Welcome to the U.S. Navy. Wagner finished his commitment one year and five days later and then returned to baseball.

Just prior to being recalled to the navy, Wagner married a pretty young schoolteacher named Gloria Larsen. They had been teenage sweethearts in Central City, where her dad had also worked for the railroad. Gloria is the perfect complement to Dick Wagner. She is warm, friendly, vivacious—someone you want to be around, a lovely person. Like Bob Howsam, Dick Wagner married well.

After his final discharge from the navy, Wagner went to work for the St. Louis Browns' San Antonio, Texas, minor-league club. From there it was on to a minor-league club in Hutchinson, Kansas. Hutchinson was a great baseball town. Wagner learned the importance of being part of the community. The local merchants held a one-day ticket drive and sold fifty thousand tickets. The club was affiliated with the Pittsburgh Pirates and that is when Wagner first got to know Branch Rickey, who was running the Pirates at the time. Hutchinson was a Class-C league team and had a good young defensive catcher with a great arm but absolutely no speed. Jack McKeon was slower than Dick Wagner. McKeon never made it to the big leagues, at least as a catcher.

After three years Wagner had interviews with several clubs for a promotion. The one from the Lincoln Chiefs, a Class-A ball club, sounded the best. Lincoln was in the Western League and that is where Wagner first met Bob Howsam. The owners assured Wagner that they had money in the bank. They did but they didn't mention the loan that they had outstanding, which was for more money than the owners had in the bank. The club had lost $76,000 the previous two years. Showing his business acumen, within the next two years Wagner had the club making a profit, the stadium renovated, and attendance increased by twenty thousand fans. Lincoln was better on the field as well, going from last to first over the two-year period. The team was led by a handsome young manager with a great baritone voice, Larry Shepard. In recognition of his efforts, Wagner was named Minor League Executive of the Year for 1958 by the *Sporting News*.

While running the Lincoln Chiefs, Wagner worked out a deal with a local radio station to carry the Chiefs games. A man named Richard ("Dick") Chapin owned the station and also was the chairman of the local auditorium committee. Impressed with Wagner, Chapin tried to convince him to come and be the general manager of the Pershing Municipal Auditorium, with a pay increase to what he was making with the Chiefs. Lincoln was a nice place and close to his roots; Wagner took the job. While at the auditorium, Wagner learned the ins and outs of running an entertainment facility. It included trying to get business lined up for a certain number of months and years down the road, besides just the regular tenants. He was always out trying to get events, booking all kinds of entertainment, and the house was frequently packed.

During one such show Wagner caught the eye of a young entertainment entrepreneur from Los Angeles. His name was John Harris and he owned an ice show. Many Americans in the 1960s will remember the Ice Capades, Holiday on Ice, and Ice Follies. Harris owned all or part of the first two. The auditorium was fairly new and had never had an ice show when Ice Capades came to the arena. As was his custom, Wagner followed Harris and the show's directions "110 percent." That impressed Harris and he asked Wagner to come to Los Angeles and help run the company. It was an opportunity that Wagner couldn't pass up; he and Gloria and their two kids packed up and moved to Hollywood from Middle America.

Wagner was learning things all along the way that would help him later with the Reds. From Harris he learned the art of promoting. Ice Capades was employing a relatively new technique, the color brochure. It may seem old hat in the twenty-first century but it was a novel idea in 1960s. Brochures, if done at all, usually contained no pictures or perhaps a black and white photo or sketch. Ice Capades capitalized on newer printing technology to prepare a brochure full of color pictures. The color stood out and caught the eye and interest of potential customers. The brochures were well distributed across the target town several weeks in advance of the show. They worked well. Wagner would later incorporate the idea into Reds schedules, which were also colorful, and spread across not only Cincinnati but also Dayton, Ohio, Lexington, Kentucky, Huntington, West Virginia, and other nearby cities and towns.

The Ice Capades job was fun at first and the Southern California area offered new attractions, like the recently opened Disneyland. Opening nights for the Ice Capades were major events attended by movie stars and other celebrities. There were live interviews as the bigwigs came to and from the show. The Los Angeles weather was also a welcomed relief from windy winters on the Nebraskan plains but business demanded late nights. Wagner and others had to stay in the office until the show, somewhere out on the road, called in the figures for the night.

After several years Harris sold the business to new owners who wanted Wagner to relocate to New York. While mulling over the move, he got a call from Dick Chapin, the radio man from Lincoln. Chapin had a radio station in Salina, Kansas, that he wanted Wagner to run. Salina sounded better than New York City and so it was off from Hollywood for the general manager's chair of KSAL.

The station was one of the biggest in Kansas and "was going Jessie," which was the parlance of the time for turning a very nice profit. He gathered radio experience that would serve him well when he started growing the Reds radio network years later.

After a short time in Salina, Wagner got a call from an old friend, Bob Howsam. Howsam had just arrived in St. Louis and wasn't real happy with everything he found on the business end. It needed some straightening out. He wanted Wagner to set up a new department over promotions and sales, handling season tickets, group sales, and the like. Additionally the Cardinals were planning to move into Busch Stadium the next year. Howsam knew that Wagner had experience with Miami Stadium, Lincoln Stadium and Municipal Auditorium, and wanted Wagner to come and help him with both projects. Wagner accepted.

Howsam and Wagner enjoyed working together in St. Louis and the move into Busch Stadium went well. The move and Wagner's resume caught the eye of a Canadian-born California businessman, Jack Kent Cooke. Cooke is best known to fans nowadays as the late owner of the Washington Redskins and Los Angeles Lakers. Many fans will remember him standing on a podium next to Joe Gibbs accepting a Vince Lombardi trophy more than once.

Cooke's paths seemed to cross with several famous Reds throughout the years. He was the owner of the Toronto minor-league club and had fired Sparky Anderson as its manager for poor performance. After he purchased the Lakers and wanted to build the Forum, he contacted Bob Howsam, then general manager of the Cardinals, for permission to talk with his assistant Dick Wagner about a job. He wanted Dick Wagner to come and oversee the project.

When Jack Kent Cooke wanted someone to work for him, he could be very smooth and persuasive. Cooke was a master at wining and dining, a great recruiter. He knew how to make someone feel special. He wooed Wagner back to Los Angeles and Wagner enjoyed much of the process— building a new facility required a lot of foresight and out-of-the-box thinking, right down to the question of how high to make a doorway. The height of doorways to basketball locker rooms are important to the Wilt Chamberlains of the world.

Building a new ballpark, stadium, or arena is accompanied by a great sense of accomplishment. You build something that is noticed and visited by thousands. It can be a high but it also has lots of headaches. People who have built their own homes know this on a smaller scale. Someone once remarked, "I'd rather live in a tent in the woods than build my own home again." Magnify that several times over and you get the idea of what building an arena is like. Additionally Cooke could be a tough taskmaster (just ask the coaches of the Redskins). While the project was still underway, Wagner was visited by Howsam who had just taken the job with the Reds. Howsam wanted Wagner to join him in Cincinnati and told him what he could pay. He wasn't specific about exactly what Wagner would be responsible for and didn't even mention what his job title would be, but that didn't matter. Dick Wagner trusted Bob Howsam and respected him — he accepted his offer on the spot. Wagner would later learn his new job title on the radio as he arrived in Cincinnati, driving across the bridge from Kentucky into Ohio.

What Howsam wanted Wagner to do was come and run the business operations for him. He also knew that the Reds were moving from Crosley Field to Riverfront Stadium and wanted Wagner to oversee that project.

After arriving in Cincinnati Wagner oversaw the successful move to Riverfront Stadium. Overall he was in charge of advertising, marketing, sales, and radio and television deals— all the business aspects of the club. One of his most successful ideas was the Cincinnati Reds Gift Shop. It was located at 580 Walnut Street and was known around town as the "580 Gift Shop." There Reds fans could purchase hats, bats, balls, posters and other Reds memorabilia. This may not seem like a big deal in an era where youngsters and adults frequently sport the garb of their favorite team; however, in the early 1970s this sort of merchandise was just beginning to be popular and was not easy to locate. It wasn't at the "local Wal-Mart" because Wal-Mart wasn't everywhere in those days and didn't carry those items—few stores did.

Each year the Reds would commission one Reds poster of a Reds player. The posters would be given out on Poster Day at the stadium. Those not attending the game could purchase their poster at the 580 Gift Shop. That year's player would be featured but one could also purchase posters depicting previous years' players. Merchandise was brought out quickly and efficiently. One could buy a world championship bat for fifteen dollars one day after the Reds won the World Series; it said so right in the big ad in the paper.

Wagner also handled most of the hiring and firing for the club. The person in that role is never the most popular person on the job but, as they say, somebody has to do it. He had hired Al Michaels and replaced him with Marty Brennaman when Michaels left for California. He had been Howsam's right-hand man but now in 1978 he was the top dog for the first time since 1958.

One of the toughest jobs in leadership is to figure out how to keep an organization at the top once it has gotten there. It is very difficult to keep the edge to stay number one. But perhaps the hardest job in all of leadership is replacing the man or woman who had led the organization to the top and is stepping aside. Trying to fill their shoes and keep the organization at the pinnacle is a daunting challenge. It has been accomplished by very few. Imagine trying to replace a Jack Welsh at General Electric or a Bill Gates at Microsoft. This person has successfully built the organization into first place in their field. The person who comes along next has to figure out new ways to continue the success. It is a tough act to follow. This was the challenge facing Dick Wagner.

Wagner was a tough-talking, no-nonsense type of guy. Loyalty was extremely important to him and he was also a stickler for details. Things were expected to be done right and done right the first time. He was very fair but if you made a mistake you were expected to answer for it. There's nothing wrong with that attitude; it helped to make the United States great.

Like any leader, Wagner had his pet peeves. Some were a bit humorous. He didn't like pipe smoking, though he enjoyed an occasional cigar. The reason for the dislike was that pipe smokers spent too much time playing around with their pipes and their bag of tobacco, so Wagner thought, while they ought to be getting something done.[4]

Another unwritten rule was never to look down at someone's desk when you were in their office. What was on their desk was their business, not yours. You were in someone's office to visit with them, not to look over their stuff. If he caught you glancing down at his desk while in his office, you got an earful if not more. True to Wagner, though, he practiced the same principles that he preached.

Once Bob Howsam called during spring training to ask Wagner a question back in the home office. The question required that Wagner go into Howsam's office to find the answer. He told the boss over the phone, "I just want you to know that I am looking in these piles of paper on your desk." He felt very awkward and wanted the boss to know it and sanction it. In a similar vein, Howsam himself was very organized and could recognize if someone had moved things on his desk, even if he had been away on a trip for several weeks.

One of Wagner's first moves was to address the pitching. Jack Billingham had been on a downhill slide for three straight years. At age thirty-five, Wagner didn't expect the trend to reverse. Coupling the slide with the fact that Billingham was never wild about pitching for Sparky Anderson, Wagner figured it was time for him to go. Wagner went the youth route, emulating the Howsam example of proven older talent for potential young talent. Billingham was sent to the Detroit Tigers for a twenty-four-year-old lefty named George Cappuzzello and minor leaguer John Valle. The trade left only little Fredie Norman from the championship rotation. Gullett had gone for the big bucks in New York, Nolan was injured and off to California, and Pat Zachry had been exchanged for Tom Seaver.

The bullpen still had Pedro Borbon, but Clay Carroll, Rawly Eastwick and

Will McEnaney were all gone. The Reds still hoped that Dale Murray, who had come over in the McEnaney deal, would show the form he'd had in Montreal. His first season with the Reds in 1977 had been a mixed bag, seven wins and four saves, but an ERA of nearly 5.00.

While Bob Howsam had left the day-to-day operations, the Reds had an old friend return. Sparky Anderson welcomed Alex Grammas back as his third-base coach. In Milwaukee Grammas had an aging Henry Aaron and a twenty-year-old shortstop named Robin Yount and little talent otherwise. (Future Hall of Famer Paul Molitor would break into the league in 1978.) After two losing seasons, car dealer and Brewers owner Bud Selig gave Grammas the boot. Anderson had missed his alter ego and invited him back, again stationing him in the third-base-coaching box.

Wagner had a strong team on the field with his position players. The 1978 everyday lineup was identical to the '77 one. Foster, as the reigning NL MVP, had been featured on *Sports Illustrated's* baseball issue cover along with Rod

Sparky Anderson's faithful and capable coaching staff. From left to right: Ted Kluszewski (hitting), Alex Grammas (infielders), Anderson, Larry Shepard (pitching), George Scherger (outfield). Except for Grammas's two-year stint in Milwaukee, all were at Sparky's side for every season in Cincinnati (photograph courtesy Roadwest Publishing [Jack Klumpe Collection]).

Carew. Everyone was hoping that the '77 season was a hiccup and that in '78 the Reds would be back as World Series champions.

Early in the season, Pete Rose reached a lofty plateau. He garnered his three thousandth hit on May 5, almost fifteen years to the month after he had broken into the big leagues. This attested to his consistency in banging out two hundred hits (another gold standard) nearly every season. Rose was the youngest ever to reach three thousand hits. It wasn't the only time his hitting would catch headlines that season. Mired in a 5-for-44 slump, Rose decided to widen his stance slightly and choke up on the bat. Immediately he began seeing the ball better. On June 14, 1978, Rose went 2-for-4 against Dave Roberts and the Chicago Cubs. He didn't stop hitting and rode a twenty-five-game streak, tying his personal previous best, into the All-Star Game at San Diego. Once again Dodgers and Reds populated the All-Star squad, with nine position players and eleven total players between the two clubs. The National League won again, 7–3.

Right after the All-Star break, Rose tied Vada Pinson's twenty-seven-game club record for a hitting streak, then broke Red Schoendist's record for a switch-hitter at twenty-eight games. Rose got his biggest scare eight days after the All-Star Game against the Phillies. When he was walked by Ron Reed in the ninth inning, it left him hitless for the game. However, Rose wasn't going to swing at a bad pitch just to get a hit. His teammates saved the day by batting around, bringing Rose to the plate again. He laid down a perfect bunt and beat the throw to first to extend the streak to thirty-two games.

Pete's streak had captured national attention. Tommy Holmes's modern National League record of thirty-seven straight was in sight. Rose passed it on July 25, 1978, with Tommy Holmes and 38,157 others in attendance. Holmes jumped down onto the field to congratulate Rose. Someone snapped a photo of Holmes and Rose tipping his helmet; it became one of the most famous of the entire streak.

Fans began to imagine the unimaginable—could Rose break Joe DiMaggio's record of fifty-six straight games? DiMaggio had actually had a longer streak, sixty-one games, for the San Francisco Seals, but that was in the Pacific Coast League, a very good league in the 1930s but a minor-league club nonetheless.

On July 28 Pete reached forty games, the only man outside of DiMaggio in the modern era (after 1900) to do so. The media circus built in size and scope; cameras and reporters were at every game, tracking every move and at-bat. Most people actually perform worse when others are focused on them but not Pete. He loved the attention. He thrived on it. Unlike most people, attention caused Rose to bear down more and focus harder. It helped his performance; it didn't hurt it. During the streak Pete's batting average rose from .267 to .315.

In game forty-one he was successful; Rose was 1-for-4 against Steve Carlton and the Phillies. He reached forty-two with a 3-for-4 effort against Jim Lonborg and Jim Kaat. Forty-three was notched against the Phillies, as well. DiMaggio's record was now roughly two weeks away. The streak had been going on for forty-seven days, with a three-day All-Star break in between. Rose had lost several pounds.

The streak moved to Atlanta, where Rose would face the Braves in Fulton County Stadium, two miles from the center of downtown Atlanta and later a baseball venue for the 1996 Centennial Olympic Games. In Game forty-four Rose would be facing Phil Niekro, the crafty knuckleballer. Unfazed by Niekro, Rose singled to keep the streak alive. The feat made Rose particularly proud; it allowed him to tie the mark of National Leaguer Wee Willie Keeler, who had hit for forty-four games in 1897 before the modern era. To Pete, it didn't matter. When a hitting record was set, he wanted to break it.

The next night, August 1, 1978, leading off the game, Rose walked against Larry McWilliams. In the second, Rose lined back to McWilliams, who made a circus catch, robbing Rose of a hit. In the fifth, Rose hit another liner, this one to Jerry Royster at shortstop. He lined to the rookie third baseman, Bob Horner, in the seventh. Would he get another shot? Six times during the streak Rose had gone hitless until his last at-bat. Thoughts may have flashed through the scorekeeper's mind — if the play is questionable do I call it an error and end the streak or call it a hit to keep the streak going?

Pete's forty-four-game hitting streak captured the nation's attention in the summer of 1978 (photograph courtesy Roadwest Publishing [Jack Klumpe Collection]).

Griffey and Concepcion singled later in the seventh inning, ensuring that Rose would get another shot in the ninth. With the Braves up 16–4, Manager Bobby Cox called on Gene Garber to close the game. Garber was one of several pitchers the Reds had tagged in the ninth inning of Game Three to sweep the Phillies in the playoffs two years earlier. He was a solid pitcher known for his twisting motion, side-arm delivery, and change-up. More than just his pitching motion looked a bit odd for the time. In an era when facial hair was not common on American men, and outside of the Oakland A's few players had mustaches, Garber had a beard, one of the few men in the league to sport one.

On the first pitch, Rose bunted toward third. He had kept his streak alive four times with bunts. The bunt rolled foul. The second pitch was a ball, as was the third. Rose foul-tipped the next pitch for strike two and a 2–2 count. Rose would later say that Garber was bearing down like it was the seventh game of the World Series. His next pitch also was foul-tipped by Rose, but caught by catcher Joe Nolan for a strikeout. Rose had struck out only five times during the six-week streak. The streak was over.

Sharing his thoughts after the game, the resilient Rose promised to start another streak the next day. He did, hitting a double, two singles and a home run, but it ended after one game. He wound up hitting .302 for the season, his thirteenth year above .300 and two hits shy of two hundred for the season.

Aside from the excitement of the streak, the Reds were once again chasing the Dodgers. It was baseball's best rivalry in the 1970s. Eight times between 1970 and '79, and every year between '72 and '78, the Reds and Dodgers finished first and second. The Reds always had the better hitting and bullpen. The Dodgers had the better starting pitching. Over that period the Reds won 953 games to the Dodgers 910 games. In head-to-head competition, the record was 97–79 in favor of the Reds.

The Reds caught the Dodgers and were in first place on August 6 but then lost sixteen of the next twenty-two games, entering September seven games back. Seaver was sound on the mound but not overpowering. He would go 16–14. Fredie Norman was still his consistent self, finishing 11–9. Bill Bonham, whom the Reds had gotten for the disgruntled Fryman, was a pleasant surprise at 11–5. However, things tailed off markedly after the top three. Dale Murray never returned to his Montreal form. Wagner grew impatient and dealt him to the New York Mets for a utility outfielder named Ken Henderson. While Murray was a bust, another reliever did emerge. Wagner had picked up Doug Bair in a deal with Oakland shortly after taking over. Bair turned into a fine closer, with twenty-eight saves and a 1.98 ERA, allowing Borbon to return to his more customary middle-relief role. Borbon, however, was not his customary self. His ERA ballooned to nearly 5.00.

The offense was not its customary self either. Morgan fell off precipitously. His average dropped to .236 and his home-run total to pre–Cincinnati levels. Worse, his stolen-base total dropped to nineteen, down from the fifties and sixties. He was fourth on the team in stolen bases, when he used to be near the top of the league. Driessen dropped from .301 to .250, while Perez was hitting .290 in Montreal. Geronimo fell to .226 and battled injury problems. Bench also battled the injury bug, getting less than 400 at-bats for the first time in his career, though he did reach three hundred career home runs in July.

On the bright side, Concepcion broke the .300 mark for the first time, Griffey was having a decent season, and Foster was still a triple threat. His home run total dropped from fifty-two to forty, but it still led the league. He also led the league in RBIs for the third straight year, only the second National League hitter in history to do so.

The Reds finished with a flurry, winning their last seven games. However it was too little too late. The Reds finished the season two and a half games back, second to the Dodgers. Theories abounded as to how the Big Red Machine could again finish runner-up to the team from Tinsel Town. The most predominant theory was age; it seemed to be catching up to them. Rose was thirty-seven now. Bench was only thirty but had eleven seasons behind the plate with a hundred or more games caught, approaching Hall of Famer Ray Schalk's record of twelve. Morgan was now thirty-four.

Pitching was another leading suspect. The starting pitching showed some age, with Seaver at thirty-three and Norman at thirty-five, along with some unproven twentysomethings. The Jack Billingham trade had turned out to be a disaster. Billingham won fifteen for the Detroit Tigers while George Cappuzzello never made the Reds' big-league roster. The pitching had been far inferior to the Dodgers and the normally potent offense had not been so good. Perhaps most of all, Perez was still in Montreal.

Wagner, however, felt that the problem might lie elsewhere, perhaps at the top. The theory had gained momentum until 1975 when it was stopped in its tracks by a World Series title. The theory gained new life after back-to-back seasons of finishing second, with nine All-Stars on the roster.

23

The Machine Stops Running
Fall 1978–October 1979

Baseball managing, like leadership, is both a science and an art. It contains tangibles: Can you handle the press? Do you know when to put on the hit-and-run? It also contains intangibles: Can you effectively communicate? Can you inspire? Do you have the players' ears? Do you have their respect? Through the years managing has become more difficult in many ways, due to cultural changes. Players, reflecting society in general, are not as willing to easily follow those in authority. When the leader says follow me, the follower is likely to respond, "I'll do it my way." It is hard to imagine a player telling that to Connie Mack or John McGraw in the 1930s.

The Reds traveled to Japan for a goodwill tour and baseball exhibition in the late fall of 1978. They did well, playing seventeen exhibition games and winning fourteen of them. Young Tom Hume showed a lot of promise by winning five games. Pete Rose hit safely in over one dozen straight games. The final game of the tour was against the Yomiuri Giants, called "the New York Yankees of Japan." Their legendary hitter and all-time Japanese home run king, Sadaharu Oh, homered, but it wasn't enough, as the Reds won, 3 to 2.

Six days after the Reds returned, on November 28, Wagner flew out to see Sparky Anderson near his Thousand Oaks home. They met for breakfast at the Marriott Hotel. During the meal they engaged in small talk about non-baseball matters. After the meal they went back to Dick Wagner's room. Wagner said, "I'm not bringing you back next year." Sparky sat there speechless and stunned.[1] Sparky Anderson was no longer the leader of the Big Red Machine.

Deciding to replace a manager is one of the toughest decisions an owner or management can make. There are many factors that one must weigh before letting someone go. What those factors were for Dick Wagner will likely forever be a mystery. There are as many theories as there are Reds fans. Some likely hold some weight, while others don't. What is clear is that the situation was complex and unclear.

The simple and straightforward reason for Sparky's dismissal was that the Reds had slipped a notch and should not have done so. As my coach and youth pastor once said, "everything rises and falls on leadership." If that is true, then Anderson was to blame for the slip. In that case maybe a change was in order.

But these things are rarely that simple and straightforward. Publicly Anderson was gracious enough to try to take some of the blame himself after the firing. He offered that maybe his leadership was getting stale. He shared an example of sitting down with Davey Concepcion who was having a bad streak. Anderson told him a story to try and pick him up. Concepcion responded, "You already told me that one." Familiarity breeds contempt. Maybe things were getting old.

Jack Billingham, safely harbored in Detroit, was the most outspoken about the firing. He felt that Sparky had let things slide in two areas. First was in his demands for physical conditioning. Billingham thought that the standard had formerly been stricter and that the players used to experience tougher spring training sessions. The players had called Sparky's first spring training, in 1970, "Stalag," after the German prisoner of war camps. Billingham said that the camps had begun to get easier and therefore that discipline and respect had taken a dip.[2]

More troublesome, Billingham felt that Anderson had slipped in his ability to deal with the superstars. He asserted there was a double standard for players that Anderson would not admit to for years. Once he did, things continued to deteriorate to the point where he would not get on one of the Big Four. In essence he began to fear them. Bench asserted as much three months earlier when he criticized Sparky for "being in awe of the superstars."

Bench later backed off a bit from those accusations, saying instead that some players had begun to take advantage of the respect from Anderson. Anderson said that he did have a double standard but that in exchange for the greater privilege and access the Big Four had greater responsibility. Disgruntled players need to see both sides of that equation.[3]

While he had his own view of how he and the rest of the pitching staff was handled, Fredie Norman was quick to point out that though he disagreed with Sparky on his philosophy, he greatly respected him and liked what he brought to the club — winning and class. Norman noted that the players didn't seem as close as they had been in the past. Perhaps it was the lessening of the discipline. Rose, Morgan, Bench, and the old lefthander Joe Nuxhall pointed out several players who had not been hustling like they had been in the past. None would name names, but they said those players knew who they were.[4]

Dick Wagner himself spent more time in the clubhouse and around the players than Howsam had. Sparky had been consistent in his philosophy that if you had a problem, you were to see your coach first. After two years of second place, some of the players began to resent the policy and complained to Wagner, "He's unapproachable; I can't talk to him; he won't talk with me." Wagner perhaps felt that this was no way to manage a ball club.[5]

Another popular theory is that Wagner wanted Sparky to fire one or more of his coaches and that he'd refused to do so, standing by his coaches. According to this theory Wagner had found that unacceptable, so he then gave Anderson the axe instead.

Sometimes two people don't hit it off; they just don't get along, for whatever reasons. Perhaps Wagner and Anderson didn't see eye-to-eye or rubbed each other the wrong way. The fact that Wagner did not go on to offer a job to coach Grammas, Sparky's alter-ego, like he did the other coaches lends credence to this theory.

The theory with the most intrigue and most potential for a made-for-TV movie involves jealousy and loyalty. Many have asserted that Wagner felt Anderson's loyalties lie with Bob Howsam, not Dick Wagner, which bothered Wagner. It was, after all, Bob Howsam who had tapped the relatively unknown thirty-five-year-old Anderson as Reds skipper nine seasons earlier. Loyalty was extremely important to Wagner, both to be given and received. If he didn't feel like he had your loyalty, you were in trouble.

Anderson felt privately and later remarked publicly, without specifics, that he thought the decision came down from "higher up." That leaves Nippert, the rest of the Reds ownership and Howsam as suspects. Howsam said that the decision or suggestion was not his, though he said that Wagner had discussed the thought of firing Sparky with him.[6] Nippert was very clear that he felt the general manager should run the club, saying "a man cannot play billiards if someone else is holding the cue,"[7] so it is unlikely that the decision came from him. All who know Dick Wagner know that he is comfortable making his own decisions, so the idea that it came from higher up has less credibility than other theories.

Sparky Anderson never asked Wagner the reason for the dismissal. Wagner said he was prepared to give it to him if he asked, but he didn't. He has never shared those reasons. In the end no one will likely know all the real factors. It was likely a combination of many of the above speculations and probably more. It remains an unsolved mystery in Cincinnati.

Now there was the question of who should replace Anderson. The winningest manager in the history of Cincinnati and the skipper of the Big Red Machine, Captain Hook, had himself gotten the hook. Wagner knew that he wanted a veteran to replace Sparky. He didn't want someone to be learning on the job. He felt that the club was still in position to take the 1979 World Series. He didn't want a rookie manager derailing that with silly mistakes.[8] He turned to a forty-six-year old former manager of the Oakland A's and San Diego Padres, John McNamara. McNamara had been around the game for a long time. He had been a minor-league catcher for years in the A's organization, never making it to the majors. Charlie Finley rewarded his perseverance with a coaching job. He knew the game; he knew the players; and he knew how to win. Wagner had met him through the baseball fraternity. In Wagner's mind McNamara liked to play younger players and the possibility of lots of younger players loomed on the horizon.

Dick Wagner (left) talks with Sparky Anderson in spring training of 1978. Nine months later he fired him (photograph courtesy Roadwest Publishing [Jack Klumpe Collection]).

John McNamara and Sparky Anderson shared some similarities that were almost eerie. McNamara's last two jobs had been with the Padres and the California Angels, same as Anderson. McNamara left a job as the Angels third-base coach to become the Reds manager, just like Anderson. In 1970 McNamara led his team to a second-place finish in their division. He said his team was one pitcher short of winning the division and that pitcher was Vida Blue, who was still in the minors and one year away from the big leagues. In 1978, Anderson led his team to a second-place finish in their division. He was one pitcher short of winning the division and that pitcher was Vida Blue, who Howsam was not allowed to have.[9] The Reds were hoping that McNamara would share another similarity with Anderson, the ability to win a World Series.

In addition to axing Anderson, Wagner also canned his four lieutenants who had served faithfully since 1970, offering all of them jobs elsewhere in the organization except for Grammas. Larry Shepard said no thanks and took the pitching coach position in San Francisco. George Scherger was given the managing job at the Reds Class-AA affiliate in Nashville, the Sounds. He was eager to get back to teaching kids the game. The Atlanta Braves called Alex Grammas and asked him to be their third-base coach. Finally, Wagner and McNamara asked Big Klu to stay on as a traveling hitting instructor for the minor leagues.

The Sparky Anderson firing did not endear Wagner to Reds fans. Another thing that cost him affection was the handling of the burgeoning problem with Rose. Rose was the symbol of the Big Red Machine, not only in Cincinnati, but across the country as well. With his determination, Charlie Hustle embodied the American ideal of hard work bringing the hometown kid from obscurity to the top. His hitting streak the previous summer had only added to the luster. His contract had expired at the end of the 1978 season. He was now eligible for free agency and Wagner had broken off negotiations forty-eight hours before he fired Sparky Anderson.

The Reds had been bitten early by Gullett's departure to New York in the first year of free agency but Rose's case would be the first test of the Big Four. It seemed inconceivable that Rose would leave his hometown and the accompanying notoriety, it was part of his identity. He was, in many ways, Mr. Red. The conventional wisdom at the time was, "He's just pressing for more money, all he can get from the Reds, but in the end he will stay." But as the months wore on, folks started to worry.

In those early days of free agency, baseball held a draft each year where a team could select the players from the free-agent pool that they intended to pursue. A single player could be drafted by up to twelve teams. It was known as the free agent reentry draft. In essence the draft was simply to narrow the field of the teams that were really interested in a player. The Reds never participated in the draft. When their turn in the draft came, they abstained. They never pursued a single free agent. If other teams had followed their example, free agency would have been seriously hampered, if not outright killed. What was required from other clubs was the self discipline not to partake. In the end everyone except Cincinnati indulged.

Sports Illustrated ran a big story as the draft approached. In the article Rose gleefully mugged for the camera as he donned baseball caps from the Dodgers, Phillies, Angels, Red Sox, Royals, Padres and more. As he donned the caps, he would outline his thoughts on each team's odds of getting his services. Wagner wanted to bring Rose back to the Reds. The negotiations with agent Reuben Katz were very tough and intense. As negotiations wore on they became more public. Money and duration of the contract were both at issue. Perhaps because each side had been through this so many times with each other over the past decade, negotiations got increasingly ugly and hurtful.

Wagner held firm on the Reds' best offer; he was not going to get held up at gunpoint by an agent — or anybody else for that matter.[10] Rose's negotiations with other teams became increasingly bizarre. The Pittsburgh Pirates owner, John Galbreath, offered Rose breeding rights for some of his racing thoroughbreds. The Kansas City Royals owner, Ewing Kauffman, offered Rose stock in his Marion Laboratories pharmaceutical company. Ray Kroc, the McDonald's and San Diego Padres owner, tried to woo Rose also while encouraging him to be loyal to his hometown. Reds fans were losing heart but in the end figured Rose's loyalty to them would win out. Their hearts were broken on December 5, 1978. Rose signed with the Philadelphia Phillies for $3.2 million over four years.

Rose's salary first made headlines in 1970 when he was the first singles hitter to make a hundred thousand dollars a year, eleven times what the average worker made. With his signing with the Phils, Rose's salary had increased 700 percent in eight years. He was now making fifty-three times what the average worker made. He was the highest-paid athlete in all of professional sports. Rose was not the only Red making a lot of money. His negotiations were just the most public and therefore the easiest to track. Rose's salary serves as a barometer for the whole team's increasing salaries. By 1979 the Reds had Bench, Foster, Seaver, and Morgan near the $400,000 level. Meanwhile Cincinnati had lost Sparky Anderson and Pete Rose in one week.

The Phillies already had a pretty good third baseman, the big red-headed guy from Dayton, Ohio, that Chief Bender had seen years earlier as a shortstop at Ohio University, future Hall of Famer Mike Schmidt. The Phillies decided to put Rose at first. In July 1979 he was selected as the National League's first baseman for the All-Star Game, his fifth different All-Star position, a record that will likely never be broken.

The Reds had a strategy for replacing Rose. For years the promising talent in the minors below had nowhere to surface. Part of it had been skimmed off in the Seaver deal eighteen months earlier but there was still plenty to tap. The Reds had a young guy who had spent time at Indianapolis, and on the Cincinnati bench, Ray Knight. He would get the first crack at Rose's spot.

Opening Day found Rick Auerbach at third (filling in for Knight who had a sprained ankle), with Concepcion, Morgan, and Driessen situated left to right across the infield. Foster, Geronimo, and Griffey filled out the outfield and Bench was again behind the plate. Geronimo was coming off of two poor hitting seasons and promised that he would bounce back to .300 in 1979. Tom Seaver got the Opening Day start. Depending on Knight's performance, the Reds still had a good team and potentially a great one.

On the field the Reds figured their chief competition for the division title was again going to be the Los Angeles Dodgers. Tommy Lasorda's ball club had made two straight World Series appearances only to lose to the New York Yankees, who were now stacked with free-agent talent.

At the All-Star break, the Reds trailed in the race by six games but it wasn't to the Dodgers. The Houston Astros were a surprising first. Knight was more than adequate filling in for Rose. He was hitting .304 at the break, identical to Rose's average. When NBC came to do a story on Knight's success, they asked one Reds fan, "Do you miss Pete Rose?" The fan replied, "Who's Pete Rose?" The Reds philosophy of replacing free-agent losses with promising talent seemed to be working. Their previous approach, to replace someone lost as a free agent with a veteran, losing Gullett and gaining Fryman, had failed miserably.

Bench, Morgan, Concepcion, and Foster were again All-Stars, but Bench and Concepcion were injured and unable to play. It was a recurring theme during the season. The Reds also had a starting pitcher selected and it wasn't Tom Seaver. Mike LaCoss had been drafted by the Reds in 1974. He had made his debut in 1978 and was a reliable starter in 1979. LaCoss was tall and lean at six four and 175 pounds. He also was outspoken. His teenage weight, fifteen pounds less than his professional weight, had scared off potential drafters during his senior year of high school in California. He was 9–3 with the National League's lowest ERA at the All-Star break.

Tom Hume, who had been so effective on the Japanese tour, eventually shared closer duties with Doug Bair. They recorded seventeen and sixteen saves respectively in 1979. It seemed that McNamara liked Sparky's idea of closer by committee. Hume and Bair had a heavier load to carry. On June 28, Wagner traded Pedro Borbon, the man with the rubber arm, to the San Francisco Giants. In return he received an outfielder named Hector Cruz. The last time the Reds traded the Giants for an outfielder it was George Foster in 1971. Cruz would prove to be no Foster. He hit a little above .230 for the Reds.

Meanwhile, Sparky Anderson was out of baseball. He was in Nashville, on a book-signing trip for his autobiography, and stayed longer to spend some time with his old friend George Scherger, who was managing the Nashville Sounds. He spent the night at Scherger's home and said goodbye the next morning as he left for the airport. He had an American Airlines flight out of Nashville with one stop, and was scheduled to arrive at home in Los Angeles around 4:30 P.M.

Several hours later, American Airlines Flight 191 taxied for takeoff at Chicago's O'Hare Airport bound for Los Angeles. As the DC-10 aircraft rolled down the runway, approaching takeoff, parts of the engine pylon flew off. As the aircraft rotated, the number-one engine dropped off the aircraft and flew up and over the left wing, falling to the tarmac below. As a result, hydraulic lines were severed to the left wing. Approximately thirty seconds after takeoff the aircraft rolled steeply to the left and the aircraft fell to the ground — all 271 people on board perished.[11]

George Scherger was panicked when he heard the news. Was Sparky okay? A few hours later, Scherger was relieved to find that Anderson's connection had gone through Dallas, not Chicago, and that Anderson was safely in Los Angeles. The Reds nearly lost an old friend.

Three weeks later, Anderson was employed again. The Detroit Tigers had a capable manager in Les Moss, who had the Tigers playing better than .500 baseball, seven games in back of the red-hot Baltimore Orioles in the Eastern Division race. He was doing a good job, but the Tigers wanted someone to do a great job. They figured that Sparky Anderson would not be unemployed for long, so they canned Moss and offered the job to Anderson before someone else got him. Moss, unfortunately, was a good guy in the wrong place at the wrong time.

Sparky jumped at the chance to get back into baseball. Even though he still looked sixty, he was only forty-five years old and missed the game. His eight-month absence had confirmed his love for the national pastime.

McNamara was doing a great job himself for the Reds. The press slowly began to stop using "Big Red Machine," and start calling the Reds "McNamara's Band." McNamara had the Reds in first going into the September stretch drive, but only by a half game. The Dodgers had fallen completely off the pace, with pitching woes of their own. Meanwhile, the Astros had risen on the strength of their pitching. Their pitching had to be great because the hitting was not. The Astros did not have a single hitter with either a .300 average or double-digit home runs playing in the mortuary known as the Astrodome. They did have speed, with eight players with double-digit steals.

The Astros also had another "Bob Gibson" type of pitcher: J. R. Richard. Richard was gigantic at six foot eight and had a long stride that made him appear to be right on top of batters when he released the ball. His hands were so big that the baseball looked like a golf ball in his palm. His weapons included a 100 mph fastball and a deadly slider. Batters feared him and struck out often against him — 313 times that year. The Astros complemented Richard with Joe Niekro, Phil's brother, who like Phil had a knuckleball.

A key series with Houston in the Astrodome loomed on the next-to-last weekend of the season. Tom Seaver had been solid all year long. He was tapped for game one of the series that would decide the division title. One of Seaver's biggest hurdles was not getting too hyped for the game. A tremendous competitor and the quintessential professional, Seaver wanted to win badly. From studies on the performance and arousal curves, it is clear that as we get more aroused (or motivated), performance increases to a point. At some level of arousal, performance plateaus. It then begins to drop off sharply. All who have played in big games know that you can get too worked up. We have known athletes that get so pumped up for the game that they actually played worse than they were capable of playing. As the result of getting too pumped up, there were some games where Seaver was worn out before the national anthem was over. Tom Seaver wanted to avoid that pitfall.[12]

The Astros countered with J. R. Richard—a classic pitching match-up. Both pitchers turned in superlative performances. Seaver was lifted for a pinch hitter in the top of the tenth inning, after surrendering just one earned run. Richard went eleven innings, fanning fifteen Reds. A seldom-used catcher named Bruce Bochy, hitting only .191, managed a bases-loaded single off Tom Hume in the bottom of the thirteenth inning for a 3–2 Houston victory. The Astros had beaten the Reds with Seaver on the mound. They were now down one and a half games with eight to play.

The next night Joe Niekro beat Mike LaCoss to become the first twenty-game winner in the National League and suddenly the Astros were only a half game back. A win the next night and the Astros would have the division lead.

The Reds had used up their top two guns and been beaten. Next up in the rotation was a young, promising right-hander named Frank Pastore. Pastore had a lot of talent but was untested. He had been a high draft choice in 1975 but this was his rookie year. He had been greeted by Johnny Bench several months earlier with these words, "Kid, there's two things you need to know about playing in the major leagues. First, it's harder to stay here than it is to get here. And second, never get too cocky or too arrogant, because you're always only one pitch away from humility."[13]

Pastore pitched a gem; he beat the Astros, 7–1, to give the Reds some breathing room and sending them on their way to sewing up the title. On the final day of the season, the Reds would win the West by the game-and-a-half lead that they'd left Houston with the previous week. Frank Pastore had been the hero of September, as he'd also beaten the Astros and Joe Niekro back on September 12, when again the Reds were only a half game up.

Despite nagging injuries to Morgan, Bench, Griffey, Geronimo, and Foster throughout the season, the Reds earned the right to play the Eastern Division champions in the playoffs. After ruling the Eastern Division for the first half of the 1970s, the Pirates had been bested by the Phillies the previous three years but they had reemerged to prove that they were again the best team in Pennsylvania and the Eastern Division. Things had come full circle over the decade, the 1979 NL playoff would look just like the 1970 edition.

Pittsburgh had a feel-good team that year. Their longtime star Willie Stargell was the ringleader and was now known affectionately around the clubhouse as "Pops" for his eighteen-year longevity in the big leagues, all in Pittsburgh.

The Pirates had a cobra in right field. Dave Parker, adorned with beard and dangling left earring, was as good as he was flashy. Parker was a Cincinnatian and had grown up a Reds fan, graduating from Courter Tech High School. He was a triple threat, hitting for average and power and stealing twenty bases in 1978 and again in 1979. He could also field. He had struck down Brian Downing from right field with a magnificent bullet to Gary Carter at the plate in the 1979 All-Star Game in the Seattle Kingdome to help secure the NL win.

The Pirates also earned the distinction of being the first team to have a starting lineup comprised completely of nonwhites. Pittsburgh had been among the first to employ men of color, including Latin American players like Roberto Clemente and Matty Alou. They were a tight bunch, calling themselves "fam-a-lee." The Sister Sledge song "We are Family" was played over the loudspeakers at Three Rivers Stadium in Pittsburgh, and the top of their home dugout was adorned with the moniker "The Family" for the postseason.

Still Cincinnati liked its chances. Seaver was on the mound for Game One at Riverfront. This would allow him to pitch Game Five of the five-game playoff if necessary, or Game Four if the Reds were desperate. The Reds' chances were severely compromised when they couldn't generate much offense against the Pirates John Candelaria, "the Candy Man." The Candy Man was tough, having no-hit the Dodgers in 1976. George Foster hit a two-run homer in the fourth inning to tie it, but the game was still deadlocked at 2–2 after nine innings. Stargell hit a three-run homer in the eleventh for the Pirates. Ray Knight later struck out with the bases loaded in the bottom of the inning. The Reds lost Game One 5–2, wasting a great Seaver effort.

Pastore got the nod in Game Two after his fabulous September. He pitched well, giving up only two runs. The Reds scored a run in the bottom of the ninth to tie the game and again it was extra innings. But Parker knocked in the winning run in the tenth and the Pirates were up two games to none and going back to their home turf.

Game Three was no contest. The Pirates jumped all over All-Star Mike LaCoss, who didn't last two innings. The pounding continued at the expense of Fredie Norman. By the fourth inning the Pirates were up 6–0. Their pitcher, Bert Blyleven, had grown up with the Minnesota Twins, starting his career at age 19. He had one of the great curveballs in the game. It seemed to drop like a ball from a table. He used it well, limiting the Reds to one run over nine innings in a 7–1 victory.

The Reds had been swept by their old nemesis, settling an old score. The Reds had swept the Pirates in both 1970 and '75, sandwiched around their classic 1972 five-game affair. As the decade came to a close, it was the Pirates' turn. They finally got past their biggest obstacle after three failures. As it happened, the Pirates would go on to face another old Reds' foe, Earl Weaver's Baltimore Orioles, with Lee May at first base.

Still the Reds could not escape the shadow of Tony Perez and the parallels to Frank Robinson. The Orioles who reached the 1979 World Series were completely unrelated to the Orioles of the early 1970s. The Baltimore Orioles had traded Frank Robinson after the 1971 World Series to make way for a young, promising hitter named Merv Rettenmund. Rettenmund never panned out like the Orioles expected he would. Those Orioles would reach the playoffs again but would not get back to the World Series. The Orioles found that what they missed more than Frank Robinson's bat was his leadership, his ability to awe and inspire his teammates—and keep them loose as the head judge of the clubhouse kangaroo court.

Likewise, Tony Perez had been traded to make way for a young promising Danny Driessen, who never panned out like the Reds had expected. Those Reds reached the playoffs again but would never get back to the World Series. What the Reds missed more than Perez's bat was his leadership, his ability to garner respect from everyone on the ball club, even the others in the Big Four, just by the kind of man he was. One trade in 1971 had opened a new chapter of greatness, while another in 1976 closed the book.

The Reds faced another obstacle during the off-season in 1979—Joe Morgan was eligible for free agency. The Reds had to deal with a new strategic reality. Their stars were getting old and the reality of free agency was growing by the season. The Reds couldn't afford to keep their best players. Though they only had a few good seasons left in them, they still commanded top dollar from the have nots around the league.

Just as the advent of the amateur draft in 1965 had fundamentally changed the way baseball teams acquired talent, free agency fundamentally changed the way that teams kept that talent. In both cases leadership's challenge was to figure out how to succeed under these new conditions. The organization that did not adapt would not stay competitive. It was critical for an organization to adopt a new framework or paradigm. The new rules required new strategies and new techniques for success.

There are other examples of organizations in industries where the playing field had been fundamentally altered. These changes can be brought on by innovations in technology or new regulations. Consider for example what happened to the typewriter industry with the advent of personal computers. Free agency did not cause changes to this extreme (the end of an entire industry) but it was close. Perhaps a better illustration is provided by modern parallels such as the impact of digital technology on the music industry. Bands still make music but how it is recorded and delivered to the consumer is radically different from two decades ago.

Free agency had a similar impact on baseball. Circumstances had changed in an extreme manner. There were still baseball players but the new way in which they could move from team to team affected contract negotiations and thus budgets, trading, and player development. At one time major-league teams had the luxury of holding a good position player in place until they could develop his replacement. Now the player can leave long before a replacement is ready.

Wagner took a different approach with Morgan than he had with Rose. Wagner had negotiated diligently with Rose's agent for several weeks before talks broke off. With Morgan, he showed little interest. Little Joe had just completed his second subpar, injury-plagued season. Wagner talked some generalities with Morgan's agent right after the playoffs but serious negotiations never took place.

Morgan, perhaps sensing the lack of interest, indicated that he wanted to play on the West Coast and Wagner let it go at that. Morgan was chosen in the reentry draft by the San Francisco Giants, Los Angeles Dodgers and San Diego Padres. The Padres then signed Dave Cash, so they didn't need Morgan. Morgan was close to deals with both the Giants and the Dodgers; however, they each signed three free agents (the maximum at the time) and suddenly Morgan had no bidders. The league held an extra free-agent reentry drawing for Morgan. This time Houston jumped in, realizing that the West Coast was no longer an option and the Reds weren't interested. His agent Tom Reich worked out a deal. Houston signed him for $225,000 plus incentives, a pay cut from the roughly $400,000 he'd made with the Reds the previous year.[14]

The Astros were willing to buy back the big fish they had let get away eight seasons prior. Harry Walker was gone. The coast was clear. Morgan would return home. The Reds employed the same philosophy that they had with Knight and Rose. This time they found two youngsters named Junior Kennedy and Ron Oester to try to fill Morgan's shoes. Oester would eventually win the job full-time.

Three of the Big Four were now gone—Perez to Montreal, Rose to Philadelphia, and Morgan to Houston. Only Bench remained in Cincinnati. Anderson was in Detroit and Howsam was in semi-retirement in Colorado. It had been a great run but with the loss to Pittsburgh in the playoffs, the Big Red Machine essentially stopped running.

There were a couple of decent seasons ahead[15] but Reds fans were left to look back at a spectacular decade: six division titles, four World Series appearances, two World Series titles, and acclaim as one of the greatest teams of all time. They were left to ponder the question, how good were the Reds?

How good were the Reds?

Sports Illustrated was the first to pose the question at a national level. After the Reds' thrashing of two strong clubs, Philadelphia and New York, in the postseason, the cover of a November 1976 *Sports Illustrated* asked explicitly, "How Good Are the Reds?" Plenty good was the answer.

Since 1976 and more so with each passing year, baseball fans have debated where the seventies Reds stack up against the all-time best. Clearly they were the team of the decade, and that was a time of pretty stiff competition. The decade began with the Baltimore Orioles dynasty at its peak but that was over by 1971. Then the Athletics fielded their strongest teams in franchise history and won three World Series titles in a row, plus two additional division championships. However their streak ran from 1971 to '75 and then stopped. The Pirates won six division titles during the decade and two World Series crowns in 1971 and '79. But in head-to-head division playoffs, the Pirates came out on the short end of the stick, losing three of the four match-ups against the Reds, two by a sweep. The Yankees are the other contender in the '70s: three straight World Series appearances from 1976 to '78. After their pasting at the hands of the Reds, the Yankees bested Lasorda's Dodgers two straight years. However, in the ten years of baseball in the 1970s, those were the only three in which the Yankees appeared in the postseason. The Dodgers meanwhile won three division and NL crowns but never took a World Series title.

The Reds were a factor across the entire decade. They had division crowns at the beginning and end of the decade, with four more sprinkled in between. Only once did they have consecutive years when they were not in the playoffs. Only once did they finish lower than first or second in the division. They won the Western Division six of ten years, with five in a seven-year period. They came within a blown game in Oakland or a Bobby Tolan catch of besting the A's in 1972. Their showing in the 1975 Fall Classic was itself an all-time classic, a win of arguably the greatest Series ever played. Finally, the pinnacle year of the Big Red Machine, 1976, has never been matched for its complete and total domination of the postseason, seven straight wins with only two tightly contested games.

Why were those teams so good? That 1976 team epitomized the Reds' greatness. Looking at the lineup, top to bottom, is revealing. Leading off was Pete Rose, the 1973 MVP and would-be Hall of Famer, who hit .323. Ken Griffey was second and nearly won the batting title at .336 with thirty-four steals. Joe Morgan enjoyed one of the finest all-around seasons of any player in history. Morgan hit third, won the MVP (.320, twenty-seven home runs, 111 RBIs, sixty steals) in 1976, to go along with the '75 honor, and wound up enshrined in the Baseball Hall of Fame in Cooperstown. Tony Perez had nineteen home runs and 91 RBIs as a future Hall of Famer. Johnny Bench hit two home runs and .533 in the World Series; he was the 1970 and '72 MVP and also went to Cooperstown.

What a lineup—and the Reds' best power hitter still hasn't been mentioned. George Foster had a great year—.306, twenty-nine home runs, and 121 RBIs; he would be the MVP in 1977. In the "weak" part of the lineup, Dave Concepcion had a .281 average with twenty-one steals and Cesar Geronimo, the former pitcher, hit .307 with twenty-two steals in the eighth slot. The Reds led the league in all twelve major offensive categories.

Why were those teams so good? Obviously talent is a big reason. If you don't have the talent, you aren't going to win in the big leagues, especially over the long run. The Reds had four Most Valuable Players, multiple Rookies of the Year and more than ten All-Stars. The statistics above provide additional evidence of the Reds' phenomenal talent but talent isn't the only reason the team won. Other teams have had talent, and lots of talent, and have not won the World Series. The Reds also had balance.

In the everyday lineup there was one switch-hitter (Rose), three lefties (Griffey, Morgan and Geronimo) and four righties (Perez, Bench, Foster and Concepcion). So against a right-handed pitcher there were four lefties and four righties in the lineup. They also had a balance of hitting for average and hitting for power. Rose, Griffey, Morgan, Concepcion, Foster and Geronimo all had high averages. Morgan, Perez, Bench and Foster most certainly had power. Bench led the league in RBIs three different years as did Foster. (Perez never did lead the league, he just knocked in more than ninety every year.) In addition to the power, the Reds had speed — every regular had double-digit steals except Rose, with nine.

The Reds from top to bottom boasted perhaps the most powerful and well-balanced lineup of all time. The 1927 Yankees are generally the gold standard by which other teams are weighed. Comparing the two teams lineups, obviously Ruth and Gehrig would start over Foster and Perez. Bob Meusel would be a toss-up with Griffey in right field. If you choose offense, go with the Yankees Earle Combs in center, but it would be hard to top Geronimo's arm and range on defense. Across the rest of the lineup, you must give the nod to the Reds.

The Brooklyn Dodgers of 1953 are the other team that could rival the Reds' hitting. The Dodgers had three big power hitters. Roy Campanella behind the plate at .312, forty-one homers, 142 RBIs had a better batting average than Bench ever did. Bench had one of his worst offensive years in 1976 but his defense would still be preferred over Campanella's. Gil Hodges and Tony Perez are a wash at first, often being compared to one another. Hodges had slightly higher numbers but not for as long a period as Perez. Duke Snider was compared to Mays and Mantle back in the day to decide who was the best outfielder in New York. He would get the nod over Geronimo. Again, in every other position, the nod goes to the Reds. Younger readers may wonder at the absence of Jackie Robinson. Robinson was on the backside of his career at this point and played mostly a utility role in the outfield.

In regard to present-day powers, the Yankees are widely considered the team with the most talent. One would be tempted to trade Davey Concepcion for Derek Jeter, but the two are close. Jeter is a little better hitter but Concepcion may get the nod for his defense. You might trade Cesar Geronimo for Bernie Williams. Williams has the better bat but Geronimo is the better defensive center fielder. Trading Ken Griffey for Gary Sheffield seems to be a good deal, Sheffield the better hitter, especially for power, but Griffey had better speed.

The most interesting and mind-boggling proposition: would you trade

Pete Rose for Alex Rodriguez at third? Rodriguez is the brightest star in the game, and if he stays healthy and keeps his head on straight he could give Barry Bonds a run for his record. Rodriguez definitely has better power numbers than Rose and his average is close. What team, though, would sacrifice Rose's leadership, determination, grit, consistency, hustle and example? In this case, I suspect you would keep Rose and just move him to one of his other four All-Star positions and still try to get Rodriguez. The other four positions clearly come down in favor of the Reds.

Defensively the Reds have few peers, as well. The Reds were not the first to hold to the philosophy of being strong up the middle. It is a time-honored baseball tradition but the Reds did it as well as anybody. In 1974 the entire middle of the Reds defense won Gold Gloves: Bench at catcher, Morgan at second, Concepcion at shortstop, and Geronimo and his cannon in center field. They repeated the trick the next three consecutive seasons.

Morgan's only weakness was that he had just a good arm, not a great arm. He made up for it with quickness and smarts. With a man on second base, he would field a ground ball at second. The normal play was a throw to first to get the runner as the man at second easily advanced to third base. Morgan had it worked out where he would quickly gun the ball to Rose to get the lead runner. This was a rare defensive play but Morgan accomplished it three or four times a season with little notoriety. It was a little thing that kept the opposition from scoring on a fly ball. Griffey had blazing speed and a great arm in right. He was very strong on the throw to third. Foster was decent in left with a good arm as witnessed by his gunning down of Denny Doyle in the 1975 Fall Classic Game Six. He also could play center field. Rose and Perez were solid at the corners. The Reds finished first in fielding percentage six times in the 1970s.

The most common misconception is that the Big Red Machine was all offense and didn't have good pitching, which ignores the facts. The Reds starters were good, if not great. They finished in the top half of the league in ERA every single year. Most teams are happy with that.

The Reds join the 1941 Yankees as being the only teams to win the World Series when no starter won more than fifteen games. This happened in both 1975 and '76; however, Gullett, Billingham and Nolan all consistently won around fifteen games each year. Jack Billingham was a workhorse, leading the league in innings pitched in 1973; no small feat when playing for Sparky Anderson. Gary Nolan and Don Gullett were among the league leaders in winning percentage on six occasions. Jim Merritt notched twenty-one wins in 1970 and Wayne Simpson was first in winning percentage and second in ERA before each hurt his arm. Fredie Norman won at least eleven games every season he pitched for the Reds.

The starters were good; the relievers were great. The Reds always had at least two guys who were proven closers (Carroll and Granger, later Carroll and Hall). In the peak years, the Reds had three men who were proven closers (Carroll, Eastwick and McEnaney) and a fourth (Borbon) who also could close but who was too valuable in middle relief to move. Borbon's rubber arm notched a franchise-record 531 appearances in his ten-year career with the Reds.

In a bullpen, where it was closer by committee, the Reds still had the league leader in saves on multiple occasions: Granger, 1970; Carroll, 1972; Eastwick, 1975 and 1976. The 1975 bullpen was full of men with impressive peak years in their careers: Carroll with thirty-seven saves, Eastwick with twenty-six, McEnaney with fifteen, and Borbon with eighteen. It was one of the top bullpens of all time. Attend most parks and if the home team is down three or four runs in the seventh inning, fans begin to file out. Not in Riverfront, not in the 1970s. With the Reds' offense, no game was out of reach. With their relievers the offense always had a shot to get the team back in the game. In essence the Reds had good starting pitching, the top bullpen of the 1970s if not of all time, and arguably the greatest offense of all time. That makes for a pretty good team.

Tremendous on the field, the Reds had a great manager and coaches in the dugout. After Sparky Anderson left the Reds, he went on to manage the Detroit Tigers for seventeen seasons. While with the Tigers he won a World Series title, two division crowns and 1,331 games, the most by any Tigers manager in history. He now leads two franchises in all-time wins. He won 863 games with the Reds. Throw out the injury-plagued year of 1971 and Anderson won at least eighty-eight games each year in Cincinnati. Sparky's .596 winning percentage is best all-time for the Reds.

His coaches were exceptional as well. George Scherger, one of his mentors, was managerial material himself, winning numerous minor-league championships. He provided wise advice to the young Anderson. Big Klu proved to be as good a hitting coach as he had been a hitter. His teams were usually first or second in runs produced, hovering around five per game. Four of his batters won six MVP awards among them. Larry Shepard, himself a former manager with the Pirates, handled the pitching staff flawlessly. Sparky didn't have to worry about it. Finally, Alex Grammas provided sage advice to Sparky before being tapped as the Brewers manager in 1976 and then upon his return in 1978. Grammas would eventually become the longest tenured third-base coach in baseball history. Grammas's replacement, Russ Nixon, was considered by Chief Bender to be one of the three best groomers of talent the Reds ever had.

To get the complete picture, and most people stop before this point, you have to appreciate the front office that assembled both the team and the coaching staff. Bob Howsam had a great front-office team. The Bowen brothers' scouting department drafted or signed twelve of the players of the mighty 1976 team. Several, like Pete Rose, Tony Perez and Johnny Bench, were signed by the Reds before Howsam's arrival. Chief Bender oversaw the development of seventeen of the players on the 1976 team in the farm system he ran. Ray Shore kept an eye on the opposition in order for the Reds to beat them on the field and trade with them effectively off the field. Wagner kept contracts under control and greatly expanded the Reds' radio reach, with great talent like Michaels, Brennaman, and Nuxhall. He also had merchandising success with Reds garb and memorabilia appearing across the land. He and Howsam did a great job in tapping Tom Seeberg and Jim Ferguson to be the publicity and media guys. The Reds routinely won honors such as MVP, Sportsman of the Year and the Hickok Belt, which can't be done unless the players' names are out in the press.

At the top of it all was Bob Howsam, as fine a baseball man and leader as the game has ever known. But Howsam's duties weren't quite over. There is another chapter to his story.

EPILOGUE

There were still some interesting twists and turns for Bob Howsam to navigate in his journey with the Reds. When he informed Mr. Nippert that he needed to step down as general manager because of health problems and the state of the game, Nippert begged him to stay on as a consultant and represent the Reds at all league meetings. Nippert appointed Howsam vice chairman of the board of the Cincinnati Reds, one step below himself. Nippert also had a stipulation put in Howsam's contract that he would help the Reds identify a new GM if Wagner were to ever leave the job.

In many ways Howsam's time with the Reds was still very busy in the late 1970s and early '80s even though he was no longer the general manager. It was a time of great upheaval in baseball as the players' union continued to flex its muscle and challenge the status quo at every turn. League meetings were frequent and Howsam was the Reds' official representative. By this time he had garnered an esteem among the ownership group, esteem that had been earned through his success with the Reds and Cardinals.

Years earlier Bob Howsam had marveled at the ability of Walter O'Malley to persuade fellow owners of the best position to take on an issue. O'Malley, a skilled orator, was able to present the facts and his case in a convincing fashion. Initially he allowed the other owners to think he wanted to do what they wanted to do. By the time he stopped talking, the position was 180 degrees from that initial position, and it was what O'Malley wanted to do. So convincing was his argument that the other owners approved his position.[1]

There were basically two full-time owners in the National League at this point, owners whose only source of income was from baseball. Peter O'Malley (Walter's son) in Los Angeles was one. Bob Howsam was in essence the second. Because of their full-time status and the fact that they could invest their attention completely on baseball, other owners often looked to O'Malley for advice on key decisions that confronted baseball. As time wore on, Howsam joined him as a sort of unofficial advisory counsel as to how the game should be run. Howsam and O'Malley were viewed by other owners as full-time guys who had baseball's best interests in mind.[2] For example, Howsam's old boss in St. Louis, Gussie Busch would often pull him aside before a meeting and ask how they should approach a certain topic. It was a proud moment for Bob

Howsam, who years prior had studied Walter O'Malley closely in an effort to learn from his communication example.

It also was quite a feather in the cap of Howsam, who was not even an official owner. It also was a tribute to Louis Nippert, a very wealthy man, who didn't feel the need to flaunt his power and wealth in order to feel good about himself. That is a rare quality among the rich. Wealthy men in particular usually feel the need to show their power. Nippert was happy to have Howsam run the show.

In 1980, the year after the sweep at the hands of the Pirates, the Reds finished third to the Astros, three and a half games back in the Western Division. Morgan had departed and rejoined the Astros via free agency. Ron Oester, a young second baseman with a light red afro, filled in nicely, hitting .277, but he didn't have Morgan's speed or power. A speedy and hustling young outfielder named Dave Collins replaced Cesar Geronimo in center. Geronimo's hitting had dropped off again. After the season the Reds dealt him to the Kansas City Royals for German Barranca. It also was Johnny Bench's last season behind the plate. Unable to take the daily grind of catching, he would search for a home over the next three seasons.

Howsam was not around to view the season firsthand. He and his wife, Janet, had returned to their native Colorado. They had purchased a home near Glenwood Springs. A small town 150 miles west of Denver, Glenwood Springs is named for beautiful hot springs that burst to the surface in town. The springs are cooled and then feed a large outdoor pool, which is suitable for swimming year-round. The water's ninety-degree temperature causes a steam to rise from its surface, especially when the pool is surrounded by several feet of snow. The scenery and long swims were therapeutic for Howsam's bad back.

The Reds were enduring a series of leadership changes. Bob Howsam had stepped down prior to the 1978 season. Sparky Anderson had been dismissed at the end of the season. Chief Bender was still running player development but Joe Bowen would leave as the head of scouting after the 1982 season. His brother Rex stayed on as chief scout.

Perhaps most importantly, a change had occurred at the very top. Louis Nippert was still vigorous and energetic but he realized that his years were advancing. As he approached eighty he didn't want his ownership of the team to result in ugly snags when his estate was settled in the inevitable event of his death. More importantly, he did not want to risk the chance that an owner would buy his beloved Reds from his estate and move it to another city. Therefore, he informed Howsam that he needed to sell the club. His decision on how to do it was truly revealing of his life and character.

Nippert declared that he wanted to put the team in a trust and be given to the city. The fact that the sale of the club, still very successful at the time, would bring him a handsome profit was of no concern. He wanted what was best for the city. He loved Cincinnati and wanted it to continue to thrive. He wanted his Reds to always remain in the Queen City and this move would ensure that they did.

While deeply admiring his motives and decision, Howsam advised him against the move. Howsam felt that letting city politicians run a baseball team would result in chaos. Nippert then turned to the next best alternative in his mind. He wanted to give the ball club to a foundation. Again admiring his devotion to the city, Howsam offered similar advice, saying that you can't have a committee from a foundation run a club — nothing would ever get done.

His top two ideas shot down, Nippert then turned to his friend and asked what he would advise. Howsam suggested that he find another owner among the ownership group who had a similar devotion and zeal for the city and for the Reds. Howsam suggested the Williams brothers, James and William.[3]

The Williams had been part of the ownership group since 1966 when the 617 Group bought the club from DeWitt. Due to their personality, as well as their minority ownership status, the Williams brothers had been mostly in the background but they shared Nippert's love for the Reds and the city. The family fortune had been earned through the Western and Southern Life Insurance Company, a company founded by their ancestors in 1888. The company had been a solid part of the Queen City for generations. It was a steady company and its claim to fame was that not one employee was laid off during the Great Depression of the 1930s. The Williams brothers were now in real estate development. Nippert agreed to approach the Williams brothers, and the brothers agreed to buy the majority of the team in 1980. The sale was finalized in February of 1981. The Williams brothers were content to leave things as they had been. "If it ain't broke, don't fix it."

Johnny Bench began playing first base in 1981, displacing Danny Driessen. The move helped Bench's bat. He was hitting above .340 when he slid into second base, breaking his ankle on May 28. A few weeks later, the union chose to strike in midseason, upset by how teams would be compensated when they lost a free agent. If a team lost a player to another team, owners wanted to choose a player from a pool of the gaining team. At the time of the strike, on June 12, the Reds were 35–21, one-half game behind the Los Angeles Dodgers. The strike lasted for fifty days. When the season resumed, the baseball powers decided that there would be a first-half and second-half champion of the season, and that they would meet in the playoffs. The Reds finished the second half 31–21, a game and a half behind the Astros. Though they had a better record than either the Dodgers or the Astros, in fact the best overall record in baseball at 66–42, the Reds did not go to the playoffs. Wagner and the rest of the Reds fans were furious. It seemed an injustice but it was the league's decision in response to the player's strike. Marvin Miller called the strike that wiped out 706 games, "The union's finest hour."

After the 1981 season, Ken Griffey was traded to the New York Yankees for Brian Ryder and Freddie Toliver. If you don't recognize those names you are not alone. Ray Knight was traded to Houston for Cesar Cedeno. George Foster's hitting and attitude began to slide and he was traded to the New York Mets in February of 1982 for Alex Trevino, Jim Kern and Greg Harris, not household names. The Reds hoped that Trevino could be their new catcher, as they had to this point not been able to replace Bench behind the plate.

After the success of 1981, unexpectedly things began to completely unravel for the Reds in 1982. The wheels fell off what was left of the Big Red Machine. Only Bench and Concepcion still remained from the glory days. Bench was moved to third base and Driessen was given the everyday first-base job again. Concepcion still manned shortstop. Seaver was still in the starting rotation, but was showing signs of his age at thirty-seven. He went 5–13 for the season. A young Mario Soto was the only bright spot in a very bleak season, the bleakest in Cincinnati Reds history. After being the winningest team in baseball in 1981, they were the worst team in 1982. They also were the worst team in Reds history, losing 101 games. Only six years earlier they had won 102 games.

Following the 1982 season, Wagner dealt Tom Seaver back to the Mets. In return the Reds got starting pitcher Charlie Puleo, outfielder Lloyd McClendon, and Jason Felice. None of them did much for the Reds. Felice never even made it to the big leagues. Seaver went on to win nine games with the Mets and then fifteen and sixteen with the Chicago White Sox. It was another poor trade for the Reds.

Unhappy with John McNamara, Wagner let him go in middle of the dismal 1982 season. He was replaced by Russ Nixon. An unfortunate name to bear while the memory of Watergate was fresh in mind, Nixon had replaced Alex Grammas as Sparky's third-base coach in 1976.

While Wagner was unhappy with McNamara, the Williams brothers were growing increasingly unhappy with Wagner. As the Reds record went south in 1982, so did attendance. From a high of 2.6 million in the 1976 pinnacle year of the Big Red Machine, it slumped to 1.1 million in the strike-shortened 1981 season. In 1982 it was 1.3 million, 50 percent of what it had been in 1976.

Dick Wagner is, if anything, a man of conviction and principle. He felt strongly that there was a certain way to run a ball club. You might not agree with him but you had no question about how he felt. He was very clear with his expectations and they were high. If you didn't meet the expectations, you would hear about it. If you didn't correct your course, you would be gone. Wagner practiced what he preached and personally kept the same high standards that he enforced.

He was similar to Howsam in that they both knew what they wanted to do. The difference was in style. With Bob Howsam you felt like you worked with him, even though you worked for him. With Dick Wagner, you felt like you worked for him — and you did. The reality, the bottom line, was the same in both scenarios but the feel was totally different. You don't have to have the "human touch" to be a great leader but it sure helps to engender loyalty from your people if you do possess it.

The other thing that Bob Howsam had that Dick Wagner didn't was an eye for talent. That is no insult. The fact of the matter is few men in the history of baseball have had Bob Howsam's eye for talent. It was developed over years of traveling the minors and working with some of the best baseball men in scouting: Jack Zeller, Billy Myers, and Branch Rickey. Wagner had very little eye for talent — it paled in comparison to Howsam's, most everyone's did.

When a ball club is winning, things are generally okay. As has been said, winning covers a multitude of sins. Owners, front-office staff, players, and managers may not have particularly liked Dick Wagner's style but they had to admit that he got results and had a strong track record. They could tolerate the style as long as they were winning. When the losing came, their tolerance for his approach quickly waned.

Things continued to get worse. The city's frustration began to boil over. Dick Wagner was quickly becoming the least popular figure in Cincinnati. A particularly embarrassing episode occurred during "Banner Night." Banner Night was an opportunity for Reds fans to show their spirit on the field of Riverfront Stadium. Fans generally made a banner on a large white sheet. They put it on a pole and it was carried by two people across the field. The banners looked very similar to the banners that parade marshals carry in front of a band or float in a parade. All the banners are inspected, of course, before being allowed on the field to ensure that they are not inappropriate. All banners passed inspection this night.

As the banners were paraded onto the field, one particularly caught the fans' eyes. It said something to the effect of "Go Reds," until the carriers flipped the top banner sheet to reveal a banner below which read "Fire Dick Wagner." The stadium absolutely erupted with applause and cheers. I can only imagine the greeting the banner bearers received when they exited the field through the hole in the right-center-field wall.

Meanwhile Howsam continued in his role as official Reds representative and consultant for the Williams brothers, just as he had for Louis Nippert. As part of his contract, he was to visit each of the Reds' minor-league teams and report back to Wagner. Howsam had been planning a trip to see the Class-AA Waterbury, Connecticut, minor-league affiliate of the Reds. He and Janet flew into New York in order to rent a car and make the short drive to Waterbury to see the game. As the plane was taxiing into the terminal, an announcement came over the intercom. "Is there a Robert Howsam on the plane? Please report to the hostess when you deplane."

Howsam identified himself to the hostess inside the terminal. She informed him that he was to call Bill Williams in Cincinnati. When Howsam reached Williams by phone, Williams told him, "We've fired Dick Wagner." Williams then asked Howsam to either get him a general manager or to be his general manager for a couple of years. Howsam agreed to take over for the interim. Before he could make a decision on the general manager's position for the long term, Howsam decided to do a little fact finding.

The Reds were in New York playing the Mets when Howsam landed in New York. Howsam decided to cancel his Waterbury trip and go over to Shea Stadium to talk with the team and watch them. Howsam felt a little uncomfortable. From the appearances it could seem that he had flown to New York knowing that he was going to be the new general manager. In reality it was just a fluke that he had been flying into town on the first stop of his minor-league scouting trip.[4] He ended up spending three days in New York, calling in Manager Russ Nixon and his coaches in order to assess the situation. He called in all the players as well, one by one. There were lots of problems and they were not all due to Dick Wagner. A common theme reported was poor chemistry on the club; it wasn't a pretty picture.

Dick Wagner left the Reds as a very unpopular figure. He was blamed by fans for letting Anderson, Rose, and Morgan all leave. He is often accused of dismantling the Big Red Machine that Bob Howsam built. I, for one, was not and am not a big fan of Dick Wagner the general manager but through the lens of retrospection nearly twenty-five years later, one must admit that he had to face some obstacles that his mentor and predecessor Bob Howsam did not. Truth be told, Dick Wagner helped build the Big Red Machine that he was accused of dismantling. His tough but professional handling of the business side of the Reds allowed Bob Howsam to concentrate on the baseball side without one worry about what was happening with the checkbook. Howsam was free of worry, business was being taken care of and taken care of very well. He could be the up-front man while someone he trusted could take care of the behind-the-scenes details.

Marty Brennaman often says that the problem with Dick Wagner was that he didn't have a Dick Wagner working for him. It implies that Dick Wagner did all the dirty work, so that Bob Howsam could be the good guy. This is not totally true. Whenever you are in charge of hiring and firing you aren't going to be the most popular person. Add to that the bulk of contract negotiations that Wagner was charged to handle and his popularity decreases further. What is true about Brennaman's statement is that there are two sides to a baseball club: playing baseball and running a business. Bob Howsam had Dick Wagner to run the business. Bob Howsam could run the baseball operations. When Wagner got the GM job, he had to wear both hats. "Had to" is probably not correct, he chose to wear both hats, which is a difficult task. If he is to be faulted it is for not choosing a top lieutenant to help shoulder the load. The rugged individualist may be glorified in American folklore but it rarely works for a leader to be a lone ranger. Wagner chose to run the whole show. A good baseball man to help with the baseball or a good businessman to help with the business would have been invaluable. In fact that is probably the most justified criticism of Wagner, his seeming failure to surround himself with good base-ball people and listen to their advice. It is hard to be a one-man show.

In a way the deck was stacked against Dick Wagner. It's hard to follow a genius. How would you like to replace Rose at third, Bench behind the plate, or Howsam behind the ball club? The Reds had enjoyed unparalleled success when Wagner took the reins. Wagner had three big issues to deal with that were just rearing their ugly heads when Howsam stepped down. The first was free agency. The Reds and many longtime fans disagreed with the entire concept. It seemed wrong to draft a player, groom him for years, get a few quality seasons, and then lose him to the highest bidder, especially when the bidders had vastly different resources. Many clubs had more resources than did the Reds.

Secondly the Reds' talent pipeline had begun to dry up. Howsam's minor-league system was highly touted. He had very good scouts whom he took care of. He had very good minor-league coaches and clubs to develop them. Wag-ner kept that system in place but it wasn't producing like it had been. Rose, Perez, and Bench had been in or through the pipeline when Howsam arrived. Concepcion, Griffey, Gullett, Nolan, Eastwick, and McEnaney followed. Ray Knight had filled in nicely after Rose's departure. Oester was adequate for Mor-gan but "nicely" and "adequate" don't win championships. Two highly touted prospects in Wagner's final months, Paul Householder and Nick Esasky, made it to the big leagues but never panned out.

That highlighted Wagner's third problem, age — and it wasn't Wagner's age that was the problem. The Big Red Machine was mostly gone and what was left was aging. Bench was thirty-five and just months from retirement. A player's peak baseball years are usually from age twenty-eight to thirty. The thirtysome-things are on the backsides of their career and some have steeper slopes than others. There are few stars like Rose, Aaron, Mays, and Nolan Ryan who can contribute greatly after age 37.

There is truth in the adage "it's lonely at the top." It is no place for cow-ards. The good ones like it that way. You make the calls the best you can and see how it pans out. President Teddy Roosevelt, known for never shying away from leadership, once said, "It is not the critic who counts: not the man who points out how the strong man stumbles or where the doer of deeds could have done better. The credit belongs to the man who is actually in the arena, whose face is marred by dust and sweat and blood, who strives valiantly, who errs and comes up short again and again, because there is no effort without error or shortcoming, but who knows the great enthusiasms, the great devotions, who spends himself for a worthy cause; who, at the best, knows, in the end, the tri-umph of high achievement, and who, at the worst, if he fails, at least he fails while daring greatly, so that his place shall never be with those cold and timid souls who knew neither victory nor defeat."[5] Dick Wagner wanted to be in the arena.

Direction is extremely important in leadership. If you have ever tried to follow someone who offered conflicting directions, directions that changed with every whim and wind, you know how frustrating that can be. That was never a problem with Dick Wagner. You may disagree with Dick Wagner's decisions— I did, many did—but you must admire him for his tenacity in sticking to his principles and having the courage to tell it like he saw it. There was no guesswork when it came to Dick Wagner; he made it very clear where he and the organization were going. If you agreed with it, you could stick around. If you couldn't, you'd better leave. In the end it was Wagner who was asked to leave. Though Reds fans can justifiably disagree with his decisions, his desire to do what he thought was best for the Reds, the way he saw it, can never be questioned.

The results of the 1982 team cannot be questioned either. It was the worst team in the 114-year history of the Cincinnati Reds with 101 losses and just 61 wins. In just one short season they went from the best record in baseball to the worst, first to worse in 365 days.

Howsam pondered what to do. He knew that going back to the GM job would entail a lot of work but he was thirsty to rebuild the club. His beloved Janny confirmed it. When he asked her opinion she was supportive, as always. She was consistently at his side and helpful to her man. Bob Howsam has no bigger fan. Janet noted a gleam in Howsam's eye that she hadn't seen in a while.[6] He was off again to run the Reds.

When the press got an audience with Howsam they wanted to know what he planned to do and how long he planned to stay. Before taking action, he made it clear that he wanted to assess the situation first. He also told them that he had promised the Williams brothers that he would stay for at least two years.

During the last few dark months of the 1983 campaign—the Reds finished last again—Howsam made his way around Riverfront. He sat in the seats and talked with fans, the few fans who were there. He sensed that something was missing but couldn't put his finger on it. He knew someone that could, however. His son Robert was in New York City working for a marketing and advertising agency. He possessed a keen marketing mind and knew how to do market research. Howsam wanted him to come to Cincinnati to get the fans' pulse. Robert said no at first, fearful of accusations of nepotism among the front-office folks. Howsam senior insisted and Robert gave in, first on a part-time consulting basis and later full-time.

Months of Robert's research could be boiled down to one recurring theme. According to the fans, it used to be fun to come to the ballpark but it just wasn't fun anymore. Winning was a big part but only one part of the equation. The excitement was gone.

Meanwhile Howsam was doing other things while in the bleachers talking with fans. He was watching the players and not just his own. One who caught his eye was the Cincinnatian he had watched in the 1979 playoffs—"The

Cobra," Dave Parker. When the Pirates were in town, Howsam often saw Parker chatting with a woman near his right-field station during warm-ups. Clearly they had some sort of relationship. One day Howsam wandered over to the woman and struck up a conversation. He asked how she knew Dave Parker. She replied that she had been his high school guidance counselor. This piqued Howsam's interest. He was always looking for someone who was good on the field (he knew that Parker was), good in the clubhouse, and good on the street. He asked what kind of student he had been, what kind of citizen, and how he was doing in Pittsburgh. The latter question was prompted by rumors coming from the Steel City that there was trouble in that clubhouse and that Parker was a ringleader.

The woman could not say enough good about Parker. A young man who did not have the best home life, Parker had gone through school with determination and a few bumps along the way. He wanted to be a pro ballplayer and had made it. Yes, he'd had some trouble in Pittsburgh but those days were behind him. Overall the counselor gave him a good report card.

Howsam filed the notes away mentally. He would retrieve them months later. He was on the verge of another major strategic decision. He was considering reversing the Reds' longtime policy of not participating in the free-agent market. Other clubs had decided not to follow the Reds' example, and as a result, salaries were escalating at a frightening pace and talent was moving around the league equally fast. It was clear that the rest of the league was not going to show Cincinnati's restraint. For better or worse, the rules were changing again and the change threatened to put Cincinnati right out of the game.

If the Reds were to participate, the question would be who to go after. They wanted to swim wisely if they were going to jump into the free-agent pool. One of the biggest names to announce that he was on the market that year was none other than Parker. At first Howsam wasn't that interested. Though he'd enjoyed the conversation with the guidance counselor, the rumors out of Pittsburgh were a bit too strong for his liking, rumors of drug use were the greatest among them.

While the Reds were researching the market in baseball and at home, Howsam's phone rang one day. It was Dave Parker's agent. He had a message for Howsam: the Cobra had an interest in playing ball in his hometown. Howsam knew the agent well, as he had represented numerous Reds. Howsam told him, "Well, I don't think I have an interest. I don't think Parker will conform to what needs to be done here if he is going to play for me." To those who know Bob Howsam, this was no surprise. If you can't follow the rules, you aren't going to play for Bob Howsam, period, end of story.

What Howsam did do was check in further into Dave Parker's background. He always did that with players. What he found was a boy from Cincinnati who was reported to be a fine young man. Parker got to Pittsburgh where a lot of things were rumored to going on but there was no solid proof that Parker was involved. Maybe he just got caught up in what was going on.

Parker's agent contacted Howsam again. "I talked to Parker and he wants to talk with you."

"Well all right, but you know what I am saying, if he doesn't want to follow what he has to do here, don't waste his time."

They set up a meeting. Howsam's secretary buzzed him and told him that Dave Parker was there. She sent him in, and in walked a six foot five mammoth of a man. He was clean shaven, wearing a three-piece business suit, with no jewelry. Parker approached the desk; Howsam got up and shook his hand and said, "Don't sit down, because if you aren't interested in following what I'm going to tell you to play for the Reds, there is no sense in you wasting your time or mine."

"Mr. Howsam, I would like to play for the Reds."

"Sit down," Howsam said, and they had a long talk.

The expectations were set immediately; the contract details were reached shortly thereafter. Too often these two events are reversed. When the process is reversed, the seeds of trouble are sown. This was not to be the case with Dave Parker.

In the press Howsam was asked about his decision to join in the free-agent game. "Baseball has changed and maybe I have a bit too." He also could have added that maybe Dave Parker had changed as well.[7]

Howsam made another acquisition in that off-season. The visits to the clubhouse that Johnny Bench and Joe Morgan had suggested seven seasons prior had reinforced in Howsam the importance of the intangible of leadership. He wanted the soul of a leader in the clubhouse. He went back to get the one he let get away, Tony Perez. He purchased Perez from Philadelphia. Perez was old for a baseball player — at forty-two, his best years were behind him — but what he brought to the clubhouse was timeless.

Russ Nixon had replaced McNamara in the middle of the disastrous 1982 year. Howsam knew and liked him, as Nixon had managed for Howsam for several years in the minor leagues. By the end of the 1983 season, though, Howsam decided that he was not the man for the job. The ball club was mired in a losing attitude and he wanted to pump life into the ball club. Howsam was faced with a similar situation that he'd had in 1970. He had inherited a manager — this time Nixon, earlier Bristol — who he did not think was the man for the job. He needed a new skipper.

For years Howsam had appreciated Vern Rapp at the Indianapolis Class-AAA club. Their relationship went back to Howsam's days in Denver. Howsam invited Rapp to join the organization when he first came to Cincinnati. Rapp had been Howsam's finisher, preparing many a Red for big-league duty. Perhaps it was time to reward his years of faithful service with the plum job of Reds skipper. Big-league manager is the aspiration of almost every minor-league manager. The choice had the additional benefit of fact that some of the Reds players had played for Rapp at Indianapolis, he was a known commodity, and so he was hired.

Halfway through the 1984 season, though, Howsam began to question his decision. The club wasn't really improving on the field; the team was playing well under .500 ball and Howsam sensed that the attitude still wasn't right in the clubhouse. Rapp's approach had worked extremely well at Indianapolis but didn't seem to be as good a fit for this different situation. His approach was a bit too tough at the major-league level.[8] Rapp did things his way and he wasn't about to change.

Howsam isn't one to rush into a decision but he also isn't one to play around when he feels he made the wrong call. He had felt that this decision had been right, just like the Sparky Anderson hiring had felt right in 1970, but it didn't turn out that way. Even the best sometimes err in decisions. Choosing the right field manager is like choosing leaders in organizations. Sometimes a person seems best for the job but isn't. You can't always tell until the person is in the job. It was unfortunate because Howsam genuinely liked Rapp and was grateful for his many years of service in Indianapolis, which made it even harder to dismiss the man from the job. It doesn't appear you are very grateful when you fire someone. On a positive note, at least Rapp had been given a shot to manage the Reds, after waiting many, many years.

For Rapp's replacement Howsam had the same philosophy after he let go of Dave Bristol. He wanted somebody to shake up the club, to bring some life and energy. He had a darkhorse in mind, north of the border. Pete Rose, the hometown boy who had left, was now in Montreal after five years in Philadelphia. Rose wasn't real happy in Montreal and his offensive output was floundering for the first time in his career.

Howsam wanted Pete to manage the Reds. If anyone could bring energy, enthusiasm, and excitement it would be Pete. Howsam made contact. He wanted Pete to retire and become the manager of the Reds. Pete was interested in managing but not interested in retiring. He would come to Cincinnati but it would have to be as a player-manager, in that order. No play, no deal. Howsam was willing to take the risk. He sent Tom Lawless to Montreal in exchange for Rose. It was like taking an organization off of life support.

Rose had reached the magical number of three thousand hits in 1978. In 1981 he passed Stan Musial's National League record of 3,631 hits. Rose reached four thousand in 1984, in his first week with Montreal, but Ty Cobb's record of 4,191 still seemed a long way off, as his performance began to slide at age 43. The trade rekindled Rose.

As a result of Howsam Jr.'s market research, the ad campaigns started, saying boldly "The fun is back." Bob Howsam was back; Tony Perez was back; Pete Rose was back. The fun was back. The Reds began to feel the excitement. The young players were in awe of Rose. In his first game at the helm he went 2-for-4, complete with a vintage Rose headfirst slide into third base. It was inspiring to the players and rejuvenating for Rose. The fun was back.

Shortly after the fun returned, the rules changed again. Another strategic decision affected Bob Howsam and the Reds. Life is full of these challenges and sometimes we just can't anticipate them. One of the owners, James Williams, got sick. Coupled with the financial losses of the 1982 and 1983 seasons, this led the Williams brothers to be ready to get out of the game. The brothers put the team up for sale.

The surprising thing was that no potential owner jumped up to bid. There was silence in Cincinnati. Louis Nippert's longtime fear began to materialize again. Perhaps the Reds would not only be sold but moved. Louisville, one hundred miles downstream from Cincinnati, was interested. They had long been the home to the Cardinals' Class-AAA club and were the first minor-league team to ever draw over a million fans. They made it clear that they would be interested in the Reds and would support them. Cincinnatians held their breath. There were several rich men in town and everyone waited for them to step up. They didn't. There was one rich woman in Cincinnati who did. Marge Schott bought the team to keep it from moving out of town.

Margaret Schott was an unknown in baseball circles. As a young woman, she had grown up in a well-to-do lumber family. She had married a rich young man named Charles Schott, who was renowned as a sort of playboy. When he died unexpectedly of a heart attack at his girlfriend's apartment, his wife was publicly embarrassed. He left her a car dealership, among other businesses, and his family fortune in 1968. Early experiences left her bitter. She was a long-time Reds fan and genuinely enjoyed the ball club, becoming a minority owner with the Williams brothers in 1981. She had expected one of the rich Cincinnati-native men to buy the club. When they didn't, she did. She wasn't going to watch the Reds leave.

Meanwhile, Howsam continued with his old practices. There were frequent surprise visits to see the minor-league teams. On one such trip, to Class-AA Waterbury, the manager informed Howsam that he was having trouble with a talented young outfielder. Howsam found the young man and sat with him on a bench. He brought the problem straight to a head. Howsam had learned to be very direct about problems, getting this from both his father and his father-in-law. In situations like this, he says that there is no reason to beat around the bush. He asked the young man how the player expected Howsam to promote him to a higher minor league or bring him to the big leagues if he continued the disruptive behaviors he had been exhibiting. Howsam then calmly and in conversational tones made it clear who was running the club and how things were to be done. Usually, he was able to straighten the situation out in this way.

Too often leaders ignore behavior problems, hoping they will go away. Often what the employee, especially a young one, really needs and wants, is someone to help them get back on track. The behavior must be addressed in a direct manner for that to happen. In this case the young man, Eric Davis, played the next day and all the days following, very well.

Howsam had promised to stay at least two years when he was hired in 1983. He had been grooming his replacement, Bob Bergesch, whom he had known since his days in the Western League. Bob Bergesch was the GM of the Omaha Cardinals when Howsam ran the Denver Bears. Howsam actually made a front-office trade with the New York Yankees for Bergesch's services. Howsam sent Woody Woodward to New York in exchange for Bergesch.

Things on the ball club were looking up. Howsam's health was going down, though. His back pains had returned; there were days that he would drive to his condo across the bridge from Riverfront Stadium in Covington and lie flat on his back for a few hours to get some relief. He would then return to his office and work some more. It was no way to run a ball club.

Baseball owners approved the sale of the club from the Williams brothers to Schott in December 1984. Shortly thereafter it became clear that the way the club was going to be run would be different under Schott. She trusted no one and liked to micromanage, without much knowledge of the business.

Howsam was uncomfortable with his back — and with the new leadership. It was time to make a change. This time he was going to retire for good. He announced his decision to retire when his contract expired in July of 1985. Bergesch would take over.

A few days before he left his Riverfront Stadium office and Cincinnati for the last time, all the Reds' front-office employees, roughly fifty of them, gathered in his office impromptu. They had a number of presents for their boss. The last one was presented by Greg Park, the accounting guy. It was a pack of baseball cards. Howsam looked a bit surprised. "Go ahead and open them, sir, see what is inside."

Howsam opened the package labeled "Topps Baseball Cards, 1985." Inside was a card of every member of the 1976 Big Red Machine. And there was one last card, a Bob Howsam card. It had been printed up specially by the group. It brought a warm smile and thank you from the boss.[9] It tells you everything you need to know about Bob Howsam's leadership style and the loyalty and admiration of his people.

Howsam's genius lay in his ability to put his philosophy, his stamp, on the entire organization. It is one thing to have philosophies, another to have them followed. His personal touch and the way he communicated and dealt with people allowed him to transfer his philosophy to each member of the organization. He also was blessed with great support on the homefront, above-average intelligence, a keen mind, wisdom, and the ability to think clearly, to recognize and attract talent, to assemble a good team, to listen, and to make decisions without worrying about how he would be perceived. He also had the good fortune to work for an owner who gave him the trust and resources to do his job and stay out of the way.

Bob Howsam had the courage to do things the way he thought they ought to be done. His decision to hire Sparky Anderson, a young, unproven big-league manager, shortly after his own contract had almost expired showed a lot of courage. Howsam had tremendous mentors who taught him the two sides of the game — talent on the field and business in the front office.

Following his retirement from the Reds, Howsam worked briefly for the Denver Zephyrs minor-league club. His son Robert was the general manager. He asked his dad to do some scouting for the Denver ball club. In a way things had come full circle; Bob Howsam was doing minor-league baseball with Denver again. By this time the old Oakland Athletics captain, Sal Bando, was the Brewers general manager. They both happened to be in the same park one evening to scout a game. Howsam asked Bando a question that had long perplexed him, "You know Sal, I always wondered how you won when you had Finley, who didn't seem to want discipline at all. He was just kind of opposed to it. You know there's no club that I have ever witnessed that didn't have discipline and ever won anything."

"Well, Bob, Finley, no, but we had discipline in our clubhouse [among] the players themselves," replied Bando. I suspect that statement overlooked a few fights involving Reggie Jackson but Bando's reply answered the question that had long perplexed Howsam.[10]

There are three players from the Big Red Machine in the Baseball Hall of Fame, plus one manager and one broadcaster. There is a man missing and I am not referring to Pete Rose. Pete's story is for another time and another place. The missing man is Bob Howsam, the mastermind of the Big Red Machine. The case is clear. If it has not been said anywhere else, let me be the first to say it. Bob Howsam should be in the Baseball Hall of Fame in Cooperstown. Period.

Consider the facts. Bob Howsam's teams won. Over a seventeen-year period, his teams had winning records fourteen times for a .565 winning percentage.[11] Before Bob Howsam came to Cincinnati, the team went to the postseason roughly every twenty years. In the ten seasons from 1967 to 1976 his teams were in the World Series six times, winning three world titles. Sixty percent of his teams went to the World Series over a ten-year period. The World Series decade of success is unmatched except by the New York Yankees. Howsam's teams were in the postseason seven times and it was his players that appeared in an eighth postseason in 1979. This does not include the 1964 World Series Champion St. Louis Cardinals, when Howsam was general manager. That team was Bing DeVine's; Howsam had only been in the job for two months. In the same spirit, the 1967 and '68 Cardinals were Howsam's, though, not Devine's. Howsam built those teams. They won the World Series ten months after he left for Cincinnati.

The 1975 and '76 Cincinnati Reds teams are considered among the best of all time and the 1976 team may indeed be the best of all time. His second stint with the Reds proved that it was no fluke. The ball club improved from seventy-two wins to eighty-nine wins in his two seasons back. Five seasons after he retired for good, the Reds won the World Championship again. Five of the eight regulars on the team, including Eric Davis and Barry Larkin, were either drafted, in the minors, or arrived in Cincinnati under Howsam's second tenure. A key starter, Tom Browning, and one of the "Nasty Boys," Rob Dibble, also fit in that category.

Perhaps the best testimonial to Howsam's leadership came from the thirty-five-year-old white-haired manager he hired in 1970. Sparky Anderson would later recall, "I didn't realize how great he was until I went to Detroit. I never got into an elevator with that man that he didn't have everyone else get in before him. That's the kind of leader he was. You ask me why the Big Red Machine was great — Bob Howsam ... he was the Big Red Machine." When Sparky's number was retired by the Reds on May 28, 2005, he thanked Howsam from the field over the public address system, remarking that he didn't know what possessed Howsam to hire an unknown quantity in 1970 and give him a chance to manage such a great team but he was thankful that he did. He ended the speech, "Never, ever forget Bob Howsam."

It is clear that Howsam deserves a spot alongside Anderson, Bench, Morgan, and Perez in Cooperstown. Greatness does not happen by accident. There are many reasons the Big Red Machine was great but chief among them was Bob Howsam.

APPENDIX: WHERE ARE THEY NOW?

The Reds Players

Armbrister, Eddie—Came over in the 1971 trade from Houston. Most famous for his sacrifice bunt and bump into Carlton Fisk during Game Three of the 1975 World Series. He was released by the Reds following the 1977 season. As of 2000, he was living in the Bahamas with an unknown occupation.[1]

Bench, Johnny—Retired from the Reds after the 1983 season. The 1968 Rookie of the Year, Bench was a fourteen-time All-Star, won ten Gold Gloves, was World Series MVP, two-time league MVP, and likely the most talented player on the Reds. Considered one of the greatest catchers of all time, if not the greatest, Bench lives in the Cincinnati area and his children are active in local sports. He is involved in several business ventures, usually behind the scenes, and also serves as a special consultant to the Cincinnati Reds. He was elected to the Baseball Hall of Fame in 1988.

Billingham, Jack—At one time considered quitting baseball to pump gas in Florida. Coming from Houston in the 1971 trade, he was the Reds' most effective pitcher in the post-season, if not always appreciated by the coaching staff. Billingham was the most adamant in his dislike for Sparky Anderson. Traded by Dick Wagner to the Detroit Tigers for George Cappuzzello and John Valle, he ended up pitching again for Sparky, when the latter was hired by the Tigers in 1979. The Tigers dealt him to Boston in May 1980 and he was released by the Bosox the next month. In 2000 he was the pitching coach for the Kissimmee Cobras in Class A. Now retired, he lives in Florida. Inducted into the Reds Hall of Fame in 1984.

Borbon, Pedro—The rubber-armed Borbon came over from the Angels in the Alex Johnson deal. He is still the Reds' all-time leader in appearances with 531. He was traded by Dick Wagner to the San Francisco Giants on June 28, 1979 for Hector Cruz. He finished that season with the Giants but was released the next April. He pitched briefly for the Cardinals in May 1980. Borbon attempted a comeback during spring training of 1995 amidst the players' strike and now serves as an itinerant minister in the Southwest.

Carbo, Bernie—The first player ever drafted by the Reds in the inaugural 1965 draft (one round ahead of Johnny Bench). A third baseman, he was converted to outfield by Sparky Anderson at Asheville in 1968. The talented left fielder was the leading hitter in all of the minor leagues in 1969. He was the *Sporting News* Rookie of the Year after his great 1970 season. Carbo fell out of favor with Bob Howsam after a bitter holdout in the spring of 1971 and horrible sophomore year. The Reds traded him to the Cardinals for Joe Hague in May 1972. Carbo went to Boston after the 1973 season where he hit his famous home run in Game Six of the 1976 World Series. Traded to the Brewers in the middle of the 1976 season, he was traded back to Boston six months later. He also played for the Indians, Cardinals, and the Pirates. Retiring as a bitter man in 1980, Carbo checked into drug rehabilitation in 1993 and became a Christian. He successfully coached the Pensacola Penguins to championships in the Independent Leagues in the mid 2000s and currently lives in Alabama where he works with youth. Carbo founded Diamond Club Ministry which helps adults and youth find freedom from alcohol and drugs.

Carroll, Clay — "The Hawk." This big reliever was one of Howsam and the club's favorites. His trade in December 1975 to the White Sox for Rich Hinton was a disaster for the Reds. He went on to pitch for the White Sox, Cardinals, and briefly for the Pirates before retiring in 1978. After playing days, Carroll worked in construction and now is retired in Alabama, his home state. Inducted into the Reds Hall of Fame in 1980.

Chaney, Darrel — One of the three possible solutions at shortstop before Dave Concepcion finally won the job, Chaney was dealt to the Braves in December of 1975 for Mike Lum. He played with Atlanta until retiring after the 1979 season. He has worked as a broadcaster in both radio and television for the Braves. Currently he's senior vice president of sales and marketing for Prime Retail Services and lives in Georgia.

Concepcion, Dave — Retired after nineteen seasons, all with the Reds, following the 1988 campaign. He was a nine-time All-Star during his career and the MVP of the 1982 game. He won five Gold Gloves and helped prepare a young Barry Larkin to be the Reds shortstop. He currently resides in his native Venezuela where he is an executive in a trucking business and a national hero. He inspired many, including Omar Vizquel, from his native land. Davey's number (13) was retired by the Reds in August 2007 and he was inducted into the Reds Hall of Fame in 2000. He hopes to be inducted into the Cooperstown Baseball Hall of Fame, now that shortstop peer Ozzie Smith has been inducted.

Darcy, Pat — The man who gave up Carlton Fisk's bottom-of-the-twelfth home run in Game Six of the 1975 World Series, Darcy pitched for the Reds from 1974–1976. Traded by the Reds to the Cardinals in March 1977, he never played for them. He is a retail and investment specialist in Tucson, Arizona.

Driessen, Danny — One of many failed solutions for the third-base problem, Driessen's bat and productive 1976 World Series convinced Bob Howsam to trade Tony Perez. Driessen never reached the promise predicted for him but had seven and a half seasons at first base before being traded in July 1984 by Bob Howsam to Montreal (where he had traded Perez) for Andy McGaffigan and Jim Jefferson. Driessen played for the Expos, Giants, Astros and Cardinals before retiring after the 1987 season. He served as the assistant baseball coach at his native Hilton Head High School through 2007.

Eastwick, Rawly — One of the Gold Dust Twins. With impending free agency, Eastwick was traded by Howsam to St. Louis on June 15, 1976, for Doug Capilla. The Mets had wanted him in the Seaver deal but were scared off by his contract problems. Eastwick pitched for the Cardinals, Yankees, Phillies, Royals, and Cubs though 1981. The Yankees made him a millionaire at twenty-seven but he never regained the glory he had known with the Reds. As of 2000, he was in commercial real estate in Boston.

Foster, George — Came to the Reds for Pat Duffy in 1971 but did not bloom until Rose moved to third in 1975. For the next half decade Foster was the hardest hitting man in baseball. Traded by Dick Wagner to the Mets in February of 1982 for Alex Trevino, Jim Kern, and Greg Harris, Foster played for the Mets and then briefly with the White Sox before retiring at the end of the 1986 season. Foster spends a lot of time in the Southeast and serves as a baseball consultant and is active in foundation activities. He runs a hitting camp for boys each summer and recently served as first commissioner of the Reds Rookie Success League. Inducted into the Reds Hall of Fame in 2003.

Fryman, Woodie — Howsam traded Tony Perez and Will McEnaney to Montreal for Fryman and Dale Murray. Along with the Carroll trade, it was the worst of Howsam's tenure. Fryman won five games for the Reds and feuded with Sparky Anderson. Along with Bill Caudill, he was traded by Howsam to the Chicago Cubs for Bill Bonham. He shortly thereafter went back to the Expos where he pitched through the 1983 season.

Geronimo, Cesar — "The Chief" came over in the 1971 trade with Houston and patrolled the outfield for the Reds from 1972–1980. Traded to Kansas City by Dick Wagner for German Barranca, he went on to play for the Royals until he retired following the 1983 season. In 2000, he served as the GM of the Hiroshima Toyo Carp of the Japanese Pro Baseball League. Currently he is involved in baseball in his native Dominican Republic. Geronimo was elected to the Reds Hall of Fame, Class of 2008.

Granger, Wayne — The Reds' sinkerball-throwing closer of the early 1970s set a team and major-league record for appearances at ninety in 1969 (later broken by Mike Marshall of Los Angeles) and was two-time NL Fireman of the Year for the Reds ('69 and '70). Granger was traded to the Minnesota Twins for reliever Tommy Hall on December 3, 1971. He went on to pitch for the Twins, Yankees, White Sox, Astros, and Expos. He finished his career with 108 saves and retired at the end of 1976. He now runs a shoe store in the southeastern United States. Wayne Granger was inducted into the Reds Hall of Fame in 1982.

Griffey, Ken — The former army private took over right field full time in 1974. The lifetime .296 hitter was a three-time All-Star (all with the Reds) and the MVP of the 1980 game. He was traded by Dick Wagner at the end of the 1981 season to the Yankees for Brian Ryder and Freddie Toliver. He played for the Yankees and Braves and then returned to the Reds as a free agent in August 1988 and played until August 1990, when the Reds released him so that he could join his son, Junior, in Seattle. He hit back-to-back homers with Junior in Seattle and retired following the 1991 season. Griffey served as the Reds' hitting coach in the 1990s and is currently a special assistant to the Reds, living in the Cincinnati area. Inducted into the Reds Hall of Fame in 2004.

Grimsley, Ross — The hero of Game Four of the 1972 playoffs against Pittsburgh, his two-hit shutout staved off elimination for the Reds. The free spirit constantly challenged both Howsam and Anderson's rules. He was traded to the Baltimore Orioles in December 1973 for Merv Rettenmund. Once with the Orioles he grew a beard and won eighteen games. He also played for the Expos and Indians, winning a high of twenty games in 1978 when he was an All-Star. He retired after the 1982 season with 124 wins. He is currently the pitching coach for the Augusta GreenJackets, a Class-A club owned by Cal Ripken Jr.

Gullett, Don — One of four players Sparky Anderson pegged for the Baseball Hall of Fame (with Bench, Rose, and Morgan), injuries derailed his brilliant career. Gullett broke into the majors at age nineteen and was gone at twenty-seven. Signed by George Steinbrenner as one of the first millionaire players, Gullett pitched well in 1977 but injured his shoulder in 1978 and never recovered, vindicating Howsam's philosophy to never offer a contract for longer than two years. Gullett fought depression after the injury, returned to farming, and became the Reds' pitching coach from mid 1993 to 2005. He now lives in Kentucky. Elected to the Reds Hall of Fame in 2002.

Hall, Tommy—An exciting strikeout pitcher with a penchant for walking the first batter, Hall came over from the Minnesota Twins in the Wayne Granger deal in December 1971. He was fantastic in 1972 and '73 but fell off precipitously after that. Howsam traded him to the Mets in April 1975 for Matt Scarce. Hall pitched for the Mets and Royals before being released by the Royals in June 1977.

Helms, Tommy—Baseball's Rookie of the Year in 1966. The second baseman went to Houston in the 1971 trade. Helms played for the Astros, Pirates, and briefly the Red Sox, where he retired prior to the 1978 season. Helms become Pete Rose's first-base coach when Rose managed the Reds. Helms was the first to hug Pete after hit number 4,192. Helms is now retired and lives in Cincinnati. Inducted into the Reds Hall of Fame in 1979.

Hume, Tommy—Emerged on the Japanese trip in late 1978 as a steady reliever. Hume led the Reds in saves for four seasons and was selected National League Fireman of the Year in 1980 and an All-Star in 1982. He struggled after knee surgery in 1982. He was traded to the Phillies after the 1985 season but returned to Cincy in mid–1987, retiring at year's end. As of 2006, he had been the Reds bullpen coach for eleven seasons.

Johnson, Alex—The temperamental and talented Johnson was shipped to the Angels for Pedro Borbon and Jim McGlothlin in November 1969. He led the AL in hitting and was an All-Star in 1970. His attitude continued to sour in California where Sparky's mentor, Lefty Phillips, quickly grew tired of it. Johnson spent the rest of his career being shipped from one team to another (Indians, Rangers, Yankees, Tigers) after a year or two. His brother, Ron, starred as a Michigan Wolverines running back in the 1970s.

Kirby, Clay—The pitcher Howsam acquired for Bobby Tolan. He won a total of twenty-two games for the Reds and was traded to the Expos for Bob Bailey in December 1975. He was released by the Expos after one season. He died of a heart attack October 11, 1991.

King, Hal—The little-used back-up catcher lit up the 1973 season like a lightning bolt and disappeared just as quickly. His pinch-hit heroics turned around the 1973 season — four of his eight hits were home runs that season. He played one more year for the Reds, hitting .176 before retiring.

May, Lee—"The Big Bopper" was the Reds first baseman from 1967–1971 when he went over to Houston as a key piece of "the trade." After the 1974 season, May was traded to the Orioles to make room for Bob Watson. He left Baltimore after 1980, as Eddie Murray was beginning to bloom. He finished his career with the Royals, retiring after the 1982 season. He was a three-time All-Star and hit 354 career home runs. He lives in the Cincinnati area, retired, but is still very active with the Reds in community functions. He was inducted into the Reds Hall of Fame in 2006.

McGlothlin, Jim—McGlothlin, who looked like "Opie" from *The Andy Griffith Show*, came over to the Reds with Pedro Borbon and Vern Geishert for Alex Johnson and Chico Ruiz in November 1969 via a Bob Howsam trade. He pitched the first game at Riverfront Stadium on June 30, 1970 and started Game Two of the 1970 World Series and Game Five of the 1972 World Series. In all he won thirty-four games for the Reds before Howsam traded him to the White Sox in August 1973 for Steve Kealey. He finished the season with the White Sox and was released the next spring. He died on December 23, 1975, in Union, Kentucky, at age thirty-two, from leukemia.

McRae, Hal—Part of the 1970 platoon with Bernie Carbo in left. His pinch hit fly out for Jack Billingham was one of several pivotal plays in Game Seven of the 1972 World

Series. McRae's desire to play every day, coupled with his defensive liability, led to the November 1972 trade to Kansas City with Wayne Simpson for Roger Nelson and Richie Scheinblum. McCrae bloomed in Kansas City where he was a three-time All-Star and won a Silver Slugger Award and nearly a batting crown. He went to the postseason multiple times with the Royals and won the World Series in 1985. He managed the Royals from 1991–1994 and Tampa in 2001–02. He is currently the hitting coach for the St. Louis Cardinals.

McEnaney, Will —One of the Gold Dust Twins, McEnaney was on the mound for the final outs in both the 1975 and 1976 World Series. He was traded to the Expos with Tony Perez in December 1976 for Woodie Fryman and Dale Murray. He never regained his 1975 form. He pitched for the Expos, Pirates, and Cardinals in successive seasons, retiring after the 1979 campaign. After his baseball career he began painting houses and as of 2000 was the manager of a refinishing company in Florida.

Menke, Denis —Came over in the 1971 trade with Houston and was thought to be the solution at third. Unfortunately he never panned out for the Reds and was traded back to the Astros where he had been solid. Howsam traded him back to Houston for Pat Darcy in February 1974. Menke played very little and retired in the middle of the 1974 season. He later served as the Astros hitting coach. As of 2004 he was living in Florida and doing occasional hitting clinics.

Merritt, Jim —Acquired by Howsam from the Twins for Leo Cardenas, Merritt was sensational in '69 (seventeen wins) and '70 (twenty wins). His September 1970 elbow injury helped doom the Reds' chances of beating the Orioles in the World Series. Merritt never completely recovered from the injury. Howsam traded him in December 1972 to the Rangers for Hal King and Jim Driscoll. Merritt toiled two and a half seasons for Texas before being released in July 1975. He won only seven games after 1970.

Morgan, Joe —"Little Joe" was the key part of the 1971 trade for the Reds. His acquisition from Houston changed the entire makeup of the ball club. Ten-time All-Star, five-time Gold Glove winner, two-time league MVP, he was likely the smartest player on the Reds. Dick Wagner allowed him to leave Cincinnati as a free agent after two subpar years. Morgan went on to play for the Astros, Giants, Phillies (where he reunited with Pete Rose and Tony Perez for a World Series run), and Athletics. Retiring after the 1984 season, Morgan was elected to the Baseball Hall of Fame in 1990. He resides in California and does baseball analysis for ESPN. Many claim Morgan would be a great manager but he has expressed no interest in it.

Nolan, Gary —A precocious talent, Nolan made the Reds as a nineteen-year-old flamethrower in 1967. Beset by injuries throughout his career, he made the All-Star team once and became a crafty pitcher after his fastball left him. Selected to start Game One of the 1970 World Series, he won eighteen games that year and fifteen each in the championship years. Traded by Bob Howsam to the Angels in June 1977 for Craig Hendrickson, he finished out the year in California and never pitched again. After retirement he worked in Las Vegas in the gambling industry. Nolan currently resides in California and works as a gaming consultant. Inducted into the Reds Hall of Fame in 1983.

Norman, Fredie —Super scout Ray Shore saw something in Norman that no one else did. His trade from the Padres to the Reds on June 12, 1973, for Gene Locklear, Mike Johnson, and cash, changed his career. He won at least eleven games with the Reds every year he pitched for them. Dick Wagner allowed him to leave as a free agent after the 1979 season. He pitched the 1980 season for Montreal and then retired. As of 2000 he was a consultant for a waste management company in Southern California.

Pastore, Frank — The hero of the 1979 stretch run to the playoffs, Pastore pitched for the Reds through 1985 and was a free-agent pickup by the Minnesota Twins in 1986. Johnny Bench had warned him that he was always one pitch from humility. Bench proved to be a prophet as Pastore's life was changed on June 4, 1984, when Dodger Steve Sax lined a fastball off his right elbow. His arm was never the same. In 1984 Pastore became a Christian. He went on to get degrees in theology and ethics as well as business administration and political philosophy. For two years he worked with Athletes in Action. He currently serves as an afternoon talk-show host on KKLA in Los Angeles.

Perez, Tony — Retired from the Reds in 1986. The seven-time All-Star (and All-Star game MVP in 1967) was likely the most admired player on the Reds. Rose said that he admired Morgan's talent but Perez as a person. Perez played third from 1967–71 but went to first base after "the trade." Perez was an RBI machine and knocked in at least ninety runs twelve times (eleven years in a row). Perez was traded to Montreal with Will McEnaney for Woodie Fryman and Dale Murray in December 1976. It was the trade that Bob Howsam regretted. Howsam brought Perez back to Cincinnati in 1985 for his leadership. He retired in October 1986. Perez served as Reds manager for the first forty-four games of the 1993 season before being fired by owner Marge Schott. He also managed the Florida Marlins on an interim basis in 2001. He currently serves special assistant to the team president of the Florida Marlins. As of late, Perez lives in Puerto Rico, unable to return to his native Cuba. Elected to the Baseball Hall of Fame in 2000.

Plummer, Bill — From 1971 to 1977 Plummer served as a back-up to Johnny Bench. Many said that he would be a starter for almost any other team. He got his chance in 1978 when he signed a free-agent contract with Seattle. He didn't start for the Mariners either and retired after the 1978 season. He went into coaching and managed the Mariners in 1992. He currently serves as the manager of the Tucson Sidewinders (Arizona's AAA club).

Rose, Pete — The Reds' team captain retired from the Reds in 1986 as a player with twenty-four seasons in the big leagues. He continued to be the team's manager until 1989. His was 1963 Rookie of the Year, seventeen-time All-Star at five different positions (2B, RF, LF, 3B, 1B), two-time Gold Glove winner, three-time batting champion, league MVP, World Series MVP, and likely the hardest working player on the Reds. On September 11, 1985, he passed Ty Cobb as the All-Time hit leader with a single to left center off of Eric Show. He finished his career with 4,256 hits. In 1989 Rose accepted a lifetime ban from baseball from Commissioner Bart Giamatti, while maintaining steadfastly that he never bet on baseball.[2] In 2005, Rose admitted to having gambled on baseball but said that he never bet on the Reds to lose. In 2000 Rose was named to baseball's all-century team. His son played briefly for the Reds in 1997. His popular ex-wife, Karolyn, still lives in the Cincinnati area. Pete lives in Southern California and makes frequent public appearances around the country, including regular appearances in Las Vegas. He is also a frequent guest in Cincinnati around Opening Day. He is baseball's career leader in games played, at-bats, and hits.

Seaver, Tom — His arrival from New York buoyed the Reds' hopes in June 1977. He was acquired for Pat Zachry, Doug Flynn, Steve Henderson, and Dan Norman in the last of Bob Howsam's great trades. He won twenty games just one time for the Reds but pitched the only no-hitter of his career on June 16, 1978, against the Cardinals at Riverfront Stadium. Dick Wagner traded him back to the Mets on December 16, 1982, for Charlie Puleo, Lloyd McClendon and Jason Felice. Seaver went on to pitch for the White Sox and Red Sox as well, retiring after the 1986 season with 311 wins. He was inducted into the Baseball Hall of Fame in 1992.

Simpson, Wayne — "The Next Bob Gibson" when he arrived with the Reds in 1970, Simpson was 13–1 with a 2.27 ERA shortly before he was selected for the All-Star team in 1970. His torn rotator cuff on July 31, 1970, began a slide for the Big Red Machine in the second half. He was unable to pitch against the Orioles in the World Series and never fully recovered from the injury. Howsam dealt Simpson and Hal McRae to the Royals for Roger Nelson and Richie Scheinblum. He pitched one year for KC, was injured in '74, pitched for Philadelphia in '75, was off in '76, pitched for California in '77, didn't make the Dodgers in '78, and then disappeared. He never won more than eight games in a season after 1970. Alex Grammas remembers him as "an awfully nice young man."

Stewart, Jimmy — Howsam's super sub who went to Houston in the 1971 trade. By the time the Reds peaked in 1976, none of those traded from the Reds (Helms, May, Stewart) was still with the Astros. Stewart played sparingly for Houston and was released after the 1973 season.

Tolan, Bobby — The onetime bright star of the Reds universe lost it all due to attitude. He led the league in stolen bases in 1970 and was 1972 Comeback Player of the Year after his Achilles tendon injury. His nightmare performance in Game Seven of the '72 Series began a slide that did not stop. Traded by Howsam with Dave Tomlin to San Diego for Clay Kirby in November 1973, he hurt his knee with San Diego, losing some of his valuable speed. He played for the Padres, Phillies, Pirates and in Japan but never hit over .270 and never stole more than fifteen bases in a season. Ken Griffey's batted ball bounced off Tolan's glove at first to score the winning run in the 1976 NLCS. He hung it up after 1979. After retirement he called Bob Howsam to ask for a coaching job. He did coach but not for the Reds. He played a bit role in the 1991 movie *Talent for the Game*. He now lives in Texas.

Vukovich, John — One of the last tries for the third-base solution in 1975, Vukovich was demoted to Indianapolis on May 20, 1975, in order to bring up Rawly Eastwick. Howsam traded him to Philadelphia in August for Dave Schneck. He retired from the Phillies after the 1981 season as a career .161 hitter. Like so many utility players, he went into coaching and was interim manager for a few games on two occasions (Cubs in 1986, Phillies in 1988). He coached for the Cubs from 1982 to 1987 and then with the Phillies from 1988–2004. Diagnosed with a brain tumor in 2001, he recovered. There was a relapse, though, and he passed away on March 8, 2007. The 2007 Phillies wore a patch on their uniforms with "Vuk" and his number (18). He was added to the Phillies Wall of Fame on August 10, 2007.

Wilcox, Milt — One of Sparky's young guns in 1970 (along with Nolan, Gullett, and Simpson), Wilcox never panned out with the Reds, as did the others. He was traded by Howsam to Cleveland in December 1971 for Ted Uhlaender. He went on to play for the Indians, Cubs, Tigers, and Mariners, retiring after the 1986 season. His best years were in Detroit where he pitched for Sparky Anderson for seven seasons, reaching a high of seventeen wins in 1984 when the Tigers won the World Series. After retirement he became prominent as a dog trainer in the Great Outdoor Games and was featured in *Sports Illustrated*. He named his dog "Sparky."

Woodward, Woody — Woodward arrived through a Howsam trade with the Braves in June 1968 with Clay Carroll and Tony Cloninger (for Milt Pappas, among others). One of three possibilities for the shortstop job, Woodward retired after the 1971 season. He did some broadcasting work for the Reds, then returned to his alma mater, Florida State, as baseball coach from 1975–78. Then he spent two years as the Reds' minor-league coordinator. He later went to work as the Reds' assistant GM from 1981–1984. Bob

Howsam "traded" him to the Yankees front office for Bill Bergesch. Woodward served as the assistant Yankees GM from 1985–86 and as GM in 1987. He was the Philadelphia GM for part of 1988 and then the Seattle GM from mid–1988 through 1999. At Seattle he drafted Alex Rodriguez and moved the Mariners into Safeco Field.

The Reds Managers and Coaches

Anderson, Sparky — "Captain Hook," the manager of the Big Red Machine from 1970 to 1978, is the Reds all-time winningest manager. Detroit Tigers manager from mid 1979 through 1995, his teams won seven division crowns and five pennants. Anderson was the first manager to win World Series titles in both leagues (Cincinnati in 1975 and 1976; Detroit in 1984). When he retired, he was third on the all-time list of managers for wins (behind Connie Mack and John McGraw). Anderson revolutionized the managerial position with his liberal use of the bullpen, a trend all managers follow today. Following retirement he did some broadcasting with the Angels, still plays lots of golf, and still lives in his long-time home in Southern California. He was elected to the Baseball Hall of Fame in 2000. His number (10) was retired by the Reds in May 2005.

Grammas, Alex — Sparky's alter-ego, according to Dick Wagner, Grammas coached third base for Sparky Anderson every year except '76 and '77, when he managed Milwaukee. He was the only coach who was not offered a position by Wagner after he axed Anderson. It didn't matter; Atlanta offered him the third-base coaching job right away. In 1980 Sparky brought him to Detroit, where he coached third through 1991. Altogether he had what is believed to be a major league record of twenty-five years in the third-base box (Pittsburgh: '65–'69, Cincinnati: '70–'75, '78; Atlanta '79; Detroit '80–'91). He has retired to his beloved Alabama where he enjoys his children and grandchildren.

Kluszewski, Ted — The former Cincinnati first baseman was Sparky's hitting coach during the Big Red Machine era. After Dick Wagner fired Sparky Anderson, "Big Klu" was given a job as a roving hitting instructor for the Reds in the minor leagues, a position that he held until 1987. Kluszewski died of a heart attack on March 29, 1988, in Cincinnati. Cincinnatians fondly remember his big muscles, the big steaks at his restaurant, and his big heart. He was inducted into the Reds Hall of Fame in 1962 as a player. His number (18) was retired by the Reds in 1988.

Nixon, Russ — One of Howsam's key player developers in the minor leagues, Nixon was chosen by Sparky Anderson to replace Alex Grammas as a coach when Grammas left for Milwaukee. Nixon stayed with the Reds until he was promoted to manager by Dick Wagner in mid–1982. He managed the Reds for all of 1983 but was let go by Howsam who felt the club needed a fresh start to regain its winning ways. Nixon went on to several major-league coaching jobs before being promoted to Atlanta manager in May 1988, a position he held until June 1990, when he was fired and replaced by Bobby Cox. Since that time he has continued to manage and instruct in the minor leagues. Currently he is a roving instructor in the Houston minor-league system.

Rapp, Vern — Bob Howsam's finisher at AAA Indianapolis. Howsam trusted Rapp to prepare his players to be big leaguers, on and off the field. Rapp himself finally got his shot at managing in the big leagues. He lasted half a season as skipper of the Cardinals in 1976 before the club revolted. He fared no better when Howsam gave Rapp a shot with the Reds in 1984. He was too inflexible for the players' tastes and Howsam let him go in midseason to make room for Pete Rose. Rapp is retired in Colorado and he and Howsam remained good friends.

Scherger, George —Sparky Anderson's first minor-league manager, Scherger was Sparky's first choice for his coaching staff. Scherger served mostly as the first-base coach (third-base while Grammas was gone) and worked with the outfielders. When Dick Wagner fired Sparky, he offered Scherger the Nashville AA job, where Scherger won the pennant. Afraid he would join good friend Anderson in Detroit, Wagner offered him a rare three-year deal to stay with the Reds organization. He continued in the minors where the 1982 Indianapolis club won the pennant. Scherger came back to the Reds as a coach for Russ Nixon, Vern Rapp, and Pete Rose. He retired after the 1986 season to be with his wife who was ill. He lives in North Carolina.

Shepard, Larry —Sparky's pitching coach during the Big Red Machine era conducted the Reds' kangaroo court and was the final word when it came to the pitchers. After Dick Wagner fired Sparky Anderson, Shepard was offered a job in the Reds organization. He declined and served as the Giants pitching coach in 1979. He then retired and settled in his native Nebraska.

The Front Office

Bender, Sheldon —"Chief" Bender served under Bob Howsam in both St. Louis and Cincinnati as director of player development. He also served under Cincinnati GMs Dick Wagner, Bill Bergesch, Murray Cook, Bob Quinn, Jim Bowden, and Dan O'Brien. He retired in December 2005 after thirty-nine seasons with the Reds. Added to his time with St. Louis, he had fifty-eight years in professional baseball. He was elected "King of Baseball" in 1996, an honor given to an individual with outstanding lifetime achievement in the game. Upon his retirement, there was not a more respected and liked man with the Reds or in all of baseball. Chief Bender passed away in Hamilton, Ohio, on February 27, 2008, at the age of eighty-eight, eight days after his good friend Bob Howsam.

Bergesch, Bill —Bob Howsam's chosen successor after his second stint as Reds GM. Howsam traded Woody Woodward to the Yankees in order to bring Bergesch over. The Reds finished second in the division in 1985 when Howsam and Bergesch split the job and second the next two seasons. Bergesch was fired by owner Marge Schott in October 1987. He returned to baseball in the early '90s as assistant GM for the Yankees and is now retired in Connecticut.

Bowen, Joe —The head of Bob Howsam's scouting program and Rex's organized younger brother, Joe Bowen was tasked to look at every single player the Reds gave serious consideration to drafting. Still the director of scouting, he was also promoted to the position of vice president by Dick Wagner and served there from 1979 to 1982. After 1982 he left the Reds and baseball.

Bowen, Rex —Bob Howsam's chief talent scout, Rex Bowen ran the scouting operation in 1968 before turning the reigns over to his younger brother so that he could return to what he did best, scout. While with the Pirates in the 1950s he signed both Bill Mazeroski and Maury Wills. He was voted one of the top ten scouts of the twentieth century by *Baseball America*. He had a fine eye for talent and was not bashful about sharing his views. He left the Reds after 1990. He passed away on December 30, 2004, at age ninety-three, in Florida.

Dale, Francis —The former *Cincinnati Enquirer* publisher put together the eleven-man syndicate that purchased the Reds from Bill DeWitt in December 1966. He was the majority owner of the Reds until early 1973 when Louis Nippert bought controlling interest after several years of negotiations. Dale was appointed by Richard Nixon to be ambassador to the United Nations in Geneva, a role he served from 1973 to 1976. He was publisher of the *Los Angeles Herald Examiner* from 1977 to 1985, commissioner of the Major Indoor Soccer League from 1985 to 1986, then president of the Music Center of Los Angeles. He died of a heart attack while visiting Zimbabwe on November 28, 1993.

DeWitt, Bill—The Reds' owner from 1961 to 1966, Bill DeWitt's refusal to consider Riverfront Stadium began a chain reaction of events that led to the Big Red Machine. DeWitt was with many teams over his fifty-year baseball career. DeWitt worked for Branch Rickey of the Cardinals and was the general manager for the St. Louis Browns (as well as the majority owner for three years), worked for the Yankees, and then was GM for the Tigers before coming to the Reds. He worked for the White Sox from 1975 to 1981. DeWitt died on March 4, 1982, in Cincinnati, at age seventy-nine.

DeWitt, Bill, Jr.—Son of Reds owner Bill DeWitt, Bill Jr. was part of the search committee that hired Bob Howsam. He continued to work for a short time for the Reds. He became very successful with a financial investment company that he started. He was instrumental in the building of Riverfront Coliseum which housed the Cincinnati Stingers of the WHA, a team that he owned. He is very active in Republican politics and was the chief fund raiser for friend George Bush's 1984 inauguration party. He purchased the St. Louis Cardinals in 1996 and is their majority owner to this day. DeWitt resides outside of Cincinnati.

Howsam, Bob—The chief architect of the Big Red Machine, Howsam retired from the Reds in July 1985, then consulted with them for a short time. Later he worked for his son Robert, when Robert ran the Denver minor-league club. Jerry McMorris hired Howsam as a consultant when he was awarded the Denver franchise. The *Denver Post* ran a poll for the name of the new NL franchise and "Denver Bears" was the overwhelming fan choice but "Colorado Rockies" was chosen by the ownership group. Howsam and his faithful wife Janny resided in Arizona until Mr. Howsam's death at the age of eighty-nine on February 19, 2008.

Howsam, Robert, Jr.—Brought in by his father for his marketing expertise in 1984, Howsam worked wonders in the mid–1980s, bringing the fun and the crowds back to Riverfront. New owner Marge Schott ran him off shortly after her arrival in 1985. He went on to be the general manager for the Denver minor-league club, employing his father as a scout. He resides in Arizona.

Nippert, Louis—Minority owner of the Reds from 1967–1972, majority owner 1973–1980, Louis Nippert was a minority owner again for a few years and also a minority owner of the football Bengals. Nippert continued his behind-the-scenes philanthropy and support of Cincinnati until his death on November 16, 1992. His wife still continues his work. They donated their Indian Hill farm Greenacres to a foundation where schoolchildren can still experience a working farm.

Shore, Ray—Bob Howsam's super scout. Through Shores' efforts, the Reds were loaded with good intelligence on the Orioles, A's, Red Sox, and Yankees in each World Series. Sparky Anderson came to thoroughly trust Shore's analysis, after declaring that neglecting his 1972 report had cost the Reds the Series. Shore continued to scout for the Reds for several seasons. He died on August 13, 1996, in St. Louis.

Stowe, Bernie—The Big Red Machine's equipment manager, Stowe made it his mission to keep Sparky Anderson humble. Stowe is still in a similar position as senior clubhouse and equipment manager, ably assisted by his two sons, Rick and Mark.

Wagner, Dick —Bob Howsam's right-hand man from 1967 to 1977, Wagner ran the business side of the Reds efficiently, turning pennies into dollars. In his career he oversaw the building of Miami Stadium, Busch Stadium, the Great Western Forum, and Riverfront Stadium. He served as general manager of the Reds from 1978 to mid 1983. Houston hired him as their general manager, a role he served in from late 1985 through 1987, when he resigned. While with the team, the Astros won their first division crown. He later worked for commissioners Ueberroth, Giamatti, and Vincent. When Bud Selig took over with a committee on an interim basis in 1993, Wagner had responsibility for day-to-day operations in New York while Selig continued to live in Milwaukee. Wagner retired in 1994. In 1999 he was involved in a serious auto accident but wife Gloria nursed him back to semi-health. He continued to live in Arizona until his death, on October 5, 2006.

Other Players

Fisk, Carlton —Boston Red Sox star catcher in the 1975 World Series. Fisk hit the game-winning home run off Pat Darcy in the bottom of the twelfth in Game Six. Young fans sometimes mistakenly think that won the Series, it did not. Fisk played for Boston until 1980 and the Chicago White Sox until he retired in mid 1993. He was elected to the Baseball Hall of Fame in 2000. To this day he still maintains that Armbrister interfered with him in Game Three and that cost the Red Sox the game and possibly the Series. In ceremonies prior to a Reds–Red Sox interleague game in June 2005, the left-field foul pole at Fenway was officially christened "Fisk Pole."

Hunter, Jim —"Catfish" Hunter met the Reds in the 1972 and 1976 World Series. He won 224 games over his career, retiring from the Yankees after the 1979 season. Hunter passed away on September 9, 1999, due to the effects of Lou Gehrig's disease. The one-time baseball millionaire auctioned his baseball spikes to raise money for his family before his death. He was inducted into the Baseball Hall of Fame in 1987. Unable to choose between the A's and Yankees, he entered the Hall with no logo on his bust.

Lee, Bill —"The Spaceman," whose words, actions, and leephus pitch garnered a lion's share of the press in the 1975 World Series, pitched for Boston for three more years. He went on to play for Montreal and finished his career in 1982 with 119 victories. He remains close to Bernie Carbo who he called "the best tenth man in baseball." Lee, along with Ferguson Jenkins and Sam McDowell, was instrumental in helping get Carbo into drug rehabilitation in 1993.

Munson, Thurman —The Yankees' star catcher who battled so brilliantly with Johnny Bench in the 1976 World Series played two and one half more seasons with New York. Munson earned his pilot license and bought a Cessna Citation. While piloting the craft at the Akron-Canton airport (near his home town) on August 2, 1979, he crashed and was killed at age thirty-two. He was dearly missed by the baseball community.

Piniella, Lou —The only Yankee player to score in Game One of the 1976 World Series. He was Rookie of the Year with Kansas City in 1969. He retired from playing as a Yankee after the 1984 season. He went into managing and has skippered the Yankees, Reds ('90–'92), Mariners, Devil Rays, and Cubs. His 2001 Mariners won a record 116 games in the regular season. He led the 1990 Cincinnati Reds to the World Series title, the first team to be in first place for an entire season, wire to wire.

Rivers, Mickey —The fleet-footed Yankees centerfielder melted down when Rose played him sixty feet away in the 1976 World Series. He went on to two and a half more years with the Yankees. Steinbrenner thought the bright lights of New York were too much for the young Rivers and he was dealt to the Rangers in 1977. He played for them until he retired after the 1984 season. Rivers now runs the Mickey Rivers Baseball Academy just outside his native Miami.

Robinson, Frank — Frankie Robinson was one of the few Reds players who wanted Pete Rose promoted to the big leagues in 1963. Traded to the Orioles for Milt Pappas in 1965, he won the Triple Crown and two World Series titles. The Orioles traded him to the Dodgers in December 1971 for Doyle Alexander, among others. In 1975 he became the player-manager for the Cleveland Indians, the first black man to manage in the big leagues. He went on to manage the Giants, Orioles, Expos, and the Nationals until 2006. He retired from playing in 1977, fourth on the all-time home run list at the time. He was inducted into the Baseball Hall of Fame in 1982. Apparently still bitter at DeWitt and the Reds, he chose an Orioles cap for his bust, though he played for the Reds four seasons longer.

Other Figures

Busch, August — "Gussie" Busch was the king of the Anheuser-Busch Company and the man who allowed Bob Howsam to leave St. Louis for Cincinnati by his lack of interest. Busch owned the Cardinals and Busch Stadium from 1953 until his death September 29, 1989. His heirs sold the team to Bill DeWitt, Jr., in 1996.

Cooke, Jack Kent — The Toronto Maple Leafs owner who hired and fired Sparky Anderson later hired Dick Wagner to oversee construction of the Fabulous Western Forum. He owned the Lakers from 1965 to 1979 and the Los Angeles Kings hockey club from 1966 to 1979. The Lakers won one title during his tenure. He also owned the Washington Redskins, winning three Super Bowl titles, and was famous for inviting the Washington elite to sit in his box on Sunday afternoons. Known as a micromanager of coaches, he passed away on April 6, 1997 after a heart attack.

Finley, Charlie — The Oakland Athletics owner who pushed for the introduction of World Series night baseball games and the designated hitter. His Oakland A's won three straight World Series (1972–74) and reached the playoffs in 1975 before falling apart. His prophecies concerning free agency were absolutely correct. He and other small-market teams were unable to afford to keep the stars they developed. Finley watched them leave for large-market teams with little in return. His team and franchise were in shambles, his wife sued for divorce, and Finley was forced to sell the team to Walter Haas, the owner of Levi Strauss, in August 1980. This may be Finley's legacy, even with some small revenue sharing among league owners; small-market teams are able to compete with their talent for only two to three years, the stars leave, and the process repeats (as has been the case with the Florida Marlins). After selling the A's, Finley's insurance companies began to do poorly as well and he lost much of his wealth. When he died due to vascular and heart disease on February 9, 1996, Finley's barn in LaPorte, Indiana, was still painted with the Oakland A's mascot.

Kuhn, Bowie — The commissioner of baseball who declared that World Series weekday games would be played at night so that kids could see the whole Series if they wanted to. His decision to move the 1976 World Series Sunday Game Two to night opened the door for the World Series to be contested in inclement weather, as long as the TV money poured in. Kuhn struggled, unable to effectively deal with the players' union chief Marvin Miller and even the owners he was supposed to lead. Granted, they were a tough bunch to lead. After the 1981 mid-season players strike, Kuhn disenfranchised enough owners, including Cincinnati's Williams brothers, that he was not reelected as the commissioner in 1982 but stayed on until his successor Peter Ueberroth was in place in 1984. Kuhn went back to practicing law and wrote some memoirs. He formed a law firm, it went bankrupt, and he moved to Ponte Vedra, Florida. He is credited with bringing increased exposure and revenue to the game, a curious legacy given the means taken to achieve those increases. Surprisingly he was voted into the Baseball Hall of Fame shortly after his death from pneumonia on March 15, 2007. Marvin Miller remembered him for his humor.

Miller, Marvin — The players' union chief whose clever maneuvering brought free agency, among other things, and fundamentally altered the way the game is run. His achievements led to great riches for the players and the union (including the chief). It also led to an era when fans no longer expect their stars to stay with the team, fans are suspicious of players' motives, and fans pay substantially higher prices ($36 for one seat in the bleachers in Wrigley Field). Miller was union chief from 1966 to following the 1981 strike. His successor was not viewed as effective and Miller was asked to return. He served until 1983. Donald Fehr, a man Miller hired as the union's general counsel in 1977, is the current union chief. Miller still resides in New York City.

Seitz, Peter — The man who decided the Andy Messersmith–Dave McNally arbitration case on December 23, 1975, opening the door for free agency in baseball. Seitz continued as a federal arbitrator for a number of years. To the day of his death on October 17, 1983, in New York City, he maintained that he made the correct decision in the case.

Steinbrenner, George — The man who bought the Yankees from CBS in 1973. His unbridled spending on free agents after 1976 led to unprecedented pay raises for the players. More than any other person, Steinbrenner is responsible for the level of salaries and high tickets prices seen today. Steinbrenner hired and fired managers almost yearly in the 1970s, '80s and '90s. Although he has mellowed in recent years, he is still willing to open his wallet to pay for the best talent for the Yankees.

The Umpires

Barnett, Larry — The umpire who refused to call interference on Eddie Armbrister after his collision with Carlton Fisk in Game Three of the 1975 World Series. Barnett and Major League Baseball continue to maintain that the call was correct. Barnett served as an American League umpire from 1969 to 1999. At the time it was a record tenure for an AL umpire. Barnett worked four World Series. He was the major-league supervisor of umpires from 2000 to 2001.

Burkhart, Ken — The umpire who made the Elrod Hendricks–Bernie Carbo call in Game One of the 1970 World Series. Burkhart retired after the 1973 season and died of emphysema on December 29, 2004, the day before Rex Bowen, in Knoxville, Tennessee.

The Announcers

Brennaman, Marty — Marty Brennaman was tapped by Dick Wagner to replace Al Michaels following the 1973 season. From 1974 to 2004 he teamed full time with Joe Nuxhall to form the longest-running announcing duo in baseball. They were known as "Marty and Joe." He continues to be the voice of the Reds on their flagship station

WLW. In 2000 he won the Ford C. Frick award presented annually by the Baseball Hall of Fame. From 2004 to 2006 he shared the booth with Steve Stewart and Nuxhall. Beginning in 2007 he was teamed with former Reds pitcher Jeff Brantley and his son Thom who moved over from the Arizona Diamondbacks. His microphone was retired by the Reds on June 10, 2007.

Michaels, Al—Dick Wagner called his hiring of the twenty-five-year-old Michaels a stroke of genius. He was the Reds' play-by-play announcer from 1971 to 1973, teamed with Joe Nuxhall. His call of the Bob Moose wild pitch in the deciding Game Five of the 1972 playoffs with Pittsburgh is one of the most famous in Reds history. He went on to call Giants baseball games and UCLA basketball games in the Wooden era. He went to work for ABC in 1976. He had the call during the historic USA–USSR hockey game, the so-called "Miracle on Ice," in 1980 at Lake Placid. In 1986 he became the voice of *Monday Night Football*. In 2006 he joined partner John Madden on *Sunday Night Football*. He resides in Southern California.

Nuxhall, Joe—The Old Lefthander was the youngest pitcher ever in the major leagues at age fifteen in 1944. He retired from the Reds as a player following the 1966 season. Soon thereafter Bob Howsam and Dick Wagner tagged him for the radio booth. He stayed there through 2004, full time, with Jim McIntyre, Al Michaels, and Marty Brennaman. He did some part-time announcing with the Reds on WLW from 2005 to 2007. Upon his death from cancer on November 15, 2007, all of Cincinnati mourned. He was inducted into the Reds Hall of Fame as a player in 1968 and his microphone was retired by the Reds on June 10, 2007.

The Parks

Bears Stadium—Located on the site of the old Denver dump, the stadium was ordered by Bob Howsam, opened in 1948, and served as home to the Denver Bears and later the NFL Broncos. It was expanded several times and renamed Mile High Stadium in 1969. It served as home to the Broncos through 2000 when the city built a new Mile High Stadium (also called Invesco Field). The Rockies played there from 1993 to 1994. Old Mile High was torn down in January 2002.

Crosley Field—The Reds' cozy home from 1912 to June 1970. The stadium stood until April 19, 1972, at the corners of Western Avenue and Findlay Street, with I-75 running nearby. It was used as the city impound lot until it was razed. Pete Rose, Jr., sat at the controls and triggered the wrecking ball, which was painted as a baseball, to begin the demolition. It is now home to a small industrial park. A plaque commemorating the park lies near the intersection of Western and Findlay.

Riverfront Stadium—The battle over this stadium inadvertently led to the Big Red Machine. It was the home of the NFL Bengals from 1970 to 1999. The Reds played there from 1970 to 2002. It was suppose to be an ultramodern stadium that would serve as the Reds' home for decades. In fact, the Reds signed a forty-year lease for the stadium, a lease they would not fulfill. After Baltimore built the successful Camden Yards in 1992, many cities clamored for "old-style" parks so they could compete. Cincinnati was no exception and Great American Ballpark was opened in 2003. Riverfront was renamed Cinergy Field in September 1996 but continued to be called Riverfront by many Reds fans. Howsam's AstroTurf was replaced with grass in 2001 and the left and centerfield stands were removed to make room for building a new park next door. Riverfront was imploded on December 29, 2002.

CHAPTER NOTES

Preface

1. From 1969 to 1994 no other team was able to sweep the entire postseason. In 1985, the playoffs were extended from a best-of-five to a best-of-seven format, requiring a team to win eight straight games to sweep the postseason. In 1995 another tier was added to the playoffs, the Divisional Series, after which a team would have to win eleven straight games to sweep the postseason.

Introduction

1. Daniel Hurley, *Cincinnati, The Queen City* (Cincinnati: Cincinnati Historical Society, 1982), 15.
2. Manager Harry Wright only considered games against National Association clubs to be official. Using his method the Red Stockings won eighty-one official games and forty-nine exhibitions in a row. *Cincinnati Reds 2004 Media Guide*, 326.
3. Eric Enders, *100 Years of the World Series: 1903–2003* (New York: Barnes & Nobles Books, 2004), 12.
4. Ibid., 154.
5. Rusty McClure, David Stern, and Michael A. Banks, *Crosley: Two Brothers and a Business Empire that Transformed the Nation* (Cincinnati: Clerisy Press, 2006) provides a nice summary of Powel Crosley's feats.
6. *Cincinnati Reds 2004 Media Guide*, 326.

Chapter 1

1. Robert L. Howsam, *My Life in Sports*, adapted by Bob Jones (R. L. Howsam, 1999), 21.
2. Ibid.
3. Interview with Bob Howsam, May 2005.
4. Howsam, *My Life in Sports*, 7.
5. Ibid., 24.

6. Interview with Bob Howsam, May 2005.
7. Howsam, *My Life in Sports*, 9.
8. Ibid., 25.
9. Ibid., 32.
10. Interview with Bob Howsam, May 2005.
11. Howsam, *My Life in Sports*, 37.
12. Ibid.
13. Interview with Bob Howsam, May 2005.
14. Interview with Sheldon Bender, May 2005.
15. Howsam, *My Life in Sports*, 34.

Chapter 2

1. Howsam, *My Life in Sports*, 44.
2. John T. Brady, *The Heisman: A Symbol of Excellence* (New York: Atheneum, 1984), various pages.
3. Later renamed the Jets.
4. Howsam, *My Life in Sports*, 53.
5. Later moved to Kansas City to become the Chiefs.
6. Officially Anheuser-Busch.
7. In the middle of his career, Richie Allen adamantly declared that his new name was Dick.
8. Howsam, *My Life in Sports*, 70.
9. "Leo Durocher." Baseballlibrary.com, http://www.baseballibrary.com/baseballibrary/ballplayers/D/Durocher_Leo.stm (accessed June 11, 2007).
10. David Gamble and Andrew Hopple were also on the search committee but did not make the trip to St. Louis.
11. Bob Howsam Interview, May 2005.
12. The median income for a household in 1967 was $7,143, therefore the St. Louis GM was making five times that amount.
13. Howsam, *My Life in Sport*, 84.

Chapter 3

1. Pete Rose, *The Pete Rose Story* (New York: World Publishing, 1970), 91.

2. Bob Hertzel, *Cincinnati Enquirer*, October 10, 1970.
3. A tradition that unfortunately was shelved in 1999 when ESPN demanded and got the right for the first game to be held on the first Sunday evening in April, teams of their choosing. The Reds still always open in Cincinnati on Monday, but the rest of the league plays as well. A fine baseball tradition changed for broadcast dollars.
4. Rose, *The Pete Rose Story*, 97.
5. Samuel O. Regalado, *Viva Baseball! Latin Major Leaguers and Their Special Hunger* (Urbana: University of Illinois Press, 2008), 156–160. Perez and other Latin stars are chronicled in this book.
6. Lee Iacocca and William Novak, *Iacocca: A Biography* (New York: Bantam Books, 1984), 167–169.
7. Kavanagh, Jack. "Chief Bender." Baseball library.com, http://www.baseballlibrary.com/baseballlibrary/ballplayers/B/Bender_Chief.stm (accessed June 11, 2007).
8. The St. Louis Browns shared Sportsman's Park with the Cardinals in St. Louis and in 1954 moved to Baltimore where they became the Orioles
9. As a side note, Bender served under Franklin Roosevelt's son, Col. James Roosevelt, in the Solomon Islands.

Chapter 4

1. Jim Collins, *Good to Great* (New York: HarperCollins, 2001), 13.

Chapter 5

1. Seeburg had grown up with Anderson in South Central Los Angeles. Therefore he referred to George as "Georgie" which is what everyone called him in the neighborhood. Sparky Anderson and Si Burick, *The Main Spark* (Garden City, NY: Doubleday, 1978), 29.
2. Interview with Sheldon Bender, May 2005.
3. *Cincinnati Post*, October 10, 1969, 22.
4. Interview with George Scherger, December 2005.
5. A Howsam observation.
6. Howsam named a pitcher by name but his identity is a long-time secret.
7. Yogi Berra, Connie Mack, and Jim Leyland are some of the men who went from catcher to field general.
8. Interview with Alex Grammas, December 2005.

Chapter 6

1. Marking the end of Ruiz's chances to once again pinch hit for Johnny Bench in the ninth inning of a game.
2. *New York Times* June 7, 1970, 171
3. Former Arizona Cardinal Pat Tillman being a notable exception.
4. Only one professional athlete died in the Vietnam War, Buffalo Bills lineman Bob Kalsu. An excellent article on this extraordinary man can be found in *Sports Illustrated* July 23, 2001.
5. Howsam, *My Life in Sports*,103.
6. "Rotator Cuff Problems." JointHealing.com, http://www.jointhealing.com/pages/shoulder/rotatorcuff.html (accessed June 11, 2007).

Chapter 7

1. *Cincinnati Enquirer*, October 11, 1970.
2. Dan Gutman, *The Way Baseball Works* (New York: Byron Preiss/Richard Ballantine, 1996), 53.
3. *Cincinnati Enquirer*, October 12, 1970.
4. *Cincinnati Enquirer*: October 9, 1970.
5. *Cincinnati Enquirer*, October 14, 1970.
6. *Cincinnati Enquirer*, October 15, 1970.

Chapter 8

1. Dick Perry, *Not Just a Sound: The Story of WLW* (New York: Prentice Hall, 1971) and William Oscar Johnson, "City of the Year," *Sports Illustrated*, December 31, 1990, 117.
2. Frank Lidz, "The Mouth Talks Back," *Sports Illustrated*, February 15, 1988, 58.
3. Interview with Dick Wagner, May 2005.
4. Daniel Hurley, *Cincinnati, The Queen City*, 79.
5. Richard Hoffer, "Dr. Harold Gores," *Sports Illustrated*, September 19, 1994, 98.
6. Interview with Bob Howsam, May 2005.
7. Interview with Sheldon Bender, January 2008.
8. Interview with Bernie Carbo, January 2008.
9. Actually the Reds' home record at Riverfront was even worse before Merritt went down on September 8.

Chapter 9

1. As of this writing, some teams are beginning to drop their advance scouts, with the advent of cable and satellite TV. Instead of sending scouts on the road, they have them sit in the

comfort of their own home and scout the opposition via television.

Chapter 10

1. The Mariners drafted a pretty good shortstop under Woodward's watch; he became known as A-Rod — Alex Rodriguez.
2. Also known as a change-up.

Chapter 11

1. Acocella, Nick. "Finley Entertained and Enraged." ESPN.com, *http://espn.go.com/clas sic/biography/s/Finley_Charles.html* (accessed June 11, 2007).
2. Lynn Henning, *The Detroit News*, July 11, 2005.
3. John Mehno, *The Chronicle of Baseball: A Century of Major League Action* (London: Carlton Books, 2000), 314.
4. Pedro Borbon was charged with the first run scored by Marquez.
5. *Cincinnati Enquirer*, October 21, 1972, 27.
6. Ibid.
7. Ibid.
8. *Cincinnati Enquirer*, October 24, 1972, 21.
9. *Cincinnati Enquirer*, October 22, 1972, C-2.
10. *Cincinnati Enquirer*, October 23, 1972, 33.
11. St. Louis Rams owner Georgia Frontiere had a great line after the Trent Green injury. When informed over dinner by the club's GM that Green was lost for the season, Frontiere said, "Don't worry, who knows maybe this Warner guy will be the next Johnny Unitas or something."
12. The author personally viewed both telecasts at the time they originally aired. The woman's name has since been lost to history. If you have any information regarding this woman's identity or her husband and children, please contact the author.

Chapter 12

1. Interview with Bob Howsam, May 2005.
2. Dick Young, *Cincinnati Enquirer*, October 10, 1970, 22.
3. Ibid.
4. *Cincinnati Enquirer*, October 17, 1975, 54.
5. Howsam, *My Life in Sports*, 35.
6. *Cincinnati Enquirer*, October 16, 1970.

7. *Cincinnati Enquirer*, July 23, 1973.
8. Interview with Sheldon Bender, May 2005.

Chapter 13

1. Bob Hertzel, *Cincinnati Enquirer*, July 2, 1973, 25.
2. William Leggett, *Sports Illustrated*, "Reds' Rookie is a Tough Cookie," August 27, 1973, 47.
3. The term became so entrenched that when Atlanta Braves closer Mark Wohlers suffered a similar loss of control, baseball people immediately said he had Steve Blass disease. Wohlers also never recovered.
4. Bennett Beach, "Surprise from the Swing Man," *Time*, June 29, 1981, 48.
5. Howsam, *My Life in Sports*, 124.

Chapter 14

1. Interview with Dick Wagner, May 2005.
2. Interview with Bob Howsam, May 2005.
3. Ibid.
4. On April 3, 1974, 315 people lost their lives to tornados. It was the second worst storm of the 1900s in America. It was a lesson New Orleans would later learn with the Superdome after Hurricane Katrina in September 2005.
5. Interview with Bob Howsam, May 2005.
6. The houses became "fronts or facades" for shooting films and television shows. You can still tour the street where Beaver Cleaver, Marcus Welby and other TV characters lived. Part of their neighborhood was actually homes from Chavez Ravine.
7. Bill Parcell's famous expression for why he was leaving the New England Patriots.
8. Gallagher, Tom. "Tommy John." Base ballLibrary.com. http://www.baseballlibrary. com/baseballlibrary/ballplayers/J/John_Tomm y.stm (accessed June 11, 2007).

Chapter 15

1. Interview with Bob Howsam, May 2005.
2. *Cincinnati Enquirer*, February 21, 1975, front page.
3. Bob Hertzel, *Cincinnati Enquirer*, May 3, 1975, 25.
4. The term was coined by Cincinnati writer Ren Mulford concerning Reds third baseman Hick Carpenter. *Cincinnati Enquirer*, June 30, 1970, Special Riverfront Stadium Section, 14.

5. Calculations based on figures in: Robert Adair, *The Physics of Baseball* (New York: Perennial, 1994).

6. Clyde King has the distinction of being the only man to manage both Hank Aaron and Willie Mays.

7. Borbon's arm was so tireless that during the 1995 baseball season when it appeared that players were going to stay on strike, he made a bid to become one of the "scab" players. He showed up at spring training at age 48 and pitched for several weeks.

8. *Cincinnati Enquirer*, May 4, 1975, 2-C.

Chapter 16

1. To date Lynn is the only man to win Rookie of the Year and MVP honors in the same season.

2. Dan Gutman, *The Way Baseball Works* (New York: Byron Preiss/Richard Ballantine, 1996), 51.

3. *Cincinnati Enquirer*, October 14, 1975, Special Section, 2.

4. *Cincinnati Enquirer*, October 17, 1975, 54.

5. *Cincinnati Enquirer*, October 14, 1975, Special Section, 2.

6. *Cincinnati Enquirer*, October 17, 1975, 53.

7. Samuel O. Regalado, *Viva Baseball!* 160–164.

Chapter 17

1. *Cincinnati Enquirer*, October 21, 1975, 2.

2. *Cincinnati Enquirer*, October 22, 1975, 21.

3. *Cincinnati Enquirer*, October 20, 1975.

4. *Cincinnati Enquirer*, October 21, 1975, 21.

5. Amazingly Carbo's first hit as a Reds rookie was a home run on Opening Day. His first hit in the World Series, against his former team, was a home run.

6. *Cincinnati Enquirer*, October 23, 1975, 47.

7. *Cincinnati Enquirer*, October 11, 1975, 25.

8. *Cincinnati Enquirer*, October 25, 1975, 25.

9. *Cincinnati Post*, October 23, 1975, 29.

10. Bob Hertzel, *Cincinnati Enquirer*, May 3, 1975, 25.

Chapter 18

1. The 1952 Report of the Subcommittee on Study of Monopoly Power of the House Committee on the Judiciary, H. R. Rep. No. 2002, 82nd Congress, 2nd Session, 229.

2. Murray Chase, *New York Times*, January 26, 1995 and Goodman, Andrew. "Sportslaw History: The Role of Marvin Miller." Sports lawnews.com, http://www.sportslawnews.com/archive/history/MarvinMiller.htm (accessed June 11, 2007).

3. Dave McNally only played part of the 1975 season with Montreal. Unhappy with the Expos and his own performance, he sat out most of the season. He agreed to stay in the case to help Miller in the advent that Messersmith dropped out for some reason.

4. Murray Chase, *New York Times*, January 26, 1995 and Goodman, "Sportslaw History: The Role of Marvin Miller."

5. *Cincinnati Enquirer*, October 26, 1975, 2-C.

6. Interview with Alex Grammas, December 2005.

7. Interview with Sheldon Bender, May 2005.

8. Interview with George Scherger, December 2005.

9. When the Reds built a new ballpark in 2003, part of the phrase was put on the outside of the stadium.

10. Interview with Dick Wagner, May 2005.

11. Interview with Bob Howsam, May 2005.

12. *Cincinnati Post*, October 23, 1975, 29.

13. Johnny Bench and William Brashler, *Catch You Later: The Autobiography of Johnny Bench* (New York: Harper & Row, 1979), 40.

14. From its inception in 1956 through 1966 there was only one Cy Young winner for all of major-league baseball. Sandy Koufax from the National League won the award in 1966. Meanwhile, Jim Kaat was pitching for the Minnesota Twins in the American League.

Chapter 19

1. *Cincinnati Enquirer*, October 15, 1976, B-1.

2. The rules would change again in 1986. Now when games are played in the American League team's ballpark the DH is used and when in the National League park they are not used, regardless of the year the Series is hosted

3. Younger brother of former Reds first baseman Lee May.

4. Calculations based on Robert Adair, *The Physics of Baseball*.

5. For a scholarly treatment of self-efficacy see: Marilyn Gist and Terence Mitchell, "Self-Efficacy: A Theoretical Analysis of Its Determinants and Malleability," *Academy of Management Review* 17, No. 2 (April 1992), 183–211.

6. *Cincinnati Enquirer*, Oct. 19, 1976, C-2.

7. Howsam, *My Life in Sports*, prologue.

Chapter 20

1. For pitchers with at least one hundred career victories. *Cincinnati Reds 2004 Media Guide*, 21.
2. The trade deadline was moved to July 31 in the 1980s.
3. Larry Keith, "Tom Terrific Arms the Red Arsenal," *Sports Illustrated*, June 27, 1977, 22–29.
4. Bench in 1970 and 1972, Rose in 1973, Morgan in 1975 and 1976.
5. Interview with Bob Howsam, May 2005.
6. *Cincinnati Enquirer*, October 19, 1976, C-1.
7. Interview with Bob Howsam, May 2005.

Chapter 21

1. After ending his stint with the A's, Burrell joined the navy. After his discharge he became the singer known as MC Hammer.
2. Howsam, *My Life in Sports*,141–143.
3. Interview with Dick Wagner, May 2005.
4. Interview with Greg Park, May 2005.
5. Ibid.
6. Interview with Bob Howsam, May 2005.
7. Ibid.
8. Ibid.
9. *Cincinnati Post*, October 10, 1969, 22.

Chapter 22

1. Interview with Dick Wagner, May 2005.
2. Ibid.
3. Ibid.
4. Interview with Greg Park, May 2005.

Chapter 23

1. *Cincinnati Enquirer*, November 29, 1978, Front page.
2. Bob Hertzel, *Cincinnati Enquirer*, November 29, 1978, 6.
3. *Cincinnati Enquirer*, November 29, 1978, Front page, 6.
4. *Cincinnati Enquirer*, November 30, 1978.
5. Interview with George Scherger, December 2005.

6. Interview with Bob Howsam, May 2005.
7. Mark Purdy, *Cincinnati Enquirer*, November 29, 1978, C-1.
8. Interview with Dick Wagner, May 2005.
9. *Cincinnati Enquirer*, November 29, 1978, C-1.
10. Howsam, *My Life in Sports*,162.
11. May 25, 1979, remains the darkest day in U.S. aviation. On that Friday before the Memorial Day weekend, American Airlines Flight 191 lost more people than in any commercial aircraft accident in U.S. history.
12. Ray Buck, *Cincinnati Enquirer*, September 21, 1979, C-1.
13. Pastore, Frank. "One Pitch From Humility." KKLA-FM, http://www2.kkla.com/frank_pastore/ONE%20PITCH%20FROM%20HUMILITY.pdf (accessed June 11, 2007).
14. *Cincinnati Enquirer*, February 1, 1980, C-1.
15. See Epilogue.

Epilogue

1. Interview with Bob Howsam, May 2005.
2. Ibid.
3. Ibid.
4. Ibid.
5. Roosevelt, Theodore. "Citizenship in a Republic." Speech at the Sorbonne, Paris, April 23, 1910. http://www.theodore-roosevelt.com/trsorbonnespeech.html (accessed June 11, 2007).
6. Howsam, *My Life in Sports*,165.
7. Interview with Bob Howsam, May 2005.
8. Interview with Sheldon Bender, May 2005.
9. Interview with Greg Park, May 2005.
10. Interview with Bob Howsam, May 2005
11. Howsam's teams: St. Louis Cardinals 1965–68, Cincinnati Reds 1967–77, 1984–85.

Appendix

1. The phrase "As of 2000" indicates the information is from *Sports Illustrated*, July 30, 2000.
2. The case against Rose is documented; it is known as the Dowd Report and was written by commissioner-appointed investigator John Dowd.

BIBLIOGRAPHY

Books

Adair, Robert. *The Physics of Baseball.* New York: Perennial, 1994.

Anderson, Sparky, and Si Burick. *The Main Spark.* Garden City, NY: Doubleday, 1978.

Bench, Johnny; and William Brashler. *Catch You Later: The Autobiography of Johnny Bench.* New York: Harper & Row, 1979.

Brady, John T. *The Heisman: A Symbol of Excellence.* New York: Atheneum, 1984.

Collins, Jim. *Good to Great.* New York: HarperCollins, 2001.

Enders, Eric. *100 Years of the World Series: 1903–2003.* New York: Barnes & Noble Books, 2004.

Gutman, Dan. *The Way Baseball Works.* New York: Byron Preiss/Richard Ballantine, 1996.

Howsam, Robert Lee, and Bob Jones. *My Life in Sports.* S.l: s.n., 1999.

Hurley, Daniel. *Cincinnati: The Queen City.* Cincinnati: Cincinnati Historical Society, 1982.

Iacocca, Lee, and William Novak. *Iacocca: A Biography.* New York: Bantam Books, 1984.

McClure, Rusty, David Stern, and Michael A. Banks. *Crosley: Two Brothers and a Business Empire that Transformed the Nation.* Cincinnati: Clerisy Press, 2006.

Mehno, John. *The Chronicle of Baseball: A Century of Major League Action.* London: Carlton Books, 2000.

Perry, Dick. *Not Just a Sound: The Story of WLW.* New York: Prentice Hall, 1971.

Regalado, Samuel O. *Viva Baseball! Latin Major Leaguers and Their Special Hunger.* Urbana: University of Illinois Press, 2008.

Rose, Pete. *The Pete Rose Story.* New York: World Publishing, 1970.

Government Report

Report of the Subcommittee on Study of Monopoly Power of the House Committee on the Judiciary, H.R. Rep. No. 2002, 82nd Congress., 2nd Session, 1952.

Articles

Acocella, Nick. "Finley Entertained and Enraged." ESPN.com, *http://espn.go.com/classic/biography/s/Finley_Charles.html* (accessed June 11, 2007).

Beach, Bennett. "Surprise from the Swing Man." *Time,* June 29, 1981.

"The Champs of '75." *Sports Illustrated,* July 30, 2000.

Gallagher, Tom. "Tommy John." Baseball Library.com. http://www.baseballlibrary.com/baseballlibrary/ballplayers/J/John_Tommy.stm (accessed June 11, 2007).

Gist, Marilyn and Terence Mitchell. "Self-Efficacy: A Theoretical Analysis of Its Determinants and Malleability." *Academy of Management Review,* April, 1992.

Goodman, Andrew. "Sportslaw History: The Role of Marvin Miller." Sportslaw news.com, http://www.sportslawnews.com/archive/history/MarvinMiller.htm (accessed June 11, 2007).

Hoffer, Richard. "Dr. Harold Gores." *Sports Illustrated*, September 19, 1994.

Johnson, William Oscar. "City of the Year." *Sports Illustrated*, December 31, 1990.

Kavanagh, Jack. "Chief Bender." Baseballl ibrary.com, http://www.baseballlibrary. com/baseballlibrary/ballplayers/B/Ben der_Chief.stm (accessed June 11, 2007).

Keith, Larry. "Tom Terrific Arms the Red Arsenal." *Sports Illustrated*, June 27, 1977.

Leggett, William. "Reds' Rookie is a Tough Cookie." *Sports Illustrated*, August 27, 1973.

"Leo Durocher." Baseballlibrary.com, http://www.baseballlibrary.com/base balllibrary/ballplayers/D/Durocher_Leo. stm (accessed June 11, 2007).

Lidz, Frank. "The Mouth Talks Back." *Sports Illustrated*, February 15, 1988.

Nack, William. "A Name on the Wall." *Sports Illustrated*, July 23, 2001.

Pastore, Frank. "One Pitch From Humility." KKLA-FM, http://www2.kkla.com/ frank_pastore/ONE%20PITCH%20FR OM%20HUMILITY.pdf (accessed June 11, 2007).

Roosevelt, Theodore. "Citizenship in a Republic." Speech at the Sorbonne, Paris, April 23, 1910. http://www.theodore-roosevelt.com/trsorbonnespeech.html (accessed June 11, 2007).

"Rotator Cuff Problems." JointHealing. com, http://www.jointhealing.com/pa ges/shoulder/rotatorcuff.html (accessed June 11, 2007).

Web Site

Dowd, John. "The Dowd Report." May 1989, http://www.dowdreport.com (accessed June 11, 2007).

Interviews

Author's interviews with Sheldon Bender, May 2005 and January 2008; Bernie Carbo, January 2008 (telephone); Alex Grammas, December 2005 (telephone); Bob Howsam, May 2005; Greg Park, May 2005; George Scherger, December 2005 (telephone); Dick Wagner, May 2005.